DECARCERATING DISABILITY

DECARCERATING DISABILITY

DEINSTITUTIONALIZATION AND PRISON ABOLITION

Liat Ben-Moshe

UNIVERSITY OF MINNESOTA PRESS
MINNEAPOLIS • LONDON

Cover description: The cover showcases a circular design on a faded yellow background. Layers of green concentric circles spiral from the center of the page and are cut off on the left side. Each circle, or circular pattern, is bigger and embedded in the next, and the whole resembles a target or growth rings on a tree. The circular pattern looks like it was drawn by hand in colored pencil. On the right side of the image are shavings or fragments that make it look like the circular pattern is being erased or shattered or disrupted by the title, as if the title is breaking through or encroaching on the circles. The title *Decarcerating Disability* is in magenta color. At the top right corner is the author's name, Liat Ben-Moshe, in green, and at the right bottom corner is the subtitle *Deinstitutionalization and Prison Abolition* in magenta color.

Leroy Moore Jr., "CAGED, Goddamn Philadelphia," SoundCloud, March 27, 2013, https:// soundcloud.com/blackkrip/caged-goddamn-philadelphia, printed by permission of Leroy F. Moore Jr.

Chapter 3 was published in a different form as "Dis-epistemologies of Abolition," *Critical Criminology* 26, no. 3 (2018): 341–55; reprinted with permission from Springer Nature, copyright 2018. Portions of chapter 4 were published in "Why Prisons Are Not the New Asylums," *Punishment and Society* 19, no. 3 (2017): 272–89.

Published by the University of Minnesota Press
111 Third Avenue South, Suite 290
Minneapolis, MN 55401-2520
http://www.upress.umn.edu

Printed on acid-free paper

The University of Minnesota is an equal-opportunity educator and employer.

Library of Congress Cataloging-in-Publication Data
Names: Ben-Moshe, Liat, author.
Title: Decarcerating disability : deinstitutionalization and prison abolition / Liat Ben-Moshe.
Identifiers: LCCN 2019027127 (print) | ISBN 978-1-5179-0442-5 (hc) | ISBN 978-1-5179-0443-2 (pb)
Subjects: LCSH: Deinstitutionalization—United States. | People with disabilities—Institutional care. | Prisoners with disabilities—Deinstitutionalization—United States. | Alternatives to imprisonment—United States.
Classification: LCC HV1553 .B46 2020 (print) | DDC 365/.6470870973—dc23
LC record available at https://lccn.loc.gov/2019027127

Contents

Abbreviations

AAAIMH	American Association for the Abolition of Involuntary Mental Hospitalization
ADA	Americans with Disabilities Act
AFSCME	American Federation of State, County, and Municipal Employees
ARC	formerly the Association for Retarded Citizens, now The Arc
BLM	Black Lives Matter
CLC	Cleburne Living Center
CMHC	community mental health centers
c/s/x	consumer, survivors, ex-patients (of psychiatry)
Dis Inc.	disability incarcerated and incorporated
DSM	*Diagnostic and Statistical Manual of Mental Disorders*
I/DD	intellectual and/or developmental disability
LGBTQ	lesbian, gay, bisexual, transgender, and queer
LRE	least restrictive environment
MHLP	Mental Health Law Project
MR	mental retardation
NAMI	National Alliance for the Mentally Ill or National Alliance on Mental Illness
NIMBY	not in my backyard
PIC	prison–industrial complex

PLRA	Prison Litigation Reform Act
PREAP	Prison Research Education Action Project
SHU	secure housing unit
SRV	social role valorization
SSDI	Social Security Disability Insurance
VOR	Voice of the Retarded

Acknowledgments

I've lived my life within one degree of separation from what Harriet McBride Johnson called the "disability gulag," the various sites in which people with disabilities are made to disappear. Over the years I have been to carceral spaces (prisons, psych facilities, institutions for people with intellectual and developmental disability labels) as a visitor, professional, and teacher, but was never captured therein. Still, the resemblance between these carceral places seemed striking. Even more striking to me were the movements and activism that refute the rationale for carcerality—the need for psychiatric hospitals, residential institutions for people with disabilities, and prisons.

The need to *write* about the connections between deinstitutionalization, disability/antipsychiatry, and prison abolition came from two pivotal encounters. The first and most influential figure to cast his enormous shadow over this project was Dr. Steven J. Taylor, who passed away in November 2014 but whose spirit and knowledge reverberate in many chapters of this book. At his memorial, I shared the following story. The first time I ever met him was during my first week in the United States, in August 2002, as a new Ph.D. student coming to study sociology and disability studies at Syracuse University. Imagine my surprise (and later delight) to meet for the first time my new American advisor, whom a few minutes prior I thought was a housing-insecure person wandering into the building for shelter, with flip-flops and raggedy clothing, and sporting a long, mostly unkempt beard. It is most telling that this humble man worked all his life to make sure that people, whatever their disabilities or labels, all had homes, real homes. Most of what I know about deinstitutionalization, as spirit, praxis, ethical stance, and process, came from him. He was not only an advisor but very much an informant for this project.

Steve was most well known for his tireless activism and scholarship advocating the closure of institutions for people with intellectual and developmental disabilities and supporting meaningful participation and life in the community. As part of that work, in which he was involved from the 1970s until his passing, he created spaces, developed courses, and provided academic support toward the development of what we now call "disability studies." His work was especially influential in bringing attention to developmental disabilities within disability studies. He exemplified not only what can be done under the rubric of disability studies but that one can be an academic and still maintain some semblance of integrity and ethics. The guiding question for all projects, grants, and writings was: Is this going to aid in liberating people?—a core question at the heart of abolition praxis and one that guides me to this day.

This question led me to the second encounter that birthed this book. In 2008, I had the pleasure of meeting Dr. Angela Y. Davis when she was visiting Syracuse University. I came to her office hours wide-eyed, trying to make connections with and between movements, prodding for any leads. After a few meetings, I asked, "Do you know anyone who is connecting disability to prison abolition in critical ways? I would like to read or meet them." She said, without flinching, "Yes, I do. You are." Her words stayed with me for two reasons. First, it was validating to hear that what I was embarking on was needed and that I (at that point an ABD student) was becoming an expert on the topic. Her words also made clear the paucity of written work (and, at that time, activist work) that connected deinstitutionalization as a form of decarceration and prison abolition. Second, it modeled for me the kind of generosity and reciprocity that was so moving coming from such a luminary, and one I try to model for my students today. It underscored how, as scholar-activists entrenched in radical political projects, we learn and build from and with each other.

This book is therefore a physical manifestation of ideas, discussions, and renumerations with scholar-activists who were and are actively fighting against the tyranny of carceral edifices. Their/our relentless efforts not only propelled me to put these genealogies of activism and resistance into printed form but also have inspired my everyday life—the kind of person I aspire to be and the kind of world I want to be a part of creating.

Beth E. Richie is a model of the kind of academic-scholar I aspire to be and has become my mentor on how, in the words of Rod Ferguson, to be "in the university but not of it," or in other words, how to be an ethical academic without losing my morals. I thank her and other abolitionist feminists like Andrea Richie, Barbara Ransby, Dean Spade, Emily Thuma, Eric Stanley, Erica Meiners, Joey Mogul, Mariame Kaba, Ruthie Gilmore, and countless others who have opened this world of activism to me as a space of co-learning and co-struggling.

Jean Stewart and Marta Russell's article "Disablement, Prison and Historical Segregation" was incredibly influential for my (and so many others') understanding of the connection between disability, incarceration, and political economy. I highly recommend that anyone interested in the topic read it. Years after the article's publication, and after Marta's death, I would come to meet Jean and call her a colleague and comrade. I thank her for the opportunity to return to that groundbreaking article in our shared writing—a process meaningful to me well beyond the page. I also appreciate the important work connecting the asylum and the prison done by Anne Parsons, Jonathan Metzl, and Bernard Harcourt and thank them for pushing this research in critical ways.

My deepest appreciation to disability studies and disability justice comrades for sustaining radical conversations over the years: Aimi Hamraie, AJ Withers, Allison Carey, Angel Miles, Angela Carter, Candace Coleman, Carrie Sandahl, Chris Chapman, Eliza Chandler, Jina Kim, Lena Palacios, Leon Hilton, Leroy Moore, Lezlie Frye, Meghann O'Leary, Nili Broyer, Nirmala Erevelles, Shelley Papenfuse, Simi and David Linton, Subini Annamma, Sumi Colligan, Tanja Aho, and Tia Nelis and many others too numerous to mention. And to the Society for Disability Studies, a much-missed home, which, just like any other home, was as cringeworthy and exacerbating as they come, but also full of cutting-edge scholarship, cultural production, beauty, and imaginative potential. Finally, membership in disability clubs had rewards!

Wonderful colleagues and mentors at Syracuse University, such as Marjorie Devault, Jackie Orr, Arlene Kanter, Beth Ferri, Rachel Zubal-Ruggieri, Zosha Stuckey, and others, helped create the spark to what, many years later, has become this book.

Colleagues at the University of Toledo's Disability Studies program have been incredibly supportive of my work and my family. In addition to building what I think is the best disability studies BA program in the United States, they have also created an intellectually stimulating and caring environment—thank you, Ally Day (and Catherine Harrington and Bob), Kim Nielsen (and Nate, Maya, and Morgan), and Jim Ferris (and family), the strongest smallest program that could. Also, thanks to Linda Curtis and colleagues at the University of Toledo, especially Sharon Barnes, Jean Kusina, and Kimberley Mack, for your friendship and collegiality. I especially thank Renee Heberlee and Susan Ford for introducing me to the painful joys of teaching in prison and, of course, all the students at TOCI for making me accountable and giving me a lot to think about.

To fearless midwestern abolitionist comrades, Sangi Ravichandran, Alejo Stark, Jackie Miller, Ami Harbin, Mike Doan, Shannon Frye, and Tia Carley, thanks for the nourishment in food, camaraderie, and thought.

I thank Beth Richie and many colleagues, staff, and students in the Criminology, Law, and Justice Department at the University of Illinois at Chicago, my new home since 2019. Special thanks to Rahim Kurwa, Susila Gurusami, Ronak Kapadia, Alana Gunn, and Stacey Krueger for their help with publication anxiety and the cover design.

Thanks to the numerous students, faculty, and others who invited me to give talks in 2015–19 and commented on different iterations of chapters, or ideas that became chapters, for their patience, feedback, and sometimes righteous anger. I was also privileged to be the recipient of the American Association of University Women (AAUW) Postdoctoral Research Fellowship for 2017–18, which enabled me to complete a partial draft of the manuscript.

Special thanks to all who offered feedback on this manuscript. H Rakes and Ray Noll were invaluable for their intellect, ongoing friendship, most enticing conversations, and finding of joy in misery. Thanks to Jasbir Puar for pushing my thinking in reciprocal, challenging, and much-appreciated ways. Craig Willse, Allison Carey, Alison Kafer, Aly Patsavas, Petra Kuppers, Jiji Voronka, Zhiying Ma, Akemi Nishida, Sue Schweik, Erica Meiners, and Mike Gill read drafts of chapters, provided generous comments, and were thoughtful editors, colleagues, comrades, and badasses. Renee Heberlee, Beth Currens, and Ally Day formed the nucleus of our feminist writing group in Toledo, and I also thank them for commenting on chapters in formation.

Since this is called "acknowledgments," I want to acknowledge at the outset that this book is long and potentially hard to read. It runs defiantly against current trends in academic publishing (short succinct books, written or revised in a span of one to three years to make them relevant and fresh, one idea per chapter, and so on). This book took more than a decade to conceptualize and many years to write. I want to be transparent about this for other struggling authors, writers, and thinkers and also for you who read this. It was a difficult book to write because of its subject matter (institutionalization, imprisonment, liberation, racial criminal pathologization and its long-lasting effects on people and communities) as well as its magnitude and scope. It was also hard due to my desire to be accountable to the movements, fading historical moments, people, and ideas that I attempt to represent here. Deinstitutionalization and prison abolition are living movements and frameworks that require the kind of nuance and heft I tried to offer here.

I want to thank the University of Minnesota Press, especially Dani Kasprzak, for not bowing down from this heft and for taking up this project in its entirety. Anne Carter was a constant throughout this process, and I want to thank her for her assistance in bringing this book to fruition. This book would not be possible without the labor of many at the Press, most of whom I do not know by name, but I wish to convey my gratitude to all the behind-the-scenes work.

Last, much gratitude to my family, chosen and otherwise. My appreciation goes to Kennedy Healy and the younger generation for whom struggles for liberation and their accompanied oppressions are always already intersectional. I especially thank her and Carrie Kaufman for queercrip camaraderie and for grounding me in what matters (sloths).

To the whole Ben-Moshe clan, much love for your support (from a "writing retreat" at my parents' apartment to harping on me to get it done). Thanks to Olivia McAdams for putting up with my lackluster cooking and long hours devoted to the actual writing of this book, and for making me think really hard. Throughout the many years of working on this book, you have turned from a smart tween to an accomplished college student.

Finally, I give my endless gratitude to my (human) love throughout this process, Dean Adams, who embodies interdependence, compassion, and curiosity, without which any discussions of liberation are futile. From *10,000 Days* to *Fear Inoculum*, thanks for reading everything I write and being my biggest and smartest cheerleader and teacher.

And to all the "we need to have a conversation abouts," the naysayers, reformers, and carceral feminists, the "we're not racists" and ableists of all sorts: you have propelled this work, its necessity and immediacy, beyond imagination.

Introduction

Intersecting Disability, Imprisonment, and Deinstitutionalization

Decarceration and Deinstitutionalization

There is no doubt that recent years have brought a surge in media, activist, and scholarly interest in mass incarceration.[1] However, the burgeoning discourse regarding imprisonment and its critique rarely covers disability or madness as a topic that merits attention, even though disability is central to mass incarceration and decarceration in the United States. This is true in terms of both the disabling nature of incarceration in prisons and the pervasiveness of incarceration (whether in so-called therapeutic facilities like psych hospitals or punitive ones like jails) characterizing the lives of many disabled people (whether they identify or are politicized as such or not).

Despite this pervasiveness, disability and madness are largely missing from analysis of incarceration and its resistance.[2] When disability or madness *is* present, it is conceived of as a deficit, something in need of correction, medically/psychiatrically or by the correction industry, but not as a nuanced identity from which to understand how to live differently, including reevaluating responses to harm and difference. This is not only a scholarly omission but also a real danger to the lives of those most marginalized, especially when many proposals for reform risk increasing surveillance over those already heavily impacted by carceral sites and logics in the United States.

Discussing incarceration and decarceration without referring to disability/madness has several pitfalls. First, it ignores the ways carceral locales and their histories of closure and abolition are interconnected. This is what Chapman, Carey, and I referred to as "carceral archipelago" or carceral matrix.[3] By *carceral locales*, I am referring to a variety of enclosures, especially prisons,

1

jails, psychiatric hospitals, and residential institutions for those with intellectual or developmental disabilities, but I am also referring to particular
logics and discourses that abolition (penal/prison/carceral) opposes. As such,
this book draws from and connects to the nascent subfield of critical carceral studies.[4]

Furthermore, analyzing incarceration and decarceration without a dis-
ability/madness lens casts away ways of understanding disability/madness
as lived identity and a way to be in and view the world (i.e., an ontology and
epistemology), as it intersects with race, gender, nationality, and other axes.
It also results in not taking disability as an analytic. Such lack of what I later
describe as a crip/mad of color critique[5] sidesteps disability/madness and
their histories of oppression and resistance as ways to inform policy and activist resolutions to vast social problems, such as incarceration. To those who
claim that prison abolition and massive decarceration are utopian and could
never happen, this book shows that they've happened already, although in
a different arena, in the form of mass closures of residential institutions and
psychiatric hospitals and the deinstitutionalization of those who resided in
them. I suggest that it is essential to interrogate deinstitutionalization as a
social movement, a mind-set, a logic to counter carceral logics. I argue that
deinstitutionalization is not just something that has "happened" but was a
call for an ideological shift in the way we react to difference among us.

Therefore one aim of this book is to construct and activate a genealogy of the largest decarceration movement in U.S. history: deinstitutionalization. Understanding how to activate this knowledge can lead to more
nuanced actions toward and understandings about reducing reliance on
prisons and other carceral enclosures as holders for people who are deemed
by society to be dangerous, abnormal, or disturbed. In so doing, we can build
coalitions between queer, racial justice, and disability justice organizing. By
connecting deinstitutionalization with prison abolition, I also elucidate some
of the limitations of disability rights and inclusion discourses and of tactics
like litigation.

Rich lessons for prison abolition are available in the history of deinstitutionalization. And yet deinstitutionalization is repeatedly blamed for the rise
of U.S. mass incarceration.[6] It is often implied that the main reason people
with psychiatric disabilities ended up in prisons and jails is the closure of
psychiatric hospitals in the early 1960s. Such claims amplify calls that con-
demn the deinstitutionalization movement as irresponsible and for "leaving

people in the streets." But as I show in chapter 4, deinstitutionalization did not lead to homelessness and increased incarceration. Racism and neoliberalism did, via privatization, budget cuts in all service/welfare sectors, and little to no funding for affordable and accessible housing and social services, while the budgets for corrections, policing, and punishment (of mostly poor people of color) skyrocketed.

Let me explain what I mean by deinstitutionalization as a phenomenon and logic. The closure of psychiatric hospitals and large state institutions for those with developmental disabilities has been a major policy trend in most U.S. states in the past few decades. The population of people with intellectual and/or developmental disabilities (I/DD) in large residential institutions (more than sixteen persons) peaked at 194,650 in 1967. By 2015, this number had declined to 69,557.[7] The number of people with I/DD labels living in institutions decreased by 80 percent from 1977 to 2015, while the number of people living in small residences (six or fewer people) increased by greater than 1,900 percent over this same time period.[8] In the last twenty years, the number of people with I/DD who receive support and services from their state while living in the home of a family member has also increased by 135 percent. As a result, by 2014, fourteen U.S. states had closed all their state-operated institutions for people with I/DD.[9] These states still have residents with I/DD labels; they have just learned how to accommodate their needs outside of the institutional framework.

An accompanying shift occurred in the field of mental health in the 1960s with the closure of large state mental hospitals in most major cities. In 1955, the state mental health population was 559,000, *nearly as large on a per capita basis as the prison population today.* By 2000, it had fallen to fewer than one hundred thousand.[10] I want to be clear here that I am not suggesting that institutionalization, hospitalization, and imprisonment in jails and prisons are the same, but I am suggesting that they all encompass carceral logics and that those who want to achieve a noncarceral society should examine one specific historical precedent of decarceration in the United States to identify potential pitfalls to avoid (such as the bureaucratization and institutionalization of deinstitutionalization, discussed in chapter 2) as well as useful strategies used during deinstitutionalization that made it happen de facto.

Deinstitutionalization has been largely defined as the movement of people with psychiatric and intellectual or developmental disabilities from state

institutions and hospitals into community living and supports. Deinstitutionalization is also the accompanying closure of carceral locales, the shuttering of large, mostly state-sponsored/funded, institutions and hospitals for
people with intellectual and psychiatric disabilities. But by understanding
it as a history of (not only but also) abolitionist practices, I argue that deinstitutionalization is not only a historical process but a logic. It was something that people fought for, and won. It was, and still is, a fraught process,
but it is also a cautionary tale of success.

This interpretation showcases the gains that deinstitutionalization made
in the ways we treat disability and madness. I mean treatment both in terms
of the impetus to therapeutically take care of disability (now outside institution walls) but also in terms of social and cultural treatment, a shift in perspective toward disability rights, inclusion, and perhaps justice. By viewing
deinstitutionalization in this way, this book brings to the forefront the social
critiques that disability/madness conjured up regarding treatment, rehabilitation, choice, and segregation. The book also offers critiques of deinstitutionalization and the ways it helped to construct a narrow liberal approach to
liberation through the framework of inclusion by adhering to specific able-
racial-gendered capitalist formations.

Genealogy of Decarceration

This book is rooted in queer, crip, and feminist of color intersectional scholarship that is indebted to the knowledge and labor of queer of color and
feminist of color scholarship. Cathy Cohen, Dean Spade, and others urge
us to frame oppression and state violence, in this case, criminalization and
incarceration, through what Roderick Ferguson describes as a queer of color
critique.[11] This critique questions traditional white liberal approaches to social
problems that call for measures like more legislation or incorporation within
the system (for example, gaining rights through same-sex marriage or the
incorporation of LGBTQ in the military). Furthermore, as Jina Kim explicates
regarding her definition of crip of color critique, "as a critical methodology,
it would ask us to consider the ableist reasoning and language underpin-
ning the racialized distribution of violence."[12] It is feminist and queer of
color not only in its interrogation of racial gendered dynamics but also in
its methodology and directive to shift "the margins to the center."[13] Crip of
color critique is also important in threading together what I term *race-ability,*

in a critical way that engages, queers (as was Ferguson's original prompt), critiques, and exceeds normative frames. By race-ability, I am referring to the ways race and disability, and racism, sanism, and ableism as intersecting oppressions, are mutually constitutive and cannot be separated, in their genealogy (eugenics, for example), current iterations of resistance (in the form of disability justice, for example), or oppression (incarceration and police killing, for example).

The analysis in this book is also deeply inspired by the work of Michel Foucault, who explored the connected power effects that operate through various regimes of truth (such as science/psychiatry/medicine/pastoral). Foucault's aim was to show that the logic of (both disciplinary and biopolitical) power operated through a variety of technologies and social as well as physical institutions;[14] his prime examples were the asylum, the clinic, and the prison, which are the sites of incarceration pervasive in the contemporary lives of those racialized and pathologized and therefore the main sites of carceral enclosure discussed here.

As Wendy Brown suggests, Foucault's work moves us from typologies of time to geographies of power.[15] Power, for Foucault, works precisely because it is not merely destructive but productive. It produces particular subject formations and, by so doing, constrains and reifies them in the very discourse that created them, for example, through the creation of the medical discourse of psychiatry. Power, in this formulation, is not a centralized external force controlled by a limited few but is inside us, making us operate in particular ways, often by benevolent means, that is, "for our own good," such as is the case with diets, psychotherapy, anger management, and rehabilitation, to name a few examples.[16]

This book strives to expand genealogy beyond analysis of instruments of power to the topography of their resistance, in this case, focusing not on incarceration and its logics but on discourses of decarceration in the form of deinstitutionalization and prison abolition. This book is especially inspired by the methodological aspects of Foucault's work. The production of psy and penological discourses and subjects (the "mentally ill," "criminals," "abnormality") are usually taken for granted or seem like they "have always been here."[17] Following Nietzsche, Foucault created the analytical tools of archeology and genealogy, which enable the critic to start taking apart these taken-for-granted notions.[18] In creating "a history of the present," the critical theorist or historian can uncover the conditions of the present circumstances in the past and create awareness of the current situation, not as transhistoric or as a continuity, but as a contingency.[19] Genealogy therefore does not attempt to capture the "true" story or the essence of an event but the local, dispersed histories attached to it. Genealogy allows the researcher to investigate imagined possibilities and carefully construct not just an alternative historiography but also a narrative of what could have been, in knowledges that have been discredited as nonscientific and forgotten.

We live now in a moment in which resistance to the current penal system, and prison abolition as a practice, is (still) contested. It is apparent to many activists in this movement that the goal of abolition is a long-term one and that we will not see this change in our lifetimes. Therefore what I offer here is about the future as much as it is about the past or present. Genealogy enables me to assess deinstitutionalization as a tactic that some see as incredibly successful in closing down repressive institutions; as an ideology that sought to change the way people with disabilities are perceived and treated; and as an unfulfilled promise seen by activists, policy makers, and social scientists. Genealogy also elucidates the contingencies in the present and future, as seen in current prison abolition work and the (as yet unrealized) vision of a noncarceral and nonsegregationist society.

This book is also genealogical in the sense that it offers a history of ideas—abolition, closure, and the critique of reform. More importantly, it reveals how one form of knowledge or tactic was discredited and seen as irrelevant and nonsensical and how relations of power made one knowledge (penal expansion, biopsychiatry, prison and institutional reform) subsume the other (discourses of abolition or other ways of reacting to harm and difference). As genealogy does not follow a progression or evolutionary model, I also demonstrate how reform and abolition are embedded in each other and live side by side, although one is often seen as legitimate and the other is discredited as belonging to a radical fringe.

To construct this genealogy, I gathered a diverse archive consisting of texts and cultural products written by scholars and activists within prison abolition as well as by those fighting against psychiatric and other forms of institutionalization of people with disabilities (including doctors, scholars, and activists in the consumer, survivor, and ex-patient movements and the field of developmental disability; self-advocates and those currently and formerly incarcerated; and disability advocates, lawyers, and family members). In other words, I look at a wide range of formal and informal players who are involved in the fight to close institutions and prisons since the 1950s and contemporarily, although the focus is on the era of deinstitutionalization and its aftermath today.

I also analyzed what was written about these abolitionary movements, as these documents provide insights into reactions to institutional closure initiatives and to prison abolition, specifically under the rubric of the "backlash" to deinstitutionalization and carceral closure. I further took up federal and state policies and case law regarding prison closures, prisoners' and inmates' rights, and the deinstitutionalization of those labeled as developmentally disabled, and I looked at policy changes to the closure of psychiatric hospitals and facilities and the shift to community care. Additionally, I analyzed protests, rallies, and testimonies during closure hearings of prisons and large residential institutions to grasp what's behind the resistance to such closures. Finally, I was able to draw from my own conversations with several key figures in these movements, including Wolf Wolfensberger and Thomas Szasz shortly before their passing as well as many current abolitionists and activists, to understand their own perspectives on "doing abolition" and its consequences.

Disability and Imprisonment

By now we should all be familiar with the figures. The United States has only 5 percent of the world's population, yet it holds 25 percent of the world's imprisoned population. Between 2006 and 2008, the U.S. incarceration rate peaked at one thousand inmates per one hundred thousand adults— a record level. By 2016, the incarceration rate was still staggering compared to the rates of other countries but was at its lowest point since 1996, at 830 inmates per 100,000 adults.[20] Another whopping 4,537,100 adults were under "community corrections," which include parole and probation.[21] Race, gender, and disability are significantly tied to incarceration rates. At its height, in 2006, whites were imprisoned at a rate of 409 per 100,000 U.S. residents, Latinos at 1,038 per 100,000, and blacks at 2,468 per 100,000. The rate for women was 134 per 100,000 residents; for men, it was 1,384 per 100,000.

Disability and impairment (physical, psychological, sensory, cognitive, learning) play a major role in this incarceration matrix. As Jean Stewart and Marta Russell show in their pathbreaking 2001 article, prisoners are not randomly selected and do not represent all strata of society.[22] The majority of prisoners are poor and are people of color. Poverty is a strong conduit to disablement and debilitation (I discuss the difference between the two in the last section of this chapter). In addition, the prison environment itself is disabling so that even if an individual enters prison without a disability or mental health diagnosis, she is likely to get one—from the sheer trauma of incarceration in enclosed, tight spaces with poor air quality and circulation; to hard labor with toxic conditions and materials; to circulation of drugs and unsanitary needles as well as the spread of infectious diseases, some of which result from environmental toxins related to the sites on which prisons are built;[23] to lack of medical equipment and medication, or at times overmedication.[24] Add to these factors placements in inhumane conditions, such as solitary confinement (which are especially pervasive for gender-nonconforming, trans, and queer or gay incarcerated people, supposedly for their own protection), and the various impairments that come with aging in prison as a result of prolonged sentencing policies, and the debilitating nature of imprisonment cannot be denied. Trauma is incredibly pervasive in carceral settings, and the trigger and disabling cumulative effects of strip searches (especially on those who experienced sexual violence previously, which is the majority of those held in women's prisoners) leads feminist abolitionists to understand them as state-sponsored violence against women.[25]

Even if they are already disabled, conditions of confinement may cause further mental breakdown for those entering the system with diagnoses of "mental," psychiatric, or intellectual disabilities. In general, although several attempts have been made to estimate the number of prisoners who have psychiatric diagnosis, it is impossible to quantify their number with any degree of precision, even if taking the label of "mental illness" as a viable construct (the critique of madness as an illness will be discussed further in chapter 2). The American Psychiatric Association reported in 2000 that up to 5 percent of prisoners were actively psychotic and that as many as one in five prisoners were "seriously mentally ill." The Bureau of Justice Statistics reports that in 2005, more than half of all prison and jail inmates had a mental health problem. The reported prevalence of "mental health problems" among the imprisoned seems to vary by race and gender. White inmates appear to have higher rates of reported "mental health problems" than African Americans or Hispanics;[26] however, African Americans, especially men, seem to be labeled "seriously mentally ill" more often than their white counterparts. It is also reported that, in general, incarcerated women have higher rates of "mental health problems" than men.[27] Gender expression that does not match people's genitals (as this is the main criterion for the sex-based separation that is the prison system) compounds these factors and leads to a psychiatric diagnosis and/or placement in solitary confinement in the name of protection.

Deaf people who are incarcerated face a vast lack of access to interpreters during arrest, trial, and imprisonment, which may lead to unwarranted incarceration due to lack of basic communication. While incarcerated, Deaf (those who are culturally deaf and use sign language as their main mode of communication), deaf, and hard-of-hearing inmates are at an extreme disadvantage. First, inability to respond to commands because of lack of access to interpreters or communication aids can and often does result in violence, especially from guards who think they are disobeying orders. Second, those incarcerated who are Deaf/deaf or hard of hearing cannot access various programming, including programs that can lead to parole, because correctional facilities or staff are reluctant to provide communication devices or competent interpreters.[28]

As Dylan Rodriguez and others suggest, it is impossible to espouse, discuss, or practice carceral abolition without an understanding of racial captivity as a core function of carceral logics.[29] The availability of black bodies (especially in what we call the United States) and indigenous bodies (especially in what we call Canada) for capture in carceral settings is not about overrepresentation but is a key feature of the carceral racial state. I want also to suggest that the disabling nature of incarceration and whose bodies are available for capture should likewise be understood as a core feature of incarceration. I therefore want to add to the important scholarship and activism around criminalization a focus that connects such criminalization with pathologization as a core feature of state violence and carceral logics.

Despite the prevalence of disability/madness in carceral locales, it is often missing from *analysis* of these sites and logics. In contrast, the framework guiding this book is rooted in the fields of disability studies and mad studies, which engage with disability/madness as an identity and culture and pivot around the knowledge of people with disabilities as a meaningful axis in questioning how we analyze and respond to carceral enclosures in the contemporary United States and historically. Centering disability and mental difference can therefore lead to a more complex understanding of both incarceration and decarceration.

In conjuncture with feminist of color analysis of incarceration, I want to offer here a disability, and especially race-ability, perspective on abolition of carceral enclosures, what could be called crip/mad of color critique of incarceration and decarceration. Crip of color critique focuses on the role of the state in trying to fix ills of its own creation and, in so doing, interpolate those it harms to seek remedies through the framework of the settler racial heteropatriarchal ableist nation-state. Crip of color critique shows that the focus on liberal approaches (legal protection, rights) ends in demands to expand existing frameworks to accommodate marginalized populations, such as disabled people of color, but not in changing the status quo. For example, demands for inclusion of people with disabilities in employment or education do not critique or change the system of exploitative racial capitalism or the settler ableist system of education but only expand it to fit more people.[30] This expansion is what abolitionists often term as reform measures, which increase the scope of harm (in this case, of incarceration as state violence on the lives of people with disabilities).

As feminist abolitionists like Beth Richie, Angela Davis, Erica Meiners, Dean Spade, and others point out, a feminist and queer analysis of what has come to be called the prison–industrial complex can shed light not only on those incarcerated who identify as women or gender nonconforming but on the entire rationale of segregation, punishment, and incarceration.[31] This illumination in turn helps organizing and scholarship that try to chip away at carceral spaces and ultimately aid those who are incarcerated and their/our loved ones and us all.

To those already interested in incarceration, prison reform, or penal abolition, I wish to offer a political look at disability as a lived experience, but especially as an analytic from which to examine, and in some ways indict, our current criminal (in)justice system.[32] The framework of disability studies provides an understanding of disability as identity and culture; it gives tools for critiquing notions of pathology and understanding their genealogy and their intermingling with criminalization and racialization. As Simi Linton explained more than twenty years ago, "disability studies takes for its subject matter not simply the variations that exist in human behavior, appearance, functioning, sensory acuity, and cognitive processing but, more crucially, the meaning we make of those variations."[33] These meanings are socially constructed through ideologies and physical manifestations (such as terminology or the built environment) and become ways of defining human experiences that take on cultural and historical meaning. I therefore utilize disability studies as a tool to surface suppressed histories of resistance and oppression, especially from those who we often do not think of as viable subjects of knowledge, people with intellectual and psychiatric disabilities, as well as the larger social movements that they constructed and that support them.

Another goal of the book is to redefine what disability studies *is,* to squarely encompass scholarship, activism, and knowledges within the field of I/DD and the knowledges, studies, and movements of those psychiatrized (including consumers, survivors, ex-patients, mad pride, and mad studies) and those critiquing psychiatry. These knowledges are usually seen as marginal to what has come to be called disability studies, often for good reason.[34] But if disability as a politicized identity is not just physical or sensory, the "studies" attached to it should not be either. Although certainly not canonical within disability studies, the early scholarship in the 1960s and 1970s of disability as socially constructed came from the fields of I/DD and mental health.[35] This is what Steven J. Taylor called "disability studies before it had a name."[36] The reexamination of early scholarship in antipsychiatry and I/DD, whose genealogy in relation to abolition of carcerality I uncover in chapter 2, is meant as an archaeological project but also as a way to reclaim what disability studies is and could be, to push its boundaries as a field and point to its early limitations and promises.

Dis Inc. and the Carceral–Industrial Complex

Even though deinstitutionalization in mental health began before the rise of the prison boom, deinstitutionalization in I/DD and the continuance of closure of psych facilities coincided with what has come to be known as the prison–industrial complex (PIC). As I suggest later in the book, one did not cause the other in a zero-sum game of "new asylums" replacing the old. What I suggest instead is that the era in which deinstitutionalization and its backlash took place as well as the rise in imprisonment and corrections was also the era of the ascent of neoliberalism. Neoliberalism could be understood in several ways—as an economic and political economic measure,[37] a shift in cultural understanding of worth and the public good,[38] and a change in state functions.[39] As an economic structure, neoliberalism manifested in austerity measures, trickle-down economy, privatization, and decimation of the social safety net. This helps account for the growth of investment in corrections (incarceration via law and order policies and financial investment) at the same time as deinstitutionalization (evisceration of social services).

The prison–industrial complex profits from racialized incarceration by transforming "prisoners" into commodities and by the construction and maintenance of prisons by construction companies as well as suppliers, catering, and telephone companies.[40] But as Julia Chinyere Oparah clarifies, "it is not, as is sometimes assumed, a pseudonym for prison labor or the private prison industry, although both of those phenomena point to the ways in which economic interests have become wrapped up in contemporary punishment regimes. Neither is it a 'conspiracy theory' that relies on surmise and suspicion of illicit deals in shady backrooms."[41] She attributes the first use of the term *prison–industrial complex* to Mike Davis, in his 1995 article in the *Nation* that described the PIC as a multi-billion-dollar prison boom in California at the time. The term was later popularized by Critical Resistance activists like Angela Davis, Ruth Wilson Gilmore, and Linda Evans. The term helps to explain the prison-building binge of the 1990s and untangles it from traditional explanations tied to crime rates, since such rates (for homicide and property crime) had either plateaued or declined (depending on the state) at that time.

The PIC is not just about profit but solves the inherent crises of racial capitalism. Gilmore's analysis of California demonstrates the intricate ways in which socioeconomic, geographical, fiscal, racial, and legal processes led the way to the biggest prison expansion in history. For Gilmore, the PIC is a geographical solution to political economic crises, and prisons are the state's attempt at fixing the crisis of surplus it is in—surplus land, people, capital, and state capacity.[42] As others put it, those of us who are not housing inse-cure or are not incarcerated are disciplined into ways of living that legiti-mate certain forms of protection and security (segregation, slow death, civil death, removal from the public) by extracting value from the abandon-ment of entire populations (disabled, unemployed, poor people of color, and so on).[43] Such analysis is not simply about privatization of incarceration or using those incarcerated for labor but is a framework from which to under-stand the current political economy as contingency and incarceration as one response to the crises it produces.

While the concept of the PIC has been incredibly useful for scholars and activists, if we also include institutionalization in the analysis, it is more apt to think in terms of a carceral–industrial complex. I am indebted here to the work of the late Marta Russell, who suggested that the forces of incarceration of disabled people should be understood under the growth of both the prison–industrial complex and the institution–industrial complex, in the form of a growing private industry of nursing homes, boarding homes, for-profit psychiatric hospitals, and group homes.[44]

Many (including policy makers) believe that disabled people are a strain on the economy, especially under the neoliberal ideology of cost–benefit analyses and austerity measures. But political economists of disability argue that disability supports a whole industry of professionals, such as service providers, case managers, medical professionals, and health care specialists, that keeps the economy afloat.[45] In the context of capitalism, disability became the category through which people are measured as need based or work based, as I discuss at length elsewhere.[46] Such interpretations dispel the common belief that people with disabilities are not productive under the capitalist system because they do not hold jobs. As Russell suggests, people with disabilities are commodified and deemed profitable, especially when occupying institutional beds. By clever capitalist alchemy, surplus populations are spun into gold. Disability is commodified through this matrix of incarceration (prisons, hospitals, nursing homes, and more).

Neoliberalism is not only an economic structure but an ideological and epistemological regime as well. As Grace Kyungwon Hong powerfully argues, neoliberalism emerged as a response to the liberation movements of the post–World War II era.[47] Disability is not often included in discussions of these post–World War II radical movements. This is for several reasons, one of which is ableism and the lack of understanding of disability and madness as (at least also) forms of identity (ontology), culture, and knowledge (epistemology). It is also perhaps because of the later emergence of these movements, which did not reach full force and become visible until the 1970s and 1980s. Because I view antipsychiatry and movements in I/DD as an (often contested) part of the larger umbrella of "disability movements" and deinstitutionalization as one manifestation of the struggle for liberation of people with disabilities, the timing and actors I look at are more varied than traditional accounts of "disability rights." Throughout the book, I show both the radical potential of such actors and movements—and their knowledges, especially as linked to abolition—but also the pitfall of disability rights as a liberal apparatus that is connected with neoliberal governance (in the form of cost effectiveness, choice, free market).

If neoliberalism is, as Hong describes, "a change in the distribution of respectability in response to the crises in racial capital as marked by the social movements of the post–World War II period,"[48] then incorporation (as social/cultural inclusion and as a form of economic incorporation, whether as commodities via incarceration or as consumers) is one of its important characteristics. As Gilmore further suggests, "intranational conflicts around inclusion and exclusion require this state to 'fix' difference in order to maintain internal pacification. . . . The 'fix' follows two general trajectories. In good times, the state remedies exclusion by recognizing the structural nature of racism and institutionalizing means for combating its effects—by, for example, extending the vote, banning discrimination in public sector employment. . . . In bad times, when deepened differentiation pacifies widespread insecurity among the herrenvolk, the 'fix' formalizes inequality. Examples of the latter include: the 1882 Chinese Exclusion Act; Jim Crow (U.S. apartheid) laws throughout the early twentieth century; . . . The oscillation between reformist and repressive 'fixes' is not a simple binary movement but rather overdetermined at the source."[49] Inclusion via and in conjunction with exclusion, therefore, is a key feature of racial capitalism and of the neoliberal carceral state.

To add disability/madness into this discussion, throughout the book, I use the concept of Dis Inc. to expand this logic to two aspects of neoliberalism: "disability incarcerated" and "Disability Incorporated." I am using the word *incorporation* to signal both the cultural and social incorporation of minority difference[50] into the status quo and incorporation as a structure of political economic profit-making impetuses, whether it is through discourses of cost effectiveness under neoliberalism or literal corporations raking in profits from incarceration and disposability under plain old capitalism, such as group homes, halfway houses, and prisons. As a concept, it simultaneously captures the corporatization of disability for profit by carceral institutions and the ways disability is subjected to incorporation in society, but only by respectability politics and assimilation (by rehabilitation, approximating normalcy, etc.). In other words, under current formations of racial capitalism and able-nationalism,[51] the incorporation of disability is twofold but equally problematic—through capitalist accumulation (on the backs of those labeled as disabled) and through erasure of the transgressive aspects of race-ability in order to be and feel included. Throughout the book, I show how the concept of Dis Inc., or the "oscillation between reformist and repressive 'fixes,'"[52] works in such cases as resistance to housing integration based on race-ability; those who fight against the closure of disability residential institutions through utilizing the concept of choice; and through the arena of litigation, which emphasizes rights to inclusion into an oppressive status quo.

Carceral Ableism and Nonreformist Reforms

Incarceration does not just happen in penal locales. In *Disability Incarcerated*, Allison Carey, Chris Chapman, and I expanded on what has come to be classified as "incarceration" to include confinement in a wide variety of enclosed settings, including prisons, jails, detention centers, institutions in the arena of intellectual disability, treatment centers, and psychiatric hospitals. We did not claim that these internments are the same, but we demonstrated and explored the ways that they enact and draw upon both similar and distinct repressive logics. In other words, we tried to explore incarceration writ large, not just in prisons but also in other spaces of confinement, such as psych hospitals, or through chemical incarceration. As we demonstrated, incarceration is not just a space or locale but a logic of state coercion and segregation of difference. And as we showed, it is a racist, colonial, gendered logic at its core.

But today, the argument that "prisons are the new asylums" is often used not as a way to connect to movements that fought to close the old asylums but instead as rationalization for the creation of new jail facilities (for "the good of" those with mental health differences) or of psychiatric wards within existing jails or prisons. As many activists forewarn, and this book details, these will likely increase the scope of incarceration. Because of the rising cost of construction and maintenance of carceral spaces, the corporate world and criminal justice and health care systems are now turning to various "alternatives" to incarceration and institutionalization. But this turn signifies the increased privatization of penalty and health care—not the decline of segregation but its intensification through other means. I want to emphasize that at issue here is not just co-optation or privatization but a change in the discourse that incorporates the punitive with the therapeutic, with vast implications for the embeddedness of criminalization with pathologization.

For example, recent critiques of solitary confinement and supermax facilities (the solitary incarceration of people in a cell the size of a closet for twenty-three hours a day for months and sometimes years) call for screening for mental health issues and the release of those with such issues from these types of confinement. Such advocacy could be a great case of coalition between prison abolitionists and disability/madness activism. But calling for certain populations to be released from jails and prisons often sends them to be reincarcerated in other institutions or by other means, including by forced drugging or by indefinite detention in detention centers, psychiatric hospitals, or psych forensic units.

In his 1974 *Politics of Abolition,* abolitionist criminologist Thomas Mathiesen follows Andre Gorz's distinction between reformist and "nonreformist" reforms, a heuristic distinction popularized by Ruthie Gilmore and used routinely in abolitionist campaigns. Reformist reforms are situated in the status quo, so that any changes are made within or against this existing framework. Nonreformist reforms imagine a different horizon and are not limited by a discussion of what is possible at present. Mathiesen states that nonreformist reforms that are effective need to be of the abolishing kind. The question is what kinds of reforms are sought and whether they will strengthen the system in the long run.[53] For instance, fighting for adequate health care for those currently imprisoned is something abolitionists often support as a nonreformist reform. However, some initiatives, such as mental health jails, are opposed by abolitionists, as these would only expand the scope of incarceration in the long haul.

My claim here, following many scholar-activists in carceral abolition movements, is that suggesting improvements or progressive alternatives is the core problem with reform and not abolition-based approaches. It increases the scope of incarceration, and instead of making the system more just, it spreads an unjust system to more people. Current examples include the increased use of e-carceration,[54] such as electronic monitoring bracelets, and the use of psych medication discussed by Erick Fabris as chemical incarceration.[55]

This is what James Kilgore referred to as *carceral humanism.*[56] He wanted a term that captured how the correction discourse changed from security to the welfare of the inmates. Kilgore characterizes carceral humanism as comprising four elements: repackaging punishment as service provisions; normalization of the delivery of social services in carceral services; reimagining of sheriffs and corrections as caring and as service providers; and innovations in new kinds of structures and providers (such as e-carceration).

Today, many manifestations of carceral humanism are embedded with ableism and sanism. *Ableism* is oppression faced due to disability/impairment (perceived or lived), which not only signals disability as a form of difference but constructs it as inferior. *Sanism* is oppression faced due to the imperative to be sane, rational, and non-mad/crazy/mentally ill/psychiatrically disabled.[57] As I show in the book, carceral humanism is compounded with carceral feminism and carceral ableism/sanism to expand the net of the carceral state and of carceral logics. Carceral feminism is the belief that the state and especially the criminal justice system can alleviate violence or abuse against women. However, such demands result in punitive measures that often harm women and communities of color.[58] Carceral ableism is the praxis and belief that people with disabilities need special or extra protections, in ways that often expand and legitimate their further marginalization and incarceration.

The example of carceral ableism and sanism regarding the critique of incarceration of people with mental health issues, especially in relation to placement in solitary confinement, bears this out. The unequivocal claims that the "mentally ill" do not belong in prison or jail only leave the carceral logic intact and even gives it more credence, as there are now clearer divisions among those who truly belong and those who do not belong under carceral regimes. In other words, if the "mentally ill" do not belong in prison, surely others do. Thus the disabling effects and legitimacy of the prison remain intact. If we take carceral abolition as an analytic, there is a need to regard prisons and other carceral enclosures as disability (justice) issues, and not just for those who are disabled or identify or are politicized as disabled in them. Abolition, and especially abolition feminism of color, offers a critique of the prison–industrial complex as a logic, one we should get rid of, not just for the benefit of one population but for the freedom of everyone.[59] This crip/mad of color critique and analysis of decarceration compose the framework that guides this book.

Etymology of *Abolition*

What is abolition then? One of my goals here is to trace the genealogy of abolition in resistance to disability-related segregation and confinement and the ways the epistemology of prison abolition is related to such a genealogy. The term *abolition,* as used in the context of penal/prison abolition, emerged from and alludes to demands to end the transatlantic slave trade. In "new/neoslavery" arguments, imprisonment is perceived as acting as a continuation of and through the lineage of chattel slavery.[60] After the American Civil War, the Thirteenth Amendment abolished slavery, except for those convicted of crimes, leading to the convict lease system in which those convicted (of mostly minor infractions meant to capture so-called free slaves, such as vagrancy and loitering) were leased for hard labor.[61] This lineage of slavery, and its supposed abolition, reverberates throughout the history of imprisonment (and therefore its resistance) leading to the present day. As historian Robert Chase remind us, if "outside the South, the discourse that prisons constituted slavery was a metaphorical organizing principle that condemned the entire prison system as a form of American apartheid," that was not the case in the South, where the rallying cry of prison slavery "had the added physical reality that southern prison farms forced unpaid prisoners to toil on former plantations in racially segregated groups to pick cotton under the supervision of white prison 'bosses' and convict guards, and the prisoners faced routine corporal punishment and state-orchestrated sexual assault."[62] This analysis offers two insights. The first is that the relation between imprisonment and slavery changes based on race and geography, and second is because it shows imprisonment not as a solution to violence but instead as de facto (sexual) violence by the state, a point echoed in various abolitionist work, work discussed throughout the book.

But there is disagreement in contemporary carceral abolition praxis and thought about how to conceptualize and whether to emphasize the slavery—convict leasing—imprisonment link. For example, political theorist Marie Gottschalk suggests that imprisonment in the United States at present is so vast that it diminishes all other phenomena in comparison, as so few blacks were actually a part of the convict lease system in the South.[63] Other scholars critique the slavery-prison nexus as an analogy and state that since only a minority of the prisoners actually get the privilege of labor or of working for wages while imprisoned, the analogy with slavery does not hold.[64]

Many prison abolitionists, however, claim that the slavery argument in abolition activism is about the lineage of oppression and segregation based on race and color in the United States, not necessarily about labor per se. These proponents do not perceive imprisonment as exactly *like* slavery but rather view incarceration as a continuation of the same racist (and I would also add settler) logic.[65] As Kim Gilmore suggests, "the point of retracing this history is not to argue that prisons have been a direct outgrowth of slavery but to interrogate the persistent connections between racism and the global economy. . . . Drawing these links has been important in explaining the relationship between racism and criminalization after emancipation, and in connecting the rise of industrial and mechanized labor to the destructive effects of deindustrialization and globalization."[66] The object of the prison–industrial complex, under these critical perspectives, is not so much profit making from prisoners' labor or private prisons as much it is containment and elimination of certain segments from civil society.[67] Therefore some draw on the framework of racial capitalism more broadly, of which white supremacy is but one manifestation.[68]

For those taking a broader approach to centering blackness in analyzing politics and resistance, what has come to be called Afro-pessimism, civil society itself is understood as a state of emergency.[69] According to such theorists, the focus is not on the excesses or crisis of the state or modernity but on its very constitution and existence. The desire of left/radical politics to anchor a politics of liberation in economic conditions, like prisons for profit, is a refusal to grapple with white supremacy.[70] Categories like exploitation, labor, progress, and hegemony are incommensurable with the black subject under these formulations. Frank Wilderson therefore asks, what does it mean to enter the anticapitalist struggle, not as a worker, but as an excess, a scandal to civil society?[71]

A related line of argument and debate can be found regarding the "New Jim Crow" thesis. The thesis, popularized by Michelle Alexander,[72] states that just as Jim Crow was a response to the abolition of slavery through the Thirteenth Amendment (and the desire for equality and black reconstruction), mass incarceration was a response to the civil rights movement, although the latter was accomplished through race baiting—claiming law-and-order policies as being race neutral—and not through the explicit racism of the Jim Crow era.[73] Though the New Jim Crow thesis has helped garner awareness of and support for critiques of the prison–industrial complex, it also falls flat on several counts; Alexander's analysis, and those who follow it, lack in intersectional analysis, especially in relation to gender/sexuality and disability.[74] Feminist activism and scholarship add a much-needed analysis of the carceral state to arguments such as the New Jim Crow. For example, regarding policing and criminalization, Andrea Ritchie offers a necessary corrective to scholarship and organizing that not only center black men's experiences and oppressions but also completely invisibilize or make insignificant any gender analysis.[75] For me, this is important to note, because men are gendered too, but such analysis does not seem to figure into the purview of documentaries like *The 13th* or books like *The New Jim Crow* and the organizing they inspire.

Another limitation of slavery or Jim Crow when used as an analogy in anti-prison organizing is that it erases the presence of nonblack prisoners of color, including the growing incarceration of indigenous, Latinx, and immigrant populations.[76] But as Chase demonstrates in regard to southern prisons, "the universality of prison abuse in the American South allowed prisoners of non–African American dissent, particularly Chicano prisoners, to share in the discourse that southern prisons created modern slavery."[77] This was not the case everywhere, but recent strikes and calls for work stoppages (for paid and unpaid labor) in U.S. prisons show that "prison slavery" offers a unique tool for mobilization and solidarity among incarcerated people and speaks to their experience, even currently.

Relatedly, Oparah offers the term *maroon abolitionists* to refer to the subjugated knowledges of activists and those incarcerated who are of color.[78] Maroon, as opposed to black–white binaries, could imply the possibility of coalitions as opposed to designations based on simplistic color lines.[79] As I foreground more in chapter 3, maroon knowledges should be centered on antiblack racism but can also apply to other fugitives, such as queer, indigenous, disabled (white or of color), and those of color who are not black.

As abolition has a lineage connecting it to slavery and to present-day imprisonment, what is its usage and weight within disability-related resistance to carceral enclosures? Within deinstitutionalization, the word *abolition* is not often used. When it does appear, it is usually referring to stopping forced psychiatric confinement and its rationale. I define abolition of psychiatric incarceration in three ways: abolition as the act and process of closing down psychiatric hospitals; abolition of the rationale for long hospitalization; and last, abolition of psychiatry. To understand the genealogy of abolition within discourses critiquing psychiatry, I discuss in chapter 2 the example of the American Association for the Abolition of Involuntary Mental Hospitalization, established in 1970 by Thomas Szasz, Erving Goffman, and George Alexander. Today there are also currents within antipsychiatry and mad movements that call for the abolition of psychiatry as a whole.[80]

Although the word *abolition* is not used as such, the first meaning of *abolition* as I defined it earlier (the act and process of closing down carceral spaces, such as institutions and hospitals) was certainly at play in deinstitutionalizing those categorized as intellectually or developmentally disabled. Early on in the history of deinstitutionalization, self-advocates (people labeled as intellectually disabled who advocate for rights and equality) called for closing down all residential institutions for those with intellectual disabilities, which they saw as form of incarceration.[81] But the word *abolition* was not and is not used as the banner for the entire movement/s that sought to close down residential and psychiatric institutions for people with disabilities or those who fought for the desegregation of those with disabilities in separate facilities (in the area of housing, services, or education). Despite the many differences between prison/penal abolition and deinstitutionalization, they share a logic that I argue is anti-carceral and abolitionary.

Race-ability and Criminal Pathologization

The insistence on abolition is rooted in knowledges and lived experiences of people of color, especially black and indigenous people, and their praxis for liberation. This book is indebted to and draws on the work of disability justice scholars/activists/cultural workers for whom the connection between race, disability, state violence, and incarceration is a given. I draw inspiration from the work of Leroy Moore, such as his poem "CAGED, Goddamn Philadelphia":[82]

Nina Simone sang in 1964
I speak my spoken word in 2013
Responding to what have brought me to my knees

Down right painful
Some people are too powerful
This is beyond shameful

Locked in a cage at a young age
Stories in newspapers
Page after page

Shit now I'm full of rage
It was Mississippi Goddamn
Now it's Philadelphia Goddamn

Locked in a basement
Sleeping & eating on cold cement
No, this is not imprisonment

Taking their SSI
Abuse and neglect from family's ties
Black on black leaving open wounds & black eyes

No brotherly love
Oppression lingers around like a stormy cloud
Can't hear the cries raining out loud

From Joice Helth being displayed in an exhibit
Now four disabled adults chained up downstairs in their own shit
This country has a nasty habit

Of treating people with disabilities
Worst than animals
Behind four yellowish walls out of sight from our communities

Shit now I'm full of rage
It was Mississippi Goddamn
Now it's Philadelphia Goddamn

We don't learn
Yesterday & today it's New Mexico, San Jose, Missouri
State by state we continue to get burn

Nursing homes to group homes to our own damn home
Where can you go when home is not safe?
Goddamn Philadelphia, where is the love

Nina Simone I hear you loud and clear
I'll speak my spoken word in everybody's ear
In the winds of oppression I'll stand solid with no fear

Children to adults
Where can we lay faults?
Because this must & will come to a screeching halt

Moore's spoken word poetic exploration of the abuse of disabled people brings to light three interrelated themes that are paramount to this book.

The first is that sites of incarceration are varied and include prisons, nursing homes, psychiatric hospitals, residential facilities for those with intellectual and other disabilities, and, at times, our own homes (or their lack). The second is the necessity to connect racial justice struggles to disability rights and movements ("It was Mississippi Goddamn / Now it's Philadelphia Goddamn"). Here Moore is alluding to Nina Simone's important protest song, which is rooted in civil rights and black freedom struggles. Moore's own work with Krip Hop Nation, Sins Invalid (a Bay Area collective of disabled performers and cultural artists, primarily people of color and gender variant), and the Harriet Tubman Collective brings the suggestion to connect these struggles to a level of imperative, one whose flag he has been carrying for many years.[83] Lastly, the poem carries with it rage and ends with a cry not for help but to action. It is not enough to point to the oppression of those incarcerated and abused; we must join in their resistance.

This book grew out of similar sentiments. Being entrenched in disability movements, cultures, and studies and becoming more involved in anti-prison and especially prison abolition movements, the lack of interface between the two was surprising to me. So was the lack of deep racial analysis within some disability rights discourses, deinstitutionalization struggles, and, especially, the literature describing these movements and processes. I refer to these intersections as *race-ability* and in more specific cases as *racial criminal pathologization*. This book is an attempt not so much to ameliorate this gap as it is to bridge, to offer necessary connections as opposed to corrections (a term that is at the core of the critique this book offers).

The call for connecting analysis of incarceration and decarceration with disability is also a call to pay attention to the lives of mostly poor people of color who are incarcerated worldwide, in prisons, detention centers, nursing homes, or institutions for those with labels of "mental illness" and/or "intellectual disability," and to bring their perspective to bear on what Chris Bell characterized as "White disability studies."[84] As I have suggested elsewhere, the history of disability is the his/story of incarceration.[85] Here I want to suggest that it is also entangled with the history of decarceration, especially in the form of deinstitutionalization. One of my hopes is that this research will create even more useful links between racial justice and critical race theory with disability/mad activism and disability studies as well as related social movements.[86] By connecting the work of prison abolitionists and theorists who critique the prison–industrial complex to disability studies and disability rights, we can begin understanding the ways in which criminalizing entails the construction of both race (especially blackness) and disability (especially mental difference) as dangerous. I do not believe one can be separated from the other. I therefore use race-ability as a way to denote this nexus. This connects with Foucault's discussion of the notion of race in the lectures published as *Society Must Be Defended*.[87] Foucault defined biopolitics as a power over life (bios) on a population level. Its aim is not to surveil bodies but to control population through managing and measuring mortality and birth rate, quality of health, life expectancy, and so on, of whole populations. Foucault claimed that with the advent of biopolitical control (i.e., the creation of a healthy populace), the state used racism as a mechanism to differentiate between those worthy of living and those who are dispensable to the "healthy" activity of the state. This can be conceived of as a mechanism of biological warfare of sorts, which is used not against an enemy but against a perceived threat to the population. There is an important link here to eugenics and Nazi ideology, which exterminated "degenerate" races and people for the "good of the population." Foucault seems to refer to race as the delineation of categories, a way to sort out or partition populations, and not only in relation to color, creed, or ethnicity. Abnormalities were conceptualized in racist terms, and those designated "abnormal" (including criminals and mad people) were made dispensable. This understanding of race links it to disability in no uncertain terms, without subsuming one into the other, analogizing them or competing in "oppression Olympics." It is this exact link that I highlight throughout this book.

I am also indebted here to the framework of DisCrit, coined by Subini Annamma, David Connor, and Beth Ferri, which connects critical race theory to disability studies, especially in the field of education.[88] DisCrit thus highlights the interdependent, intersecting, and mutually constitutive aspects of race and disability. Such intersectional analysis in the field of education, for example, repeatedly demonstrates the overrepresentation of students of color in special education and their labeling in "soft" disability categories such as emotionally disturbed, attention-deficit and hyperactivity disorders, and historically also "mental retardation" and now intellectual disability.[89] As critical educators Dean Adams and Erica Meiners suggest, classification as special education masks segregation and pathologizes students of color.[90] In other words, as Ferri and Connor show, after *Brown v. Board*, which prohibited segregation based on color, segregation in education is being justified using disability but disguised as race and gender neutral.[91]

If this understanding of the interlinking of race with disability still seems farfetched, I want to propose one avenue from which to understand why these constructions are inseparable—the processes of criminalization and pathologization. Let's take the notorious shooting of Mike Brown by officer Darren Wilson in Ferguson, Missouri, in 2014, which ignited a slew of protests and massive organized resistance after a grand jury refused to indict Wilson in the shooting. If we look at the transcripts of the evidence presented, we get a picture from Wilson of what criminal pathologization is. Wilson said about trying to subdue Brown that "the only way to describe it is that I felt like a five-year-old holding onto Hulk Hogan." Wilson was only slightly shorter than Brown, but of course, Brown is described as something not quite human. Wilson testified, "I've never seen anybody look that, for lack of a better word, crazy.... I've never seen that. I mean, it was very aggravated, ... aggressive, hostile.... You could tell he was looking through you. There was nothing he was seeing." Brown is described here not just as animalistic but as crazy, pathological, abnormal. Race is coded in disability, and vice versa. It's impossible to untangle antiblack racism from processes of pathologization, ableism, and sanism. Together they justify what Jelani Exum calls "death penalty on the streets."[92] Even if Brown had not been killed in that fatal night, he would have most likely ended up subsumed by the prison–industrial complex. He was criminalized as soon as Wilson laid eyes on him.

Andrea Ritchie offers an important critique and supplement to such accounts by focusing on the stories of women and gender-nonconforming people of color who are criminalized and brutalized by policing and incarceration. For example, Ritchie highlights parallels between police officers' public rationales of their murder of Aurora Rain Rosser and Michael Brown: both are described by their killers not just as inhuman/superhuman but as crazy, pathological, abnormal. Race is coded here in disability, and vice versa. Ritchie's intersectional analysis and storytelling approach show that if we were to center the experiences of these women of color, we would also be talking about and resisting on behalf of those "living while elderly, disabled, black, female, and poor ... and the role that controlling narratives of 'deranged' black women of inhumane or superhuman strength play out" in relation to racial profiling and police violence.[93] Ritchie quotes Mia Mingus as pointing out that women of color are already understood as mentally unstable.

What I term as racial criminal pathologization has a long history, from eugenics, to resistance to slavery being diagnosed as drapetomania, to projecting the trope onto indigenous people, particularly women who resisted the state when it wanted to take their children to Indian residential schools. As Ritchie illustrates, race and gender/sexuality encase perceptions of disability and, accordingly, police responses to so-called disorder. As Jin Haritaworn implores, "I wish to propose that we further expand our abolitionist imagination by asking how hate is ascribed in tandem with not only crime but also pathology, in ways that defend and expand not only the prison but also psychiatry and other institutions of 'care' and reform. In particular, I argue that hate always already emanates from racialised bodies and 'minds' in ways that call for their assimilation and segregation in the form of treatment, education, policing, confinement and deportation."[94] Therefore pathology and criminalization cannot and should not be separated in analysis and abolition praxis. I take Haritaworn's call seriously and advance it throughout the book. I am also indebted to the work of Nirmala Erevelles, Subini Ancy Annamma, and Ashley Taylor,[95] who also connect race to ability (especially intellectual dis/ability) and racialization to pathologization in important ways.

Turning to another highly publicized case of police shooting, in summer 2016, a North Miami police officer shot Charles Kinsey, a behavioral therapist and a black-appearing man, who was laying on his back with his hands raised up.[96] This incident might not have garnered as much media attention, or any attention from the disability community, if not for the fact that Kinsey was accompanied by his autistic client, Arnaldo Eliud Rios Soto, a person of color who was holding a toy truck. At the time of their encounter with the police, Kinsey was bringing Rios Soto back to the group "home" from which he had (literally) escaped. When the police were first called, it was Rios Soto who was believed to be dangerous by the caller, identified as "holding something like a gun."[97] What drew attention and outrage from most in disability communities was that the police dared to shoot at a young person with autism, who obviously was not holding a weapon but a toy. Some outrage was also generated that even caregivers are now unsafe, especially if they are of color. But as disability and Deaf justice advocate and legal scholar T. L. Lewis urges, "when a Black Disabled person is killed by the state, media and prominent racial justice activists usually report that a Black person was killed by the police. Contemporaneous reports from disability rights communities regarding the very same individual usually emphasize that a Disabled or Deaf individual was killed by the police—with not one word about that person's race, ethnicity or indigenous roots. In the wake of Charles Kinsey taking a bullet marked for Arnaldo Rios this week, I am renewing the call for Disability Solidarity. Disability solidarity means disability communities actively working to create racial justice, and [nondisability] civil rights communities showing up for disability justice."[98]

I want to think through two factors that should cause as much outrage among disability communities and communities of color, and especially their intersections. First, as a result of the shooting, both men were even further disabled, both by the trauma of the encounter, which ultimately led Rios Soto to be reincarcerated in a psych facility, and by the shooting that injured Kinsey. But I want to suggest that even if the encounter would have not been disabling, those in disability communities should make incarceration and policing a top priority in their activism. This is also because, second, state violence, including through slow death, incarceration as social death, and state killing, should be on the agenda of disability scholar-activists as much as it is of concern for those seeking racial justice. We therefore must think about *incarceration* as a form of state violence, not only the shooting. Why has Rios escaped from his "group home"? Did he see it as a home? Why are people with disabilities, especially poor and of color, forced to live in a variety of carceral enclosures? Why are these forms of incarceration and state violence not on the agenda of those advocating for racial or gender justice?

In other words, the framework of racial criminal pathologization is also about understanding policing,[99] incarceration, and its alternatives as disability issues, with everything such reformulation entails—from refiguring alternatives to diagnosing the crisis. It also entails centering the experiences of disablement and ableism in criminal, racial, and social justice movements, for example, the trauma and disabling effects of detention and incarceration.

Cathy Cohen, Dean Spade, and Roderick Ferguson envision a queer politics through a coalitional lens that is related to one's positionality in relation to power and not identification. Instead, they urge us to understand vast social problems through an intersectional lens that has a broader analysis of what we come to call freedom and what liberation might be, not just for the inclusion of some but for the connected liberation of us all.[100] Following such a

framework, I ask what a disability justice or crip of color critique of incarceration and decarceration would be.[101] I suggest that race-ability as linked
to a mad/crip of color critique of incarceration and decarceration is not just
about those who identify or are politicized as disabled people of color who
are caught up in these systems (although it's important to recognize the high
numbers of disabled men, women, and trans folks, especially those of color,
in carceral systems, including policing). Such framework entails theorizing
the disposability of certain populations and their susceptibility to premature
death, which is Ruth Gilmore's definition of racism,[102] to understanding the
nature of systems of capture and exclusion, to discussing alternatives to these
systems and envisioning shared horizons. It is also an understanding that
antiblack racism is composed of pathologization and dangerousness, which
lead to processes of criminalization and disablement, for instance, constructing people as Other or as deranged, crazy, illogical, unfathomable, or scary.

Crip/mad of color critique and disability justice urge us to move from
approaches that look at violence and discrimination as related to individual
acts and instead focus, through an intersectional lens, on systemic issues and
structural inequalities. The point is not to look for the bad apples and then
punish them using the same tools that oppress marginalized communities to
begin with. The criminal justice system, psychiatry, and legal-based rights
discourses are therefore not seen by these frameworks as the solution to the
plight of queer, disabled, or poor persons or of people of color, immigrants,
and so on, but are in fact seen often as the source of the problem. Sensitivity
training and ensuring diversity within these systems (police, corrections, psy
professions) are not a panacea.[103] Instead, we must seek new ways of reacting
to one another, or as disability justice advocate Mia Mingus explains, we
need to "change the framework."[104]

Debility, Disablement, and Disability

Much of disability studies came out of the disability rights movement, which
in some sense is the strength of the field: it emerged out of a desire for liberation of disabled people and articulation of their/our unique epistemology. This link to disability rights and pride is also the field's limitation. The
pride framework (love yourself, flaunt your disability and difference) is both
powerful and a reversal of power differentials. But there is no denying that it
is not a framework rooted in intersectionality theoretically or embodied and

it does not account for questions of who does not and, in fact, *cannot* participate in disability rights and pride—who, essentially, rains on the (disability pride) parade.

The desire to depathologize dis/ability from notions of deficiency, which is at the core of a critical disability studies stance, gets complicated when an intersectional analysis taking account of race, gender, sexuality, class, and other constructs is being introduced. It is important to highlight the tension between the desire to untangle disability from medicalization and diagnostic categories and reclaim it as an identity and culture—and the ability (and sometimes desire) to even become a subject under the medical gaze. As Sandy Magaña and I suggested elsewhere, for many people of color or those who have no access to quality medical care, not being diagnosed is due less to viewing disability as a source of pride or as a fluid state and more to disparities in service provision and the ability to access doctors and medical services, such as therapy, medication, and early detection, because of inequalities based on class, color, language, or geographical barriers.[105] It is clear from the literature that people of color are at greater risk for losing ability capacities, often in conjunction with a lower socioeconomic or an immigrant status. There are also numerous barriers for disabled people of color to obtaining quality health care services.[106]

Jasbir Puar's work is of interest at this juncture. She moves us from discussions of disability pride, rights, or even disablement to centering the biopolitics of debility, in which debilitation is "the slow wearing down of populations" of "the bodies that are sustained in a perpetual state of debilitation precisely through foreclosing the social, cultural, and political translation to disability . . . the tension between targeting the disabled and targeting to debilitate."[107] In more Foucauldian terms, some are folded into life while and because others are targeted for premature death (Gilmore's definition of racism) or slow death (per Lauren Berlant[108]).

This distinction between disability identification and biopolitics of debilitation pushes a conceptualization of disability as an aspect of biopolitical population management. This is a shift from the seemingly axiomatic statement about "overrepresentation," of children of color in special education or of people of color in prisons, to understanding this debilitation and forces of what I call racial criminal pathologization as a core of institutions that uphold settler racial "democracies." Puar shows that disability under capitalism and empire is not overrepresented, as if this is an unfortunate side effect of these regimes. Rather, it is the core function of the system as is—to incapacitate, punish, contain.

Beyond critiques of disability studies and culture as being "white disability studies," Puar adds an analysis of the *incompatibility* of the disability pride framework with the experience of poor people of color (in the United States and globally), especially those who acquired their disabilities by violence, most often due to state violence or negligence (which is also violence). As Puar suggests, following Australian theorist Helen Meekosha, the disability framework that resists discussion of the prevention of disability due to pride frameworks lacks the nuance to talk about these complex experiences, especially in relation to the Global South.[109] Puar writes, "The analysis of 'southern disability' is not simply 'left out' of disability studies; it is rather a constitutive and capacitating absence."[110]

Puar offers the triangulation of debility, capacity, and disability to discuss how disability "is about bodily exclusion that is endemic rather than epidemic."[111] Disability and debility in this formulation do not counter each other but are in fact interdependent—the discourse of rights and empowerment relies on the same economy (i.e., neoliberalism, colonialism, and racial capitalism) that capacitates certain bodies (makes them available for identification) and makes others available for injury. I show how this works in the context of labor in chapter 6, disability litigation and rights in chapter 7, and the rejection of "others" into the (white) community in chapter 5.

Puar's analysis stresses the importance of centering both disability and debilitation to understand the workings of empire and their central role in the maintenance of statehood and state violence. As I show throughout the book, these sites of violence (prisons, psych hospitals, and other carceral locales and logics) are incredibly disabling and, as Puar shows, sites of targeted biopolitical debilitation. But at the same time as I critique debilitation through state violence (through incarceration) and critiquing rights and pride discourses, I want also to insist that disability cannot be articulated solely through the lens of pathology. The potential peril of discussing disability solely on the level of the biopolitics of debilitation is that we are left with prevention and assimilation discourses as the only available frameworks that can account for ways of effectively living with disability. The biopolitics of debilitation can't explain or account for what becomes of/to people on the level of activism or ontology once they are disabled/debilitated.

Such analysis can result in reproducing a zero-sum game of two nodes of disability exceptionalism–disability as assimilation (rehabilitation and rights, as Puar critiques) or prevention (in this case, as prevention of the conditions of debilitation). I worry that calls to close carceral enclosures because they are disabling can be taken up as a biopolitical tool by state and social justice agents through what I am calling carceral ableism/sanism to "improve" or extend carceral locales. This could look like, for example, stopping the debilitating conditions of confinement by providing better health care in sites of incarceration or even releasing those with debilitating conditions but not others—all of which will result in increasing the net scope of carcerality and state violence.

It can also result in furthering ableism, especially through the frame of racial criminal pathologization, the results of which strip those who are disabled of their epistemology and ontology as disabled. If disability is understood through the lenses of avoidance or pathology, those who are already disabled and debilitated lose the opportunity to understand their disability or impairment as part of their identity, which can result in lack of efforts to collectivize based on their/our shared culture and histories. Therefore it is imperative to connect the analysis of state violence and its resulting population level slow death and targeted debilitation, including by carceral apparatuses and logics, to disability as identity and culture. Disability as a political entity is important because it offers a site of collective resistance to such violence—in the form of deinstitutionalization, antipsychiatry, and self advocacy.

Disability studies offers the powerful idea of disability as empowering, enabling, productive, and political. Not everything disability produces is beautiful, but as a productive force, in the Foucauldian sense, disability produces specific sensibilities and discourses. I want to affirm the life that's already here in the form of the knowledges of disabled and mad people, at the same time as calling to end violent debilitation and the conditions that make them viable. This book therefore understands disability as an (intersectional) optic that deconstructs the normative body/mind and uncovers the radical potential of living otherwise. In other words, I wish to ask, what can be gained from the presence of disability, or from disability justice or crip critiques of the carceral emanating from disability/mad movements, especially those related to deinstitutionalization, anti-prison, and antipsychiatry?

Road Map and Suggested Usage

I want to be clear that I am not suggesting that prison/penal abolition is about facility closure; it is about abolishing a society that could have prisons. More precisely, as contemporary abolitionists Angela Davis, Beth Richie, Ruth Wilson Gilmore, Mariame Kaba, and other black feminists discuss, abolition is about creating a world without the necessity and footprint of incarceration and segregation, with all that entails for distribution of resources and social values. Thus prison abolition insists not only on ridding ourselves of imprisonment but of imagining a "new world order" in the absence of the carceral archipelago. As Davis further advises, "the call for prison abolition urges us to imagine and strive for a very different social landscape."[112] This book takes up only one string of this complex web. I acknowledge that incarceration is not merely a place (the prison, the institution). But it's *also* a place. Decarceration is certainly not the only route to carceral abolition, as carceral logics reside outside of specific locales, but this diffusion does not dissolve the necessity to coalesce against walled carceral enclosures and demand their closure. Connecting, and distinguishing between, the ethics and politics of capture and enclosure of those whose incarceration is legitimated by "care" versus "punishment" is another implicit goal of this book.

The first part of the book *conceptualizes* decarceration, as I trace the genealogy (origin story, birth narrative, history of ideas) of deinstitutionalization and epistemologies (knowledges) of abolition. I begin with a two-part genealogy of deinstitutionalization. The first part excavates and complicates the hegemonic narrative of deinstitutionalization in mental health and intellectual disabilities as occurring due to exposés, policy changes, financial factors, and psychiatric drugs. Chapter 2 adds an emphasis on expert knowledge that moved the pendulum of reform toward abolition in deinstitutionalization. I specifically focus on Wolf Wolfensberger's theorization of *normalization* in the field of intellectual disability and Thomas Szasz's view of the *myth of mental illness* within antipsychiatry and showcase how such theories were perceived, taken up, and entangled in deinstitutionalization, its consequences, and its backlash.

Chapter 3 conceptualizes what abolition is, especially as it applies to carcerality. There are various critiques laid out against prison abolition and deinstitutionalization. They can be summarized into three main prongs: that this form of activism is abstract and does not focus on prescriptive and specific solutions and alternatives to incarceration; that it is an optimistic and uto-pian vision of the world; and that it is unrealistic to share this worldview in the world we currently occupy. In this chapter, I demonstrate how these cri-tiques can be conceptualized as strengths as a dis-epistemology of abolition. The second part of the book focuses on *resistance* to decarceration. Here my case studies are the prevalence of those defined as mentally ill in prisons and jails and the ways deinstitutionalization was blamed for it; resistance to community living and integration in housing; and resistance to closure of carceral enclosures, especially institutions and prisons. In chapter 4, I analyze discourses that were used to construct a particular (punitive and medical) narrative around the "homeless mentally ill" and "jails as the new asylums," which created a backlash against deinstitutionalization and prison abolition. I deconstruct these claims and discuss what is at stake in such discourses now, decades after the closure of psychiatric hospitals.

In chapter 5, I interrogate various forms of resistance to community liv-ing also known as the not in my backyard (NIMBY) phenomenon and the way it relates to criminal pathologization and race/ability. I also demonstrate how desegregation (or inclusion) in the disability arena followed, paralleled, and intersected with racial desegregation in the 1960s and 1970s.

Chapter 6 focuses on the triad of parents of those institutionalized and incarcerated, unions, and employees of these facilities in advocating for or fighting against closure of carceral locales. It examines who supports car-ceral enclosures (especially institutions for those with intellectual disability labels and prisons), why others advocate for their closure, and how the ratio-nalities embedded in such efforts are part of political and affective econo-mies related to discourses of safety/danger, innocence, choice, community, care, and labor.

I end the book with the vexed relation between abolition and decarcera-tion. In chapter 7, I investigate the role class action litigation played in the closure of carceral enclosures (prisons and institutions) and the consequences of utilizing it as a technique of decarceration. I contest the belief that disability-related litigation replaced prison reform litigation and instead point to the ways gender and disability became primary avenues from which to legally critique imprisonment. I also critique such approaches by discussing the potential ableism entrenched in this form of litigation. I conclude the book by summarizing how decarceration and excarceration worked, or not, in dein-stitutionalization and show what can be learned from deinstitutionalization for prison abolition, and vice versa. I also caution against current "alternatives" that expand the carceral state through the decarceration–industrial complex and carceral ableism and sanism.

In sum, this book is a call to address incarceration and decarceration as disability issues, whether those oppressed by it are disabled or identify or are politicized as disabled or not. On the flip and related side, I show the need to view radical mental health and disability justice and organizing as carceral abolition issues. Activists and scholars of imprisonment and incarceration need to be more versed in the lived experience, history, and culture of mad, disabled, and Deaf people to chart a way out, which I demonstrate through the historical example of deinstitutionalization. But it also requires being attentive to forces of carceral ableism and sanism that seek to expand the carceral state in the so-called service of disability/madness (such as accepting people with disability into community housing and services as long as they are "not criminals").

As a scholar (trained in the social sciences) and activist (in prison abolition and disability arenas), this call for connecting decarceration, disability, and deinstitutionalization runs on dual tracks. The first is the need to construct a more critical genealogy to add to research on deinstitutionalization, one that encompasses the complexity of its history and origin story (beyond the public imagery of "dumping people in the streets" and "jails as the new asylums"), and that focuses on the closure of residential institutions for people with intellectual disabilities in tandem with the closure of psychiatric hospitals. Connectedly, I want to put deinstitutionalization as part and parcel of discussions on decarceration, inclusion, and abolition. The second track is a call to those of us who engage in social change work to understand these genealogies, movements, and knowledges as connected so we can implement their lessons and the spirit of dis-epistemology in our own work.

How can creating coalitions around the need for community mental health and affordable and accessible housing in the community be aided by understanding the shift that occurred in the 1970s onward that decreased the social safety net while increasing the reach of the carceral state? What if we understand these forces in tandem as opposed to causal effects, that is, deinstitutionalization caused the rise of incarceration and the rise of the "mentally ill" in prisons and jails? What if categories like the "mentally ill" are not simply taken for granted in research or activism but understood as constructed categories contested and changed over time, changes that both necessitated and hindered a force like deinstitutionalization? What if, as I suggest following activists in these movements, deinstitutionalization is not merely a process or policy change but a mind-set, a logic? What were the limits and gains from using strategies like exposés and litigation in gaining people's freedom from sites of incarceration? Who resists decarceration and deinstitutionalization, and how can coalitions be created to oppose such resistance? How would understanding deinstitutionalization as a form of residential desegregation that paralleled and intersected with racial desegregation aid in making white policy papers on disability relevant to the lives of disabled people of color?[113] What can be gained from taking up an abolitionist perspective? How did the concept of abolition play out in different arenas of incarceration—in antipsychiatry, the field of intellectual disabilities, and the fight against the prison–industrial complex? I hope this book incites some of these questions and provides some answers that can be activated in other contexts and struggles for freedom.

1

The Perfect Storm

Origin Stories of Deinstitutionalization

I argue that deinstitutionalization should be reconceptualized as being, at least partially, about abolition of disability-related carceral spaces and logics. As such, deinstitutionalization is the biggest decarceration move and movement in U.S. history. But how and why did deinstitutionalization happen? What conditions made it possible? This chapter is devoted to examining but not resolving the debate among policy makers, social scientists, historians, and activists about what led to or was the deciding factor in deinstitutionalizing mental health and I/DD (intellectual and developmental disabilities, historically "mental retardation," or MR). What was the perfect storm that led to mass decarceration of disability confinement in the United States?

There is agreement that the most important factors leading to deinstitutionalization are/were shifting public opinion about institutionalization, which included exposés of conditions of living in these carceral locales (institutions and psych facilities). There is also agreement that policy changes (such as the creation of Medicaid and Social Security Disability Insurance, or SSDI) made a big difference and enabled community living and community mental health to become a possibility. Cost-cutting measures are also discussed as a major motive for the closure of psych hospitals and institutions for those labeled as I/DD. Lastly, in the arena of deinstitutionalization in mental health, psych drugs are seen as a major contributor that enabled the release of psych patients. There is no agreement in the literature regarding which of these factors was more important in pushing toward deinstitutionalization.[1]

I want to stress that I will complicate this origin story of deinstitutionalization as opposed to providing a definitive answer as to what "caused" it. A

confluence of factors in the 1950s and 1960s created the conditions of possibility for deinstitutionalization, and they cannot all be accounted for or
replicated. I conceive of the emergence of deinstitutionalization as an un-
predictable convergence of factors that permitted unexpected, often accidental, outcomes. Much of it was about a discursive shift, which I will discuss
more fully in the next chapter regarding the prevailing theories in I/DD and
antipsychiatry that advanced a new conceptualization of human worth and
difference that made deinstitutionalization necessary and possible. For those
looking to reactivate this "effective history" of deinstitutionalization,[2] these
conditions of possibility are crucial to learn from; but the confluence of
all these factors, the "perfect storm," cannot be repeated or replicated. This
caveat follows the spirit of dis-epistemology of abolition, as I discuss in chapter 3, which calls for abandoning attachments to clairvoyance and certainty
and instead embracing the local and the unfinished.

Here, then, I map a genealogy of the origin story of deinstitutionalization. By genealogy, I am referring to a specific methodology adapted by
Foucault from Nietzsche. Genealogy calls into question the conditions constructing our present moment, becoming a "history of the present," interested in possibilities for the future, by exposing what appears as self-evident
in the present and tracing the various ways these contingencies were constructed in the past. The conditions of possibility and the hegemonic narrative of the emergence of deinstitutionalization are the topics of this chapter,
while the next chapter conjures out some of the discarded knowledge that
led to deinstitutionalization.

I suggest that the hegemonic narrative of deinstitutionalization as one
of progress based on scientific means (advent of drugs, more accurate diagnosis criteria, cost-effectiveness, and humane policies) as the major engine
that led to the closure of psychiatric hospitals and large residential institutions for those with I/DD labels, and progression of history more generally, should be questioned and not be taken for granted. Foucault notes
that genealogy "opposes itself to the search of origins."[3] Much of what is
conceived of as advancement—for instance, the shift from torture to imprisonment as a form of punishment, releasing people who are mad from asylums and jails and into psychiatric hospitals to become patients, and the
subsequent release of mad patients into community settings—are in fact not
signs of progress. Moreover, they are not so much the result of planned
actions as they are an accidental outcome of unrelated changes, or of multiple

unidentified processes colliding or passing through. Therefore a genealogist is looking for contingencies, not causes.[4] In other words, history and our interpretation of events as historical are full of events that could have happened.[5]

Psychiatrization, for example, is not natural or God given; it is a specific discourse arising in a particular historical moment that had come to be seen as ahistorical and inevitable. Imprisonment as a form of punishment is also a contingency, as is punishment as a result of crime or wrongdoing. These discourses have not "been there forever and will always be there," as some are led to believe. States' ability to control and measure their populations is a contingency, as is the modern nation-state to begin with. The narrative I offer herein therefore is much more fragmented and critical. In this chapter, I chart the hegemonic origin story of deinstitutionalization as often told, concerning shifts in policy, the role of exposés of institutions and psych facilities, austerity and budgetary measures that led to the closure of disability carceral spaces as being non-cost-effective, and the advent of therapeutic measures like psych drugs. I will offer a more complex retelling of each component, paying close attention to the tendency to reform these carceral enclosures, in addition and sometimes in opposition to calls to close them down, which will culminate in the next chapter.

What Is Deinstitutionalization?

I define deinstitutionalization as a three-pronged phenomenon. First, as many others understand it, it is the process of closing down carceral locales, such as psychiatric hospitals and residential institutions for people labeled as intellectually and/or developmentally disabled. Second, deinstitutionalization is not only about spaces but about people. It is therefore also the movement of people with disabilities (psychiatric, intellectual, physical) from segregated spaces of "treatment" and warehousing to community living (whether or not these carceral spaces close). Such a view of deinstitutionalization enables a more complex understanding of what happened when (or whether) carceral enclosures closed down. Lastly, and perhaps most importantly, I conceptualize deinstitutionalization not only as a movement of people from one locale to another but as a *social* movement, an ideology opposing carceral logics, a mind-set. This understanding of deinstitutionalization as a step toward abolition of the carceral is not discussed in the literature and origin narrative of deinstitutionalization. It is this effective history that I am aiming to bring to light.

Although the controversy and backlash around deinstitutionalization still rage on, this is an important moment to take stock of what had been accomplished so far in the largest decarceration effort in U.S. history. Deinstitutionalization in most U.S. states is a reality today. Many closures of psych facilities and residential institutions for people with I/DD labels have already happened; others are under way. In 1955, the state mental health population was 559,000, nearly as large on a per capita basis as the prison population today. By 2000, it had fallen to fewer than one hundred thousand, a drop of more than 82 percent.[6] The population of people with intellectual disabilities living in large state institutions peaked at 194,650 in 1967. By 2015, this number had declined to 69,557.[7] As discussed in the previous chapter, the trend in deinstitutionalization for people with intellectual disabilities was accompanied by institutional closures across most states. By 2013, fourteen states had closed all their large (more than sixteen people) state institutions for people labeled I/DD.[8] Other states have not closed any public institutions. Overall, 140 closures were completed or were under way between 1960 and 2010.

Deinstitutionalization is not an unrelated and inconsequential phenomenon to issues of decarceration and abolition but one with historical, contemporary, and tactical significance. As discussed in the introduction and elsewhere,[9] incarceration happens not only in prisons but also in other sites of carceral enclosure, such as psychiatric hospitals, detention centers, nursing homes, and residential institutions. Although these sites are different in their rationale (treatment versus and alongside punishment), it is important to discuss them in tandem. As legal scholar Bernard Harcourt[10] suggests, what we now call "mass incarceration" or the rise in incarceration barely reaches the level of institutionalization that the United States experienced at mid-twentieth century. In other words, when the data on mental hospitalization are combined with the data on imprisonment for the period 1928–2000, the highest rate of aggregated institutionalization occurred in 1955, when almost 640 per 100,000 adults over age fifteen were institutionalized in asylums, mental hospitals, and state and federal prisons.

But I want to go a step further than Harcourt, whose important research connects incarceration and decarceration in mental hospitals and in prison, to discuss the continuity of confinement.[11] Throughout this book, I contend that if we are to discuss decarceration writ large, we need to look at all aspects of deinstitutionalization, including the arena of institutions for those labeled as I/DD, which Harcourt and most scholars who discuss deinstitutionalization and decarceration do not mention. The literature and discussion on deinstitutionalization have so far been singularly oriented, focusing only on mental health, so much so that when deinstitutionalization is mentioned, the only example people conjure up is psych facilities that closed down (leading to blaming activists for the "failure of deinstitutionalization," which I will deconstruct in chapter 4). Deinstitutionalization in mental health is often taken as prototypical or the only deinstitutionalization that happened. Its centrality in terms of popular culture, scholarly attention, public imagery, and historical accounts serves to obscure the fascinating, liberatory, and contentious process and discourse of deinstitutionalization in I/DD.

The book's goal is to combine analysis of deinstitutionalization, as decarceration, in both mental health and I/DD for several reasons. It is imperative to understand institutionalization and therefore deinstitutionalization in all its forms. The breakdown and categorization of people and services into discrete categories, such as "mentally ill" versus "mentally/intellectually disabled," is a particular historical form of subjugation created by specific therapeutic/managerial/medical discourses prevalent in each era. For example, prior to the nineteenth century, there was no apparent distinction between intellectual and mental disability.[12] The poorhouse in the early nineteenth century did not simply provide shelter for the indigent. It was a catch-all for all who were deemed dependent, unproductive, or dangerous. This system of warehousing together all the needy populations lasted in various degrees until the 1930s.[13] In addition, during this eugenic era, the category of "mental defectives" emerged as a way to distinguish those with intellectual disabilities from other "defectives" and general "degenerates."[14]

In terms of confinement and carcerality, these categorizations—mentally ill, mentally defective/degenerate, feebleminded—resulted in segregation and often institutionalization, albeit in different carceral enclosures in various eras, such as asylums, poorhouses, and then separate institutions such as jails, psychiatric facilities, and residential "schools." Many reformers and progressive associations did not distinguish between various dependent populations and their underlying circumstances. For instance, the National Conference on Charities and Corrections, founded in 1874, became the nation's leading association dealing with pauperism, insanity, delinquency, prison reform, immigration, and feeblemindedness.[15] At that time, there was no clear policy segregating the "worthy" (aged, widows, orphans, disabled) and "unworthy" dependents (poor, unemployed, criminals). Such separation began at the turn of the mid-nineteenth century, when different facilities were beginning to be sought for different populations. With increased authority of medical knowledge, there was a move from notions of punishment to notions of medical and moral treatment of those previously deemed as deviant and now seen as "abnormal." The idea was to reform people, to correct them, and to do so in separate facilities adequate for their lot in life, such as poverty or illness. Because of the later separation between so-called mental illness and mental retardation, the causes and outcomes of deinstitutionalization in each arena were related but also different. I discuss these outcomes at the end of this chapter. First, though, I discuss deinstitutionalization writ large, combining I/DD and mental health, when feasible.

Formation of New Policy

According to the literature and the hegemonic origin story of deinstitutionalization, one of the most impactful changes that led to the ability to care for disabled people in the community and to deinstitutionalization and closure of facilities was policies and the promise of accompanying funding to do so. Although federal policies certainly created the infrastructure that enabled deinstitutionalization, I suggest that such policies were one contingency among the conditions of possibility that created what we have come to call deinstitutionalization, but contingencies are not causes, as Foucault reminds us. The first was the proposed creation of community mental health centers and "community facilities" for those with intellectual disabilities, and the second was the creation of federal support programs such as Medicare and Medicaid.

The hegemonic story focuses on legislation and policy changes beginning with the Kennedy (and Shriver) family, culminating in John F. Kennedy's presidency. This is for good reason, of course. President Kennedy had intimate ties to issues of mental health and intellectual disability. His sister Rosemary was labeled as "mentally retarded" after being lobotomized in the 1940s, when she was twenty-three. The lobotomy was initiated because she had exhibited erratic behavior and was seen as disabled since birth.[16] After her botched lobotomy, Rosemary spent most of her life in an institution away from the public and her family, who only acknowledged her condition after JFK was elected president.

In 1961, JFK formed the President's Panel on Mental Retardation, which comprised professionals and experts, mostly medical, educational, and legal in the field of MR. In 1962, they presented 112 recommendations for a comprehensive federal approach to intellectual disabilities and urged him to "think and plan boldly." Among the recommendations were to boost educational programs, improve social services, improve facilities for care, and increase educational opportunities to learn about so-called mental retardation, which was done through legislation to establish research centers in universities that study I/DD. It also introduced a new legal and social concept of mental retardation, which is discussed in the next chapter and has been much debated since.[17] It is important to note that the recommendations were couched in medical discourse and that those with intellectual disabilities (and for the most part their families) were absent from the analysis and from the body making the recommendations. The report was promoted as one to "combat mental retardation," and the focus, in addition to programming, was on prevention and cure.

In 1963, President Kennedy gave a "Special Message to the Congress on Mental Illness and Mental Retardation." In it, he proposed three key areas of focus: "First, we must seek out the causes of mental illness and of mental retardation and eradicate them. Here, more than in any other area, 'an ounce of prevention is worth more than a pound of cure.'" Second, he proposed a focus on staff by providing aid for education and creating a more skilled workforce. "Third, we must strengthen and improve the programs and facilities serving the mentally ill and the mentally retarded. . . . Services to both the mentally ill and to the mentally retarded must be community based and provide a range of services to meet community needs." This created a major shift of funding from institutionally based responses to treatment of disability to community-based ones. This push from then president Kennedy is seen as the sounding bell for deinstitutionalization, or at least its infrastructure.

The same year, the Mental Retardation Facilities and Community Health Centers Construction Act authorized federal grants for the construction of fifteen hundred public and private nonprofit community mental health centers (CMHCs) nationwide. Each center was required to provide inpatient services, outpatient services, consultation and education on mental health, emergency response, and partial hospitalization. The promise of the creation of these CMHCs never really materialized. But ideologically, the act showed promise in shifting the discourse of institutionalization to focus on community support and provided an impetus for closure of institutional settings.

Mental health and I/DD policy changes emerged as part of broader social welfare reforms during the 1960s when Medicare and Medicaid were established through passage of the Social Security Amendments of 1965.[18] The expansion of Social Security (income based) and Social Security Disability Insurance also provided some financial resources for people discharged from hospitals and institutions. To take advantage of these financial incentives, states moved patients out of mental hospitals and into community-based outpatient facilities. Thus the cost of care in mental health and I/DD was shifted from states to the federal government, which, at least in theory, had more funds. The passage of later legislation, such as Section 504 of the Rehabilitation Act in 1973 and the Education of All Handicapped Children Act in 1975, would push the pendulum even further against segregation and toward inclusion of adults and children with disabilities.

The same policies and financial incentives credited with leading to deinstitutionalization also led to its inability to be realized de facto. For example, to date, there is inherent institutional bias in programs such as Medicaid, due to their funding stream, strong political lobby and staff organizations, and (often underutilized) unions.[19] This bias means that money, in the form of benefits or waivers, goes toward institutions, nursing homes, or group homes but not to the person who benefits from these services directly. The introduction of Medicaid money mostly applies to alternative institutions (nursing homes, hostels) and not to alternative care or forms of mutual care. As a result, these policies that were seen as an engine to deinstitutionalization actually provide incentives against it and against services like nonsegregated long-term treatment or advocacy and support for living in the community.

There is no doubt that however one measures the impact of these policies and reimbursement procedures, especially in the arena of mental health, they indeed had a large impact on those institutionalized and on the ability to prevent further institutionalization en masse.[20] But I want to underscore that the pendulum toward deinstitutionalization did not *begin with* these policies, although they were certainly initially solidified by the availability of such public funds. Remember that the institutionalized population in psych facilities started declining from 1955 (when the hospitalized population was at its peak). So, although the advent of such policies decreased the reliance on long institutionalization and psych hospitalization, these policies did not begin it. Some of these changes had already been under way since the post–World War I period. In 1954, governors of all states, except for Nevada and Arizona, met in Michigan to discuss what to do about "the problem of the chronically mentally ill."[21] Although it is unclear if the proceedings resulted in changes in all states, the convening itself resulted in heightened public attention to an issue that was not previously perceived to merit national intervention.

In addition, in 1955, JFK commissioned a federal study on the state of mental health in the United States, long before his speech to Congress. The Joint Commission on Mental Illness and Health was created, in 1955, by the American Psychiatric Association and the American Medical Association.[22] The joint commission's report, *Action for Mental Health*, came out in 1961, after five years of deliberations, and provided the first comprehensive analysis and recommendations on issues of mental health. It concluded that community-based treatments were essential and recommended a continuum of community-based and hospital services. I critique this continuum approach in the next chapter and in chapter 5, but suffice to say that while hospital services continued to be recommended and funded, the funds and ideology had not shifted to community-based approaches.

While these recommendations were beginning to be digested by Congress, policy makers, and advocates, the decrease in psych hospitalization was already under way. If we again follow Foucault, we can see that the origin, the birth story as narrative, masks the chain of singular events, events of error, discontinuity, and chance. In her polemical book on deinstitutionalization in mental health, Ann Braden Jonson acts much like a genealogist and suggests that deinstitutionalization was never really planned; rather, it happened because of a variety of circumstances that were not closely related or arranged.[23] The process was not even named until about twenty years after it started to happen. Johnson maintains that it was the backlash and critiques against psych hospital closures in the 1960s and 1970s that gave deinstitutionalization a name for a phenomenon that began in the 1950s.

Importance of Exposés

Deinstitutionalization was a confluence of many factors, including growing critiques of carceral logics of disability-based incarceration, which is one component of my definition of deinstitutionalization. One of the most impactful factors that led to questioning the efficacy of psychiatric hospitals and I/DD institutions was a slew of exposés in print and visual media.[24] The emergence of photographic journalism, of the documentary form, at that time aided in the popularization of visual exposés. As the word suggests, these documents *exposed* conditions of living in these carceral spaces. But they also exposed the general unaffected publics to the fate of many of those "out of sight and out of (their) mind."[25] Exposés brought the plight of those institutionalized into headlines in widely read magazines and later to American TV screens. They were certainly *affective* tools and formative for many of that generation, as they appealed to people's emotions (empathy, horror, humanity, anger) and therefore went beyond arguments about policy or fiscal matters, which the general public was neither interested in nor aware of. But despite their sustained affect, I contend that they were not a factor leading to deinstitutionalization, as much of the literature on the origin story of deinstitutionalization suggests, although they were important for other reasons, which I discuss later. Instead of leading to deinstitutionalization, the focus on conditions of confinement resulted in *reforming* and not shuttering these facilities.[26]

Numerous and repeated exposés of mental hospitals and institutions have been conducted by journalists, professionals, and scholars since the turn of the twentieth century. They became more widespread during and after World War II, largely because of the placement of conscientious objectors in hospitals and I/DD institutions as a civil service substitute to military service.[27] These exposés presented residential institutions as deplorable, as inhumane, and as serving warehousing functions, often alluding to concentration camps in their imagery and textual references. The allusion to concentration camps would also coalesce later around demands for their closure. As historian Anne Parsons suggests, during World War II, politicians could overlook the conditions in these places, but public outrage after the war made them impossible to ignore any longer.[28]

The establishment of the National Mental Health Foundation by conscientious objectors during World War II aided in exposing mental hospitals as "snake pits" during the 1950s. A prominent exposé of that era is of interest here, both for its damning content but also for the analysis of reform it can offer. In 1946, *Life* magazine published the article "Bedlam 1946: Most U.S. Mental Hospitals Are a Shame and a Disgrace." It was written by Albert Q. Maisel and was based on his interviews with conscientious objectors at Byberry Hospital in Pennsylvania.[29] In 1951, *Life* published a follow-up article based on Maisel's recent visits to thirty psych hospitals around the country, titled "Scandal Results in Real Reforms." Both articles were accompanied by damning images, and both were widely read.

Maisel's second article is interesting, as it begins clarifying the pendulum swing between discourses of reform and of abolition. In the 1951 follow-up article, Maisel applauded the increased budgets most states designated to psych hospitals since the original 1946 exposé and the increase in hospital staff, which he described as hopeful steps. He also emphasized the decrease in admissions to psych hospitals for the first time in a century. Maisel describes an interesting conundrum emerging between what he called "brick-and-mortar" reformers, who advocated for more construction and staffing given to hospitals and institutions, versus those who advocated for intense treatment that would enable patients to return to the community faster. Maisel does not resolve the quandary, but he does present it as a dilemma between policies and (perhaps) values. Reform here is presented as nuanced, what I explain in later chapters as nonreformist reforms, and we can begin seeing the pendulum between reform and abolition of these institutions.

The article was accompanied by photographs, one of which depicted the governor of Minnesota in 1949, Luther Youngdahl, burning straitjackets to symbolize the end of the inhumane congregate treatment of the insane. This image is reminiscent of eighteenth-century reformer counterparts Philippe Pinel in France and William Tuke in England, who began to remove mad people's restraints after exposing their treatment in chains as inhumane. They then began treating mad people as mental patients in (what would become) hospitals, as Foucault documents.[30] Burning straitjackets is meant to signal to the reader of Maisel's exposé an end to a decrepit and premodern time in which the mad were treated as pariahs or in punitive ways. The fire indicates that modern societies had moved to new modern, scientific ways of understanding, not madness, but *mental illness*. When the mad became mental patients, Foucault claims that moral chains, feelings of inadequacy and guilt, replaced the physical chains of an earlier epoch. The institutions became

Minnesota governor Luther W. Youngdahl burning straitjackets on the grounds
of a state hospital in 1949 to symbolize mental health reform in the state. Courtesy
of the Minnesota Historical Society.

a monument for a new discourse—that of science, of reason, which now no
one could escape, not even into madness. Instead of being sinners and morally objectionable, people who were deemed deviant were now viewed as
pathological, in need of therapy, rehabilitation, correction.

Such narratives of progress as symbolized in the photograph from Maisel's
essay should not be conceived of as an epoch of moving from repression to
liberation. As Foucault warns, reforms such as releasing the mad from their
chains is what brought us the advent of incarceration in specialized facilities.
The social processes that led to increased confinement of a variety of populations did not only come about from above, whether from kings or govern-
ments, but also came out of the vigorous advocacy of *reformers*. Psychiatric
hospitals in the United States were founded partially out of efforts of religious reformers, such as Dorothea Dix, who sought to liberate the "mad"
from oppressive conditions in which they were kept, in chains and squalor, and instead provide them with therapies in hospital-like confined settings. Therefore such imagery of "freeing the mad" by releasing them from
chains or burning their straitjackets shows not only a hegemonic narrative

of liberation but a long history of reform, which ended up increasing the net scope of incarceration, not shrinking it.

These journalistic condemnations of the plight of those incarcerated due to their disability were not limited to psych facilities. If, up until the 1960s, exposés of institutions focused on hospitals for the "mentally ill," in the late 1960s and 1970s, exposés of state schools and institutions for those labeled as MR (now I/DD) became more prominent. In 1965, Senator Robert Kennedy made unannounced visits to New York's Willowbrook and Rome state schools for people labeled as MR. What he saw there shook him and led to a series of proposed changes. Kennedy's visit was widely broadcast; in his statement, printed in national newspapers, he likened the conditions at Willowbrook to being worse than housing animals in cages in a zoo, "living amidst brutality and human excrement and intestinal disease."[31]

Many objected to his depiction of what he saw in these institutions. In response, Burton Blatt, then a professor and educator at Boston University who was becoming a leader in special education and the field of MR, decided to prove that the conditions Kennedy described were not an anomaly but the essence of what institutionalization had become. As he wrote in 1966, "in fact, we know personally of few institutions for the mentally retarded in the United States completely free of dirt and filth, odors, naked patients groveling in their own feces, children in locked cells, horribly crowded dormitories, and understaffed and wrongly staffed facilities."[32] In 1966, Blatt enlisted the help of his friend and photographer Fred Kaplan to take candid photographs in back wards of four institutions for those labeled as MR in the Northeast. Kaplan would use a camera held onto his belt or briefcase to take pictures on tours of institutions, unbeknownst to most or all of the staff and residents. The appalling account of what they saw was published as *Christmas in Purgatory*.[33] The book begins with the now infamous lines "There is a hell on earth, and in America there is a special inferno. We were visitors there during Christmas, 1965." Blatt ends the introduction with his characteristic pathos: "It is fitting that this book—our purgatory in black and white—was written on the 700th anniversary of the birth of Dante."

Part I of *Christmas in Purgatory* is a damning photographic display of black-and-white candid photographs depicting half or fully naked incarcerated adults lying, sitting, and staring aimlessly in barren but overcrowded rooms. Blatt and Kaplan chose quite different scenes for part II. It displays pictures, taken with permission this time, at Connecticut's Seaside Regional

Center, a smaller, newer facility housing 250 residents with intellectual disabilities and 100 staff. The residents had access to employment (sheltered workshops), education (segregated classrooms), and one-on-one care (for eating, bathing, and other activities). There was still no privacy, and the cribs looked like cages, but the walls were decorated, there were stuffed animals on the beds, everyone was fully clothed, and some were smiling. The point of this part of the book was, in Blatt's words, "our way of communicating our deep conviction that many of the severe conditions with which you are about to become involved are not necessary consequences of the fact of institutionalization of mentally retarded individuals. These problems are largely the result of inadequate budgets, inferior facilities, untrained personnel, and haphazard planning."[34]

In other words, the disaster shown in part I is of our ("society") doing, not about the capacity of people labeled as disabled to learn. And it is on us to change part I to appear more like part II nationwide. At that point in time, Blatt and Kaplan constructed their call for action in terms of reform, but they also presented a (literal) picture of what could be done otherwise, not in the future, but a future that is already here. Because of the affective, material, and aesthetic differences between the two parts of the exposé, the second part is presented without any critique. This, the readers are poised to surmise, is progress, humane segregation done right. As we shall see in the next chapter, Blatt would come to abandon this reformist position later in his career and call for the abolition of all such facilities.

One year later, in 1967, Blatt published a version of the exposé in the widely distributed *Look* magazine. It garnered much attention from the media and the public, including many professionals who all agreed that the conditions in institutions were deplorable and in need of serious change. In 1974, Blatt received the Humanitarian Award from the American Association on Mental Deficiency (now the American Association on Intellectual and Developmental Disabilities) and was elected to serve as the association's president in 1976. But large residential institutions for those with I/DD labels and other disabilities were still pervasive, despite the reach of Blatt's work.

There were other news stories over the years in a variety of publications, but they did not elicit any more significant changes. The late 1960s and early 1970s brought with them exposés in another visual medium, the television, which brought about a national moment of reckoning for U.S. publics about the reality of institutionalization. In 1968, a local TV channel in Philadelphia broadcast its exposé of Pennhurst, the infamous large state institution for those with I/DD labels. Under the name *Suffer the Little Children*, the televised exposé brought the issue of institutionalization, and especially the conditions at large spaces of enclosure like Pennhurst, to the public's attention, especially locally. It also created an outcry that eventually led to the lawsuit that necessitated the closure of Pennhurst, discussed more in chapter 7.

But it was not until 1971 that an exposé made national news and brought the issue of institutionalization to every home in America. The exposé targeted Willowbrook, the same institution visited by Senator Kennedy and Blatt a few years earlier. The focus on Willowbrook was not surprising, considering that by the mid-1960s, the institution housed about six thousand people with intellectual disabilities and was the biggest such institution in the United States. The timing is also not surprising in hindsight, as all the factors lined up to produce the conditions of possibility for a major national outrage. In 1971, budget cuts and therefore a hiring freeze were announced in a facility that was already understaffed. Tension and pressure were already in the air when a few residents and doctors at the facility decided to break the story nationally. After getting nowhere with the administration, Bronston and Wilkins, two physicians working at Willowbrook, called their acquaintance, then journalist, Geraldo Rivera, who took a cameraman and visited Willowbrook unannounced.

To give an account of what transpired at the facility at the time is chilling (and potentially triggering, read with care). Bronston described the conditions in the institution at the time: "The place was pandemonium all the time, shrieking, stench, chairs flying, people unconscious, asleep on the floor after being drugged daily, burned both from laying against the radiators and injured by the daily detergent concentrate used to swab the floors . . . nudity and humiliation the norm, violence the norm. I mean, all the time. It was all blamed on 'mental retardation.'"[35] What Rivera's exposé did was to bring the issue of institutionalization to the homes of everyone with a TV in the United States. It stayed on the news for months, and many remember it to this day. Rivera's televised exposé on ABC opened the door for more reports in the *New York Times* and the *Village Voice*. This resulted in heightened public interest in Willowbrook and the conditions at mental institutions more generally, leading to lawsuits.

Blatt published his monumental and striking photographic exposé in 1966. In 1979, eight years after Rivera's televised exposé, Blatt revisited these same institutions and found no great improvement; they were just "mildly cleaner snake pits." The setting was smaller, much cleaner, and the inmates were clothed. But just like Maisel's follow-up article in 1951 (to his original exposé from 1946), scenes of idleness, boredom, and inhumanity abounded. Rivera also went back to Willowbrook a year after his exposé in 1972 and found that the conditions were not much improved. As Blatt wrote in his introduction to the follow-up book, "As you will see, everything has changed during the last decade. As you will see, nothing has changed."[36]

Although there is no doubt that these exposés did indeed lead to some measures of reform at least in some places, they did not lead to the desire to *abolish* these spaces, only to change the conditions of confinement. As Steve J. Taylor writes in his expansive and revealing book *Acts of Conscience* regarding cycles of reforms in institutions for people with intellectual disability,

> perhaps the institutions had changed between the 1940s and the 60s, but then what is change? A day room of 100 or 150 half-naked people is probably better than one of 250 or 300 naked people. A room with some benches and chairs and a television is probably better than one with none of these things. A ward staffed by three or four attendants is probably better than one staffed by one or two. A punch or a slap is probably better than being beaten with a pipe or a rubber hose filled with buck shot. None of this, though, should be confused with real change in how some of the most vulnerable people in our society are treated.[37]

I am quoting this passage at length not only to give a disturbing picture of the conditions of confinement in these institutions at that time—and certainly not to make the reader fall into a false sense of progress portrayed in these exposés. These notions of progress, arising from exposing conditions inside and comparing them to seemingly humane policies, are more about the stories we tell ourselves about progress in relation to dealing with difference than they are about the actual lived reality of those incarcerated. In addition, what Taylor and his book, as well as my analysis of Blatt's and Maisel's exposés, point to is the slippage between reform and status quo, as opposed to abolition. Changes within the carceral apparatus did little to abolish it and especially to abolish its logic, to question its necessity and its underlying rationale for confinement and segregation of people because they are different and seen as dependent.

In addition, such shock-and-awe campaigns, presented through these exposés, can further ableism in several ways. Because of the sheer abjection and lack of agency presented, such exposés can further the oppression of incarcerated disabled people by viewing them as inherently incapable of life outside these carceral spaces, despite the goals of Blatt and others. It can also lead viewers away from solidarity or understanding they are part of shared communities of struggles, for example, the larger nascent disability rights (which focused on physical disabilities) and human rights communities. Lastly, because these exposés were mostly done by nondisabled (or not cognitively or psychiatrically disabled) white men, they did not focus on disability as a cripistemology,[38] as a framework from which to create social change. As I suggest throughout the book, disability as a political condition can be mobilized for social change not as a deficit but as a possibility for being and living otherwise. For this reason, in the next chapter, I briefly discuss self-advocacy and mad movements that critiqued institutionalization from within.

My broader contention is that the focus on deplorable conditions may have assisted in shaping the public's view as to the abuses taking place but it did not lead to abolishing these spaces of confinement; instead, it led to calls to reform them, which often aided in prolonging and justifying their existence. As Rachel Herzig and other abolitionists suggest regarding campaigns focusing on alleviating prison conditions, such measures perpetuate the myth that the system is broken and therefore in need of improvement.[39] But the system is not broken;[40] it performs based on its espoused rationales (segregation, confinement, incapacitation), and only once the rationales have been disputed can meaningful change occur.

I suggest therefore that deinstitutionalization should be conceived not only as a process, of people exiting hospitals and institutions for a variety of reasons, or as a form of progress from warehousing to reforming carceral enclosures to be more humane spaces of confinement. Instead, if deinstitutionalization is at least also a demand for the abolition of disability-based confinement, then exposés could be seen as a step in the direction of questioning the efficacy of such carceral locales, but not necessarily as a critique of their rationale and raison d'état. I discuss the latter—deinstitutionalization as a call for abolition—more in the next chapter.

Class Action Lawsuits

The legal arena was a major battleground on which deinstitutionalization started to be implemented de facto. Important class action lawsuits came as a result of these exposés and took the battle over conditions of confinement into the courts. In the 1960s, and more strongly in the 1970s, public interest law gained prominence, and numerous lawsuits were brought against psych hospitals, residential institutions for those with I/DD, forensic psych facilities, and prisons. In addition, several organizations were established that specialized in disability and mental health law. Since the early 1970s, there have been more than forty-five lawsuits filed against state institutions for people labeled as MR.[41] There is a high correlation between litigation and reduction in institutional populations. For instance, the five states that ranked highest in depopulating mental institutions between 1988 and 1992 had court orders or consent decrees in place at that time.[42]

I devote chapter 7 to detailing the genealogy of institutional reform litigation, its effectiveness and consequences, why it waned over time, and the ways litigation regarding prisons is connected to institutions, but I would be remiss not to include a few trailblazing cases in deinstitutionalization litigation here. *Wyatt v. Stickney,* in Alabama, was one of the first legal challenges to confinement in psychiatric and MR institutions. It was filed initially on behalf of an employee and a patient at Bryce Hospital, for people with mental illness, in 1970 and expanded to include Partlow State School for people with MR in 1971. The *Wyatt* case became a landmark case because of two major factors. First, in his ruling, the judge affirmed that people labeled with mental illness and MR who are committed to institutions have a right to treatment (in the case of mental illness) and habilitation (in the case of MR). In doing so, he created standards of treatment for those confined in psych hospitals and institutions, which later became national standards.

Second, because the ruling affirmed that those confined have a right to treatment and because it also created standards for such care, it could then be utilized as a deinstitutionalization (and not just institutional reform) strategy. As Steve J. Taylor suggests, the hypothesis of the lawyers in the *Wyatt* case, and other deinstitutionalization cases, was that the prohibitive cost of rehabilitation and treatment would necessitate the release of patients into other settings and ultimately result in the closure of the institution,[43] which was a novel strategy in class action litigation. Third, the *Wyatt* case was also a landmark because it lasted thirty-three years, making it the most litigated and costly mental health lawsuit (estimated over $15 million in litigation costs).[44]

Another landmark case came in relation to and following the pervasive and damming exposés described earlier, the 1972 Willowbrook case *New*

York State Association for Retarded Children v. Rockefeller in New York. In it
the court ruled that the right to protection from harm entitled those confined to Willowbrook to safety, a tolerable living environment, medical care,
and freedom from conditions that "shock the conscience."[45] It took three
years from the start of the suit until the consent decree, which was a watered-
down attempt to decarcerate Willowbrook residents in phases. Willowbrook
finally closed in 1987, fifteen years after the suit was filed.[46]

It was not until the *Halderman v. Pennhurst State School and Hospital*
case, filed two years later, that the *institutional logic* itself was placed on trial.
In it, the judge opined that "the confinement and isolation of the retarded
in the institution called Pennhurst is segregation in a facility that clearly is
separate and not equal."[47] He therefore ordered Pennsylvania to provide
community living arrangements for those at Pennhurst and, by extension,
to close down the institution. The suit was brought on by David Ferleger
and colleagues at the Mental Health Law Project. As their name suggests,
they were quite knowledgeable in issues of psychiatric hospitalization and
its legality, but Pennhurst was one of their first forays into litigation in the
arena of I/DD. This chasm, again, speaks to the social differences between
I/DD and mental health. Ferleger wrote that he was familiar with the abuse
and conditions in institutions for the so-called mentally ill but was unaware
of what was happening in institutions (ware)housing people with intellectual disabilities at the time. After all, he recounts that "the letters and phone
calls ... received from people confined as mentally ill were not echoed by
people confined as retarded."[48]

Overall, these cases had some effect, especially in making states implement plans to reduce reliance on institutions. It is estimated that about two-
thirds of those with mental disabilities were deinstitutionalized in the 1970s,
and court orders due to class action litigation and its resulting consent decrees
certainly facilitated this outcome. In 1975, New York State signed a consent decree that required it to relocate the 5,323 residents of Willowbrook to
community-based settings at a rate of about 50 people per month. A similar
consent decree was signed in Massachusetts in 1977, and in 1978, Washington, D.C., ordered the city to release residents from its thirteen-hundred-bed
institution for those with intellectual disabilities.[49] A decade later, in 1985,
Maryland promised to increase community residential services through a
consent decree, and Minnesota was required to limit the number of institutionalized people with intellectual disability in a 1987 settlement.[50]

The lessons here are useful for institution and prison abolitionists and reformers. While expanding and investing in carceral spaces ("just for right now," "until alternatives emerge," "for their own good"), one perpetuates the system, financially and ethically. Limiting institutionalization is an important decarceration strategy, but it still legitimates confinement as just one among other seemingly equal options and as such rationalizes carcerality and neutralizes its logic.

In addition, the legal battle in some of these cases, such as *Willowbrook* and *Pennhurst*, went on for decades as the state refused to comply with the consent decrees or to close down the institution. Taylor and Searl point out that as late as 1983, more than ten years after the initial suit was filed, there were still about one thousand residents living in Willowbrook in squalid conditions.[51] As can be seen from the length of time these cases were (and still are) litigated and the ways they were (not) implemented, they were not necessarily a successful decarceration strategy.

Willowbrook is an exemplary case as, I argue, it represents the inherent problem of trying to achieve abolition through reformist means. Those who pursued the suit (particularly the activist lawyers) wanted nothing short of a revolution in the way mental disability was perceived and treated, socially and medically. They wanted to achieve a total shift from institutional to community care, while the department of mental health subscribed to what I discuss later in the book as a continuum approach, by which institutions will be used alongside community placement and group homes. Thus, as Rothman and Rothman showed, the *Willowbrook* legal decree was full of contradictions, asking for huge financial investments to be made in the institution at present by reforming it but requiring its closure in the near future.[52] In other words, much like with the strategy of exposés, these suits and especially their consent decrees often ended in reform measures, which enabled new facilities to be erected, new technologies of governance to be used, and further legitimated the logic of institutionalization. They did, however, also have other important effects like mobilization and politicization, which are discussed in chapter 7.

Financial Factors Leading to Deinstitutionalization

Cost-cutting measures, austerity, or what became known later as neoliberalism is one of the major contributors to the eventual closure of psych

hospitals and institutions. The cornerstone of neoliberalism is privatization and austerity measures or budget cutting, especially to social services
provided by the state, which go against centralized state spending on large
institutions. As a result, the push to close down state institutions came as
an attempt to cut down public expenditures on social services more generally. Of course, this same move would also make services in the community and affordable housing scarcer than ever. With deinstitutionalization
come measurable savings—this was the main idea pushing for closures based
on cost-effective calculations, which are the epitome of neoliberal thinking. But is it cost-effective, even through the lens of neoliberal calculations?
This is also where we can see the gray line between closure, reform, and
abolition. As we shall see, even while (some) carceral spaces closed, the discourse and the budgets still went toward a costly institutional and segregationist agenda.

These fiscal decisions conveyed the rising costs of care within congregate
settings. The increase in costs came as a result of legislation and court litigation that mandated institutions to increase their quality of care and service
and thus made them more expensive. In addition, many of the institutions
were already dilapidated at the time the ideology of community living was
taking hold, and there was little sense to spend more money on bringing
them up to par with current codes and standards. Once the process of releasing people from institutions and hospitals was underway, the rising costs per
person in these institutions made politicians think about closure of these
money pits.

In the 1980s, and in some states to this day, the spending on mental health
has only increased post deinstitutionalization, and most of the budget still
went to psychiatric centers and hospitals.[53] This was due to the lingering
hold of institutional and segregation-based ideologies but also due to the
inherent institutional policy bias described earlier. Even when these carceral
enclosures close down, the budgets of each institution do not go directly into
community services. Monies that used to be utilized for the care of people
with disabilities either disappear from the budget altogether or go to the up-
keep of institutions even when the number of residents is very small. In the
1970s and 1980s (and in some states to this day), traditional institutional facilities receive the bulk of the mental health budget, even while the institutionalized population has shrunk significantly over the years.[54] In addition, as
mad activists point out, even when the budget of mental health does not go

directly into institutionalization, it still goes into expanding biopsychiatry and medical intervention, which often intersect with surveillance and punishment, especially for racialized and low-income populations. This contributes to what I call carceral sanism, which are forms of carcerality that contribute to the oppression of mad or "mentally ill" populations under the guise of treatment.

Although institutional bias in budgets was prevalent in both mental health and I/DD, the sum of the budgets themselves did differ significantly between the two forms (I/DD and psych) of deinstitutionalization over the years. Until the 1970s, mental health budgets overshadowed those for I/DD services significantly—in 1955, during which psych hospitalization peaked, the mental health population was four times more than the I/DD population. But by the early 1980s, the budgets had equalized. Not all the money went to community services, especially in the 1970s and 1980s; much money was spent on reforming institutions for people with I/DD, and that is still the case today in many states. However, spending for community services since the 1980s has been significantly higher for those labeled as I/DD than for those with psych disabilities.[55]

Why did state and federal budgets go to congregate carceral facilities even during and after efforts to deinstitutionalize? The short answer is reform. There was (and is) interest in upgrading the old facilities, which have closed down or were underutilized. Many states had included in their mission statement of deinstitutionalization the desire to improve the conditions of institutions for those who will "need them." In the arena of mental health, these reform efforts not only raised the mental health budget overall but also decreased funds for community programs and less restrictive placements.[56] Jerry Miller, who closed down juvenile prisons as Commissioner of the Massachusetts Department of Youth Services in the 1970s, remarks that while thousands of patients were left with little housing or treatment options in the community, the budgets for the depopulated hospitals actually increased at the beginning stages of deinstitutionalization in New York State and Pennsylvania.[57] He sums up the situation by remarking that although most people were deinstitutionalized in past decades, the staff, resources, and budgets remained institutionalized. This idea of "institutionalized budgets" is apt and again shows that reform often leads to an expansion of carceral logics and budgets and not to their decrease.

Other than shifting budgets, there was another financial factor that led to the desire for and necessity of closing down I/DD institutions especially. Over the years, carceral institutional settings lost one of their major labor forces: the institutionalized. Superintendents and administrators had to release those labeled with mild disabilities from hospitals and institutions and thus lost their greatest pool of unpaid laborers. This trend was solidified in 1973 with a court ruling, *Souder v. Brennan,* prohibiting the use of unpaid labor of inmates in "non-federal hospitals, homes and institutions for the mentally retarded and mentally ill."[58] In *Disability Servitude,* Ruthie-Marie Beckwith shows that one of the major economic causes of accelerated deinstitutionalization was ending the practice of unpaid forced labor in these institutions. This practice, based on lawsuits and enforcing fair labor laws within disability carceral spaces, meant that the cost of maintaining institutions increased after the 1970s. I wouldn't go as far as to state that these factors led to deinstitutionalization per se, but they accelerated a phenomenon already in place. In effect, the impetus behind these lawsuits came from self-advocates who were institutionalized and, when decarcerated, discovered that they didn't have retirement savings, Medicare, Social Security, or back wages and sued the institutions. In that sense, deinstitutionalization was ushered by and contributed to bringing these peonage lawsuits.[59]

Closure of carceral enclosures based on neoliberal mandates and policies, or cost-cutting measures more broadly, poses a poignant quandary for decarceration supporters. Ronald Reagan's policies are a case in point. Although not one to be at the forefront of the movement to promote equality and civil rights, Reagan nevertheless supported the closure of large institutions and psych hospitals, both as governor and then later as president. Population decline in psychiatric hospitals was in full swing by the 1970s, when Reagan became governor of California. This decline, coupled with his neoliberal policies, led to his infamous decision to close down all the state hospitals in California. Reagan is cited as referring to institutions and psych hospitals in California as "the biggest hotel chain in the state."[60] Although he was not ultimately successful, the vast majority were indeed shuttered.[61]

These tactics, although financially and politically motivated, could be construed as making inroads toward decreasing the power of psychiatry and institutionalization and therefore as empowering and favorable steps on the way to abolition of institutions and their logics. This scenario offers an important cautionary tale about closure versus abolition, however. Can we call the deinstitutionalization that resulted from such neoliberal ideologies, which show no concern for quality of life or life itself, a win? Is it abolition if the closure is done solely through neoliberal racist ideology? The answer to these questions is not just theoretical. Many of the facility closures happened in response to state fiscal crises and the need to shift costs to the federal government as well as the desire to cut budgets for mental health treatment and any social support altogether. And Reagan was, of course, not alone in setting these priorities, as Nixon famously cut budgets for many social services, including mental health. As is clear in the prison arena, closures and decarceration measures motivated by carceral logics end up increasing the scope of the carceral state. This was certainly the case here, too. A growing industry of privately run nursing homes and board and care facilities began to emerge with the phase-out of the hospitals and in some cases gained a lobby that advocated proactively for closure in order to increase their profits, leading to the modern-day institutional and *deinstitutional* industrial complex.

The Great Cure: Psych Drugs and Deinstitutionalization

Last but not least, one of the most pervasive claims made in histories of deinstitutionalization and in public opinion is that the availability of psych drugs, especially Thorazine, was a major engine for deinstitutionalization of psych hospitals. It is cited in almost every study, historiography, or overview of deinstitutionalization in mental health, with some discussing it as *the* engine for change, and some as secondary to fiscal decisions leading to closure of psych facilities. It is used to discuss both the how and the why for deinstitutionalization in mental health. Many scholars, and laypersons, believe that deinstitutionalization happened mostly, or solely, due to the invention of psychotropic drugs, which enabled patients to leave the hospital and manage outside of an institutionalized environment. Although there is some merit to such claims, especially in relation to the perceived timing of both events, this causal relation should be questioned especially since the decline in the institutionalized population began before the wholesale use of psychotropic drugs.[62]

As an important side note, I want to emphasize that psychopharmaceuticals' use in I/DD institutions was rampant, and in some cases, such as at Willowbrook, *all* residents were on Thorazine at some point.[63] But in the hegemonic story of deinstitutionalization, psych drugs were seen as a factor only in the field of mental health and are almost never discussed in the origin story of deinstitutionalization in the field of I/DD. In other words, the use of Thorazine and other psych drugs in I/DD institutions is not perceived as leading to their closure, even though they were widely used. Therefore my following discussion mainly centers on the hegemonic story of the closure of psych hospitals and not I/DD institutions.

From the chain of events described, it is clear that there were many reasons for psych facilities to close (and be replaced by other mechanisms for treatment and control), including exposés, lawsuits, policy changes, and the ideological push from scholars and activists under the umbrella of antipsychiatry, discussed in detail in the next chapter. But why has the advent of psychopharmacology been suggested as a forerunner of such complex processes and ideologies? Some suggest that the story of the efficacy of psych drugs was needed to justify the closure of psych hospitals or to accelerate reform in psych facilities that was already on the way.[64] Johnson goes further to suggest that this origin story was carefully constructed and maintained by the drug companies that invented and patented these drugs, although their efficacy remained contested.[65]

In contrast to popular opinion, the drugs, especially Thorazine, were not seen as a panacea, not just by those psychiatrized but by psychiatry itself. Johnson constructs a careful genealogy of the marketing of Thorazine in the United States, based on the work of Judith Swazey, who detailed its "discovery" and ascendance in psychiatric practice.[66] As they show, Thorazine was initially suspect in the United States, and drug companies had to be persuaded to take it up from the French pharmaceutical company that owned the patent for it. Once Smith, Kline, and French decided to take on the drug, they discovered that most office psychiatrists were resistant to prescribing drugs to their patients and that mental hospitals that could have used the drugs were reluctant because their use would entail increases to budgets that were already strained due to overcrowding. As a result, starting in 1954, the company began to lobby state legislators on behalf of mental hospitals to increase their budgets, especially for drug treatments. Smith, Kline, and French created a "Thorazine task force," which included hiring sales reps who would be housed in almost every major psychiatric hospital in the country. In addition, they created research briefs that demonstrated the lower overall cost of custodial care with Thorazine compared to staff turnover and maintenance of infrastructure without the drug. In essence, they tried to sell it to legislators as a cost-effective measure of institutional-ization (not *deinstitutionalization*).

Following three clinical trials that showed favorable outcomes with use of the drug, Smith, Kline, and French saw a spike in uptake of the drug, which went to 2 million consumers in a short eight-month period. The studies in question were questionable by today's standards, but as some have proposed, they were shoddy even for the 1950s. Some even go as far as to attribute cur-rent research protocols for drug trials to the fast introduction of Thorazine, a drug that was tested on a few hundred people without any understanding of long-term effects and was then given to people en masse—people who, I might add, had very little ability to refuse it, as it was given mostly in insti-tutional settings.

But not everyone swallowed the pill. There were opponents to this "psy-chiatrization from within" from the get-go. Some opposition came from sur-prising places. In their 1961 report, the Joint Commission on Mental Health commented on the use of psychotropic drugs. They did not mince words by stating that the use of drugs in psychiatric institutions is "the greatest blow for patient freedom, in terms of nonrestraint, since Pinel struck off the chains of the lunatics in the Paris asylums 168 years ago."[67] Mad activists seem to agree with this assessment. The late antipsychiatry activist Judie Chamberlain discussed Thorazine as a chemical straitjacket, and contempo-rary mad activist Erick Fabris contends that the introduction, and enforce-ment, of psychiatric drugs acted as a form of literal (not figurative) chemical incarceration that enabled populations that were deemed dangerous to live outside of an institution. These forms of chemical incarceration do not signal the liberation of the mad but their increased surveillance by other means—what I have termed *carceral sanism*.

As noted in the 1961 report, as well as other studies and reports of those psychiatrized, the most visible outcome of using these drugs is that they make patients quieter and easier to manage, especially in larger wards with their intense noise levels. Unfortunately, this was seen as proof of their overall efficacy and has served as justification for their use in hospitals to this day. In other words, as Johnson explains, if Thorazine was useful for anything, in the eyes of psychiatry, it was because it made people more amenable to other forms of therapy—made them quieter, more introspective, open to talk or group therapy. But then, "other forms of therapy" was the part cut out of the equation, and the drugs were soon seen as a form of treatment on their own.

In regard to the hegemonic story of deinstitutionalization in mental health, it is also interesting that these drugs were seen as effective and successful solely because people assumed they were a major cause of deinstitutionalization. So, the tautological argument goes, thousands of people were able to leave psychiatric hospitals beginning in the 1950s; this was because of psychiatric drugs; hence the drugs must be effective in treating mental illness. Of course, each part of this axiom has been disputed by psychiatric survivors and antipsychiatry activists: whether patients were leaving hospitals because they were well, because they did not feel they needed to be there in the first place, or because of budgetary and other reasons unrelated to their mental health status; whether deinstitutionalization was caused or aided by the advent of psychopharmacology and the level to which this was related to patients' well-being; and whether there is such a thing as mental *illness* and to what extent it is therefore treatable by drugs or other biological interventions.

The latter point is an important one, because it helps answer the question I posed earlier: why has the advent of psychopharmacology been suggested as a forerunner to deinstitutionalization? The short answer is that this narrative of curing or even treating an entity called "mental illness" cemented this entity as taken for granted instead of a contingency arising from a specific historical discourse, as Foucault suggests.[68] In other words, psych drugs fitted within the rational and scientific discourse of biopsychiatry, which saw mental illness as an illness.[69] This is a factor related to deinstitutionalization that not many discuss because of just how hegemonic the conceptualization of madness as illness had become. Most studies of deinstitutionalization in mental health refer to the "mentally ill" to discuss how and why deinstitutionalization happened, without even giving pause to their construction as a category of scientific inquiry and surveillance, that is, the construction of madness as a medical category.

Therefore the advent of psych drugs is related to and an important part of the genealogy of how biopsychiatry, the transformation of madness into mental illness, became hegemonic. Post–World War II, the sentiments of national triumph were coupled with strong notions of scientific progress. This was because of advances in medical science and more specifically the successful campaign against polio in the United States during the 1950s. The National Institute of Mental Health and key psychiatrists were so confident of the prevention and cure approaches brought by new medical technologies that they were led to declare that "mental illness might be brought under control in a generation or so."[70] Psychiatry had other grandiose hopes in the 1950s, as it was hoping to become a major player intervening in and fixing all social ills—from criminality to schooling. Therefore the process of institutionalization (i.e., treatment) and *deinstitutionalization* (via the narrative of madness and mental illness and the "discovery" of psych drugs) can be traced genealogically to the idea of scientific progress and reform.

This discourse of scientific progress should be a part not only of the genealogy of deinstitutionalization, as I have suggested here, but also of the difference between the discourses of mental illness and I/DD with which I began the chapter. As Bagnall and Eyal contend, the difference in the perception of the two forms of deinstitutionalization was due to different framings of social worth, in which those labeled with I/DD were seen as "forever children" and in need of guardianship, protection, and education, while those with labels of mental illness were constructed as "autonomous citizens."[71] Because mental illness was perceived as an illness and postwar sentiments believed in cure, people with psych labels were seen as self-reliant individuals who were only temporarily in need of assistance. Therefore deinstitutionalization could be justified (even though, as suggested earlier, deinstitutionalization as a concept only emerged after psych facilities began their decline).

If people can be treated, even if not fully cured, for their "mental illness" via drugs and other therapies in a noninstitutional setting, there is no need for prolonged hospitalization. Despite this liberatory potential, this idea cemented further the power of biopsychiatry and brought forth even more psychiatric interventions into the lives of those diagnosed as "mentally ill" and those not so diagnosed.[72] The other consequence of the hegemony of biopsychiatry is the hierarchy of disability it created. For psychiatry to become a legitimate profession, let alone a science, a separation was created between those who can be treated (the "mentally ill") and those labeled as incurable (feebleminded and then intellectually disabled).[73] Another way to put this in context is that part of the easy acceptance of the hegemonic story of psychopharmaceuticals leading to deinstitutionalization is the underlying presumption that some form of social control of disability and abnormality is necessary. The so-called success of drug treatment validates this story. But the rationale and taken for grantedness of biopsychiatry are contested by those psychiatrized and those in the arena of antipsychiatry, who also pushed for deinstitutionalization, but through other, subjugated knowledges, which are the topic of the next chapter.

Deinstitutionalization Outcomes: Mental Health and I/DD

Deinstitutionalization in I/DD is generally perceived to be more successful and had seen less backlash than deinstitutionalization in the field of mental health. Some of the differences are due to the public's perception of mental illness versus I/DD. In the hegemonic discourse, "mental illness" is seen as analogous to danger—for example, in connection with mass shooters or mad Muslim terrorists[74]—and therefore containment and segregation are legitimized, as those labeled as "mentally ill" are seen as posing "a danger to themselves or others." These claims are entirely unfounded and have been rebuked by scholars and mad activists, but they still form the basis of current commitment laws and prevailing media narratives, creating moral panics around the figure of the mentally ill as dangerous, especially through a racialized and gendered prism: as a lone bad apple, the mentally ill is a white man; as inherently depraved due to group association or background, the terrorist is sick and nonnormative, and also male—what Puar characterized as inherently queer.[75]

In contrast, the image of the "mentally retarded" is of the eternally innocent, in need of understanding, compassion, education, and specialized treatment. In essence, the person with intellectual disabilities is seen as an eternal child having "special needs." In terms of social treatment, this leads to paternal and infantilizing attitudes as well as the denial of agency. This could result in loss of reproductive rights, voting rights, freedom, and legitimation of segregation and incarceration in the name of treatment; the innocent is only dangerous to himself or herself and therefore requires care. Connecting the ethics and politics of custody of those whose incarceration is legitimated by "care" versus "punishment" is one goal of this book. Many disabled people experience both discourses at the same time, as I discuss through the prism of criminal pathologization throughout the book, but the distinction between danger and infantilization did help in crafting a different narrative and outcome for deinstitutionalization in I/DD versus mental health.

The timing for each process of institutional closure was also quite distinct. Deinstitutionalization in the field of developmental disabilities occurred about twelve years after the deinstitutionalization of psych hospitals, and the rate of reduction of use of these facilities was also significantly different. In the first ten years of deinstitutionalization for institutions for those labeled as MR, the institutionalized population was reduced by 30 percent and then averaged about 11 percent a year during the 1970s. At its height between 1955 and 1965, deinstitutionalization in psychiatric hospitals reduced the inmate population by 15 percent only.[76]

Because deinstitutionalization in mental health happened first, and because of the close ties between the policies and factors leading to both, the tactics and discourses used in each were often quite similar. This was a deliberate strategy. Deinstitutionalization activists and supporters would often use deinstitutionalization in the other field as a tool to advocate for facility closure or to advocate for different types of deinstitutionalization. Since deinstitutionalization in I/DD happened decades after deinstitutionalization in mental health, closures of psych hospitals, and often the backlash against them, were used as cautionary tales to ensure that funds actually went toward community living for those with disabilities, that plans were in place for every person who was released, and so on. In short, those in the field of I/DD translated the lessons of deinstitutionalization in mental health into desired policy and practice. But this strategy often relied on reproducing the harrowing (often exaggerated, moral panic inducing) stories of the "failure of deinstitutionalization." Those in the mental health arena, on the other hand, would often evoke I/DD policies and imageries to push for deinstitutionalization. Since people with I/DD started to be seen as deserving of rights and protections, those advocating for antipsychiatry or closure of mental health facilities evoked the nascent developments in the field of I/DD. This was because deinstitutionalization in I/DD is seen as less controversial and people with I/DD as innocent, not dangerous, and more "deserving" of institutional reform, as we shall see in the following chapters.

Owing to the different negative perceptions of "mental illness" versus I/DD, the consequences of each form of deinstitutionalization were quite different as well. Although the phenomenon of NIMBY, not in my backyard, which I discuss in chapter 5, raised its ugly head in both arenas (I/DD and mental health, as well as other carceral spaces), there is no doubt that more often than not, those with I/DD fared better in their move into community living. Although there was often fierce resistance to the construction of group homes, for example, the resistance usually subsided (of course, this is not true in all cases). As I discuss further in chapter 5, race and white supremacy had a lot to do with the ways resistance to community living took shape. But I will only mention here that terms like *innocence* have connotations of whiteness, whether or not the people themselves are perceived as white, as the resistance was often toward an unknown group of people before they moved in and terms like *danger* have connotations of color or racialization, particularly springing out of antiblack racism (again, often related to, but not always representative of, the actual reality of who is or is not categorized as "mentally ill").

The kind of deinstitutionalization that occurred, as a process, was also different in each arena. Admissions and discharges in I/DD facilities had been declining steadily since the 1970s, while admissions at psych hospitals fluctuated—between their peak in 1955 and complete overhaul in the 1970s, admission rates had actually doubled. In essence, deinstitutionalization in I/DD was more about the *prevention* of institutionalization, as Taylor and others suggest.[77] This mostly related to the prevention of institutionalization of young people or children. The professional opinion changed so significantly that now one would be hard-pressed to hear a doctor order the institutionalization of someone with I/DD as an infant, never to be seen again, which was commonplace for most of the twentieth century. Bagnall and Eyal also discuss the role parents played in the push for their children's institutionalization in the 1940s and 1950s, as part of a desire to adhere to ideals and norms of the (white) middle-class family. In the mental health arena, however, deinstitutionalization was more about transferring adults, some of whom were elderly, to other spaces of confinement and less about the prevention of institutionalization of young people.

As the largest decarceration move in U.S. history, deinstitutionalization in I/DD and mental health was a great victory for anti-institutionalization activists, for disabled people and their families, and for those pushing for a policy of inclusion as opposed to segregation and containment. In the next chapter, I offer an analysis of a factor hardly discussed in the literature about deinstitutionalization, which is the subjugated knowledges and social movements that pushed for deinstitutionalization. To be clear, I am not saying that these movements and shifting perspectives were the deciding factor leading to deinstitutionalization; I believe it is a futile battle to find *the* factor leading to deinstitutionalization, and I explain why by utilizing Foucault's genealogical approach. What I want to emphasize is that these subjugated knowledges are often dismissed as by-products of other factors, or they are ignored and forgotten altogether in accounts of deinstitutionalization. As I suggested here, deinstitutionalization was a piecemeal phenomenon, one that was not even named until decades after it happened. It came from many directions at once, many of which cannot be replicated. But there are important lessons in the genealogy of deinstitutionalization, for example, the ways exposés and litigation created public outrage and awareness of the horrors of disability-based confinement but did not ultimately lead to decarceration as an abolitionary practice, or the ways alternatives such as psychopharmacology are hailed as a panacea leading to deinstitutionalization when such interventions were actually initially marketed to increase institutionalization. As part of a critical genealogy of deinstitutionalization as a piecemeal phenomenon coming from multiple directions, I focus in the chapter that follows on the pendulum between the push for reforming carceral institutional spaces and the desire to abolish them, that is, deinstitutionalization as a process that happened versus deinstitutionalization as a movement toward the abolition of disability-based segregation.

2

Abolition in Deinstitutionalization

Normalization and the Myth of Mental Illness

Despite sustained critiques of institutionalization, deinstitutionalization did not occur en masse in the United States until the mid-1950s for mental health and until the mid-1970s for intellectual and developmental disabilities (I/DD). I contend that one of the reasons why is that it wasn't until the abolitionary approach to confinement in the disability arena took hold that deinstitutionalization could have occurred or even been imagined. Earlier attempts to achieve change (through exposés or litigation, for example, discussed in the previous chapter) were not successful because they did not develop an alternative *logic* to institutions. But how did this shift from trying to reform carceral enclosures in the disability arena to demanding their abolition occur?

In this chapter, I discuss two case studies of outliers in the deinstitutionalization of I/DD institutions and psychiatric facilities that pushed not for reform but for abolition: the work of Thomas Szasz and his call to abolish psychiatry as a medical field and Wolf Wolfensberger's principle of normalization or social role valorization, as well as their milieu and those who took up their concepts. Each theory was then taken up differently in each field and led to policies, class action lawsuits, and establishment of organizations that called for the abolition of spaces of enclosure for disabled people. Although the ideas these scholars proposed did not necessarily originate from them, as white male academics, they were able to popularize these ideas of abolition and were both despised and valorized for their distribution. While I am focusing here primarily on the influence and work of these professionals, and their contemporaries, such as Burt Blatt and Erving Goffman, throughout

69

the chapter, I also center activist movements anchored by those most affected, such as self-advocacy, psychiatric survivors, and more.

This genealogical excavation of abolition within deinstitutionalization discourses follows and nuances Foucault's conceptualization of genealogy, which is largely about uncovering subjugated, disqualified knowledge. Foucault identifies two elements within this term. First, it is the buried histories that have been subsumed by "formal systemization."[1] It is these excavated "blocks of historical knowledges" that have been obscured that he terms *subjugated knowledges*. The second meaning of subjugated knowledges, besides being buried, is forms of knowing that had been disqualified, considered nonsensical or nonscientific. It is "the knowledge of the psychiatrized, the patient, the nurse, the doctor, that is parallel to, marginal to, medical knowledge, the knowledge of the delinquent, what I would call, if you like, what people know."[2] By stating that it is the knowledge of what people know, Foucault is not referring to the taken for granted or dominant form of knowledge circulating but localized, particular, specific knowledges, what we might also call marginalized, experiential, or embodied knowledge.

It is important to note that Foucault included under the prism of subjugated knowledge the epistemology of both the doctor and the patient. It is not only the person who became the object of knowledge and was subjected to medical authority but the one who administered it as well. Because medical discourse is authoritative and has the power to tell us the truth about ourselves, it is exclusionary to other medical knowledges as well. I therefore focus on the subjugated knowledges of people like Thomas Szasz, who, although being a psychiatrist, was a strong advocate of abolishing psychiatry as a medical profession. For Foucault, the seemingly paradoxical nature of grouping together scholarly, meticulous, buried historical knowledges and localized disqualified experiential ways of knowing is what gives this coupling its critical efficacy. What is at stake in both these forms of subjugated knowledges is a history of struggle and resistance, "a memory of combats."[3] This coupling of erudite (scholarly) knowledges and embodied (popular) knowledge is what Foucault refers to as *genealogy*.

I now turn to two such blocks of knowledge that shift between erudite, discredited as nonscientific, and back again, which were subsumed by the hegemonic narrative of deinstitutionalization as failure. I begin this excavation with Wolfensberger and the field of I/DD because the field of I/DD is less discussed as part of the history of disability studies or deinstitutionalization (which is often characterized as the closure of psychiatric hospitals only), and I want to bring this knowledge to the forefront, literally. Also, abolition of residential settings and logics was more successful as an ideological and policy shift in the I/DD arena than it was in the field of mental health. Therefore the principle of normalization provides an important case study of what happens when calls for abolition get institutionalized themselves and taken up by State apparatuses. In other words, I aim to show not just the (economic, cultural, political) price of exclusion but that of inclusion.

If exclusion resulted in segregation that encompassed the creation and retrenchment of carceral enclosures, what is the price of *inclusion* of disability into the mainstream? This is what I am calling *Dis Inc.,* disability incarcerated and incorporated. The time frame of deinstitutionalization, the 1960s for mental health and the 1970s and 1980s for I/DD, also signaled this impetus toward incorporation more broadly. The reaction to 1960s and 1970s radical and revolutionary social movements, including black power, antipsychiatry, and radical gay, lesbian, and feminist (and gender nonconforming or queer before queer was an oft-used term) political activism, was reactionary and repressive. But the sediments and attempts to quell radical movements of these eras also brought new forms of incorporation under the rubric of inclusion, multiculturalism, and, later on, diversity.[4] Much had been said to critique this incorporation in relation to discourses of multiculturalism, as well as diversity.[5] But less had been discussed about this shift in relation to inclusion and disability or race-ability.

Inclusion itself carries very specific meanings within disability cultures and social movements. It often refers to the desire and policies that call for the integration of disabled students into mainstream (compulsory state-funded and mandated) K–12 education in the United States. It began as a push from disabled people, or mostly parents of disabled children, to provide kids proper education that is equal to and in conjunction with their peers. This demand can be viewed as an antisegregationist measure, akin and related to civil rights struggles and especially racial integration in education.[6]

Sometimes this process is erroneously referred to as mainstreaming, incorporating disabled students into regular (i.e., not marked as special) education, into the mainstream. But radical inclusionists contest this conflation and assert that inclusion is about changing the whole structure of education and its infrastructure so that it will better accommodates all students' abilities, including those who are labeled or identify as disabled.[7] It is not about "dumping" children into oppressive and unsustainable educational environments in a survival-of-the-fittest kind of strategy. Instead, some activists and theorists ("radical inclusionists") conceptualize inclusion as, not a place, but a mind-set, a logic.[8] Therefore inclusion does not equate into incorporation into the status quo but to changing the structures, in this case, the field of education, for everyone's benefit.

In this sense, I am using the word *incorporation* to signal both the cultural and social incorporation of minority difference[9] into the status quo and incorporation as a structure of political-economic profit-making impetuses, whether it is through discourses of cost-effectiveness under neoliberalism or literal corporations raking in profits from incarceration and disposability under plain old capitalism, such as group homes, halfway houses, or prisons. The questions I pose in this chapter are, therefore, what are the costs of the incorporation of specific knowledges that were discredited into practice and policy? What occurs to abolitionary theorizations and demands when they travel across fields and across times and audiences? What are potential consequences when professionals or so-called experts push for populations who were until now excluded, via institutionalization and psychiatrization, to get incorporated? What happens when abolitionary theories are actually successful in shifting the institutional framework, and what kind of technologies of governance are produced outside and instead of the institution? What happens when such theories are not incorporated into expert knowledge and are countered with more so-called scientific theories?

Normalization: From Subjugated to Erudite Knowledge

In the field of I/DD, one of the crucial factors leading to deinstitutionalization was new professional knowledge in the field, which was then utilized to push for community integration. Although many, including me, would come to critique these theorizations, these forms of social scientific and professional knowledge were crucial in turning the tide against a century-old practice of institutionalization and disability-based segregation. These early conceptualizations included the concept of the therapeutic community, which was used and spread by various scholars and professionals in the 1950s and 1960s;[10] Harold Garfinkel's (1956) analysis of degradation ceremonies that could be applied to institutions;[11] Erving Goffman's *Asylums* (1961), which coined the concept of the "total institution";[12] and David Veil's

Dehumanization and the Institutional Career (1966).[13] These were all popular frameworks in social sciences in the 1960s, although none of them was specifically referring to developmental disabilities in relation to institutionalization or treatment.

The question I find interesting in regard to activist knowledges that pushed for an end to the institutional framework is, how did such theories move between being discredited to being regarded as erudite/scientific/expert knowledge? And how had that changed the discourse about people labeled as I/DD and their construction as subject of expertise? How has liberation from the confines of institutional confinement for those with I/DD labels been bound with new forms of subjection? And how and why did the pendulum in professional knowledge shift toward the abolition of the institutional mind-set or carceral logics?

In the I/DD literature, later activated in courts, policies, and laws, none was more influential than the principle of normalization. The concept of "normalization" in the context of I/DD came from Scandinavia, where it was originally suggested in the 1960s by Neils Bank-Mikkelsen from Denmark and Bengt Nirje from Sweden,[14] who became prominent figures in the professional field of I/DD research and advocacy and also what would become known as the parent movement for those with "mental retardation" labels.[15] What popularized this framework in the United States was the report for President Kennedy's Panel on Mental Retardation, which was coedited by Wolf Wolfensberger and published in 1969 as *Changing Patterns in Residential Services for the Mentally Retarded.*[16]

Although this principle is often perceived as the desire to normalize people, the goal was to aid those with disabilities, especially intellectual disabilities, enhance their quality of life so that it resembles the lives of those without disabilities. In short, it was about normalizing and equalizing conditions and environments. What was meant by normalization then? Nirje specified the following components to the creation of normalized environments: they should have normal rhythm of the day (eating, sleeping, working, etc.); normal routines and settings for leisure, schooling, sleeping; a normal rhythm of the year, including holidays, weekends, and so on; opportunities to undergo normal developmental experiences of the life cycle; the choices, wishes, and desires of those labeled as "mentally retarded" themselves have to be taken into consideration as often as possible, and respected; the ability to live in gendered (male and female) environments; maintaining comparable economic standards as their peers; and lastly, ensuring "that the standards of the physical facilities, e.g., hospitals, schools, group homes and hostels, and boarding homes, should be the same as those regularly applied in society to the same kind of facilities for ordinary citizens."[17]

When one reads over this list of criteria today, one has to wonder what was so innovative about this approach. But the idea that people with intellectual and developmental disabilities should be raised in and live in "normalized settings" resembling those of their peers was an idea that was fiercely resisted at its time and is not universally accepted to this day. It is therefore important to pause here and think about this professional critique of disability-based segregation as connected to other abolitionary demands. The idea that those with I/DD could and should be educated and reside with their (non-disabled) peers was a paradigm shift that seemed almost unimaginable in the 1960s and early 1970s, for several reasons. Wolf Wolfensberger, who popularized the principle of normalization in the United States, attributes this resistance to the lingering effects of eugenics, which, alongside the Holocaust, troubled him and Nirje and led to their utmost disdain of any type of segregation, especially in enclosed, camplike settings, such as residential institutions for people with I/DD.[18] It was therefore hard to dissipate ideas and ideologies that were entrenched since the end of the nineteenth century and led to the creation of segregated facilities based on disability as well as social policies related to the confluence of ability, race, sexuality, ethnicity, and so on.[19]

Moreover, the principle of normalization was published during the height of institutionalization of those with labels of I/DD, the rate of which peaked at 1967, when almost two hundred thousand people were housed in large state institutions.[20] Lifelong institutionalization of those with I/DD was a widespread practice in that era, so that those institutionalized were often there for decades, some for life. Living a segregated life in an enclosed setting was more the rule than the exception for many people with disabilities. One could say it was normal.

I also want to anchor the importance of the ways reform-based thinking obscured people's imagination regarding the potential living and educational opportunities for those with I/DD labels at the time. The prevailing solutions to the problem of mass institutionalization of that era were focused on improving or reforming institutional living by creating smaller settings that would be better managed or pushing for more money for segregated housing and special education to improve them. The notion of abolition, or that people with disabilities should not be segregated in the first place, was almost unfathomable.

To grasp the importance of this new approach in the genealogy of deinstitutionalization, we need to understand its critiques of institutionalization. In his seminal book *The Origin and Nature of Our Institutional Models,* Wolfensberger theorized his disdain for institutional settings and discussed their historical origin and function. He simultaneously identified the various tropes under which people with intellectual disabilities (then MR) are treated.[21] These two processes go hand in hand, according to Wolfensberger. Institutionalization creates a self-fulfilling prophecy by which if you are placed in an abnormal environment for life, such as the institution, you are perceived as and potentially will become deviant. This also works the other way around: when someone is seen as disabled, she will be placed in an institution-like setting. Wolfensberger further classified the various dehumanizing perceptions of people with disabilities: subhuman or menace, sick, object of charity, subject of pity, or holy innocent. These perceptions (or roles) are what then determine the expectations of and placements for people with intellectual disabilities. His book is filled with enlightening examples and observations of this process of dehumanization and pathologization, leading to institutionalization. Wolfensberger offers here a kind of social constructionist perspective of disability, especially the ways that the label one is assigned and the environment in which one is put reinforce each other. This kind of professional knowledge is what I called in the introduction, using the phrase coined by Steven J. Taylor, "disability studies before it had a name."[22]

Normalization also differed from other therapeutic approaches to "mental retardation." At the time, the two main prevailing discourses regarding "treatment" of those with I/DD were centered on either cure (by prevention or various "treatments") or rehabilitation. According to Eyal et al., the principle of normalization thus filled the gap that was created by futile attempts to find a cure or an etiology to "mental retardation" and psychiatric treatments, which most often resulted in custodial placements.[23] Under the new conceptualization of normalization, cause or "treatment" in the traditional way was not the objective, biomedically or otherwise; rather, normalization itself (resemblance to peers, elevating the expectations and roles of those labeled as I/DD) was the goal.

The Iron Cage of Normalization

These types of professional knowledges, which Foucault refers to as subjugated, were fiercely resisted at the time and discredited as utopian, unscientific, and dangerous. But over the years, normalization has moved from being discredited to being hegemonic knowledge in some circles. I posit that what has tilted the scale toward adherence to these theories of normalization was their acceptance over time as erudite and *scientific* knowledge.

Wolfensberger critiqued early formulations of normalization, like Nirje's, because in his view, they were not empirical but instead ideologically based. It was important to him to tie the theory into social scientific language and, in his words, "take it out of folk language."[24] Wolfensberger claimed that such understandings of normalization were too open to interpretation and that without more specifics, they can lead to reforms but stop short of the abolition of institutional structures. Wolfensberger therefore decided to put the emphasis not on the environment but on the role, actual or perceived, that is given to an individual and to ensure that this role is a valued one.[25] Therefore he renamed normalization theory social role valorization, or SRV,[26] defined as "the pursuit of the good things in life for a party by enhancing their competency and image, by the application of empirical knowledge, so that these roles are positively valued in the eyes of the perceivers."[27] The emphasis on empiricism is in the very definition of SRV.

Because *reform* of institutions was the hegemonic discourse of that time, Wolfensberger and others felt that the only way to become a counterdiscourse within the field of I/DD policy was to "speak its language." He therefore designed an empirical tool to evaluate the way normalization is implemented, so that it would not just increase the net effect of institutionalization into smaller "homelike" institutions or educational settings. Wolfensberger called this empirical quantitative measurement tool PASS—Program Analysis of Service Systems—and it is still used today to evaluate the system's or program's impact on various variables, such as positive interpretation, integration, or age-appropriate and culturally appropriate programming.[28] Service providers began codifying normalization/SRV into policy, mandating it in training, and so on.[29] But in most instances, it was taken up by service agencies as one more guideline that needed to be followed and not as a paradigm shift. In short, it became an iron cage.[30] For example, Wolfensberger wrote in 1975, "To this day, food and drink may be served in unbreakable tin reminiscent of prison riot films of the 1930's. Often no knives and forks are permitted."[31] But his poignant observations about daily living for those in prison-like "abnormal settings" had evolved into a set of checklists that disabled people and their caretakers get measured on, such as eating with a fork (as opposed to a spoon or hands) or not having stuffed animals in one's room.

In other words, once SRV, or normalization, reached the level of policy or iron cage of technocracy, it had created a shift in the lived experience of many disabled people. What I am interested in here are therefore the costs of integration, assimilation, and normalization. What happens when normalization and SRV are actually successful in shifting the institutional framework? What kind of subject is produced in these newer living arrangements for those with I/DD outside of the institution?[32] The work of Chris Drinkwater is instructive here.[33] Drinkwater presents a Foucauldian analysis of group homes for those labeled as intellectually disabled to show that although these represent alternatives to institutional living, they do not guarantee emancipation for those who live in them. He demonstrates that what is produced in these settings are indeed people with valued social roles or well-integrated citizens. This is achieved by a variety of disciplinary techniques in which the person with an I/DD label needs to prove their civility and compliance. These include cultivating bodily regimens in relation to hygiene, conduct, sexuality, and so on in order to resemble peer like behavior. It also includes different techniques of surveillance of the resident and their actions and the constant monitoring and recording of their compliance.

In summary, along the way to its instrumentalization, the perspective changed from a focus on the environment (what would later be called the social model of disability[34]) to a focus on the person (assimilation). Paradoxically, it was this shift to focusing not on fixing the environment, i.e., reforming institutions, that brought forth abolition of the institutional model. By focusing on the individual with disability and their needs, though, these theories simultaneously entrenched a more deficit-driven individual model of disability, even if the outcome was the liberation of people with disabilities from institutional life.

Professionals not only learned about SRV or normalization and how to implement it, technocratically, but also became gatekeepers and held this knowledge above the embodied knowledge of those with disabilities who were not professionals, those who were now called "clients" or "consumers." Put differently, one of the reasons why the normalization principle caught on so far and wide is that it galvanized commonsense ideas that were already circulating but put them in the hands and language of "experts."[35] Although Wolfensberger does not claim that SRV was the only factor that led to deinstitutionalization, he nonetheless claims that it "broke the back of the institutional movement" and that without it, "there would have been massive investments in building new, smaller, regionalized institutions."[36] But community living, according to the late disability studies theorist Mike Oliver,[37] and as demonstrated throughout this book, also reproduces the control of the capitalist state (and I would add racial and settler State), especially since professionals, who as a class make money off controlling the lives of disabled people, remain intact in their position of power. This is the second part of Dis Inc., the work of incorporating disability through literal corporations who understand disability as a commodity, especially under the prism of the institutional–industrial complex and, as I alluded in the introductory chapter, also the decarceration–industrial complex.[38]

Contesting Normal(ization)

The main critique of the normalization principle is of course questioning what gets to count as "normal." Disability theorist Lennard Davis argues that there is a difference between normalcy and normality, in which normality is the actual state of being normal or being regarded as normal, and normalcy is the discourse that controls and normalizes bodies.[39] It is the ideology behind normality. Normalcy is embedded with bourgeois and white cisheterosexual and male norms.[40] These processes are also colonial imperatives, quite literally. As theorist Sylvia Wynter has poetically argued, (ethnoclass) Man overrepresents himself as if he is *the human* itself. A specific, Western bourgeois settler heterosexual white Christian, version of being human is enveloped into modernity as a universal category of Human.[41]

Nirje and Wolfensberger discuss how disabled lives should resemble the lives of peers through normal rhythm of the day, normal setting, and so on. But as critical legal scholar Fiona Kumari Campbell rightfully points out, Wolfersberger's examples for a "normal" course of life were resolutely middle class, cisgendered, and heteronormative.[42] As part of SRV, for example, there are guidelines for the evaluation of "valued sex roles," which refer to gendered expectations in behavior and appearance as well as to sexuality. Other than some forms of asexuality, queerness is disavowed, while cisgender and hetero forms of disability are to be valued and incorporated. These are also entrenched in race and class assumptions and privileges—discussing the "normal life course" as one leading to parenthood, marriage, education, or employment implies that the disabled person's peers actually have access, let alone equal access due to class, race, gender, etc., to such pathways, or that these are the desirable paths to pursue. These assumptions around "valued" and "normal" written by Eurocentric white heterosexual men were then taken to be universal.

This is a prominent example of Dis Inc., disability incarcerated and incorporated. The inclusion and incorporation of disability away from sites of incarceration, such as large state institutions for people with I/DD labels, contributed to the production and reproduction of a variety of techniques of management, governance, and surveillance over people labeled as disabled (and often over their careworkers as well). In segregated settings like group homes and sheltered workshops, all life's activities, including eating, hygiene, sexuality, and intimacy, are policed and surveilled constantly. As Mike Gill puts it, "professionals working with individuals with intellectual disabilities become authorized to regulate sexual behaviors, even if no behaviors are present."[43] This is what Gill calls sexual ableism.

In the educational and self-advocacy arenas for people with I/DD, self-determination is a much-discussed concept and is similar in its implementation and logics to normalization. As critical education theorists Phil Smith and Christine Routel argue in their discussion of educational policy in the United States, concepts such as self-determination, normalization, autonomy, and independent living are colonial, white, masculine, Western constructs.[44] Disability related policy relies on notions of autonomy and individualism, a form of self-reliance that is foreign to many indigenous and non-Western communities. This crip/mad of color analysis shows not only some of the reasons why indigenous, black, and people of color don't often find themselves "at home" in disability rights or independent living movements and discourses but also that the State itself is not home, in other words, that incorporation within settler ethnocentric norms is not the solution but the problem.

The concept of self-determination has a different but perhaps related meaning in the context of native sovereignty. In the native context, it is about decolonialization, sovereignty, and the rights of indigenous people under the settler state. But as Dina Gilio-Whitaker writes, "self-determination is reduced to the ability of a tribal nation to be merely self-governing.... It is still a paternalistic relationship with tribes generally thought of as incapable, if not undeserving of the type of self-determination reserved for nation-states."[45] Smith and Routel critique self-determination from the perspective of indigenous groups who experience it as a white colonial apparatus. As they explain in the context of education, "the notion that self-determination (having choice, control, and power in one's life) can be taught to others strikes us as a uniquely colonialist idea—some ingroup (teachers, people who describe themselves as not having disabilities, as being normal) has it, and can teach the out-group (students, people with disabilities, people who are by definition not-normal) how to get it." In this sense, the technocratic iron cage of professional knowledge in the field of I/DD is not only colonial in that it erases (nonprofessional) disabled people's culture, knowledge, and experiences but is also a literal tool of reproducing Western colonial white hegemony.

More broadly, normalization and rehabilitation are colonial impetuses to correct deviant and backward bodies and minds, stemming from particular Eurocentric assumptions on both an individual level (disciplining) and population level (civilizing as a biopolitical mode of governmentality). Crip/mad of color (especially one that includes indigeneity) critique underscored the ways that values perceived as inherent in the modern liberal subject (such as independence) are then used to scapegoat populations (cognitively disabled people, women, indigenous people, black people, and their intersections) as pathological and in need of corrections. Independence, self-determination, and other modernist individualist values are then constructed as skills or traits that can be mandated, regulated, and taught to those (backward, retarded, primitive, degenerate) who are then assessed whether they "have it." The burden of proof is on the person who needs to be as normal or comparable as possible to their peers, but not on the peers or social system that creates segregation from those deemed as nondisabled.

This is also the work of Dis Inc.—the need to integrate and be included, but only as a liberal civilized subject under white settler middle-class heteropatriarchal norms. The costs of not being integrated correctly (and I am using corrections here deliberately) are the veiled threats and often realities of institutionalization or returning to segregated congregate living (for those who were deinstitutionalized). There is always the shadow of the adverse consequences if one does not conform or comply—what I called elsewhere the institution yet to come.[46] The specter of incarceration is inherent, as a promise or threat, in mechanisms of liberal inclusion.

Furthermore, I suggested in the introductory chapter that we should view disability as an analytic as well as a political category of identification and material reality. Because disability status (but not necessarily diagnosis or label) and conditions of debilitation are more pervasive in families of color and those of low income, the gap between professional expectations of something like "social role valorization" and the reality of those most prone to debilitation is even larger. But I also want to state that disability is both an ontology and an epistemology. As an epistemology, disability, to some, signals a defiant stance, one that (nondisabled) theorists such as Goffman and Wolfensberger did not even imagine.[47] In other words, a crip/mad of color analysis of social role valorization and other professional theories can show, as I argue here, that embedded in such theories in the field of I/DD is the assumption that people would want to assimilate and be included, as opposed to celebrate their difference, as demonstrated by the tenets of neurodiversity,[48] disability culture,[49] mad pride, and frameworks such as neuroqueer.[50] As Campbell suggests, "we are denied a deliberative capacity to adopt a resistive positionality."[51] Therefore inclusion, via assimilation, does not allow the production of disability culture and epistemologies. Because the goal is to reduce stigma and assimilate (to be like one's nondisabled universal subject peers), these theories are already rooted in a specific racial, ableist, heteronormative discourse.

The Pendulum between Reform and Abolition in the Field of I/DD

It was not only professionals and academics that pushed for the shift from reform to abolition in the field of I/DD. Although discredited to this day, the knowledges and activism of disabled people themselves had been a major force in turning the tide as well. When institutions began to shutter, people with I/DD labels sought others who shared their experiences of learning to (re)live in the community. These were the sprouts of many developing self-advocacy groups and associations. In turn, these groups became the most vocal abolitionists, who advocated for the closure of more (or all) institutions and the move of all their peers into community living. As they were the most affected by institutional closure, self-advocates became the most insistent voices in the fight for the abolition of institutions for people with disabilities.[52] For example, former residents of Pennhurst in Pennsylvania established Speaking for Ourselves, headed by Roland Johnson, with the goal of ensuring that all people get out of institutions and receive services in the community.[53] Another prominent group at the time was People First Nebraska, or Project Two, as they were known then.

As described by Williams and Shoultz,[54] Project Two in Nebraska began when a few people with I/DD labels who were deinstitutionalized from Omaha's Beatrice institution started meeting to share their struggles of living in the community after institutionalization. One of them was Ray Loomis, who was confined in Beatrice from 1953 to 1963.[55] In 1977, Project Two members were instrumental in making their voices heard regarding their desire to live in the community and close institutions in the state. In a public forum held by Eastern Nebraska Community Office of Retardation, with which Wolfensberger also worked, they spoke up about their negative experiences living in Beatrice, often speaking to and against parents who were in favor of institutionalization as an option.[56] They were the only organization in Nebraska at that time that called for the abolition of the institution and of similar institutions.

Much like normalization, the origins of self-advocacy as an organization and ideological framework came from Sweden in the late 1960s.[57] The first North American convention took place in British Columbia, Canada, in 1973. The conference was attended by representatives from Oregon who had already formed their own support groups comprising mainly people who were deinstitutionalized from Fairview Hospital. In 1973, a joint committee was formed of self-advocates who still resided in Fairview and those who were already deinstitutionalized, in order to start organizing a national convening. The conference took place in 1974 in Oregon. A whopping 560 people came, more than double what was expected. It was a conference that sparked, and was sparked by, a movement, the People First movement.[58] The name People First was chosen to indicate that people with I/DD labels (at the time, "mentally retarded people") were people deserving of human rights.

What led to the development of self-advocacy groups in the United States in the 1970s?[59] Parents' groups were gaining prominence, especially associations like The Arc,[60] which, by the end of the 1970s, (mostly) supported community living and deinstitutionalization as a matter of policy. As such, they began to include and interact more with people with I/DD, who were now more active in the community.[61] Second, the pendulum toward abolition of institution-alization in professional opinion played an important role. The principle of normalization and other new ideologies were starting to be taken up in ser-vice provision agencies and among professionals (such as case managers and social workers) who were in direct contact with people with I/DD labels.

By the 1970s, a small number of professionals in the field of I/DD started to promote the notion that reform of institutions is a futile enterprise, and they should not be restructured alongside other living arrangements but abolished altogether. As Burton Blatt wrote in 1979, "if there is hope in what we have learned in our examination of institutionalization, it is not in any improvement of institutional life—imprisonment and segregation can be made more comfortable, but they can never be made into freedom and par-ticipation."[62] Blatt, a leader in special education (what would become known as the inclusion movement), was also an early critic of residential institu-tions for people with I/DD and exposed them in *Christmas in Purgatory*, described in the previous chapter.[63] When he first exposed the institutions, Blatt advocated for institutional reform and the humane treatment of resi-dents. By the mid-1970s, he had given up hope that institutions could be reformed. In *The Family Papers: A Return to Purgatory*, he wrote:

> A decade or so ago, we went to five state institutions for the mentally retarded, the purpose then not as clear as the purpose for our return last year. Then, we found little to give us hope but we were reluctant to admit that the concept of "institution" is hopeless.... We convinced ourselves that by making them smaller, providing more resources, developing ways to insure proper inspec-tion and accountability, by working at improving things, we could make good institutions out of bad institutions. The subsequent years and this most recent round of visits convince us that those were foolish ideas. *We must evacuate the institutions for the mentally retarded.*[64]

In his book *Acts of Conscience*, Steven J. Taylor, who worked and studied with Blatt and continued his legacy in many ways, constructs a historiogra-phy of exposés of mental institutions from the turn of the century, focusing on the 1940s onward.[65] Exposé-driven reforms, as suggested in the previous chapter, resulted in change in the degree of squalor presented in the insti-tutions, but the qualities of the institutions essentially remained intact. It was not until the call was made for the elimination of such institutions that a change in the institutional mind-set, its carceral logic, was sought. It was the coupling of these exposés with the ideology of normalization, labeling theory, and antipsychiatry that ultimately led to a change in perspective—from institutional living to a community-based model and calls for the closure of all such disability-based carceral enclosures.

In addition, in 1971, the Center on Human Policy was formed by Burton Blatt at Syracuse University.[66] It served as a progressive academic and advocacy center to promote inclusion and counter discrimination against people with disabilities, especially those with I/DD labels. In 1979, the Center on Human Policy wrote *The Community Imperative*, a declaration supporting the right of all people with disabilities to community living.[67] *The Community Imperative* was written in response to organized opposition to deinstitutionalization and community living. Specifically, it was intended to counter a 1978 memorandum submitted by ten national experts in hearings in the *Wyatt* case in Alabama, discussed in chapters 1 and 7, that argued that community living and training programs were only beneficial and appropriate for a small and select few. The *Imperative* contends that all people can and should benefit from community living. It was endorsed by more than three hundred parents, people with disabilities, and professionals and was part of the changing tide toward the abolition of segregated living based on disability.

The same year that the *Imperative* was being drafted, Wolfensberger penned his two-part article "Will There Always Be an Institution?"[68] In it he predicted that "institutions will be phased out because of five trends: development of nonresidential community services; new conceptualizations of and attitudes toward residential services; increased usage of individual rather than group residential placements; provision of small, specialized group residences; and a decline in the incidence and prevalence of severe and profound retardation."[69] The development of alternatives (nonresidential services, small group homes) is not the only thing that will bring forth deinstitutionalization or the decline of the institution. As he suggested, new ways of thinking about segregation, institutionalization, and disability have to accompany these policy changes. But as I indicated in the genealogy of deinstitutionalization in the previous chapter, many factors contributed to this perfect storm. In Nebraska, where he advocates and about which he wrote extensively, establishing community living and closing institutions for those with I/DD labels was due to a shift in perspective but also localized values[70] that cannot necessarily be generalized or replicated.[71]

But the shift from trying to reform I/DD congregate institutions to advocating for their complete abolition was not just a top-down process. One of the most significant factors leading to the creation and evolution of self-advocacy in the United States had to do with deinstitutionalization and its abolitionary spirit. Even though many institutional residents began to meet "inside" while confined, that was not always possible or feasible. It was not until people got out of institutional placements that they came together to discuss their hardships or to meet socially. By doing so, they also developed a political consciousness. This activism, in the field of I/DD, is not often mentioned or cited in literature reviews and histories that discuss disability activism and the disability rights movement. The disability rights movement was gaining momentum in the 1970s, but not for all people with disabilities. At the forefront of the movement were people with physical disabilities (mostly white men, but not only) who were promoting the removal of architectural barriers, increased employment for people with disabilities, and independent living. Later, women and feminists within the movement would characterize this agenda as phallocentric, as most of them experienced barriers related to childcare, obtaining substantial disability benefits as mothers who do unpaid labor, and also value not so much independence as interdependence.[72] Such goals for independence and employment seem to have little relevance for people with I/DD at the time, who were either living at home or in institutions, and some principles seem to be at odds for professionals and parents who did not think that people with MR labels can make decisions about their own lives and live independently. Furthermore, as Allison Carey shows, the tactics used by the disability rights movement, such as street protests, marches, and civil disobedience (tactics taken from civil rights struggles), did not seem to suit parents and professionals who did not want to bring undue attention to themselves or their family members or be seen as radicals or troublemakers.[73]

The disability rights movement on its part did not go out of its way to include people with I/DD or parents' organizations. As the main principle of the disability rights movement was the ability for the disabled person to control their own life, the inclusion of people with I/DD required a leap of faith, not to mention a change in the practices and tactics used by such a potential coalition, both of which were not on the agenda of the major players at the time. Moreover, it is possible, as Baynton showed in regard to first wave feminists and slavery abolitionists, that to gain rights, marginalized groups need to distance themselves from the stigma of disability.[74] Even though the rights in this case are for people with disabilities, the stigma of mental disability seems like something that activists with other disabilities would like to avoid. In *The Autism Matrix*, Eyal et al. claim that theories like the normalization principle helped to democratize the field of developmental disabilities by putting psychiatry, experts, and administrators on the same playing field.[75] Parent activism, which turned against the medical establishment in the 1960s, was seeking allies and found them in the more marginalized professions, such as social workers, speech and occupational therapists, sociologists, and special educators. Ironically, this breaking down of the monopoly of medical expertise would eventually lead to a new monopoly of technocrats and bureaucrats in regard to prescribing and administrating benefits and services, as the pendulum shifted from notions of medical cure to notions of habilitation. But this shift now meant that all these professionals, with their varying expertise, had to share the table with parents, advocates, and, later on, self-advocates.

The "institutionalization," if you will, of integration and anti-institutionalization theories via the acceptance of normalization or SRV acted as a double-edged sword. Once instrumentalized, these conceptualizations were used as a way to increase the management of those it originally thought to liberate (those exiting institutions and those with disabilities living in the community), paradoxically through the operationalization of concepts like self-determination and inclusion. Through checklists and increased technocratic surveillance, normalization was solidified as a policy and a way of policing difference. It policed caretakers (the majority of whom are underpaid people of color, and many of whom are women) but also a variety of people with disabilities. Many no longer resided in institutional settings, but were they free?

Abolition in Antipsychiatry

Deinstitutionalization in mental health is often taken as prototypical (or as the only deinstitutionalization that happened), but it is deeply intertwined with deinstitutionalization in I/DD and its knowledges. As I argued, some of the differences in professional knowledges, and its resulting deinstitutionalization, are due to the image of "mental illness" as one of danger versus "mental retardation," which is more of an eternal innocent child (with

exceptions to each stereotype, of course). But madness was not only perceived under the discourse of danger. During and contributing to deinstitutionalization, mental ill health was also perceived as a productive and creative
entity, which led not only to its disavowal but also to its romanticization.
The allure and romanticization of madness in the 1960s and 1970s in radical and progressive circles (the mad genius, social outcast, political dissident)
are in sharp contrast to the figure of the mentally "retarded" or developmentally disabled in that era. Although the figure of the intellectually disabled
was not as hidden as it was in previous decades, when some didn't even
know they had a family member with I/DD label, often due to institutionalization, there was certainly no desire to romanticize or *become* intellectually
disabled. It was not seen as a metaphoric condition for social dissonance and
was not taken up as a distinct figure of the 1960s. The case was much different in the arena of mental health. Riding on post–World War II fears of
authoritarianism and the State, increasing waves of liberation movements—
from feminist to civil rights (and later black power), gay (and later queer),
and others—critiqued and tried to break apart oppressive structures related
to their subordination. Under this purview, according to historian Michael
Staub, mental illness was seen as a social disease, a symptom of its era with
its social and cultural upheaval.[76]

It is no surprise, then, that the early 1960s saw an explosion in books
critiquing psychiatry. In 1961, the Joint Commission on Mental Illness and
Health's report *Action for Mental Health*, the American Bar Foundation's *The
Mentally Disabled and the Law*, and sociologist Erving Goffman's *Asylums*
were published.[77] Michel Foucault published his *Histoire de la Folie*, which
characterized the birth of psychiatry as creating a chasm between madness and reason, and he sought to provide "an archeology of that silence."[78]
The year 1961 was also when psychiatrist Thomas Szasz's *The Myth of Mental Illness* and fellow psychiatrist R. D. Laing's *The Divided Self* were published.[79] In 1962, Ken Kesey's *One Flew over the Cuckoo's Nest* came out
to wide acclaim.[80] Although a fictional portrayal, it was this novel and its
subsequent movie in 1975 that gave the critique of psychiatric hospitals popular appeal.[81] Another influential cinematic portrayal of the era was the
1966 influential *Titicut Follies*, Fredrick Wiseman's first documentary.[82] It
was a bleak, graphic, and utterly disturbing depiction of incarcerated life at
Bridgewater State Hospital for the Criminally Insane in Massachusetts, with
scenes of naked inmates in barren cells bullied by guards, strip-searched,

and force-fed. Film critic Roger Ebert wrote that "the film leaves us with the impression that institutions like Bridgewater are causing mental illness, not curing it."[83] Taken together, the two films added to the growing critiques of psychiatry as an agent of social control and of institutionalization as an inhumane and brutal practice.

Most of these early critiques of psychiatry ignored or at least did not emphasize the profound role that gender had in the construction, diagnosis, and treatment of madness. But American women took up the challenge. The posthumous publication of Sylvia Plath's *The Bell Jar* in 1963 marked a growing critique of psychiatry from a feminist perspective.[84] In addition, the intellectual works of sociologists like Thomas Scheff, Ervin Goffman, and Dorothy Smith also contributed to the creation of erudite knowledge critiquing psychiatry and leading to deinstitutionalization in mental health. In *Being Mentally Ill,* Scheff developed labeling theory to assert that the process of stigmatization and categorization actually produced a person as mentally ill.[85] In a related fashion, in "'K Is Mentally Ill,'" feminist sociologist Dorothy Smith extrapolates the ways mental illness is constructed as factual by people who do not acknowledge its constructed nature.[86]

Taken together, many of these books were best sellers, produced as cheap editions for mass audiences. Whatever their merit in changing the psychiatric landscape, and regardless of their authors' intent, their influence traversed into a wider social critique, which made them appealing to the lay public of their day.[87] In these seminal texts, the psychiatric hospital was being attacked and critiqued as the modern epitome of social control, as a total institution and producer of regimes of power/knowledge. It is also important to note that many of these scholarly works and critiques (especially Szasz, Goffman, and Foucault) connected the psychiatric hospital to other loci of incarceration, such as prisons, a point foregrounded throughout this book. This corresponded with important historical intersections of radical activism that connected antiprison activism and critiques of medicine and, sometimes, psychiatry.[88]

Although, in this chapter, I am focusing only on abolitionary knowledge in antipsychiatry that was taken up by mainstream audiences and affected deinstitutionalization policy, I would be remiss not to mention the entanglement between radical movements, including antiwar, feminist, gay liberation, and black power movements that were also critical of psychiatry.[89] Queer and gay movements in particular had a complex relationship with psychiatrization, one that still affects the diverse movements encompassing queer or gay liberation. Gay and lesbian activism offered one of the most pronounced critiques of psychiatry, which desired to unlock homosexuality from medicalization and therefore from its pathologization (and resulting criminalization).[90] Organizations like SNCC (Student Non-Violence Coordinating Committee), black power organizations and individuals, and SDS (Students for Democratic Society) were involved in multiple campaigns and multicause struggles. The organization Psychologists for a Democratic Society, for example, was formed as an offshoot to the organizing of SDS.[91] Many also distributed newsletters and zines offering criticisms of the "system" (capitalism, imperialism, militarism, sexism, and so on). In them, aspects of psychiatry and its control function are critiqued. An important site in which critiques of psychiatry and radical movements intersected was in the black power and queer movements, especially in the 1970s.[92] Although not discussed as antipsychiatry knowledge by black power scholars or Black Panther Party members themselves, I want to suggest that the goal was the same—to delegitimize the expertise of psychiatric knowledge, to denounce it as biased and unscientific, and to put forth their own framework of how to "diagnose" harm, violence, and difference and how to "treat" it. In the same era, the militant collective the George Jackson Brigade (armed self-defense in the service of liberation of various oppressed peoples, including native, gay, women, third world, and those incarcerated) was resolutely against electroconvulsive therapy and sensory deprivation as part of its agenda to support and free those incarcerated.[93] Emily Thuma also presents a fascinating account of the Coalition to Stop Institutional Violence, an alliance of prisoners, mental patients, and feminist organizations and collectives in the Boston area in the 1970s that opposed the creation and expansion of medicalization and securitization in prisons and psych hospitals.[94]

I want to anchor these movements' work toward deinstitutionalization as it offers a complex picture of critiques to psychiatry. But since they arose after the height of deinstitutionalization and did not directly contribute to its creation (although their critique of psychiatrization was incredibly valuable), the rest of the chapter is devoted to analysis of abolitionary strands of scholarly knowledges in the critique of psychiatric confinement that led, at least in part, to deinstitutionalization in mental health. I define abolition of psychiatric incarceration in three ways: abolition as the act and process of closing down psychiatric hospitals; abolition of the rationale for long hospitalization; and lastly, the abolition of psychiatry. Not all mad or ex-patient movements are antipsychiatry, and not all critiques of psychiatry or antipsychiatry movements are abolitionary or agree on what should be abolished, not to mention how, in regard to psychiatry and its practices.[95] Even fewer were resolutely abolitionist in all three ways.

For the rest of the chapter, I will focus on one of the main U.S. figures to symbolize the abolitionary approach to psychiatry in all its facets: Thomas Szasz and the American Association for the Abolition of Involuntary Mental Hospitalization (AAAIMH). My focus on Szasz is not meant to reproduce the idea of the white man scholar as an all-knowing universal subject, but quite the contrary. As Dylan Rodriguez defines in a different context (referring to Foucault and the GIP[96]), "white academic raciality, in these terms, is both an epochal, disciplining knowledge-project and a laboriously contrived, transparent racial subject position,"[97] making it *the* position to produce and authorize knowledge as proper. Furthermore, as Jane Ussher claims, white men psychiatric dissenters, like Szasz and Laing, were miles away from the actual lives and experiences of mad women, who were the majority of those psychiatrized and institutionalized in most of the twentieth century.[98]

As a genealogical study wedded to historical content, I want to both critique and retell the hegemonic story of ideas that were engaged with or dismissed as erudite by the mainstream establishment. I am not focusing on Szasz because he was the perfect poster child of what has been called "antipsychiatry" (a term he despised) but because I want to show the limits and limitation of abolition done through a normative settler white frame— and because historically, his writings were incredibly influential for radical and revolutionary thinkers and movements. In his extreme and simplistic way, he popularized views that then circulated and traveled elsewhere. For better or worse, his theories probably did more to push for and later bring backlash against deinstitutionalization than those of any other person.

I therefore turn now to analyzing Szasz's theories as one specific example of abolition in the context of psychiatric confinement to illuminate a set of questions that are historically significant, as well as their potential consequences for organizing: What were the effects of absorption or rejection of abolitionary critiques of psychiatry and psychiatric confinement? How was abolition utilized in these discourses critiquing psychiatric confinement? Was it taken up, by whom, and in conjunction with what other frameworks? How had the attachment to abolition waxed and waned, and what was the relation between such changes and the closure of psychiatric facilities? Finally, what were the effects of deploying these critiques as a single issue, as opposed to intersectional frameworks more broadly?

The Founding Fathers of the American Association for the Abolition of Involuntary Mental Hospitalization

Even though Szasz himself might be well known in critical circles, a rarely discussed chapter in the genealogy of antipsychiatry and deinstitutionalization is the establishment in 1970 of the AAAIMH by Thomas Szasz, Erving Goffman, and George Alexander. Histories and genealogies of antipsychiatry do not mention, let alone discuss or analyze, the AAAIMH. I want to focus here on two of the founders of the organization, Szasz and Goffman, who had much clout in the popular imagination of their time and used it to change the public's perceptions of the necessity of psychiatric confinement.[99]

Szasz's work is foundational to any historiography of antipsychiatry, although Szasz himself disliked and distanced himself from this term.[100] His basic premise, discussed first in 1961 in *The Myth of Mental Illness,* and elaborated in his prolific writing until his death in 2012, is that mental illness is a metaphor, as there isn't and could not be an illness of the mind.[101] Unlike other fields of medicine, Szasz claimed, psychiatry created new criteria for diagnosis of disease: alteration of bodily function instead of bodily form. Now doctors only need to observe behavior to diagnose, not find evidence of lesions or viruses. Therefore, in psychiatry, diseases are invented, not discovered.[102]

Szasz does not object to the views purported by psychiatrists but to the fact they express their views as medical experts, as to him, psychiatry is a belief system, not a branch of medicine. People are free to believe in what they choose, but the problem with psychiatry is that it is coercive, and one lacks a choice of whether to engage in it or not once one is forced into treatment, hospitalization, and medication. As he famously put it, "incarcerating people and talking to them are not medicine."[103] Moreover, as a libertarian, Szasz opposed the power that the State and its agents have to engage in people's behaviors, beliefs, or conduct, as bizarre as they might be. The theocratic State of the past was essentially replaced by a therapeutic State, according to Szasz.

An obvious critique of Szasz's work is that he seems to fall back on the age-old distinction between "medical" (or physiological) symptoms and "mental" (or psychological) conditions, reifying the traditional mind–body split.[104] The former (physical) is seen as real and can be verified by scientific means, whereas the latter (mental) is perceived as constructed and cannot be assessed by scientific means. Medical categorization is seen by Szasz as objective, yet not applicable to psychiatric or psychological assessment. The essential character of medicine as objective, apolitical, and scientific is never questioned a priori by Szasz and Szasz-minded antipsychiatry scholar-activists, except in relation to mental symptomology.

Thus Szasz might be a critic of psychiatry, but it is not surprising that his work had not been taken up more broadly in disability studies, as for him, "mental illness" is manufactured, but physical disability or the category of MR or intellectual disability is "real."[105] These mind–body as subjective-objective diagnostic criteria would lead to some thorny divides between antipsychiatry and disability activism for years to come.[106] In other words, Szasz's views, and the views of those following him, cemented the idea that violence in the cloak of treatment should not befall those labeled as "mentally ill," which was a paradigm shift leading, among other things, to vocal critiques of institutionalization, further leading to its eventual abolition in the form of closure of psychiatric hospitals. However, the same liberatory spirit was not extended to other disability categories and their respective social movements.

Although Szasz had been the main propeller of the AAAIMH, the other "celebrity" who landed the organization its notoriety was famed sociologist Erving Goffman. Although Szasz acknowledged that Goffman's greatest contribution to the organization was giving his name and seal of approval to the enterprise,[107] it was Goffman's popular scholarly work that connected him to the goal of abolition of psychiatric hospitalization, as well as a personal familial connection (Goffman's first wife had a label of mental illness and took her own life). His writing circulated widely and led to critiques of institutionalization in both I/DD and mental health. Erving Goffman and Howard Becker were among the first in the social sciences to offer a reconceptualization of disability and other identities as not inherently negative but a product of successful labeling as deviant. This notion freed the bearers of these identities or labels from guilt and shame and placed the process of Othering in the social realm.[108] This liberating aspect of their work is what gained scholars of labeling theory notoriety, not just among academics but among progressive social movements, such as the disability and anti-psychiatry movements. It also contributed to the not-yet-formed field of disability studies.

Goffman got his notoriety in disability studies with *Stigma: Notes on the Management of Spoiled Identity,* in which he conceptualized criminality, disabilities, bodily changes and modifications, queerness, and so on as social flaws and referred to these traits as either discredited (flaws that are visible and known to others) or discreditable (differences that are not yet visible to others), and his central concern was how to manage these "spoiled identities" (his term).[109] The tensions in Goffman's work (its liberatory potential and its stigmatizing assumptions) would come to reverberate in some factions of the social movements of those with these discredited identities, what I jokingly call "spoiled identity politics," who would take up the mantle of crip, queer, or mad to flaunt it, not hide it. The major problem in Goffman's work, though, is that he does not consider that difference can be quite empowering.[110] Difference may cause one to be regarded as inferior, but this constructed inferiority can be rejected, not just managed.[111] His stigma approach (and related frameworks by labeling theorists) assumes that whenever possible, people would want to conform to social norms, even if these norms are actually the ones that label them as different. This rejection of normalcy would become a hallmark of the LGBTQ movement, especially in its queer factions, as well as fat/phat activism, disability/crip, mad pride, and others who find not only spoilage but pride in their labels and construction, as the adage of "who wants to be normal?" can attest to. Choosing to embrace one's spoiled identity is something Goffman did not envision.

But the biggest contribution to the anti-institutionalization and antipsychiatry movement was probably Goffman's other critical and often cited book, *Asylums,* published in 1961.[112] In it, he analyzes a specific structure, an ideal type, in the Weberian sense, of the total institution, defined as "a place of residence and work where a large number of like-situated individuals, cut off from the wider society for an appreciable period of time, together lead an enclosed, formally administered round of life."[113] What makes total institutions unique, and socially interesting, is that they are sites in which people reside 24/7, sleeping and eating and working in the same place, with the same people. Goffman adds that "handling of many human needs by the bureaucratic organization of whole blocks of people—whether or not this is a necessary or effective means of social organization in the circumstances—

is the key fact of total institutions."[114] In Goffman's account, people in total institutions also fill strict roles, as either inmates or staff.[115] Goffman's book did not just remain a topic for scholars to ponder but was widely read by those in the "helping professions" as well as the general public. For example, Taylor and Bogdan concluded from their participant observations of four institutions for people with "mental retardation" labels between 1970 and 1977 that there wasn't a single official who was unaware of Goffman's critique of asylums.[116] Goffman, Scheff, and other labeling theorists should be credited for at least starting a conversation about an issue that was not part of scholarly discussion before—institutionalization and the dehumanizing effects of labels, especially in relation to labels of disability and mental illness.

The back-and-forth between abolition and reform can also be seen in the platform of the AAAIMH. While the platform of the AAAIMH, as its name suggests, with its focus on opposing the involuntary aspects of psychiatric practice, may seem narrow, the involuntary nature of psychiatric hospitalization (which Szasz saw as a form of incarceration) became for Szasz the defining characteristic of psychiatry as a medical discipline. As Szasz famously stated, "committed mental patients do not 'come to see' coercive psychiatrists; they are brought there against the detained person's will, typically in restraints."[117] Szasz claims that there is no such thing as voluntary commitment to a psychiatric hospital because you are not the person who decides when you get out. Once you are committed, getting out is always determined by medical experts, regardless of how you entered the hospital. If you cannot get out voluntarily when you choose, how can it be called voluntary commitment? Thus, for Szasz, modern psychiatry always stands for coercion. Abolish that, and the raison d'état of psychiatry crumbles.

However, the AAAIMH, in its language and platform, does not seem to call for the abolition of psychiatry as a field, as Szasz does in his sole authored writings. Some of this tension might be due to pragmatic reasons—the desire to appeal to larger segments of the population or the need to focus on a specific and achievable goal while espousing a larger, long-term agenda. But it could also be attributed to the differences between the cofounders of the organization. Despite his own critique, Goffman could not envision a society free of asylums. As he states, "if all the mental hospitals in a given region would close down today, tomorrow relatives, police and judges would raise a clamor for new ones; and these true clients of the mental hospitals would demand an institution to satisfy their need."[118]

In an interesting turn of events that shows the influence of Goffman and his milieu's writing at that time, this exact passage became a battleground for and against deinstitutionalization. As Susan Schweik discusses, this passage from *Asylums* appeared in a legal brief in the *Wyatt* case about the right to treatment in Alabama's institutions for those with intellectual disability labels.[119] One would think that passages from *Asylums* would be used as evidence for the inhumane conditions of institutionalization (for which Alabama was notorious), but as Schweik shows, Goffman's work was used as ammunition by the defense to argue that the state had no obligation for quality care in its institutions because the main service they provided was essentially segregation and their main clients were the "relatives, police and judges" who wanted respite, not people with disabilities who needed care and education. Ultimately, as Schweik remarks, "this misreading of Goffman didn't hold up. The court ruled: 'It is fairly clear that Professor Goffman's intent, in calling "relatives, police and judges" the "true clients of the mental hospitals"' was harshly critical."[120] Even though Goffman himself could not foresee an end to the commitment of people to mental hospitals, and certainly not to a noncarceral society, his work nonetheless fueled the growing antipsychiatry and anti-institution movements in the 1960s and 1970s.[121]

The AAAIMH: The Pendulum between Reform and Abolition

AAAIMH's founders saw the organization as "a beacon," to show the way to others who oppose psychiatry, and especially the coercive aspects of psychiatry as a medical field. The organization also attempted to assist people who were involuntarily committed to seek legal advice and help.[122] AAAIMH published a newsletter titled the *Abolitionist* to promote the association's goals.[123] The AAAIMH newsletter was distributed about once a year to members of the association, which at its peak was almost one thousand.[124] Based on analyzing the artifacts left by the AAAIMH (newsletters, position statements, and conversations I had with Szasz), it seems that one of the aims of the organization was to provide a counterview to psychiatry that does not take it as neutral and scientific (i.e., objective and empirical) but instead as coercive. It seems equally important that this viewpoint was presented by men of science advocating not for changes and reforms in the field but for its abolition. As Szasz explained, "the practice of involuntary psychiatric interventions—epitomized by civil commitment—is a moral atrocity, similar to the practice of involuntary servitude. This makes the abolition of that practice a precondition of so-called psychiatric reform."[125] Two things are of note here. The first is that Szasz alludes to the abolition of slavery as an analogy, hence the use of the term *abolition* in the name and platform of the organization. As I will show in the next chapter, this is also how the term is used by prison abolitionists, only in that case, it is seen as a continuation of the work of slavery abolition and not as an analogy. This is because white supremacy and racial capitalism are central to the theoretical understanding of prison abolition, which is not the case here. Second, Szasz, and, by extension, the AAAIMH and its members, saw the difference between abolition and reform, in which abolition of one practice (involuntary hospitalizations) should be a prerequisite for any profound change in psychiatry and its eventual dissolution. In this case, ending involuntary hospitalization would be a nonreformist reform, one that leads to abolition of psychiatric confinement. The impetus toward the intentional use of abolition in the organization's name and platform merits attention, as I posit that this shift toward abolition of hospitalization and institutionalization was one of the tipping points for enacting deinstitutionalization, not just as policy, but as an ideology and logic.

Like prison abolition, whose goal is to untie the Gordian knot between crime (its production, crime rates, and the construction of criminality) and incarceration, Szasz's goal was to untie the knot between deviance/abnormality and biomedicalization, leading to psychiatric confinement. Other antipsychiatry activists took up this mantle as well. Judi Chamberlin was one of the most prominent contemporary critics of psychiatry, whose work also circulated extensively in the 1970s and early 1980s. Chamberlin critiqued the mantra that is often recited by activists and professionals that "mental illness is like any other illness" or that the way to combat the oppression of those psychiatrized is in fighting against stigma.[126] Given the current laws in relation to involuntary hospitalization, mental "illness" is not like cancer or a heart attack, according to Chamberlin. Altered states, anger, and pain should not be characterized as illness but as a consequence of a system of power and inequality that denies people their basic human needs. In addition, stigma is not perceived by Chamberlin to be the force that most oppresses those psychiatrized; psychiatry itself is that force.[127]

Szasz's demand for the abolition of psychiatry and its coercive aspects was useful for a variety of liberation movements, including gay rights, feminist thinking, and civil rights/black power, in critiquing the power of psychiatry to define what is "normal" behavior as well as diagnose and "treat" accordingly. From the disavowal of "homosexuality" as a diagnostic criterion in the *Diagnostic and Statistical Manual of Mental Disorders (DSM)* to the critique of hysteria as applied to nonconformist women or schizophrenia as a category to label and restrain black men at the height of the black power movement,[128] there is little doubt that the idea that mental illness is a social construct and not a medical or biological reality was useful to these liberation struggles in more ways than one. For example, within gay activism in the 1970s, Szasz was a cause célèbre. Abram J. Lewis shows how madness was both taken up and disavowed within gay activism of the era. Gay print media cited Szasz extensively, and radical reading groups took up Laing's and Szasz's work alongside Marxist critiques. At the same time, mainstream gay activists of the 1970s era who wanted to take out homosexuality as a classificatory category under the *DSM* saw madness and disability as pathological and did not want to associate with them for fear of medicalization or criminalization. In other words, according to Lewis, declassification activists looked at the diagnosis of homosexuality as an error in an otherwise scientific profession of psychiatry.[129] By so doing, declassification activism aided in the legitimation of psychiatry as scientific knowledge, an assertion that was cemented at the end of the 1970s.

Since Szasz was an abolitionist who founded an organization devoted to the abolition of psychiatric confinement, he was disappointed that some of these movements, such as feminist and gay rights, did not take his critique of psychiatry in its entirety and only contended that it did not apply to them, and he thus perceived such movements as only adding to the legitimization of psychiatry. The *Advocate* ran an interview with Szasz in 1977 that called on gay liberation activists to denounce psychiatry wholesale, not just for the psychiatrization of homosexuality.[130] In another example, Szasz berated feminist psychologist Phyllis Chesler for not working for the liberation of women from psychiatry but instead working to liberate some women by saying they were not really insane.[131]

In other words, Szasz saw reform efforts as a way to increase the net of the therapeutic State and of psychiatry as a field. In Szasz's conceptualization of abolition, this idea of chipping at the margins (excluding a specific group from psychiatric purview based on one characteristic) would not work to destabilize the center unless the group also becomes critical of psychiatry for everyone's sake. This is interesting in light of recent calls for antipsychiatry to adopt the attrition model, which espouses exactly such claims. "Abolition by attrition" was described by Knopp and colleagues in their seminal manual written in the mid-1970s in regard to prisons.[132] According to the attrition model, the function and power of prisons will be slowly worn down by working to decarcerate as many prisoners as possible, one strategy and population after another. Longtime antipsychiatry activist Bonnie Burstow recently suggested that antipsychiatry needs a unified plan and theory to guide toward abolition.[133] Burstow suggests several reasons why antipsychiatry as a movement is currently floundering; among them are the strength of biopsychiatry and a lack of shared vision of a way forward. She emphasizes that antipsychiatry is not only a stance against psychiatry but the understanding that psychiatry is untenable and will never be tenable, with any amount of reform. The goal is the abolition or end of the system of psychiatry. Burstow proposes that the movement could benefit from the insights of prison abolitionists, especially as formulated by Quakers in the 1970s. Following the recommendations of Knopp et al., Burstow recommends that the short-term goals of antipsychiatry activists, such as reform efforts, be kept as such—as steps on a road that is not yet fully formulated, the unfinished road of abolition. At any given time, the work should not be aimed at reform but should have goals for concrete and direct partial abolitions on the road to long-term change. This attrition model has had its detractors, even from abolitionist circles, who see it as a glorified reform strategy.[134] Decarcerating or removing from psychiatry's control by attrition would mean that some populations would be closer to freedom, as in the case of demedicalizing certain conditions such as homosexuality or hysteria, but the system and its power imbalance remains; we are still left with a punitive and vengeance-driven system of capture, only now it does not apply to one population or another. Instead of attrition, what Szasz and others suggest is the liberation of all by abolishing, not just taking one category from the purview of psychiatry but by advocating its abolition as a field of medicine and taking its power to incarcerate and institutionalize.

The AAAIMH did not last very long, and perhaps its biggest effect was to spread the gospel of Thomas Szasz and his critique of the "therapeutic State." By the time the AAAIMH was disbanded in 1979, the landscape of psychiatric incarceration had changed—commitment laws were much more stringent, and other organizations were established to safeguard against coercion in psychiatry. Therefore both Alexander and Szasz agreed that the goal of the organization, to serve as a beacon and rallying cry for others, was accomplished.

The AAAIMH also disbanded because of strong currents blaming so-called antipsychiatry for the failure of deinstitutionalization. As I show in chapter 4, deinstitutionalization was blamed for the rise in mass incarceration, the increase in homelessness, and the abandonment of mentally ill people to live without supports. This was an ironic and paradoxical process, as antipsychiatry (and especially Szasz) was seen as esoteric and at the same time was blamed for deinstitutionalization in mental health and all that came with it. In other words, Szasz and those critiquing psychiatry caught the brunt of the backlash against deinstitutionalization while being discredited as irrelevant at the same time. Antipsychiatry theories were under attack almost from their inception, especially by "men of science." But from the late 1970s, the twilight of deinstitutionalization, they came under further critique and scrutiny in a more organized fashion. For instance, media campaigns that ridiculed the position that mental illness is a myth were very effective at garnering public support as well as serving as the impetus for the formation of organizations such as the National Alliance on Mental Illness (NAMI).[135]

Yet, just like the incorporation of normalization as a critique that was meant to liberate people from institutionalization and coercion, the incorporation of some of the critiques of hospitalization were taken up and then subverted as modes of regulation on the lives of disabled people. One of the consequences was that it embedded psy powers in the law. This created two important secondary effects: the entrenchment of expert knowledge (legal, scientific) over the lives of those psychiatrized and reinforcement of the power to define who is "really" mad. This created a discourse the led to criminalization of mental illness and contributed to the expansion of racial criminal pathologization, which also led to more people of color being institutionalized when psychiatric hospitals started to shutter.

After the jurisdiction was given to courts to decide who can be hospitalized (based on being a danger to oneself or others), a trend of racialization of those confined to psych hospitals occurred.[136] Since dangerousness was predicated on risk assessments, and those were based on raced and gendered assumptions, psychiatrization and institutionalization of people of color increased in that era post deinstitutionalization. As historian Anne Parsons details, by the end of the 1970s, all U.S. states had restrictions based on whether one posed a danger, whereas in 1960, only five states had restricted involuntary hospitalization to measures of danger.[137] Therefore a shift occurred from involuntary hospitalization based on psych diagnosis to one based on psychiatrists' and courts' opinions of dangerousness, which was racial, gendered, and intertwined with sexuality. This is related to the discourse of racial criminal pathologization, as I called it, which sorts danger based on racism-induced fears and norms. This change fostered a criminalization of mental ill-health, as now the courts played a major role in funneling people into jails and prisons. It also aided in racially coding "criminals" and the "dangerous" in an age in which racially based classifications were heavily critiqued—what Michele Alexander calls "mass incarceration in an age of colorblindness."

Such litigation and protections from civil commitments also deepened the separation of "dangerous" mental patients from the "nondangerous" ones, reinforcing the idea that people who are deemed dangerous by psychiatrists and/or the courts should indeed be imprisoned and are not entitled to the same level of civil liberty as so-called nondangerous mentally ill individuals.[138] In 1975, the U.S. Supreme Court ruled on the constitutional right of a "nondangerous mental patient" in *O'Connor v. Donaldson*. In a unanimous decision, the Supreme Court ruled that Kenneth Donaldson, a "nondangerous" mental patient, had a constitutional right to liberty. The judgment relayed that it was not constitutional to incarcerate a person who is deemed nondangerous and who can safely live by himself or with the support of others. This was viewed as a milestone, as such rights are not usually associated with or guaranteed to those institutionalized. But I argue that at the same time, the ruling reinforced the notion that those who are so-called dangerous (i.e., criminalized, imprisoned) are not deserving of such rights and freedoms, which set a treacherous legal precedent and also created a chasm between psych patient advocacy and prisoners' rights.

In turn, legal changes that sought to determine the level of "illness" or dangerousness of individuals as prerequisite for confinement also increased the demand for so-called professional expert knowledge that judges can rely on in their deliberations, and the likes of Blatt, Wolfensberger, and their theories were called to testify in court cases to defend the opposite stance, that people should not be institutionalized. In other words, there became a market and necessity for "scientific" assessment of danger to institutionalize people based on new criteria established after psych hospitals began to close.

This idea that one can detect "mental illness" is exactly what Szasz and others feared.

Szasz claimed that the AAAIMH's critical work was co-opted and then subverted by other organizations that claimed to do similar work but were reformist and essentialist in their tactics and goals, particularly public interest law organizations, such as the New York Civil Liberties Union and the Mental Health Law Project (MHLP), which was a primary stakeholder in many deinstitutionalization cases, especially in the 1970s.[139] Szasz, and other advocates in antipsychiatry, claimed that although the MHLP brought on landmark cases that protected the rights of people with mental and developmental disabilities, at the same time, these cases reified mental illness as a medical category and a "real" inherent condition, as opposed to a behavioral or cognitive difference based on normative standards. To create protection under the law, these cases reinforced social notions that ground disabled/mad people as in need of extra protection and cemented their status as requiring medical treatment or corrections. As I suggested earlier, this was part of the price of incorporation as liberal subjects deserving of rights. To guarantee protections under the law, mental illness had to become an entity that can be categorized and seen as inherent in people and not a result of relations of power.

The disconcerting aspect of such changes was the exclusion and delegitimization of activist voices, especially of those who are most affected. In seeking more scientific theories, the lived experiences of those psychiatrized were left to the margin of the debate and were seen as only supplemental, at best, in determining policy and the contours of the debate over psychiatric treatment. In some sense, they returned full circle to the relation between madness and reason described by Foucault in *Madness and Civilization*.[140] Even though those psychiatrized are invited to the table in many policy deliberations, (consumer) councils, and public debate, the voices and authority of professionals override their concerns within such discursive locales.[141]

Reform with Abolition: Consumers, Survivors, and Dis Inc.

In the 1970s, a loose mental patients' rights movement was emerging, including the Insane Liberation Front, the Mental Patients' Liberation Project, the Mental Patient's Liberation Front, and the Network against Psychiatric Assault. The fragmented networks communicated through the annual Conference on Human Rights and Psychiatric Oppression (held from 1973 to 1985), the ex-patient-run Madness Network News (from 1972 to 1986), and the annual Alternatives conference funded by the National Institute of Mental Health for mental health consumers (from 1985 to the present). During the 1970s, the antipsychiatry and survivors' movements were growing but were also experiencing what Linda Morrison characterizes as a "crisis of representation" between dissenting professionals, like Szasz and many social and mental health workers who considered themselves allies, and those who are psychiatrized themselves.[142] This followed suit with other (spoiled) identity-based social movements, including the larger disability rights movement whose motto was "Nothing about us without us."[143]

After and during deinstitutionalization of psychiatric facilities, ex-patients of institutions demanded a right to participate in programming related to community mental health. In part, this activism was spurred by the realization that many community programs reproduce the same problematic features that they experienced in institutions and hospitals, such as forced medication and a general attitude of paternalism.[144] But some sought state funding and focused on developing self-help groups and/or advocated for improvements within the mental health system, while others insisted on grassroots approaches and advocated for more radical changes, which created a chasm within the movement.[145]

Another facet of the change in the ex-patient and antipsychiatry movement was the adoption of the term *consumer* into the mix. Beginning in the 1980s, *health care consumer* became interchangeable with *consumer* in mental health discourses. *Consumer* connotes two aspects: the commodification of health care and the idea that one has resources to purchase and consume. Second, and especially under an ideology of neoliberalism, it connotes the ability to choose, under a free market ideology. According to Nancy Tomes, patients initiated the use of the consumer language in the 1960s and 1970s because they viewed it as "a liberating alternative to the traditional doctor–patient relationship they believed to be hopelessly mired in paternalism."[146] During the first Alternatives conference in 1985, a schism between ex-patient groups started to surface between those who were adamant about opposing involuntary treatment and those who supported more cooperative approaches.[147] The former group became known as the psych survivor group and the latter as consumers. In the same year, 1985, NAMI established its own "consumer council."

Here, too, the price of disability inclusion (as in the discourse of Dis Inc.) needs to be problematized as much as its exclusion. With Dis Inc., I am not referring to co-optation of these groups in the traditional sense (although

that may have been part of the process as well). I follow here the illuminat-
ing work of Grace Kyungwon Hong, Lisa Duggan, Roderick Ferguson, and
others who show that the ascent of liberalism, as a policy and epistemology,
is tied to the incorporation of minority difference.[148] In this case, I want to
add "the mad" or "the disabled" into the mix, as the category intersects with
race, gender, sexuality, and so on. What happens when mental health difference, often codified as mental illness, gets incorporated into existing structures of settler racial capitalism? The language of *consumer* within the larger
and heterogeneous mental health movements is a great case in point.

Historically, Hong argues, neoliberalism emerged as a response to the liberation movements of the post–World War II era: "A new neoliberal order
arose based on selective protection and proliferation of minoritized life as
the very mechanism for the brutal exacerbation of minoritized death."[149] In
other words, protection of some leads to (as opposed to prevents) the deval-
uation of others in a cruel but seemingly neutral zero-sum game. As Ferguson claims, this is the "affirmation of difference," whereby certain previously
excluded groups become protected under the state and certain antiracist, anti-
homophobic ideas become hegemonic. A related phenomenon that follows
due to this incorporation is the commodification of difference. It should come
as no surprise, then, that the pharmaceutical industry was among the first to
embrace both the family movement and the new consumer movement in
mental health.[150]

For these reasons, antipsych activist Judi Chamberlin did not view the
mental health consumer movement as a liberation movement.[151] For her,
community mental health is growing alongside traditional psychiatry and
therefore is not aiding in its elimination. If anything, it broadens the scope
of psychiatric power to those who were previously free of its grasp. In the
same vein as critiques of the LGBTQ movement, from self-identified queers,
for instance, the conceptualization of "the movement" as consumer driven
is beneficial to a small section of its constituency, mainly middle-class, white,
American men. It is also highly problematic to call individuals who are
forced into "treatment" by the state, consumers. Many psychiatrized people
are forced to take medication, undergo electroshock "therapy," or reside
in institutions. For antipsychiatry activists, forced psychiatric treatment is
not a service that people consume; it is a violation of their autonomy and
freedom.[152]

Szasz mocked the mental health consumer movement as an oxymoron.
According to Szasz, if people want to see a psychiatrist without coercion,

with full consent, that is their choice. But because, in psychiatry, that is not "a choice," he advocates for its exclusion from medicine as a field. Szasz stated that the "rights" that mental patients gain by becoming the subject category "mental patient," such as the right to treatment, the right to live in the least restricted environment, as "instead of liberating the mental patient from domination by the coercive psychiatrist, these measures had reinforced the legitimacy of psychiatric oppression as medical care."[153]

He does say, though, in his simplistic and analogical polemical way, that just as some slavery abolitionists still believed in the inferiority of blacks but still fought for their liberation from bondage and servitude, so does the fact that some people, including ex-patients, believe in the category of mental illness does not need to preclude them from fighting against psychiatric coercion. In his books, Szasz discussed witch hunts, the inquisition, slavery, and other atrocities, often to compare them to the social control function of psychiatry, to prove it as a pseudoscience with immense power to control and oppress. A prime example can be found in his book *Psychiatric Slavery* and its later formulation, *Liberation by Oppression: A Comparative Study of Slavery and Psychiatry.*[154] He defines psychiatric slavery as the practice of depriving people of their liberty by psychiatrists (usually by confinement) under specific legal and moral justifications. In that sense, to Szasz, it is a reprehensible system akin to slavery. He also writes that both the slave and the mental "patient" are perceived as potentially dangerous and therefore in need of segregation and control, which is what the police were established to do. His conclusion regarding abolition is hard to overlook: "For more than forty years, I have maintained that psychiatric reforms are exercises in prettifying plantations. Slavery cannot be reformed—it can only be abolished."[155]

But it's important to note that his definition of slavery does not even include the words *race, black, property,* or *labor* and therefore is shockingly lacking in any racial analysis, although he does see chattel slavery as only one category of slavery. Szasz's dangerous downplaying of racialization, colonialism, and especially antiblack racism, white supremacy, or racial capitalism within discussions of slavery is not unique to his other writings or later critiques under the rubric of antipsychiatry, as shown by mad studies scholars such as Tam and Kenani.[156] By comparing those psychiatrized to slaves, he suggests that there were no intersections between the two. Unfortunately, such strands regarding the abolition of psychiatry would outlast Szasz.

Therefore, in addition to incorporation of minority difference, commodification, and bifurcation within the movement/s, another factor leading to
the decline of radical and abolitionary antipsych was its seeming irrelevance to the lives of mostly poor people of color who did not have access
to psychiatry to begin with or do not identify with antipsychiatry, consumer,
or mad pride.[157] The push to abolish psychiatry can seem very privileged
when some, especially racialized people, gender nonconforming people, poor
people, and their intersected oppressions, don't have access to any meaningful form of mental health care, including psychiatric diagnosis that provides
access to other state services (in such avenues as education, employment
accommodation, SSDI). Although not condoning the coercive aspects of such
services and often using them quite strategically, the antipsychiatry movement and philosophy have had little appeal among communities of color.
Recall that after deinstitutionalization, the populations who were psychiatrized and institutionalized were composed more of people of color. Therefore
one can say that such communities were psychiatrized in larger proportion
but did not find their way into antipsychiatry.

As Rachel Gorman claims about current-day mad pride organizing, it is
hard to decenter whiteness in mad organizing if people of color can't afford
to take up the mad identity, because of a variety of reasons, including already
living under surveillance by medico-judicial apparatuses, not having access
to mental health care, and the seeming irrelevance of mad movements to
the lived experience of racialized and colonized people.[158] Liberation from
psych oppression (mad activism) cannot come at the cost of further state
violence. Puar further notes that some (queer, racialized) cannot be read
as mad, disabled, or mentally ill. Such subjectivities are only legible (if tan-
gible at all) as crazy, deranged, terrorist, dangerous.[159] Louise Tam elaborates
that without a serious engagement with the ways psy disciplines pathologize
and order people differentially, indigenous and people of color won't be able
to see themselves as part of any mad movement, especially ones that "add
them" in.[160]

In other words, those who are rooted in an understanding of race-ability
and its relation to State violence do not see the incorporation of madness (as
or in addition to mental illness) into communities of color or the inclusion of
people of color within mad and antipsychiatry discourses as the goal. As Tam
elaborates, what is needed is not an additive model regarding settler status,
race, gender/sexuality, and disability but one that considers how discourses

that construct each of these subject positions are related to each other and how the oppressions that result from such constructions build on each other. Mental illness or madness is not a trait of the mind but a relation to others and a result of relations of power.

Gorman's concern is that "mad" identity (in its formulation within mad movements and mad studies) "will be absorbed into white middle class narratives of disability."[161] These politics of disability Gorman identifies posit disability as an identity (or fixed ontological state, as Gorman puts it) that (some) people claim as opposed to being a relational frame. Such distinctions pit those who are "disabled already" (part of disability rights/culture/movements/identities) against those who are disabled because of disabling or debilitating conditions (war, poverty, violence, incarceration). In short, Gorman asks, "Whose interests are being served by the expansion of political identities afforded by the shift to mad organizing?"[162]

I don't want to suggest that current-day mad activism is monolithic (i.e., white, or on the other hand reflective and intersectional in its understanding of oppression) or that it is identical to the antipsych movements of the 1970s. Much had been said about the differences and connections between the c/s/x (consumer, survivor, ex-patient) movement and current mad pride and activism. Since this is a genealogy, I would just say that mad activism is a newer, and different strand, of organizing by those psychiatrized, and as such can fall into some of the pitfalls I contoured in this chapter in regard to Szasz and antipsychiatry. But there is also the hope for newer and more nuanced critiques of oppression as well as conceptualizations of liberation that might emerge from current movements.

Abolition in Deinstitutionalization and Its Aftermath

Deinstitutionalization in I/DD and in mental health (especially in the form of antipsychiatry) had a strong abolitionary stance from an ideological standpoint. In its ultimate vision and praxis, the ideology behind deinstitutionalization was very radical for its time and advocated for the delegitimization of the rationale that people with psychiatric and intellectual disabilities should be segregated and institutionalized. It contested the power of medicine and theories in education and I/DD that espoused carceral logics. In the field of developmental disabilities, the abolitionary vision seems to have won the battle, and most U.S. professional organizations in the field of I/DD today believe in deinstitutionalization and community living for all. There are still many factions who advocate for reform or even for reinstating residential institutions (which I discuss in chapter 6), but even mainstream organizations like The Arc have moved to an abolitionary approach and advocate for community instead of institutional living for those with I/DD labels.[163] In the field of psychiatric disabilities and the movement to abolish psychiatry and its institutions, the picture is murkier. There were some gains made as a result of deinstitutionalization and closure of many psychiatric hospitals, which allowed hospitals to become a place of last resort, not a first option for people who were labeled as mentally ill. But deinstitutionalization in the field of "mental illness" remains controversial to this day, and the backlash against it is still palpable, as we will see in chapter 4.

The result of the many factors outlined herein (governmental funding, heterogeneity of those psychiatrized, and the mental health movement and its relation to antipsychiatry, as well as the ascent of neoliberalism and the incorporation of minority difference and consumerism) was that the fiery antipsychiatric message of the early years was heard less and voices calling for alternatives and reform were heard more. Since many of those who identify as ex-patients distanced themselves from what they saw as radical antipsychiatry, it is perhaps no wonder that the lay public took up their arguments as proof that this discourse was irrelevant and nonsensical.[164]

One of the reasons for this difference in outcomes of deinstitutionalization in mental health and I/DD is that abolition became accepted as policy in the field of I/DD. This is, I argue, at least partially, because theories like normalization/SRV were seen as (social) scientific breakthroughs of their time, as best practices in the field. They helped to make the field of I/DD more empirical at a time when "curing" those with mental disabilities gave way to "treatment." For psychiatry to become a legitimate profession, let alone a science, a separation was created between those who can be treated and those labeled as incurable. Since the introduction of new technologies of managing the "mentally ill" (especially psych drugs) in the 1960s, both in and out of asylums, psychiatry cemented itself as a medical field, and madness was completely subsumed by "mental illness." Any critique to this axiom was seen as ludicrous, and the call for the abolition of psychiatry as a medical field, or at all, had not been taken seriously, to put it mildly.

One of the critiques of Szasz's work is that "he went too far" by claiming that all psychiatric disorders are metaphorical and in essence nonexistent as medical conditions.[165] These critics argue that if he had limited his claims to the fact that some conditions are overdiagnosed or that there are too many different psychiatric diagnoses, and they are increasing each time the *DSM* is revised, then his critique would have been heard by many psychiatrists. Unlike many activists in the antipsychiatry movement, Szasz wanted to be considered a legitimate scientist and expert in his field but was ostracized by his own milieu because of his views. But I do not think it is true that his analysis was not heard in the medical community; rather, it was simply not taken up by them. In other words, the sheer number of times in which he is mentioned in the medical and academic literature should alert us to the fact that although his work was never taken up as hegemonic, it is definitely not "buried knowledge" in the field of psychiatry, at least for the time being, but instead should be characterized as "disqualified knowledge."

These professional theories, although contributing to deinstitutionalization, also ushered in new forms of surveillance and control against disabled people. Incorporation did not automatically lead to liberation but to other, not necessarily worse, but different, forms of carceral entanglements. As I asked at the beginning of the chapter, if exclusion resulted in the kind of segregation that included the creation and retrenchment of carceral enclosures, what is the price of inclusion of disability or Dis Inc., disability incarcerated and incorporated? This critique is also very useful to discussions today on community corrections, for example, as extension of the carceral state and not its opposition.[166]

During the era of the "asylum," the only potential benefit from psychiatry was that those outside of the walls of the asylum were free from psychiatric intervention, according to Szasz. Now, after deinstitutionalization, psychiatry, and especially psychiatric coercion, lay everywhere. Today those who were discharged or never institutionalized are still under the surveillance of the therapeutic State, but it has furthered its reach—adhering to strict drug regiments, living in semi-institutions (group homes, halfway houses), and subjected to a variety of outpatient commitment laws and policies. For example, touting chemical incarceration as a panacea for the liberation of the mad from their (institutional) chains is described by self-identified mad folks as a form of State violence.[167] This situation is similar in the field of I/DD. The iron cage of normalization ushered in surveillance in group homes and segregated settings that are now in the "community."

The line between institutional living and not is a contextual one. In response to both the self-congratulatory tone of some and overtly critical tone of others, Blatt reflected on the success of deinstitutionalization as a movement. In an undated essay, he sarcastically writes:

> You have heard about the scandals in the field, the exposes, the litigation, the progress. There has been talk of a "Revolution." To be sure, there have been reforms and there has been a "revival of conscience." The institutions have been improved, refinanced, made smaller. The community programs that serve them now are larger (or smaller; I forget which, but in whatever direction they are taking I've been advised that they and we are better for the change). Now we are left with the question, "Are the new smaller institutions better? And if so, are they better than other arrangements? Better than no institutions? Better than what?"

This critique might make Blatt a remarkable figure in the field of I/DD, but it also points to the slippages inherent in pushing for systemic social change. As Blatt points out, these are moral, philosophical, and ethical questions. They cannot be resolved by policies, checklists, or state-funded solutions alone. Abolition and theories of abolition leading to deinstitutionalization are against carceral logics, but through frameworks of inclusion and incorporation, they became invitations (or even mandates) for State interventions into the lives of disabled people.

Today there are certainly currents within antipsychiatry and mad movements that call for the abolition of psychiatry as a whole, but they are small and still seen as a "lunatic fringe" (as the AAAIMH was described years ago).[168] Some antipsychiatry activists advise looking to the prison abolition movement for models of how to proceed, especially the attrition model.[169] In the name of showing analogies, however, just like with Szasz's writing, any intersectional analysis (I mean intersectional as coming out of women of color feminism, grounded in a discussion of the intersecting oppression of race, class, nationality, and sexuality/gender) is being quashed and averted.

In addition, abolition is not about specific locales or even practices but about ridding ourselves of logics. It is about building, not alternatives to oppression (psychiatry, institutionalization, incarceration), but different ways of being in the world. Therefore the following chapter highlights how intersectional analysis and maroonage positionality (fugitive knowledge) expand understanding on abolition of carcerality. In addition, as I suggest throughout this book, deinstitutionalization was about closure of carceral enclosures, the movement of people who were in them into community settings, and a social movement. The next chapter is about movement and its meaning in the context of abolition more broadly; the movement toward the unknown; and the rejection of ways of knowing that are rooted in prescription, universality, and certainty. It is also about how being a "radical fringe" could be construed as a strength of abolitionary approaches to freedom and liberation.

3

Abolition as Knowledge and Ways of Unknowing

W hat can be learned from doing abolition about the nature of resistance to carceral enclosures and carceral logics? Abolition is a political framework, an analysis, and an agenda for action. But I suggest, following other abolitionists, that abolition is also a specific epistemology and an ethical position. Prison/penal abolition, deinstitutionalization, antipsychiatry, and other disability movements that go beyond rights frameworks strive to envision and create a noncarceral and nonsegregationist society and showcase "fugitive" knowledges.[1] By "carceral enclosures," I am referring not only to physical spaces of containment but to particular logics and discourses that (penal/prison/carceral) abolition opposes.[2]

There are various critiques laid out against prison abolition and strands of deinstitutionalization and disability activism that manifest in the push to close psychiatric hospitals and residential institutions for people with disabilities. They can be summarized in several main prongs: that this form of activism is abstract and does not focus on prescriptive or policy recommendations; that it only critiques but does not suggest specific solutions; that it is based on a utopian vision of the world and of human nature; and that it is unrealistic to espouse this worldview in the world we currently occupy. I hope to demonstrate how all these critiques of abolitionary movements, who work toward a noncarceral society, can be conceptualized as strengths and provide a unique strategy, epistemology, and ethics of resistance to incarceration in the form of abolition.

For example, in the wake of renewed attention to the nexus of police brutality and racism in the United States in the summer of 2016, grassroots organizing and analysis under the banner of Black Lives Matter (BLM) provided an assessment of how antiblack racism operates. One prevailing critique of the BLM movement/s can be found in a recent online op-ed titled "How to Go from #BlackLivesMatter to #BlackPolicyMatters."[3] The subheading reads, "Instead of demanding a series of changes, we should focus on one achievable reform that could significantly reduce police violence and lead the way for other policy changes." Under the framework espoused by such critics, "reform," "achievable," "reduction," and "policy" are the desired goals and are viewed as the only means of making "real" social change (as the subheading of the article suggests). I am offering this op-ed as one out of endless examples of intentionally devaluing the gains and worth of insurgent decentralized activism and the kind of ethical stance articulated in abolitionary demands and analysis.

This chapter comprises two parts. The first discusses abolition as a unique epistemology with specific focus on how intersectionality and maroonage complicate and complement abolitionary knowledges and the concept of abolition itself. The focus on erudite and subjugated knowledges, which began in the previous chapter, will be complemented with an affective understanding of epistemology, emerging from feminist and queer theory, particularly queer/feminist of color scholarship and other abolitionist knowledges, which will comprise the first portion of this chapter. The second part is devoted to understanding abolition as rejection of specific ways of knowing—of "knowing alls" (in the form of experts, prescriptive solutions), of certainty, of rationality and finality. Finally, I will suggest that painting abolition as utopian and unrealistic is actually a strength of this unique form of resistance. My hope is that this theoretical mediation foregrounds a way toward a noncarceral future.

Maroon Knowledge for Abolition

If abolition is an ethic and (dis)epistemology, as I am suggesting, where does abolition knowledge come from? Although there might be different pathways to becoming an abolitionist, I want to underscore here the kinds of intersectional fugitive/maroon abolitionist knowledges that originate and take into account those who are most affected by State violence and capture, those for whom abolition for the future is already rooted in survival of the now. As Robert Fanuzzi describes in his brief etymology of the term, "'abolition' is a word we use when we want to activate scholarship with a sense of urgency, relevance, or potential for the future"—the key word here being *urgency*.[4]

Even though abolition alludes to slavery, not all forms of abolition center antiblack racism or racial capitalism. Fanuzzi contends that under its nineteenth-century conceptualization, abolition was about the liberation of humanism, humanitarianism, and *white* sensibility that degenerated due to the immorality of slavery. In that respect, "the nineteenth-century 'colonization movement' . . . was an abolition movement in the eighteenth-century sense of the word, to the extent that it identified both slavery and enslaved Africans as obstacles to the moral and national development of whites in the United States."[5] It was not until a decade, or more, later that abolition (of slavery) would take up the broad coalitional liberation movement and concept that it connotes today.

Through a discussion of the congruence and continuity of slavery and penal abolition, Vivienne Saleh-Hanna shows how abolition that is rooted in color neutrality or white supremacy, as these are interchangeable for her, is a failure for liberation.[6] To show this, Saleh-Hanna discusses the notorious case of Margaret Garner, an enslaved African American woman who killed her daughter because she did not want her to be returned to a life of captivity. Through this historical case (later fictionalized in Toni Morrison's *Beloved*[7]), Saleh-Hanna shows that connections between prison abolition and abolition of slavery are not just semantic.

White slavery abolitionists advocated for Margaret to be tried for murder, as this would establish her and her deceased daughter as human beings and not property, while white pro-slavery advocates wanted her to be tried for theft or simply returned to her owner for punishment (which is what eventually happened). No side even remotely suggested freeing Margaret from bondage. Therefore, Saleh-Hanna suggests, "though seemingly diametrically opposed, each White side of this bloody tale stands firmly rooted in anti-Blackness driven and legitimated by their own images of White superiority. On one side of White colonialism's coin stand slaveholders and their plantations built on stolen lands hanging on, by any means necessary, to a White supremacist slave economy of anti-Black exploitation. On the other side of capitalism's racist coin stand White (self-proclaimed) anti-slavery abolitionists and their criminal justice system built upon a stolen sense of justice, hijacked and replaced by imperialist and racialized constructions of crime and criminality."[8] As Saleh-Hanna shows, abolition of slavery in this and other instances did not lead to abolition of penalty, nor to liberation more broadly.[9]

While white abolitionists were fighting against slavery out of moral, religious, and ideological convictions, "maroon abolitionists" were fighting for their communities' liberation and survival. Julia Chinyere Oparah's insightful work on present-day "maroon abolitionists" continues in the praxis of the black radical tradition and brings to light the unique prison abolition perspectives of gender oppressed and activists of color who are rooted in African diasporic traditions of resistance and spirituality.[10] Maroon also implies the resistance of nonblack populations such as indigenous and exiled whites. Through this fugitive knowledge, these activists therefore rejected the call for gradual emancipation and called instead for an immediate end to slavery, not just on moral or ethical grounds but based on their desire to stay alive, as do present-day imprisoned intellectuals[11] and maroon abolitionists.

Avery Gordon further alludes to this sense of urgency of abolition demands that are rooted in maroonage and suggests that the core of abolitionism is its refusal to wait.[12] According to Gordon, and following Toni Cade Bambara, abolition efforts must take place while people are still enslaved. She states, "Abolition time is a type of revolutionary time. But rather than stop the world, as if in an absolute break between now and then, it is a daily part of it."[13] Emancipation is ongoing work and cannot wait until the time is ripe for it. Slaves, captives, or prisoners, and those fighting for their freedom, cannot wait for a new world order to be free of incarceration or bondage. They cannot wait until the right conditions emerge and the desired future begins.

This characterization of abolition could also be seen in the case of deinstitutionalization activists who insisted on a noncarceral and inclusive world and demanded to close all institutions for those with intellectual disabilities and all psychiatric hospitals much before alternatives to institutionalization were in place, as I have shown in the previous chapter. The goal was to close down institutions at present and refute the segregationist discourse while the alternatives were not ready-made and indeed could not have been, as such a framework did not exist at that time.[14]

The feminist antiviolence movement offers another interesting case study. Emily Thuma presents a fascinating account of the Coalition to Stop Institutional Violence, an alliance of prisoners, mental patients, and feminist organizations and collectives in the Boston area in the 1970s that opposed the creation and expansion of medicalization and securitization in prisons and psych hospitals in the 1970s.[15] Much like modern-day feminist abolitionists, they saw the State as a source of violence, not a protector or guarantor of rights, and thus offered a different kind of feminist analysis and epistemology about violence against women. They named what they thought were the sources and conditions of violence in their lives—gendered, sexualized, and racialized oppression and incarceration and medicalization. Thus they viewed the prison and the psych hospital as irredeemable and intimately connected sites of violence and normalization.

But by the end of the 1970s, the most vocal sections of the feminist antiviolence movement would demand increased policing, laws protecting women from intimate partners, and other legal and fiscal demands that would lead to the racist expansion of the carceral state. It created a different vocabulary and epistemology of crime and violence in which women were "victims" and sought remedy from the state from harm perpetrated by individual "criminals."[16]

Beth Richie shows how antiviolence feminists' demands of the state resulted in specific policy changes: domestic violence shelters opened, professional counseling began to be offered to women experiencing intimate violence, and legislation and legal changes followed suit, including the enactment of the Violence against Women Act of 1994. But these policy shifts did not lead to the liberation of all women; instead, they became an apparatus of the State and assisted in the buildup of the prison nation.[17] Specifically, it was a white liberal version of feminism seeking the liberation of women from patriarchal violence under the umbrella of the "universal woman," which is by default white, cisgender, heteronormative, and middle class. As Richie contends, "when the national discussion became organized around 'it could happen to anyone,' 'it' was reduced to direct physical assault from household members and stranger rape, and 'anyone' came to mean the women with the most visibility, the most power, and the most public sympathy, the citizens whose experience of violence is taken most seriously."[18] In essence, the focus became white ideals of womanhood and the need to protect them from either intimate assailants or strange men of color (stranger danger[19]). As Priya Kandaswamy asks in relation to the antidomestic violence movement, "what kind of identities are we forced to adopt and police when we engage in state centered politics? . . . And finally, what passes as politics in an era when incarceration and/or normalization are increasingly represented as the only solutions to social problems?"[20]

A corollary trajectory can be described in regard to disability rights movements, most of which do not center race analysis (especially antiblack racism), and that is one of the shortcomings of their approach to abolition. The consequences of not engaging in abolition from an intersectional lens rooted in maroonage is that it becomes irrelevant to the majority of those it seeks to liberate,[21] both demographically (as it is not based on the lived experience of people of color) but especially epistemologically and methodologically, by not underscoring race as a lens rooted in black radical tradition that critiques the state as violent and not the arena to seek remediation to injustice. The result in deinstitutionalization was decarceration, but often in the form of transcarceration (moving people from large institutions to smaller group homes, for example).

Abolition as Counterhegemonic Knowledges

As subjugated knowledge, one can view abolition as a specific epistemology, one that is counterhegemonic, that is, opposing the status quo and taken-for-granted assumptions. The hegemonic discourse is about the need to segregate others in the name of safety (from themselves or the people who might encounter them), in the name of punishment, and as a form of justice and rehabilitation. Abolition counters these discursive frames with the kind of vision it encourages—of a world in which carceral and segregated locales are viewed as senseless and commonsenseless. Abolition is not merely about closure of prisons or institutions; it is a revolutionary framework that transforms the way we analyze and understand forces that shape our histories and everyday lives.[22] Abolitionist knowledge reconceptualizes notions like "crime" or "innocence" (what gets to be defined as crime, and who gets defined as criminal); disability or madness (as an identity and politics, not only a medical diagnosis) and rehabilitation (which is seen as a form of assimilation and normalization, not just as benign "treatment"); ideas of punishment (transformative justice vs. revenge or retribution); notions of freedom and equality (whether we can feel free and safe without locking others away); and, on the other hand, concepts of danger and protection (Whom do we protect by segregating people behind bars in psychiatric hospitals and prisons? Is it for "their own good"?).

The prison–industrial complex is more than the sum of all the jails, prisons, and internment camps. It is "a set of symbiotic relationships among correctional communities, transnational corporations, media conglomerates, guards' unions, and legislative and court agendas," as Angela Y. Davis suggests.[23] The prison has direct implications for all, in terms of morality, ethics, surveillance, commodification, criminalization, inequality, and oppression based on race and class.[24] For those engaging in an abolitionist critique of incarceration, the most powerful relevance of the prison abolitionist stance is to analyze the prison as a core structure that shapes social relations in society, not just for those affected directly but for everyone.

Although I can give numerous examples of the ways carceral abolition knowledge is counterhegemonic and provides building blocks for alternative ways of thinking about a variety of issues, I will give here three brief examples: knowledge on crime and who/what gets defines as criminal; abolitionist critiques of corrections; and abolitionist approaches to the question of "the dangerous few," otherwise known as "what should be done with mass murderers" in a noncarceral society?

Abolitionists' Perspective on Crime

The social construction of crime is dependent on power relations (in relation to race, sexuality, nationality, class, ability, gender) and state definitions of who gets to define what is a crime and who gets to be defined as a criminal. Crime, like insanity/disability, is one of many definitions that can be attached to a behavior or event but must be legitimated by a professional—you are not officially disabled or a criminal until a doctor, judge, court, psychiatrist, or the paper says you are, despite your own description or contestation. Therefore some prison abolitionists do not refer to illegal or other acts as crimes, unquestionably, but discuss "criminalizable events" instead.[25] In a similar vein to labeling theory, prison abolitionist Ruth Morris contends that "the criminal justice process is not about justice, or truth . . . it is the process of making a person feel and become a criminal."[26]

The line between the "righteous and free" and "the dangerous" is seen as socially and politically drawn and is perceived as a continuum rather than a binary.[27] These boundaries serve a purpose, so that those who are not currently imprisoned can feel like we live in a free society and to justify the rationale for caging others for some sense of freedom. As those who critique racist and imperial state violence note, life outside of prison often resembles a prison if one lives in "the projects,"[28] when one is a freedom fighter or fugitive,[29] or even sites of education with their metal detectors and barred windows.[30] As Zayd Shakur famously remarks as a Black Panther member in the 1970s— America is the prison.[31] Incarceration under this framework is about racial gendered class warfare, not individual acts.

In a similar vein, abolitionists untie the Gordian knot between lawbreaking and criminality. Slavery, for example, was not considered a crime and was in fact a legal apparatus. Eurocentric laws and codes were forced on native peoples in Turtle Island since the colonial encounter. These laws made native customs and culture illegal.[32] Sodomy laws and regulations against gender nonconformity (such as restroom use or dress) are still currently on the books in various locales in the United States. Laws are not given from above but are human-made. Therefore the assertion that people who "broke the law" are the ones in prison or need to be, does not give premise to how laws are enacted, enforced, and utilized as tools of oppression and state control.

Other current facts that exemplify this false connection between lawbreaking and incarceration are that most defendants in the United States take a plea bargain and never go to trial, largely because they cannot afford a lawyer. And many current occupants of jails are there not because of a conviction but because they could not afford bail and are awaiting trial (several community bail funds have sprung up in recent years as abolitionary initiatives for this very reason). Furthermore, the overrepresentation of people of color in prison is not due to increased criminality but to being targeted more rigorously by law enforcement, judges, laws, and economic policies. Most instructive are recent cases of driving/bbqing/being pregnant/parenting "while black," targeting transgender and gender nonconforming people for living or being in public,[33] and racial profiling more generally.[34]

Under current criminal "justice" logics as produced in the popular imagination (from Law and Order the longest-running TV show to law and order the actual policy), the following individual drama is constructed: first, individuals are sorted into criminals and survivors/victims. Survivors/victims are eternally wounded and vulnerable, and perpetrators are dangerous and punishable. To rectify the harm, the "victim" has to become a plaintiff, an individualized subject that the state deems as deserving of their day in court. Only two parties are involved, and they are oppositional and do not know each other. They are both passive, while their lawyers, prosecutors, and other experts and professionals are active. Then comes a trial, and then justice is served. There is no discussion of the ways the community might be harmed or a part of creating the harm and therefore a part of the process; there is no mention of accountability or healing or even agency.

Prison abolitionists, however, demonstrate that social and media-based fear of street crime, particularly of men of color, diverts attention from other harms—within the family, from acquaintances and corporations, and from crimes induced by the State, including the harm of incarceration itself.[35] As Heiner and Tyson succinctly put it, "criminal justice responses treat non-state violence as *individual pathology* that calls for the incapacitative disappearance or rehabilitative reformation of criminalized subjects, rather than as a *social practice* (connected to state violence), the abolition of which will require the invention and proliferation of alternative social institutions and practices . . . or in the case of Native peoples, the decolonial resurgence of traditional Indigenous ones."[36]

Abolitionists insist that denying the a priori existence of crime should not entail the denial of the painful consequences of a harmful event or behavior. This is where community accountability processes come in, with their own understanding of harm and how to prevent and address it as a collective process.[37] As Ana Clarissa Rojas Durazo states, the goal of community accountability as an abolitionist practice is to transform the roots of violence.[38] There are also models of transformative justice that look not only at restoration but at transformation of communities and social structures as a measure of prevention of future harm (e.g., eliminating poverty or ensuring gender affirming health care) and as addressing current harms in ways that do not contribute to the expansion of oppression as status quo (i.e., through policing, imprisonment, and so on).[39]

Disability studies and this abolitionist perspective share a critique of essentializing and instead focus on the cultural and social creation of harm, crime, disability, and impairment. The constructed nature of crime is related to the social constructionist approach in relation to disability and mental distress, which also sees them as culturally and socially produced, but having very real consequences for their bearers, including pain. Just like deconstructing notions of crime as harm does not negate the harm or its consequences, recent disability studies literature, especially from feminists, has insisted on bringing back the lived body/mind into this discourse, to raise discussions around issues of pain, for example, which cannot necessarily be mitigated by social interventions. Feminist disability studies scholars' focus on embodiment challenges the medical model of disability, which conceives of disability as a lack and deficiency inherent in nonnormative bodies. It also challenges the social model of disability, which encourages us to focus solely on processes of disablement or debilitation (disability as harm produced by state violence) as a critical framework that will end the oppression of disabled people.[40] In other words, pain or harm, or trauma from harm as disability, makes it clear that individualizing, medicalizing, or exiling the symptom does not get to the social issues at hand, and vice versa.

Critique of Corrections

Prison abolitionists emphasize that the primary functions of prisons are punishment, control, and incapacitation, not rehabilitation.[41] Even if rehabilitation is used, rhetorically or in praxis, it is about fixing individual people through oppressive normative frames, a trend that began with the colonial encounter. Both disability studies and those critiquing imprisonment or carcerality share a critique of rehabilitation, of disciplining bodies,[42] of normalization through civilization and the colonial roots of such practices. In sum, they are both epistemologies that are against "corrections," whether of what had come to be aptly called the "corrections industry," via criminal (in)justice systems, or physical/psychiatric/behavioral rehabilitation and modifications pushed on those considered abnormal (such as neurodiversity critiques of applied behavioral therapy, for example[43]).

The impulse to rehabilitate, felt most potently in the mid-twentieth century in the criminal justice system was entrenched in colonial impetuses. In North America, this discourse continued the attempt to assimilate indigenous communities in order to "civilize" them, first through training schools and continuing in prisons.[44] As Captain Pratt put it at the time, the goal was "to kill the Indian but save the man." That's what prisons and institutions for people with disabilities were created for in the first place. Those aspects of humanity that fell outside of the narrow conception of normalcy (i.e., white colonial heteropatriarchy) were to be eliminated, but not by physical eugenic or genocidal means, as in the past. It was now believed that this could be done on an individual basis through training and rehabilitation, as part of the civilization process.

When discussing the cultural genocide of Native American culture through incarceration, the enforcement of rehabilitation as a Western white tool of subjection becomes clearer, and the prison can be seen as a site of reeducation and normalization. In Foucauldian terms, I would say that normalization works through both techniques of power—disciplining and making docile bodies (anatomo-politics)—and regulation of whole populations (biopolitics). The norm and the normal distribution could be applied to both the body you want to discipline and the ones you wish to regulate. These techniques seek to categorize, define, and control any social anomalies. They work through the prism of what I called racial criminal pathologization, as both pathology and criminalization could be utilized as forms of corrections on a disciplinary level (via incarceration/criminalization or medicalization/incarceration) and/or biopolitical levels (racialization, debilitation, etc.).

In *Inventing the Savage*, Luana Ross discusses rehabilitation as a form of control and cultural erasure for Native American women, not a benign therapeutic practice. For women, rehabilitation in prison is designed for conformity with Eurocentric ideologies that espouse, among other things, sexist notions of how a "proper woman" should act. Training and education in prisons that follow these rehabilitation ideals are usually provided in such areas as clerical work, cosmetology, and food service. In addition to reproducing strict gender roles, these trainings "prepare" those incarcerated for low-status and low-paying jobs once they are released.[45] Prisons are also sites of gender construction, as there are only men's and women's facilities and only gender presentations that conform to the binary rules of the facility are allowed.

This logic of assimilation and normalization operates through rehabilitation when dealing with disability as well. Institutionalization, which, in its early days, was meant as a way to treat people with a variety of conditions—a benevolent goal—later turned to warehousing people without even a facade of training or treatment. As Chapman, Carey, and I discussed in *Disability Incarcerated*, New York's Utica State Lunatic Asylum began construction in 1837, and the first American large institution for the "feebleminded" was established in Albany, New York, in 1851. These developments occurred out of French-inspired American understandings that intellectually disabled people, as a population, could learn. Although there were widely divergent effects on the groups incarcerated in these various settings, including the emergence of prisons, there was a loosely shared political rationality, which stated that under the right conditions, degenerate, disabled, criminalistic, or uncivilized peoples can be corrected and brought up to acceptable social standards. As Lennard Davis suggests, everybody was, for the first time, now theoretically capable of achieving, and in fact was expected to achieve, normalcy.[46] EveryBody was now measured against it, and the effects of this new discourse of normalcy, as opposed to the earlier one of the "ideal," still have detrimental effects for all, but especially for those who are scapegoated as unable to achieve this illusive normalcy.[47]

Similarly, Elizabeth Whalley and Colleen Hackett recently stated that "correctional institutions adopt a 'culture of treatment' . . . thereby assuming that impoverished and racially marginalized women need to be protected and fixed in the first place," and for "crimes" and traumas made by the state itself.[48] The need to treat and normalize is also rooted in racially based heteropatriarchy and specific gendered norms, in this case, women needing to be protected. As abolitionists show, racialized policing around gender and sexual norms was a founding principle in the making of the United States, through colonialism onward.[49]

To add to such critiques, as those incarcerated or formerly incarcerated contend, rehabilitation was never perceived to be a major force in the everyday life of the American prisoner, as educational and other programs were few and far between. Their purpose was always contested by those incarcerated themselves, who are critical of the "rehabilitation" discourse espoused by prison administration.[50] Yves Bourque offers as an illustrative example the fact that a sign of rehabilitation by the parole board is that the incarcerated person has accepted her oppression and the system as a whole, from her sentencing and treatment while imprisoned to the need for her incarceration in the first place.[51] Such understandings of "rehabilitation" are nothing more than attempts to assimilate those incarcerated.

In addition, both disability studies/culture and those critiquing imprisonment or carcerality also share a critique of individualizing social issues and instead demand a focus on systemic analysis and solutions instead of correcting or reforming individuals. In disability studies, the push is to shift the perspective from fixing people to approximate normalcy (through surgery, speech therapy, physical therapy, etc.) to focusing on changing environments (social, cultural, economic, physical) to make them more functional and accessible for everyone. For example, curb cuts and elevators are access features that anyone can use (including parents with strollers, delivery people), but making a paralyzed person walk with expensive devices will not grant others the same access.[52] The focus, then, moves from rehabilitation and corrections under ablenationalist and assimilationist norms to social change on a collective level.

In disability studies and disability culture there are vast critiques of notions of cure and rehabilitation of disabled people. Some see it as a way to normalize people to fit particular societal norms regarding bodily function, behavior, and appearance, which are not necessarily shared by those whom medical professionals try to "rehabilitate." According to philosopher Henri-Jacques Stiker, rehabilitation is the cultural desire for identification, for making things identical: "This act will cause the disabled to disappear and with them all that is lacking, in order to assimilate them, drown them, dissolve them, in the greater and single social whole."[53] In Stiker's critical formulation of rehabilitation, integration of disability always necessitates assimilation, as the integration is to a society under its own terms.

Similarly, in penal corrections, the focus is much the same. In their seminal call for prison abolition, the American Friends Service Committee stated in 1971 that if something needs rehabilitating, it is the system of punishment, and not the person. "It says 'if we can fix the person, we can fix the problem.' This is a fundamental fallacy; Rehabilitation is reliant upon indeterminacy; the individual is released when he or she is 'cured' of criminality." It is imperative to ask, in the context of the prison–industrial complex as well as in the disability context, what rehabilitation means when it is decontextualized from discussions of inequality, inequity, and social justice, or from deconstructing the discourse and materiality of racial criminal pathologization as a pillar of the colonial nation-state. Isn't "rehabilitation" or "treatment" (in regard to addiction, psych, parole, etc.) another apparatus of the carceral state to make people in its own image (white, proletariat, hetero, masculine, able-bodied, sane/rational, and so on)?

The "Dangerous Few"

By far the most common question asked of abolitionists is, but what should be done with those deemed as having the most challenging or dangerous behaviors? In prison abolition circles, this discussion is known as "what to do with the dangerous few" (i.e., "serial killers," "rapists," etc.), and in the realm of developmental and psychiatric disabilities, it is the question of "what to do with the most significantly/profoundly disabled."[54] In both cases, the general assumption is that these are the populations that will not be able to "make it on the outside" and therefore will always require some sort of segregation and restraint, either for their own or the public's good.

As other abolitionists suggest, the current focus in criminal justice reform on "non non nons" (nonviolent, nonserious, and nonsexual offenses) eschews the approach at the heart of abolition work. Such critics suggest that this

narrow focus augments rather than shrinks the carceral state and reproduces the borders of innocence and guilt as well as who is worthy of liberation.[55] It also eschews the question of who is not deemed a danger, who is not
criminalized, who or what is considered not violent or serious. In short, this
focus on the "non non nons" masks the violence of the state and lets state
apparatuses define what violence means. Incarceration and institutionalization are not considered violence against a person or group of people, such as
boarding schools for indigenous people, while spitting on an attendant or
guard is considered an act of violence. As Saleh-Hanna sharply put it, "only
by segregating our definition of serial killing from historic and contemporary acts of genocide, enslavement, and colonial domination can criminologists conclude that the dangerous are 'few' and that they have become
a-typical actors of violence."[56]

A similar commitment comes out of strands of queer theory, and especially crip theory.[57] Robert McRuer has described crip theory as a combination of disability/crip and queer studies, reclaiming the positions of crip
and queer as critical, as opposed to derogatory, positions and subjectivities.
Crip theory, therefore, draws "attention to critically queer, severely disabled
possibilities in order to bring to the fore the crip actors who ... will exacerbate in more productive ways the crisis of authority that currently besets
heterosexual/able-bodied norms."[58] By "severely disabled," McRuer is referring not merely to the level of impairment a person is presumed to have but
to a queer position, a position that questions, a mark of defiance. By reclaiming severe as "fierce" or defiant, McRuer reverses able-bodied standards that
view people with severe disabilities as those who will never be integrated
(reflecting the adage "everyone should be included, except for ..."). From
their marginal state, "severe disabilities" and queer subjects are positioned to
reenter the margins and point to the inadequacies of straight and nondisabled
assumptions.

Translated to praxis, some prison abolitionists and activists in the fields of
developmental disabilities and antipsychiatry indeed begin birthing alternative social arrangements from the positionality of "severe" cases. It is partially
this abolitionist position that prompted those advocating for community
inclusion to begin with the most "severe" cases when calling for and implementing the move out of institutions. A lesson learned from successful deinstitutionalization closures is, therefore, that those labeled as having the
most significant needs should move to community placements early on in

the process. If left to the end, they would most likely be placed in segregated settings because of a lack of skills, experience, ability, or desire in the community to support them. For example, those deemed the most violent and dangerous youth became commissioner Jerome Miller's symbol as he closed juvenile facilities in Massachusetts in the 1970s and were the first to be decarcerated.[59] In the prison arena, the work of Fay Honey Knopp is especially relevant here. After working to draft the abolitionist manual *Instead of Prisons*, Knopp sought to engage with the "toughest" cases, and she devoted the rest of her life to working with so-called sex offenders and sexual abusers. The thought behind this commitment was that if she can demonstrate the ineffectiveness of prisons for this segment of the imprisoned population, there will be no doubt that prisons should not be the response to lesser criminalizable acts like property or drug offenses.

I want to suggest that through the lens of abolition, we can use the question of the "challenging/severe/dangerous few" to start developing the "very different social landscape," as Angela Davis called it, that is a noncarceral world—in other words, to use feminist, black freedom dreams[60] or queer of color critique to chart a way for the liberation of us all.[61] This can be observed in bell hooks's formulation of the need to shift the margin to the center, as she urges us to do about feminist work more broadly. As the motto of the BLM movement urges, for all lives to matter, black lives must matter; for all black lives to matter, black trans lives and black women's lives must matter, and so on. This is a deeply feminist praxis. To do the work of liberation means to leave no one behind. Here we can also learn from abolitionist campaigns that might center one person but ultimately call for freedom for all, such as the self-defense campaigns that feminists engaged in the 1970s, as Thuma demonstrates.[62] It also entails beginning with those most marginalized. This shifting of the margins ("the few") to the center would lead to shifting the core for everyBody, especially all those marginalized. Beginning from the "few" (the severe, the so-called violent, etc.) as opposed to beginning with the "nons" would, and did, enable advocacy and praxis to move into the kind of building from anew that are the work of abolition as dis-epistemology.

Abolition Dis-epistemology

My second claim in this chapter is that abolition is a radical epistemology of knowing and unknowing. Therefore the second meaning in which abolition operates as an epistemology is as giving way to other *ways* of knowing. I term this *dis-epistemology*, letting go of attachment to certain ways of knowing. This means not only letting go of hegemonic knowledge (of crime, of corrections and the dangerous few, for example) but letting go of the idea that anyone can have a definitive pathway for how to get rid of carceral logics. It is this attachment to the idea of knowing and *needing to know* (clairvoyance) that is part of knowledge and affective economies that maintain carceral logics. I suggest that abolition is dis-epistemology in three ways: it is about letting go of attachments to forms of knowledge that rely on certainty (the definitive consequences of doing or not doing); prescription and professional expertise (tell us what should be done); and specific demands for futurity (clairvoyance, or what will happen).

A key characteristic of abolition dis-epistemology is rejecting absolutism, foreclosing certainty (what must be done, what will lead to the best results for a noncarceral future). In his 1974 *The Politics of Abolition,* Thomas Mathiesen conceptualizes abolition as an alternative in the making: "The alternative lies in the unfinished, in the sketch, in what is not yet fully existing."[63] Abolition, therefore, by definition, cannot wait for a future constellation when appropriate alternatives are already in place. This is inherently impossible because alternatives cannot come from living in the existing order but will come from a process of change as a result of a transition from it.

The characterization of abolition as rejection of certainty is also connected to feminist philosopher Ami Harbin's conceptualization of *disorientation,* which she defines as "temporarily extended, major life experiences that make it difficult for individuals to know what to do."[64] In other words, it involves experiencing serious (prolonged and major) disruption so that one does not know what to do. The hope generated by Harbin's analysis is that these experiences of disorientation, although often unpleasant and jarring, can also be productive.

Richie eloquently details this phenomenon in relation to the incorporation of the feminist antiviolence movement in the United States in her aptly named chapter "How We Won the Mainstream but Lost the Movement."[65] The title of the chapter is as telling as its analysis. Going mainstream is counter abolitionary, and that is one of the points that Richie artfully makes. But I want to pause at the use of the term *movement* here. One interpretation is the loss of the social movement, the grassroots coalition that sought to stop violence against women. But another interpretation seems to me to be relevant here. It is not just the coalition that was lost but movement itself, the act of moving. Abolition is always in flux, an ongoing struggle, and therefore, when we stop moving, the social movement and the movement toward abolition die. The goal of abolition is therefore not finality but process itself, trial and error, and understanding disorientation as generative.

Prescriptive Solutions and Reform

Abolition efforts are often described as not being prescriptive and not offering specific solutions and therefore as being not useful. Some opponents (be it progressives who believe in reform or those wanting to maintain the status quo) posit this stance as "if you can't offer a specific solution, then you are part of the problem." But as an epistemology and ethical stance, abolition politics invites us to abandon our attachment to knowing and especially to knowing all.

Following Mathiesen, abolition is triggered by making people aware of the necessary dilemma they are faced with—continuing with the existing order with some changes (i.e., reform) or transitioning to something unknown. The question becomes not "what is the best alternative" in its final formulation, but how this new order shall begin from the old. In this sense a question that emerges from the "unfinished" as alternative, is how to maintain it as such, a sketch, not a final result but a process.[66] It is precisely for this reason that scholarly work such as Mathiesen's has often been criticized for lacking any concrete suggestions for penology or even activism, and therefore perceived as abstract and detached from specific activist and policy stances. The *common* sense (commonsense gun policy, common sense policy, common sense policing) obstructs the *undercommons* as Moten and Harney refer to it.[67] Reclaiming abolition as dis-epistemology and its lack of certainty would solidify abolition as fashioning new ways of envisioning the world and opening up opportunities that are not closed off by ready-made prescriptions.

Abolition critiques the carceral system and carceral logics, but also critiques any efforts to *reform* carceral sites, because some of the factors leading to the growth of the carceral state were the direct result of attempts to reform the system. In practice, reform and abolition are on a continuum, as discussed in relation to nonreformist reforms in the introductory chapter. But, critics say, if everything offered can be conceived as or become reformist, what solutions does the abolitionist offer? I suggest that this question is rooted in the kind of ready-made prescriptive thinking that is contrary to abolition in the spirit of dis-epistemology. This demand to only enter the debate if one can "offer solutions" only makes sense from privileged positionality and not in intersectional subjugated knowledge, or maroonage, as those already oppressed do not feel secure in the first place.[68]

In short, as Sara Ahmed explains, this is the work of the feminist killjoy: "Feminists, by declaring themselves feminists, are already read as destroying something that is thought of by others not only as being good but as the cause of happiness."[69] Feminists, and other affect aliens, as Ahmed refers to them, including abolitionists, "hence [bring] others down, not only by talking about unhappy topics such as sexism but by exposing how happiness is sustained, by erasing the signs of not getting along."[70] If we take this one step further to intersectional struggles, "The angry black woman can be described as a killjoy; she may even kill feminist joy, for example, by pointing out forms of racism within feminist politics."[71]

The call of "don't talk about it unless you have a solution" assumes there is a monolithic answer to the question of "what is to be done." As Angela Y. Davis contends, we can't think about substitutes to prisons or incarceration, but instead should conceptualize a world without the footprint of incarceration.[72] That is exactly the problem with carceral enclosures—such as detention centers, psych hospitals, prisons—that they become catchall solutions to diverse social issues. One of the difficulties of conceptualizing a world without prisons is that many think about a monolithic system that will replace the punitive one we have now. But harms and their effects will be handled in a myriad of ways instead.

Abolitionists work on a case by case basis in their campaigns, research, and calls for action. They are often in a position of not knowing what to do but they try to break new ground nonetheless, while building collectively and relying on movement memory to learn from historical examples in a similar context. For example, successful campaigns to stop the building of a new jail can be discussed among abolitionists nationally but there is no assumption that such campaigns could be replicated in a different locale or context. The knowledge of abolition is therefore accumulative on a movement level. And the movement as unfinished is key. This conceptualization of abolition puts it with other radical and revolutionary traditions, especially those that anchor prefigurative politics. Prefiguration refers to the need to ground the goals of the movements with its means and create (prefigure) the society that is desired by so doing.[73] In other words, in order to create the different social landscape, there is a need to ensure that the ways of getting there are done using the same principles as the desired goals. Or put differently, the journey is as important as the destination—noncarceral society will not be achieved through punitive and segregationist mind-sets or praxis. Abolition dis-epistemology as movement, as the unfinished is about breaking new ground in "the shell of the old," as the anarchist saying goes.

I am not suggesting therefore that abolitionists know nothing, about how to organize, how to respond to harm without reliance on state harm or how to build alternatives. In fact, dis-epistemology is about particular ways of knowing while letting go of certain attachments to other (perhaps more commonsense) ways. It is not about not knowing but about having the strength and humility to collectively experiment while creating the world anew.

Abolition, Optimism, and Futurity

In addition to letting go of attachments to certainty (knowing what to do in its final formulation), I suggest that another characteristic of abolition dis-epistemology is letting go of attachment to clairvoyance, or the ability to see the future. Here I want to focus specifically on attachment to optimism in relation to futurity. To counter the vast critiques and sheer repression that come from holding abolitionist views, there is a temptation to be overly optimistic about what a noncarceral future might bring. (And just for full disclosure, I use this trope myself as well.) To critique the present, the claim that is often made is that whatever a noncarceral future holds, it will surely be better than what we have now. So even if we close down all prisons, residential institutions for people with disabilities, and other segregationist locales, the argument goes, that act by itself alone would be better than the present system of state capture. Even just this act will be progress, improvement, and movement.

The critique over such affective registers should be familiar to those attuned to recent debates on futurity in queer theory and disability studies.[74] Specifically, it is related to the stream of queer of color critiques of the "It gets better" campaign.[75] The campaign played on the same affective register of "the future is better no matter what" that can be found in some abolitionist discourses. The 2011 campaign came as a response to the high number of suicides of LGBTQ and gender-variant teens. Don't give up now, "it" will get better, it signifying here a person's life chances, progress, proximity to assimilation, that is, success, as opposed to *it*, the material conditions of oppression. But "it" only gets better from a certain privileged locale, and reliance on such tropes forecloses other important queer affects, such as failure or unhappiness.[76]

My argument therefore is not to suggest that there is no possible answer to the question posed by Lenin at the turn of the last century and conjured up by Ruth Wilson Gilmore in 2011 in regard to prison abolition—"What is to be done?" Quite the opposite, I want to suggest that there are perhaps infinite answers to this question. But they are made invisible in our current paradigms (of criminal "justice" or corrections, as I highlighted in the first part of the chapter).

In suggesting the perhaps infinite possibilities abolition conjures up, I am using the term *perhaps* quite intentionally, following theorist Sara Ahmed. At the end of her essay on the feminist history of (un)happiness, Ahmed argues that "the word happy originally meant having 'good "hap" or fortune,' to be lucky or fortunate."[77] But in relation to the feminist killjoy, Ahmed suggests that "in refusing to be constrained by happiness, we can open up other ways of being, of being perhaps. The word perhaps shares its hap with happiness. . . . To deviate from the paths of happiness is to refuse to inherit the elimination of the hap."[78]

I therefore posit that living in the "perhaps" is the position of the abolitionist. Not knowing how things end up is not a disadvantage but in fact opens up possibilities of other life worlds that cannot be imagined right now. Refusing narratives of happy endings and living in "perhaps" does not equate hopelessness, though—quite the opposite. As Ahmed suggests in relation to Audre Lorde's writings in *The Cancer Journals,* the positionality expected of Lorde while battling and coming to terms with living with cancer is to stay positive, look at the bright side, not be an angry black woman, not be a feminist killjoy. This disabled/wounded positionality that Lorde occupied during this time allotted her the foresight to refuse demands for certainty and futurity, as well as the ableist trope of "getting over it" and "it gets better." In fact, she refused the whole individualistic discourse, which she found stultifying and baffling. In Lorde's words, "looking on the bright side of things is a euphemism used for obscuring certain realities of life, the open consideration of which might prove threatening to the status quo."[79] What do we lose, then, when we foreclose the future with optimism? How do we conjure up a noncarceral future without repeating the pitfalls of this world?

The Necessity of the Utopian

From the inception of prison abolitionism as a movement, its activists were being dismissed as utopian and unrealistic. In *Cruising Utopia*, queer theorist José Esteban Muñoz suggests that "we must strive, in the face of the here and now totalizing rendering of reality, to think and feel a then and there."[80] For Muñoz, "the here and now is a prison house."[81] The connection to prison abolition is conjured by this affirmation from Muñoz, and not simply because he brings up prison as the ultimate metaphor for stagnation and lack of imagination. Muñoz further discusses Ernst Bloch's distinction between concrete and abstract utopias, explaining that concrete utopias represent collective hopes and are the blocks upon which hope can exist. As Bloch writes, "hope's methodology . . . dwells in the region of the not-yet."[82] The "not-yet," as Bloch refers to it, seems akin to Mathiesen's formulation of the "unfinished" in relation to the work of the abolitionist.

When one is called "utopian," this usually connotes something degrading, a naïveté of sorts, that makes one look foolish or dangerous, depending on the context. In any case, utopia is not often a feature that makes one be taken seriously. However, Muñoz suggests that despite these possible consequences, "a certain affective reanimation needs to transpire if a disabling political pessimism is to be displaced."[83] This suggestion only works, of course, as long as "disabling" connotes something destructive and not affirmative. It might be useful to connect this statement with an earlier one in which Muñoz suggests that the way out of stagnation is that "we must dream and enact new and better pleasures, other ways of being in the world, and ultimately new worlds."[84]

I want to suggest here that one way to reclaim utopia is to reclaim this "disabling political pessimism." Following disability theorists such as James Overboe, David Mitchell, and Sharon Snyder, imagining "other ways of being in the world" is the gist of disability culture.[85] Disability and madness, as a lived reality, in a world that often cannot contain it, allows for reformulations of in/dependence and community. Mitchell and Snyder term this the capacities of incapacity: the potential to produce knowledge/praxis that is only possible from a disabled embodiment or eminence, or as McRuer and Johnson discuss in a different context, cripistemologies.[86]

A noncarceral way of living would be unimaginable without these reconceptualizations and celebrations of "other ways of being in the world." I am not suggesting that these "other ways of being in the world" are currently materialized, but I am suggesting that their effects could provide useful models for social transformation in the spirit of abolition as a utopian stance. As Patricia Berne states in regard to the formation of the paradigm of disability justice (which critiques liberal rights frameworks), "a Disability Justice framework understands that all bodies are unique and essential, that all bodies have strengths and needs that must be met.... We are in a global system that is incompatible with life. There is no way stop a single gear in motion—we must dismantle this machine."[87] The goal is not to be integrated within the existing framework but to work toward the liberation of us all from it.

Activist-scholars and longtime abolitionists Angela Y. Davis and Dylan Rodriguez describe prison abolition as much bigger than a critique of incarceration but rather provide a broader critique of society.[88] Thus prison abolition insists on ridding ourselves not only of imprisonment but also of carceral logics, while at the same times imagining a "new world order" in the absence of the carceral archipelago and its logics. As Davis suggests, "the call for prison abolition urges us to imagine and strive for a very different social landscape."[89]

Abolition is not just an agenda for demolishing but also for building. As Gilmore suggests, "in other words, the goal is to change how we interact with each other and the planet by putting people before profits, welfare before warfare, and life over death."[90] When a system is abolished, there is a danger that other systems that fulfill the same functions would arise to fill in the void left by the abolished system. Famed sociologist W. E. B. Du Bois, in his book *Black Reconstruction*,[91] discusses (slavery) abolition not as a mere negative process, one of tearing down; it is ultimately about creating new institutions and a new society that values them. Du Bois was insistent that to abolish slavery in modern times, new democratic institutions had to be established and maintained. Because that did not occur, slavery found a new home in Jim Crow, convict lease system, segregated education (by race and today by race-ability), and mass incarceration. Thus the abolition of slavery was only successful in the negative aspect, but few new institutions were created to successfully incorporate black people (freed slaves and those not enslaved) into the existing social order. The carceral state today has thrived precisely because of the lack of such resources that Du Bois was arguing for. Angela Davis reminds us, via Du Bois, that incarceration today cannot be abolished until the project of abolition democracy is accomplished.[92] She thus connects Du Bois to current abolitionary struggles within the black radical tradition.[93] Like Moten and Harney state, the goal is the abolition of a society that would have prisons and building a new one from the rubble. Being free of chains is only the beginning.

Abolition could be conceptualized as a radical form of activism in the full sense of the word, meaning going to the root cause of issues, in both content and form. As I argue here, abolition can be further conceptualized as a strategy beyond resistance, as it does not acknowledge the structure as is but envisions and creates a new worldview in which oppressive structures do not exist. It goes beyond protesting the current circumstances to creating new conditions of possibility by collectively contesting the status quo. It does so by means of movement, the unfinished, trial and error, but without recapitulating to affective necessities of state expansion, optimism, prescription, and clairvoyance. Reclaiming utopia, unhappiness, uncertainty, as liberatory dis-epistemologies would conceive abolition as helpful, and hap-full, in fashioning new ways of envisioning and being in the world.

As I have shown, there are vast connections between disability, deinstitutionalization, and prison abolition as epistemologies of abolition (critique of corrections, maroon knowledges) and dis-epistemologies (refuse certainty, embrace the unfinished, prefigure). But the connections between these realms are often taken up quite differently in the public imagination. Because deinstitutionalization is not perceived as an abolitionary movement, and because abolitionary movements for liberation are still very much contested (as utopian, crazy, unrealistic, and dangerous, which are the exact categories they contest), the backlash against them had also been fierce. In the next chapter, I discuss this backlash, especially the claim that deinstitutionalization led to the rise of mass incarceration.

4

Why Prisons Are Not "the New Asylums"

Deinstitutionalization as a demand for abolition of all carceral facilities for people with disabilities (especially psychiatric hospitals and institutions for people with intellectual disabilities) did not happen without much debate and backlash. One such attack came in the form of the seemingly neutral claim that deinstitutionalization was a major contributor to the rise of mass incarceration. I continue here the genealogy of deinstitutionalization I began in previous chapters by contesting this hegemonic narrative, and the social scientific expert knowledge that made it seem so commonsense. By so doing, I paint a more complex picture of the relation between disability/madness and mass incarceration.

"Prisons Have Become Warehouses for the Mentally Ill" reads a recent headline in Slate.[1] Over at the Wall Street Journal, the title is "The New Asylums: Jails Swell with Mentally Ill."[2] The titles change only slightly, but the message is similar: mass closure of psychiatric hospitals in the United States led to waves of homelessness and to prisons becoming the new asylums. Another oft-heard proclamation is that "Jails have become the largest mental health providers in the United States." These two axioms are heard from activists, journalists, and service providers on a nearly daily basis. But I suggest that these slogans provide a reductionist political stance that flattens complicated historical and socioeconomic realities.

Populations in psychiatric hospitals started rapidly declining at the end of the 1950s, as I explained in the first chapter. But why is deinstitutionalization of psychiatric hospitals, whose heyday was decades ago, still blamed for social realities in the 2010s? Why is it taken for granted that deinstitutionalization is relevant to an analysis of the current phenomenon of mass incarceration? And why *are* there so many people with mental health differences behind bars currently, if not for deinstitutionalization? I will answer these questions by returning to the era in which the "new asylum" thesis first arose: the end of the 1970s and into the 1980s. My aim is to interrogate and destabilize the seemingly neat connections that are being drawn between deinstitutionalization, homelessness, and imprisonment. My second goal is to reveal why these counterhegemonic readings, which I offer here, did not gain traction, in other words, what discourses and realities were erased by maintaining the "new asylum" thesis.

I offer a three-part analysis of the hegemonic narrative deinstitutionalization → homelessness → imprisonment, which I call the *new asylums* thesis. I do this counteranalysis not only to create a more nuanced genealogy of deinstitutionalization and mass incarceration but also to show the dangers of current calls to reopen psychiatric hospitals because jails are not appropriate as "new asylums." I begin by discussing the medicalization of housing insecurity and the ways social science research tried to prove the connection between deinstitutionalization and housing insecurity by uncritically constructing and reifying the category of the "homeless mentally ill." I then briefly discuss the criminalization of housing insecurity to provide a counterexplanation to the nexus of homelessness → imprisonment. To answer the question of the prevalence of incarcerated people with mental health difference, I examine the disabling effects of imprisonment as well as the lack of mental health treatment while incarcerated. At the end of the chapter, I critique the dangerous consequences of the narrative deinstitutionalization → homelessness → imprisonment, or the new asylums thesis.

To untie the Gordian knot between imprisonment, deinstitutionalization of psychiatric hospitals, and homelessness, I will bookend the chapter with scenes from the 2005 PBS *Frontline* episode appropriately titled "The New Asylums."[3] The episode showcases life behind bars for those with severe mental health differences in a supermax prison in Ohio. It opens with a collage of vignettes from the episode with a grim voice-over inquiring, "Why have American prisons become the new asylums?" The thesis's case is made in the first few minutes of the episode that, indeed, prisons are the "new asylums," and the only question is how it came to be this way. The first scene in the *Frontline* episode introduces us to an African American man in an ambulance being questioned by paramedics and police. Then the narrator informs us, "Scenes like this have become all too familiar throughout

America. As the nation's psychiatric hospitals shut down, police departments everywhere were left to handle the growing number of mentally ill on the streets." How did it come to this? Fred Cohen, prison mental health consultant, says, "Once you had hundreds of thousands of people leaving the mental hospitals, they suddenly, obviously, didn't become mentally healthy. They went to the streets, they became homeless, and then they eventually began to cycle into the system that cannot say no."

If you are watching this episode online or reading the transcript, at this point, you are prompted to click on "What happened to mental hospitals?" This link takes you to the page "Deinstitutionalization: A Psychiatric 'Titanic.'"[4] It is an excerpt from *Out of the Shadows: Confronting America's Mental Illness Crisis* by psychiatrist E. Fuller Torrey. Torrey is the founder of the Treatment Advocacy Center.[5] The center supports the psychiatrization of those with mental health differences and their hospitalization, a point to which I shall return at the end of the chapter.

One does not even have to read the excerpt to understand the implications embedded in the title of the piece offered by PBS to its viewers as an answer to the question "What happened to mental hospitals?" The juxtaposition of deinstitutionalization (as a *Titanic* disaster–like event) and the scene of taking a person experiencing mental distress to jail solidifies for the viewer the main thesis—that the irresponsible closure of psychiatric hospitals nationally led to massive homelessness and to a revolving door leading those same populations to be scooped up by criminal justice apparatuses. Precisely because this narrative seems so commonsense, it requires further examination as to how the "new asylums" became the prevailing discourse around deinstitutionalization and imprisonment.

Untangling Housing Insecurity from Deinstitutionalization

Although there are variations to this idea, the hegemonic story is that deinstitutionalization led to "dumping people in the streets" or to "mentally ill" people living in the streets or in jail via being homeless. We are media inundated with new stories of the "homeless mentally ill" who ended up on the streets since psych hospitals closed and are now showing up in prisons and jails across the country. Add to these news stories the stack of scholarly books written on the topic, such as Dear and Wolch's *Landscapes of Despair: From Deinstitutionalization to Homelessness,* Isaac and Armat's *Madness in the Streets,* and E. Fuller Torrey's *Out of the Shadows* and it becomes clear to any layperson that the connection between deinstitutionalization in mental health, imprisonment, and homelessness is indisputable.

The *Frontline* episode "The New Asylums" is not from the 1970s, however, when deinstitutionalization was at its heyday, or even the 1980s or 1990s, when homelessness was on the political agenda. The episode was made in 2005 and is not the only current artifact calling attention to the phenomenon it dubs the "new asylums."[6] So why is this connection still evoked, and for what purposes? What is at stake in this discourse of imprisonment as the new asylums, via homelessness? What I hope to show is how such discourse reduces a much more complex process and points the blame toward an easy target—deinstitutionalization—and away from discussions of neoliberal policies that led simultaneously to the growth of the prison system and to a lack of financial support for people with disabilities to live in the community. In essence, the new asylums discourse medicalizes, pathologizes, and psychiatrizes what is a deeply political and socioeconomic issue.

Counting and Accounting for the "Homeless Mentally Ill"

What is at odds, then, with the pervasive narrative of deinstitutionalization leading to incarceration via homelessness, or the narrative expression deinstitutionalization → homelessness → imprisonment? To begin with, closure of psychiatric hospitals and the growth of housing insecurity as a national phenomenon did not happen at quite the same time. Deinstitutionalization in mental health began in the 1950s and continued in earnest in the 1960s, and although in some states it continues to this day, nationally, the major waves had waned by the beginning of the 1970s. Therefore, from the mid-1980s, most of those classified as mentally ill have not been institutionalized.[7] In terms of home loss, increasing rates of people seeking public shelter did not appear until the early 1980s, with an increase in percentages throughout that decade. In the public's eye, it seems that deinstitutionalization is a major cause of homelessness, even though during deinstitutionalization, the major population affected by home loss were families with small children, which are not necessarily the same populations affected by deinstitutionalization.[8] If deinstitutionalization occurred decades before the mass waves of housing insecurity and affected a slightly different population, why does this narrative presented in the episode "The New Asylums" and elsewhere seem so clear-cut?

One basis for the thesis is that in sociological and public health literature, it seems that one of the most commonly researched aspects of the phenomenon of housing insecurity is not lack of shelter or the causes leading to home loss but measuring the pervasiveness, or lack thereof, of mental illness (and, secondarily, drug use) among "the homeless." In these sociological studies, estimates of the percentage of mental illness among the so-called homeless vary extensively, from 30 to 90 percent.[9] I suggest that these statistics, and their huge variance, in counting the "homeless mentally ill" serve a cultural, political, and social purpose.

As sociologist Martin De Santos argues, social statistics often transform quanta of information into powerful collective representations. In that sense, it does not matter if they were "biased" or "exaggerated," but what matters is how they get embedded in social meaning and become a part of what de Santos characterizes as "statistical imagination." For our purposes, then, the notion of exactly how many people are or are not homeless and mentally ill is almost inconsequential to the larger question of how such statistics became powerful cultural agents in the fight for and against deinstitutionalization. Since such statistics have been circulating in the media quite frequently since the 1980s, they have become symbolic objects.[10]

As social/cultural studies scholar Craig Willse suggests, instead of focusing on housing and poverty alleviation, most studies of the last twenty years had focused on counting and studying "the homeless." This is done especially through a lens of pathology and medicalization in relation to psychiatric disability and drug use. As Willse puts it, "what to do with the homeless, rather than what to do about housing, has become the obsession of government policy, social service practice and social scientific inquiry."[11] In fact, it seems that trying to accurately measure the percentage of the mentally ill among the homeless has become somewhat of a social science obsession, and one that is still debated among scholars and policy makers.

Much time and money went into trying to "accurately" count the homeless mentally ill, and much less effort went into rethinking or ameliorating the root causes of housing insecurity as well as lack of quality community or peer mental health care. This counting was not a pure exercise in futility, however, but a major economic and policy battleground between state, cities, and the federal government. Willse shows in his genealogy of housing services that housing programs have traditionally been grouped under public assistance and not federal programs. From the beginning of settler colonialism in the United States, housing was seen as an issue for local authorities or charities to take care of. The federal government did provide program assistance in the 1930s, as part of the New Deal, but since then had relied on states or private agencies to administer services.[12] In essence, the battle over services is thus: if the homeless are considered a welfare issue, then the city would need to address the issue; but if it could be proved that it is a mental health crisis, then states will bear the financial responsibility of taking care of the problem (or making the problem less visible). Perhaps needless to say, states had more funds than cities; therefore, there was a lot at stake in trying to "prove" the connection between deinstitutionalization of psych facilities and homelessness.[13] This statistical imagination is therefore embedded in political economies related to biopolitical management of ability/mental health status, as related to other axes, such as gender/sexuality, which are already embedded in class status and its relation to housing insecurity.

Disablement and Housing Insecurity

There is another factor that accounts for the high percentage of, and vast variance in, accounts of the "homeless mentally ill," which is that the "homeless mentally ill" is not a neutral group of people but a constructed category of analysis. As discussed by mad/psych survivors/ex-patients and activists in the recovery and antipsychiatry movements, mental illness is not a biological diagnosis but a social construction based on normative assumptions that are gendered/raced/classed, as discussed in chapter 2.[14] For instance, the late activist Judi Chamberlin critiqued the mantra that is often cited by activists and professionals that "mental illness is like any other illness." Given current laws in relation to involuntary hospitalization, mental "illness" cannot be characterized as being like cancer or a heart attack, according to Chamberlin. Altered states, anger, and pain should not be characterized as illness but as a consequence of a system of power and inequality that denies people their basic freedoms and needs.[15]

If diagnosing so-called mental illness seems intangible and subjective, add to that the very act of living unhoused. One cannot prove a causal relation between mental illness, deinstitutionalization, and homelessness, because the very definition of homelessness conflates with that of mental illness, such as the inability to care and provide for oneself.[16] Thus many of the behaviors and responses exhibited by people who are homeless can be attributed to that fact alone, such as being depressed, being agitated, mistrusting authority, having eating difficulties, and being unresponsive, but these are all taken as signs of the prevalence of "mental illness."[17]

The conflation of homelessness and psychiatric disabilities was probably compounded by the fact that some of the most visible people who are unsheltered might also be regarded as mentally ill.[18] The figure of the homeless person talking to herself and shouting out in the streets of urban neighborhoods had become the archetype of homelessness at large. Without trying to erase the existence of people with altered states of mind who live on the streets, it is also important to remember that just because something is visible and vocal does not mean it is predominant. Most people who are considered to be homeless blend in with passersby or are bunking up with friends or relatives. In essence, the majority of those who are housing insecure are invisible.

In addition, the connection between housing insecurity and so-called mental illness is not unidirectional, in which one (mental health difference) leads to the other (home loss and eventual incarceration). One needs to call into question the assumption that there is anything normal about being housing insecure in such an affluent society. This questioning will lead to focus on the disabling effects of being housing insecure, which then cannot be traced to deinstitutionalization because they are intrinsic conditions of living on the streets. As Stewart and I suggest, homelessness by itself disables. The streets, or shelters or living day to day without housing security, are disabling psychologically as well as physically. The constant noise, diesel fumes, cold/heat, lack of privacy, anxiety of not knowing where the next meal will come from, fear of attack, and fear of being removed or arrested by police are part and parcel of the everyday reality of living without permanent shelter.[19]

But if there is no identifiable causal relationship between deinstitutionalization and homelessness, then what were the reasons such a connection was evoked, by whom, and to what effects? The U.S. discussion on homelessness becomes a way to psychiatrize what is a deeply political and socioeconomic issue.[20] As we have seen, this diversion serves to shift responsibility from the state and its fiscal and welfare policies into the human service sector as a way of ameliorating the problem with interventions in mental health. But it is not just a matter of policy but the political economic governance of life itself.

As a category, the "homeless," like the "mentally ill," becomes socially and economically productive through what Willse calls surplus life. In terms of political economy, much like and in conjunction with the category of "prisoner" or "disabled," "homeless" becomes a commodity, to be managed by its own industry. This is part of Dis Inc., which refers to disability incarcerated and disability incorporated. As a term, it aims to capture the ways disability is subjected to incorporation in society but only by respectability politics and assimilation to normative expectations of race-ability, as I demonstrated in previous chapters regarding the inclusion of people with disabilities in social arrangements and community living during and after deinstitutionalization.[21] The other side of Dis Inc. is the corporatization of disability for profit by carceral institutions, such as nursing homes, halfway houses, and prisons, or incarceration for economic and social gain. In other words, as a term, it offers a crip/mad of color analysis that connects a critique of not just normativity but also state and capital.[22] In this case, the psychiatrization of homelessness enabled it to be captured by two systems of incarceration—criminal justice (jails and prisons) and psychiatric facilities. As Russell and Stewart argue, in postindustrial times, disablement has become big business.[23] Connecting the institutional- (including psychiatric-) industrial complex with the prison–industrial complex, as I showed in the book's introduction, helps to account for the state's investment in punishment, which grew in sharp contrast to the cuts in other areas of social policies under neoliberal calculations, a point to which I will return.

The corporatization and commodification of madness and homelessness are not an aberration of capitalism or (post)modernity but a key feature of it. As a social and political economic phenomenon, the production of homelessness en masse makes life in neoliberal societies possible. Those living in industrialized nations are disciplined, in this stage of late capitalism and neoliberal governance, into ways of living that allow for certain forms of protection and security by extracting value from the abandonment of entire populations.[24] This explains why and how the management of the "homeless" and not the eradication of housing deprivation became the goal of policy and service delivery, according to Willse. In other words, housing insecurity cannot be explained by mental health status or deinstitutionalization because it is endemic to neoliberal life, not a side effect of it.

So how and why had deinstitutionalization become a scapegoat of housing insecurity? The "new asylum" thesis puts the blame on an easy target, deinstitutionalization, and away from discussions of neoliberal policies that led simultaneously to the growth of the prison system and to lack of accessible and affordable housing. Populations in psychiatric hospitals began to shrink in the mid-1950s and were already low when Reagan became governor and was the first to close down all the state hospitals in California, referring to them as "the biggest hotel chain in the state."[25] The money that was saved from closing down these facilities was supposed to be used to support community mental health centers, which never materialized because of austerity measures that cut publicly funded services. It is important to remember that the Reagan administration introduced a fundamental change in public housing in the early 1980s, which was a significant shift from previous U.S. policy, and included a $30 billion cut in housing assistance.[26] At a time when workers' wages were eroding, Reagan tightened eligibility requirements for federal assistance programs, including unemployment benefits.[27]

Historian Michael Staub demonstrates how deinstitutionalization and antipsychiatry became a perfect scapegoat on which to pin the housing crisis of the 1980s. Despite evidence to the contrary, Staub suggests, "there developed nonetheless and almost all at once other ways to tell the story of deinstitutionalization that effectively erased any perception that people living on the streets had suffered from the callous disregard of the Reagan administration."[28] In other words, the alchemy of individualizing structural inequalities and using the statistical imagination of the figures of the "homeless mentally ill" (and the "mentally ill in prison" discussed later) gave credence to deinstitutionalization as an explanation for a whole host of socio-politico-economic problems.

To add to these economic shifts, local changes in housing markets work to displace many populations. Such changes include gentrification of urban neighborhoods, inflated rents, coupled with decreasing welfare benefits, and "urban renewal" projects or evictions.[29] In addition, as I discuss in the next chapter devoted to housing desegregation, at its root, both housing security and deprivation are distributed not simply in terms of economic resources but along racialized and gendered lines.[30] Therefore the issue of housing insecurity and deprivation is a phenomenon much larger and more complex than can be gleaned from the discourse of the "new asylums."

Did Deinstitutionalization Lead to the Rise in Incarceration in Prisons and Jails?

Housing Deprivation and Incarceration

In addition to the complexity of the phenomenon of counting the "homeless mentally ill" and its relation to deinstitutionalization, that is, the axiom of deinstitutionalization leading to a rise in the homeless population, we are still left with the second part of the deinstitutionalization → homelessness → imprisonment construct, which is the relation between home loss and incarceration. As in the rest of this book, it is vital to understand the connection between housing deprivation and incarceration through the lens of criminal pathology, and especially racial criminal pathology. Housing insecurity, and specifically those who experience it or the "homeless," had not just been medicalized and psychiatrized, for reasons discussed above, but criminalized in the process as well. While the criminal pathologization of the livelihood (as "beggars") and sheer existence of visibly physically and psychiatrically disabled people on the streets predates processes of urbanization,[31] the processes of criminalizing life on the streets have certainly morphed and intensified in recent decades. Acts such as sleeping in public spaces or asking for money or even food from passersby had been restricted, including the ability to share food with others in public spaces, and are now punishable offenses in certain jurisdictions. This is part of what Katherine Beckett and Naomi Murakawa refer to as the "shadow carceral state"—the conflation of criminal punishment with civil codes and administrative pathways to incarceration.[32] More specifically, in *Banished*, Beckett and Herbert show that many U.S. cities are increasingly deploying social control tools that involve spatial exclusion, such as "off-limit" orders, trespassing, stay out of drug areas and stay out of areas of prostitution orders, and gang injunctions, which meld in essence civil codes with criminal laws.[33] Beckett and Herbert therefore signal the genealogy of banishment as a form of punishment, even though many propose these ordinances as *alternatives* to punishment, because they are meant to compel people to leave a locale and thus supposedly avoid imprisonment or connection with "criminal" activity, such as drugs or sex work. But such ordinances only increase the scope of the carceral state. Therefore it is no wonder that being housing insecure is such a strong conduit to imprisonment, regardless of mental health diagnosis or deinstitutionalization.

The nexus of criminal pathologization helps clarify how the conflation of mental illness and homelessness allowed city and state officials to remove unsheltered individuals from public spaces by using a discourse that emphasizes the connections between danger and mental illness. The medicalization of homelessness delegitimized the plight of those who were homeless and redirected any public discussions away from poverty and the retrenchment of welfare to focusing on medication noncompliance and reinstitutionalization of the "mentally ill." Deinstitutionalization became a perfect scapegoat on which to pin the plight of the so-called homeless mentally ill and, by affiliation, homelessness itself.[34] In short, the discourse that pits confinement in institutions and prisons against living on the streets or being unhoused creates a false equation since there are, and should be, more than either the medico-punitive discourse of social control (institutionalization) or biopolitical discourse of social abandonment (housing insecurity).

From Asylums to Prisons?

I want to move us now to the second part of the construct deinstitutionalization → homelessness → imprisonment, mainly, the axis of imprisonment. The move from one carceral space to another has been termed *transincarceration* and is much debated in the sociological literature. When looking at general trends, it is easy to surmise that medicalization gave way to criminalization over time, that is, that psychiatric hospitals closed and then prisons boomed.[35] This relationship, of reversal of the trends between the mental health and the criminal system, is hardly new, however, and had been studied over the years by many social scientists, who nicknamed this phenomenon the "balloon theory," in which populations seem to exit one carceral space only to enter another, like air in a balloon.[36] As early as 1939, Penrose suggested that social control evolves from incarcerating people to treating people, therefore suggesting an inverse relationship between the mental health and prison systems. Since then, much like the measuring of the percentage of mental illness among the homeless, this hypothesis had been tested numerous times, with inconsistent results.[37]

It is certainly true, though, that from the 1960s, the mental inmate population decreased but the prison population increased. The shrinkage of the safety net from the Reagan era to the 1990s, coupled with increases in federal expansion of corrections operations, created a trade-off between social services (which shrunk) and incarceration (which exploded). Many scholars, especially in social sciences, thus argue that there was a shift from medical and social services to penal and surveillance measures and that these changes can best be viewed when examining the treatment of people with psychiatric disabilities.[38] But such arguments are not value-free and reiterate the claims that deinstitutionalization resulted in reincarceration of mentally ill people in jails and prisons—or the new asylums hypothesis.

This idea of psychiatrization or medicalization *giving way* to criminalization doesn't take into account those who are people of color who are and were psychiatrized. As I showed in previous chapters, the population in psych hospitals during deinstitutionalization came to comprise more people of color, especially black and brown. For people of color, this is not an either/or form of social control but both at the same time. This balloon theory also fails to capture the carceral archipelago or carceral continuum especially when looking through the lens of racial criminal pathologization, which sees these processes as emanating from one another and inseparable.

Taking incarceration in its broadest terms, that is, in relation to both prisons and institutions, would entail deconstructing the categories that are used by criminologists, psychiatrists, and social scientists.[39] The goal will not be to reproduce socially manufactured categories, such as the "mentally ill" or the "homeless," in prisons and jails but to ask questions that take into account the interconnected discourse of criminal pathology. To not do so is to look at only a partial picture of both confinement and incapacitation, as Harcourt suggests, and also not to take seriously the theoretical and historical perspectives that conceptualize incarceration more expansively, viewing psychiatrization and institutionalization as forms of incarceration as well.[40]

One of the dangers of supporting the new asylums thesis is that then it seems obvious that unsheltered people with mental health issues as well as those in mental distress more generally end up incarcerated because they can't be in psychiatric hospitals. Since psychiatric hospitals in the 1950s and 1960s were warehouses for people with mental health diagnoses, indeed, the people who resided there were less visible to those outside these institutions. But that does not mean that these were places of quality care and treatment or that those psychiatrized consented, in the broadest sense of the word, to having their freedom taken in order to be in these enclosures. So especially during this time, the United States didn't have to contend with extreme variance in behavior, thought, or mind, as many people were "out of sight, out of mind" of the public's eye. But it does not logically follow that people who were psychiatrized were better off in such locales in the "good old days" of massive confinement in the field of mental health and developmental disability.

Connecting deinstitutionalization to, not to mention blaming it on, the rise of the U.S. prison nation also leads one to believe that psych hospitals closed and led the same people to be incarcerated in prisons. But this claim cannot be corroborated in terms of demographics, as Harcourt shows.[41]

Over the years, the gender distribution of those in mental hospitals tended to be either equal or trending toward overrepresentation of women. However, in terms of imprisonment, the majority of those newly imprisoned are male. There are differences in terms of age and race as well. Although there is some evidence to suggest that during deinstitutionalization, the proportion of those identified as nonwhites had increased among those admitted to mental hospitals, the number was still at about one-third at its highest point.[42] As should now be clear to anyone familiar with the prison system in the United States, nonwhites are highly overrepresented, reaching over 50 percent in the early 1990s. Put differently, generally speaking, the inmate population in mental hospitals tended to be white, older, and more equally distributed by gender than the prison population.[43] Therefore we are not speaking about the same population that simply transitioned from the mental hospital to the prison but of ways in which the social control function of incarceration retained its importance, although for differing populations. It is not about medicalization giving way to criminalization but about the nexus of racial criminal pathologization, a nexus that is intersecting at its core.

Prison Is Maddening

My last claim concerns another part of the deinstitutionalization → homelessness → imprisonment construct, which is the reality that many incarcerated people do have mental challenges, and some are quite severe, as "The New Asylums" episode painfully shows. But this does not mean that deinstitutionalization caused a rise in the population of the "mentally ill" in prisons.[44] If the population of those with mental health differences behind bars is substantially large, I contend that that should warrant an indictment of the system of incarceration and not of deinstitutionalization.

The *Frontline* episode focuses on instances of psychosis of those incarcerated, but I want to begin with the less visible mental health challenges of depression and suicide. As Stewart and I show, suicide remains the leading cause of jail inmate death; the picture is not much different in state prisons.[45] According to the Bureau of Justice Statistics, between 2001 and 2010 suicide was among the five leading causes of death in prison in all but two years.[46] Why is the suicide rate so high in carceral spaces? Much of the scholarly research on suicide rates in prison had focused on the individuals incarcerated and their characteristics. As Meredith Huey and Thomas McNulty state, this focus is related to the medicalization of suicide more broadly, in which the causes for suicide are seen as reflective of personal pathology and not as related to the environment, even in a repressive setting, such as a prison or other total institutions.[47] Perhaps the case discussed by Stewart of Howard Andrews, a disabled California prisoner who requested physician-assisted suicide, might shed further light. Andrews requested assisted suicide not because he found life as a quadriplegic unbearable but because he found life as a quad *in prison* unbearable. Rather than address the issues of abusive treatment and deplorable conditions raised by his case, the judges granted him permission to end his life. Interestingly, by the time of their decision, Andrews had apparently changed his mind and opted for life, but in an ironic bitter twist of fate he died anyway, unintentionally, due to prison conditions (a botched catheterization).[48] Thus disablement and imprisonment converge and intertwine.

There is some acknowledgment that prison itself is disabling from the prison administration in "The New Asylums" episode. Gary Beven, chief forensic psychiatrist in Ohio correctional, comments that it is very hard to treat inmates in a maximum security prison because they get depressed and turn to suicide or self-mutilation. In solitary confinement they start hallucinating and become psychotic. Fred Cohen, a prison mental health consultant in the episode, admits that if you go into segregation with mental health issues, they will get worse; and if you go in without them, you will likely come out with mental health challenges. Thus, conditions of confinement may cause further mental deterioration among those entering the system with diagnoses of "mental" or intellectual disabilities.[49]

In "The New Asylums," those incarcerated understand this reality all too well. Toward the end of the episode, Carl M.,[50] one of the men incarcerated in Lucasville, the supermax prison in Ohio, turns to the camera and asks the viewers to consider what he calls the "environmental factors that come into play before making a diagnosis or a misdiagnosis," in his words. "Before discussing or taking a miracle drug that supposed to be a cure all," he says, "let's find out what's going on, and being in prison," he continues, "that is one problem." Carl puts the crux of the issue on the prison itself. The narrator tells us his story as an example of other prisoners' circumstances that landed them in the supermax. A "story" that I interpret to be a result of the entanglement of incarceration and disablement, through biopolitical (population level) control, that is, racism (which Gilmore defines as the "state sanctioned or extralegal production and exploitations of group-differentiated vulnerability to premature death"[51]).

Carl was convicted of burglary initially and then returned to prison for violating his parole by taking someone's bicycle. The narrator says that then Carl began disobeying officers, which after a decade landed him at Lucasville, the maximum security prison. Indeed, many so-called mentally ill prisoners came to the prison from minimum security prisons, but because they were seen as disruptive, they ended up in Lucasville, which the episode's narrator describes as the "basement for the very mentally ill in Ohio." Because of this entanglement of criminalization and pathologization, Carl has been in prison more than thirteen years beyond his original sentence, which is not an uncommon occurrence. The racist nature of criminal pathologization becomes evidently clear when we learn at the end of the episode that Carl had finally been granted parole, but because he came from Jamaica as a child, he was detained by immigration and deported to Jamaica, a country he barely knew.

Another disabling effect of incarceration, one unrelated to deinstitutionalization (although it could be attributed at times to previous forms of institutionalization, incarceration, or police harassment), is in relation to the nature of trauma. Women, trans, and gender-variant folks who are incarcerated report high levels of trauma, both before and during their incarceration. This previous experience with trauma is hardly taken into account either in sentencing or during their incarceration. Terry Kupers, who is a prominent psychiatrist and advocate for racial justice and prison reform writes that an estimated 80 percent of women behind bars had experienced domestic violence or physical or sexual abuse before incarceration.[52] This trauma is then triggered and retriggered by the further violence within prison, such as the common practice of body cavity search (i.e., state-sanctioned daily sexual assault). Even if one believes that people who are incarcerated "deserve" their sentence, they were not sentenced to daily sexual assault in the form of strip searching and cavity searching. If they had been previously assaulted, this practice has a further cumulative effect. As mentioned in other parts of the book, this had led feminist abolitionists to refer to incarceration as State-sponsored violence against women (and trans and gender-nonconforming people).[53] In addition, there is also a racial and gender bias in the *interpretation* and diagnosis of mental health differences in prisons. Prisoners of color who experience emotional breakdown are more likely than their white counterparts to be sent to segregation; to be thought of as malingering, stubborn, or violent; and to be denied treatment. This is part of the discourse of racial criminal pathologization as well, especially when interlinked with gendered and sexually based oppression. In addition, those incarcerated who are identified as mentally ill or who exhibit "disruptive behaviors" are often sanctioned to "administrative segregation" in separate units (often referred to as the SHU, or secure housing unit).[54] These are isolation units resembling a closet, in which one stays for twenty-three hours a day. People who are "mentally ill," queer, gay, gender nonconforming, and Other are often placed in the SHU as a form of "protective custody," often "for their own good."[55] These segregated forms of incarceration are likely to cause or exacerbate the mental and physical ill health of those incarcerated, regardless of their mental state prior to incarceration.[56] Legal scholar Kathryn DeMarco goes a step further to argue that since confinement in supermax facilities almost guarantees the creation of a mental disability, such confinement violates the Convention on the Rights of People with Disabilities, which was approved by the United Nations in 2006.[57] In a tragic cyclical way, as Keramet Reiter and Thomas Blair point out,[58] the very presence of seriously mentally ill people in jail or prison has become a primary justification for the use of solitary confinement, which, in turn, creates or exacerbates mental distress.[59] As Carl says in "The New Asylums," "being involved in a solitary situation . . . is like being placed in a prison's prison. And that's—that's worse than simply being taken from society and placed in prison."

Prisons in Ohio, where the episode was filmed, are currently (since 2012) subject to the tiered system of segregation and confinement, a system that enshrines solitary confinement. Much like the continuum approach discussed earlier in the book in relation to services for people with intellectual disabilities, the tiered system assigns each incarcerated person to a level of security that ranges from 1 to 5b (ten levels overall) that they have to go through in order to have more privileges. Levels 5b, 5a, and 4b are variations of solitary confinement.[60] To move between the levels, those incarcerated have to demonstrate "good behavior" for a few months. Therefore, if someone is classified as 5b, it will be two years before they can be with other people, under the best of circumstances. For those who are incarcerated and are directly unable or seen as unable to "follow orders," which is a critical aspect of surviving in a carceral locale, including those with hearing, intellectual, or psych disabilities, the ability to move between the tiers and regain more privileges is much diminished. One of the implications is that those incarcerated spend much of their sentences in various levels of solitary confinement, which is likely to lead to mental and physical disablement. In summary, in contrast to the thesis of deinstitutionalization leading to people with mental differences and crisis behind bars, and as those incarcerated tell us in "The New Asylums," one of the reasons why there are many people with mental health issues in prisons is because of the nature of confinement and incarceration.

Setting the Scene: Lucasville

The reason why "The New Asylums" was shot in Lucasville and adjacent correctional facilities in Ohio, we are told, is because Ohio is innovative and at the forefront of dealing with "mentally ill" prisoners. What the episode does not show, however, is the background behind what made Ohio a so-called leader in treating the mentally ill behind bars. Needed changes in treatment options for people with mental health differences inside Ohio prisons did not come about because of the benevolence of the criminal justice system. They came because the incarcerated fought for them, combined with the efforts of professionals (activist lawyers, mental health experts) mostly in the form of lawsuits on behalf of those incarcerated and psychiatrized.

Although not as high profile as other prison uprisings, and although not mentioned at all in the episode, Lucasville is the site of one of the most extensive prison rebellions and takeovers in the United States. In April 1993, nine inmates and one prison guard were killed during an eleven-day occupation of the Southern Ohio Correctional Facility by its inmates. In his account of the uprising, Staughton Lynd, the renowned activist and lawyer, paints a much more critical picture of Wilkinson, the director of the Ohio Department of Rehabilitation and Correction at that time, who is interviewed at length in the episode.[61] After the rebellion, inmates sued the state for negligence because of practices like double celling (the practice of putting more than one person in a prison cell, which is against regulations), overcrowding, and not complying with reforms that had been mandated since 1990.[62]

One of the reasons behind the uprising, according to testimonies by those incarcerated, is that Arthur Tate, the new warden at the time, wanted to make it into a supermax prison, but his request was denied by the Department of

Correction. Tate was appointed as warden after a schoolteacher who came to the prison to help inmates with their General Educational Development test (GED) was killed by a "mentally unstable" inmate. Tate instituted "operation shakedown" in the facility by cutting off all opportunities for programming, treatment, and social interaction. At the time of the rebellion, 1,820 were incarcerated in Lucasville (about 300 over capacity), with 804 double-celled. Moreover, 75 percent of those recommended by prison staff to be reclassified to medium security, and therefore eventually transfer out were denied by the Department of Correction. This fact, the conditions of confinement, the lack of programming, and the limit of one five-minute phone call permitted per year created an environment of total suppression and hopelessness among those incarcerated.[63] Even though Tate's request was denied, after, and by some accounts because of, the uprising, the state of Ohio built its first supermax, the Ohio State Penitentiary in Youngstown, adjacent to Lucasville in 1998.[64]

The following November, a class action lawsuit, *Dunn v. Voinovich*, claiming that prisoners with serious mental illness in Ohio were not provided with a constitutionally adequate level of psychiatric care, was filed in federal court. The suit, filed on behalf of twelve thousand prisoners with psychiatric disabilities, also claimed that they were sometimes chained to their beds and beaten, much like their counterparts at the turn of the twentieth century, as demonstrated in exposés and lawsuits I discussed in chapter 1. In June 1995, the state and the defendants entered into a consent decree, and Fred Cohen was brought in to monitor progress.[65] The kind of mental health treatment shown in the episode "The New Asylums" came as a direct result of this lawsuit and of activism by those incarcerated. But the "treatment" provided should hardly give Ohio reasons to be proud.

Treatment While Incarcerated

A common claim among those who call prisons the new asylums is that prisons and jails had become de facto the biggest mental health treatment facilities in the United States. To be regarded as a mental health facility, though, and not a warehouse for all kinds of indigent populations, carceral spaces need to actually provide mental health treatment. As we shall see, this claim is highly suspect. A related claim is that people who are destitute and in crisis are often so lacking in choices that they want to end up in prison or jail to get proper treatment (at times, this is also said regarding food, physical health, and shelter). But this claim also merits further scrutiny. In the *Frontline* episode "The New Asylums," for example, an officer points out that many of the prisoners get much better care inside prison than they would on the outside. Wilkinson, then director of the Ohio Department of Rehabilitation and Correction, further states in the episode that he knows a judge who sent people to prison because this is where the judge thought they would finally get the help they needed. Therefore, to understand and critically assess such statements, one needs to examine the problematic nature of mental health care behind bars.

So what does treatment behind bars look like? At the very beginning of the episode, we are brought into Lucasville Prison in Ohio in an unprecedented way, we are told, and shown a group therapy session. Most of the participants in this group therapy scene are black, all are men, and each is sitting in an individual crate resembling a bird cage. This is not hyperbole but mere fact. Each of the participants in this therapy session is in a small cage with bars and locks, including chains around their ankles (where they would escape to in their tiny cages, we are not told). The presumed therapist (who looks phenotypically white) is sitting outside the cages, which are positioned in a circle, asking the men who are lined up in a row of cages how they are doing, how they progressed this week, inquiring about new body injuries he can observe, and so on. A guard is constantly circling the cages.[66] This is treatment, we are told—a level of treatment some of them had never experienced on the outside. This scene is a representation of a talk therapy session, the *best-case* scenario in Lucasville and many prisons like it.[67]

In another scene, we are brought into the prison infirmary, in which a psychiatrist is talking to an incarcerated person in distress through the tiny slot in the door, intended mostly for meal delivery. They are trying to calm him down and convince him to take his medication. This is not uncommon. When prisoners are seen by a so-called specialist, it is often for a period of time amounting to a few minutes a week or a month, depending on the facility. Of course, those incarcerated there are not likely to be very candid with their answers to such public queries through a meal tray or with other caged people. This "treatment" might be combined with psychotropic medication, but there are no other forms of treatment available.

Behind bars, even though psychiatric medication is discussed as voluntary, refusal to take it can often result in punitive measures. Psycho pharmaceuticals as a mandate in "treating" psychic difference or distress has been heavily critiqued by consumers/survivors/ex-patients/mad identified people, as was discussed in earlier chapters in relation to a broader critique of the effects of a biopsych approach that remakes madness into "mental illness."[68] The point is not to criticize people who take psychiatric medication but to alert to the fact that it is a first and often *only* course of action when dealing with psychic harm, as opposed to peer counseling or knowledge and other options. As Kupers suggests, at the very least, the person being "treated" should be educated about the therapies they are given, the rationale for treatment, and so on, which very rarely happens in carceral spaces.[69] Since medication has varying effects on the people who consume it (some of which are perceived as worse than the symptoms of distress, and some would have long-term and irreversible bodily and psychic effects), the lack of other alternatives and the compulsory nature of the drug regimen are even more pronounced.

Psychiatric drugging, sensory deprivation, and lack of human contact are not humane ways of treating people, especially those in psychiatric crisis, but ultimately anyone. For psychiatric incarceration, in psych facilities or wards, this form of "treatment" is being justified as therapeutic, for the incarcerated's own good. In prisons and jails, such treatment is justified on the basis of security, for the inmate's own good but also for the good of the other prisoners and ultimately of those not imprisoned. In fact, there is acknowledgment of this fact even by correctional personnel. In prison, security regimes trump so-called treatment in almost every way, since it is governed by top-down hierarchies in which medical staff are much lower than correctional personnel. Here again, criminalization is entangled with and ultimately triumphs over pathologization in ways that are often deadly. When someone who is imprisoned is in crisis or is acting out, the response comes from security guards and not mental health professionals. If someone seeks mental health aid, correctional staff are often reluctant (because they think the person is faking it or is manipulative), unwilling (because of what they deem as security risks), unable (because even if they see those imprisoned as human beings, they, like the rest of us, have been deskilled in dealing with human variation and put it on so-called experts, who are only available for a few hours a month in any given prison), or tentative (refusal to let a prisoner see a professional until they disclose some information, such as who started a fight) in their decision to "allow" an inmate to be given access to even request treatment.

For example, throughout the episode, we are shown horrifying scenes of what is often called "cell extraction." Cell extraction is a brutal practice in which numerous helmeted guards dressed in riot gear remove a single person from their cell by force. These occur in supermax prisons or in lockup, places where prisoners with mental health issues are overrepresented. Since the person is already locked within a single cell and isolated, one wonders what the rush is to extract them and for what possible reason. Cell extraction can happen due to any prison rule violation, including not returning the tray to the slot in the door when told or throwing excrement on the walls or door. These acts are not seen as a cry for help or a root of a much deeper problem with the conditions of confinement (or its rationale) but instead are viewed as a violation of security that requires further punitive measures. In other words, spitting on the wall or a guard is seen as a violent offense requiring punitive measures, while the actual placement of human beings in these cells is not. This also is treatment inside.

In addition to lockdown facilities, such as Lucasville, the episode "The New Asylums" depicts other ways of treating mental health crisis behind bars. Oakwood Correctional Facility is the local forensic psych hospital, built on the ground of an older psychiatric asylum in Ohio. There we meet Donnie, an inmate who has been sent there for the eighteenth time. He says that when he is there, he feels better. But when he is stabilized and starts feeling more human, he is released back into the prison. In his meeting with his caretakers and doctors, they discuss releasing another prisoner back into Lucasville. He asks them if that is in his best interest. They say that of course it is, he has been a model patient and his treatment had been successful. He asks if that will be the case in a different setting; they say it is only up to him to keep it up. It is unclear from the episode if the treatment team had ever been to Lucasville themselves. If they have, they would know how incarceration itself leads to further mental distress and disablement.

This reliance on individualistic discourse ("don't commit crimes," "behave and be rewarded") to address structural oppression (including the very nature of and rationale for incarceration) is at the heart of "treatment" behind bars. When enshrined in medical discourse, as opposed to and in addition to security discourse, such treatment is discussed as if it occurs in a vacuum, and not in the most inhumane and repressive setting possible. At its core, then, under the "new asylums" thesis, prisons and jails can be thought of as places of treatment ("the largest mental health facilities in the U.S.").

But as I have shown, they are, more often than not, places of disablement that create and exacerbate mental ill health. Discussing them as places in which people can or do get treatment is not only inaccurate but also ethically and ideologically problematic, as it legitimizes incarceration and makes it appear needed and normalized. The plight of those experiencing mental health issues while incarcerated should concern us, but I want to suggest that the reason is because of the detrimental effects of incarceration and not because people need to be in psychiatric hospitals instead. It should also lead to indicting disablement, but without falling on models that only see disability as deficit. We need to work to end disablement as a form of state violence but without ending disability or madness as a way of life or way to view the world. As I suggested in the previous chapter, it is exactly these knowledges of those in disability and mad movements that created the largest decarceration movement in U.S. history, deinstitutionalization. Instead of blaming this huge victory in how we treat and understand difference, we would be better served by learning from these knowledges to critique and abolish prisons and jails, not just for those who are disabled or mentally ill therein but for everyone.

Rediscovering the Asylum: Consequences of Prisons as "the New Asylums"

I want to end with a discussion of the potential political effects of the new asylums thesis currently. The thesis posits that "deinstitutionalization → homelessness → imprisonment." As I hope this chapter has demonstrated, institutions and psych hospitals are and should not be residential placements or alternatives to housing. People are unsheltered because of lack of economic equalities that left them unhoused. Blaming deinstitutionalization for that diverts attention from these structural inequalities, the production of precarity on a biopolitical level, reliant on many mechanisms, including disablement through and in conjunction with racism (premature death) and criminalization. It also makes it appear as if hospitalization and institutionalization were a panacea for such social problems, although decades of fighting against these carceral enclosures and logics by those psychiatrized and their allies had shown otherwise.

It is exactly the success of deinstitutionalization, in terms of facility closure, that had led to the backlash that the new asylum thesis purports. The

construction of deinstitutionalization as dangerous and as a failure resulting in people living on the streets and in prison has had material consequences for those most affected by psychiatrization and incarceration. One
of the major effects of such backlash and critiques of deinstitutionalization
are growing calls for a return to institutionalization as a way to alleviate the
suffering of the "mentally ill" on the streets and in prison.

In a recent editorial in the *Journal of the American Medical Association,*
three renowned bioethicists called for "a return to the asylum," presenting
every claim I have discussed here: that jails and prisons are becoming the
new asylums, that they are the largest mental health facilities in the United
States in the absence of psychiatric hospitals, and citing statistics of the
number of mentally ill in prison and as homeless, stating that deinstitutionalization has failed and led to people being homeless and funneled into the
criminal justice system—and therefore the only way to correct it is to reinstate
psychiatric hospitals.[70] The first author of the article (Sisti) then reappeared
in a *New York Times* forum about the "mentally ill in prison," reinstating these
same claims.[71]

Not only are the claims made almost identical to the critiques of deinstitutionalization heard since the 1960s but the critics have remained the same
as well. In 1984, a special task force of the American Psychological Association was calling deinstitutionalization in mental health "a major societal
tragedy." The chair of the committee who wrote the 1984 report would then
become a major proponent of the reinstitutionalization of mental patients,
including authoring a recent, 2016, editorial urging practitioners to "re-
discover the concept of the asylum."[72] E. Fuller Torrey, head of the Treatment
Advocacy Center, continues to author and lecture about the dangers of deinstitutionalization. It is quite troubling that almost every document written about this axiom of prisons as the new asylums and the "mentally ill in
prison/jail" since the 1970s has referenced, was authored, coauthored, shadow
authored by, or otherwise involved Torrey or the Treatment Advocacy Center
(including the links in the *Frontline* episode "The New Asylums"). If the
players are the same, and the claims have been the same for half a century,
one should ask, why is the debate over deinstitutionalization as a culprit for
criminalization still raging on?

At the time of writing this chapter, President Donald Trump has tweeted
about the need to reopen psychiatric hospitals to better control the so-called
"violently mentally ill" who are responsible, in his opinion, for mass shootings

in the United States. Because his claims are based on this thesis of the "new asylums," they were accompanied by editorials in the *New York Times* and the *Atlantic*, endorsed by psychiatrists and health care professionals.[73] No similar endorsements were heard from people who are or have been psychiatrized or from social movements led by those psychiatrized or criminalized. The danger is that such public appeals are often followed by specific policy changes, which, taken together, could become a reality of reinstitutionalization of those who are labeled as mentally disabled. Wolch, Nelson, and Rubalcaba characterize these calls as a "new asylum movement," especially within psychiatry.[74] Such policies include the construction of new homeless shelters (which have many restrictions and house unsheltered people only temporarily); the upgrading and reform of state mental hospitals; and the segregation of those labeled as mentally disabled in the criminal justice system, especially by the creation of new facilities or beds in existing prisons and jails. This increase in state capacity toward reinstitutionalization and away from community living and adequate services in the community or peer support or noncoercive and affirming health care is joined by various measures that increase social control over those who are psychiatrized and criminalized. These measures include bills that attempt to alter involuntary commitment laws and the increased use of transfers from the criminal justice system to the mental health system.[75]

It is therefore baffling that some advocates use the plight of mad and disabled prisoners as a rallying cry for reincarceration in psychiatric beds or hospitals as a solution, and not a continuation, of the problems inherent in incarceration. As discussed throughout the book, incarceration and especially carceral enclosures should be thought of in the broadest way, including nursing homes, psych facilities, and other segregated spaces in which one does not control one's life. Others call not for psychiatrization outside but for increased treatment options within the prison as a way to address at least some of the distress experienced by prisoners with mental health differences. But if the problem is endemic to incarceration itself, creating more psychiatric units or options in prison is not a solution but part of the problem. If incarceration disables and exacerbates mental health conditions, as I have suggested here, then "treatment behind bars" is an oxymoron.

In essence, policies that follow the "new asylum" axiom increase the scope of incarceration, albeit in different locales. By painting deinstitutionalization as the culprit in the plight of people with mental health differences inside and outside of prisons, the disabling effects and legitimacy of the prison remain intact; this is the real danger of this discourse, disguised as common sense and apolitical in nature. This is why I contend that it is important to conceptualize deinstitutionalization as a logic, a mind-set, a movement, and not just as a social and historical process. It is not something that "happened" but a potential ideological shift in the social response to difference. It was not successful on all fronts, and I critique the movement and its consequences throughout the book, but it was obviously radical enough to create a backlash counterdiscourse, one so successful that it is taken as an axiom.

The *Frontline* episode "The New Asylums" reinforces these tropes that call for "a return to the asylum." Much like the discourse on housing insecurity, here the audience is left with the false choice between reinstitutionalization (medical pathologization) or criminalization as the only two axes to deal with harm and extreme mental distress, both leading to different forms of incarceration and both individualizing and pathologizing what is a deep socioeconomic problem. Any discussion of alternatives to these so-called choices is left out of the episode and out of most current discussions of mental health in prisons, or outside of prison, or the plight of those who are housing insecure. The viewer surmises that deinstitutionalization created not only a lack of options for the "mentally ill prisoners" that led them to prison but also created danger to the community to which they were hastily released. This panic-inducing discourse of danger of those deinstitutionalized is the topic of the next chapter, about resistance to integration in housing in terms of race-ability, another discourse of the backlash against deinstitutionalization.

5

Resistance to Inclusion and Community Living

NIMBY, Desegregation, and Race-ability

Once deinstitutionalization was under way, the urgent question became, where should those deinstitutionalized live? Where should people who need support reside if not in carceral locales? One of the proposed solutions at the time was the creation of group homes in residential neighborhoods. But this was not done without a fight. In 1986, the *New York Times* ran an editorial about ongoing clashes over the construction of group homes in the state, especially in suburban communities:

> As state agencies are trying to establish hundreds of additional group homes over the next few years under the policy known as "mainstreaming," disputes and protests are intensifying in New York City's suburbs and other parts of the state.... To many residents of such communities, mainstreaming means the threat of falling property values, diminished personal security and more frequent encounters with the disabled than they might wish.... The disabled "have as much right as anyone else to live in the community of their choice," said Margaret Deutsch, president of the Special Education Parent-Teachers Association Council of Western Suffolk. Attempts to keep the disabled separate, she said, are tantamount to "*an apartheid.*"[1]

To understand how and why this resistance to disability desegregation was "tantamount to an apartheid," as the editorial suggests, this chapter focuses on the ways resistance to integration in housing relates to criminal pathologization and race-ability. Although deinstitutionalization had been discussed, researched, and conceptualized as a move toward community

161

integration, almost no systemic study to date relates it to racial integration that preceded it.[2]

These forms of resistance to community living (especially the construction of group homes or facilities in the community for so-called special populations, including those exiting prisons and institutions and drug and disability rehabilitation programs) as posed by those currently living "in the community" are often referred to as NIMBY (not in my backyard). I show how NIMBY was composed of various affective economies that resisted integration, such as safety/danger, paternalism, change in the makeup of the neighborhood, and fear of decreased property values, all couched around notions of heteronormative racial-ableism. To combat NIMBY and what I term reverse gentrification (when undesired and less resourced populations move into the "neighborhood"), advocates supporting community living in the 1970s and 1980s utilized affective economies of innocence and likeness to (re)gain acceptance and inclusion. I analyze this tactic and show the price of being included/incorporated through adherence to normative assumptions of race-ability as Dis Inc. I also analyze deinstitutionalization as a desegregation measure, one that paralleled and intersected with racial desegregation in the United States.

Desegregation, NIMBY, and Race-ability

In previous chapters, I began to chart a genealogy of deinstitutionalization of psychiatric hospitals and residential institutions for people with intellectual and developmental disabilities. I continue this track here to showcase what happened after institutions and psych hospitals closed. Together with the previous chapter and then continued into the next chapter, on resistance to closure of carceral enclosures, I construct a genealogy of the *backlash* to deinstitutionalization. The previous chapter focused on the negative reaction to the closure of psychiatric hospitals, leading to outcries about prisons as the new asylums. Here I focus on backlash to the closure of institutions for people with intellectual and/or developmental disability (I/DD) labels. This backlash took the form of vocal and violent resistance to the integration and incorporation of disabled and deinstitutionalized people, and this resistance looked eerily similar to struggles against racial integration in housing.

I therefore posit that desegregation (or inclusion) in the disability arena followed, paralleled, and intersected with racial desegregation. Deinstitutionalization could therefore be conceived as a desegregation measure, as a way to provide services, housing, and education to people with disabilities in the same location and manner as is provided for nondisabled people. This was the core of the normalization principle in the field of I/DD at the time, which stated that people with mental disabilities should be living in a way as similar to their peers as possible, in all areas of life.[3]

This NIMBY discourse was justified based on recurring affective registers. The resistance to the construction of group homes, halfway houses, rehab facilities for those dealing with addictions, and community living for those exiting prisons and for people with disabilities (especially psychiatric, developmental, and cognitive) can be grouped into a few themes: affective use of fear of crime or danger (toward residents or those moving in); unwanted change in neighborhood infrastructure (traffic, noise, pollution, garbage); decrease in property value; and significant change in the current makeup of the neighborhood.[4] As I will show, race-ableism, class/income, and criminal pathologization are at the heart of this moral panic over the "new neighbors."

The connection between segregated populations (people of color, particularly black, and people with disabilities—and, of course, disabled people of color) was discussed in previous chapters, especially through the lens of racial criminal pathologization, but suffice to say that segregation in separate facilities was, and in many cases still is, the rule and not the exception in relation to race-ability, whether in segregated housing, recreation, or services. Hence the allusion to apartheid in the editorial with which I began the chapter is not far-fetched, although it is used there only in an analogical way, as was often the case. For instance, in the *Cleburne* court case, discussed later in the chapter, Judge Marshall expressed his opinion about the institutionalization of people with disabilities in this way: "A regime of state-mandated segregation and degradation soon emerged that in its virulence and bigotry rivaled, and indeed paralleled, the worst excesses of Jim Crow. Massive custodial institutions were built to warehouse the retarded for life."[5] In this example, Jim Crow and institutionalization are seen as distinct from each other but moving on parallel tracks and logics.

By conceptualizing deinstitutionalization as desegregation, my intent is not merely to allude to an analogical inference between the two, as in this court ruling. In fact, in what follows, I detail the dangers of such analogies, as opposed to *intersections* of race and disability in calls for integration (in this case, in community services and housing). However, I believe it is essential for both desegregation movements to take stock of the vast similarity between the virulent resistance to housing integration based on race-ability.

Many of the sentiments, tactics, underlying logics, and in some cases similarly situated groups of people used to defy and actively resist racial integration were also used during attempts to create integrated housing for those with disabilities, including disabled people of color.

Resistance to Racial Integration in Housing

Resistance to racial integration in housing took many forms, from the implicit, including glares, intolerance, not associating with people of color who moved in, to outward violence. The latter included a variety of intimidation tactics, such as destruction of the properties of prospective buyers, threats, arson, demonstrations in which rocks or other objects were thrown, heckling, intimidating phone calls, and more. These acts of violence were coordinated and not a sporadic phenomenon. In *As Long as They Don't Move Next Door,* Stephen Grant Meyer shows how, from the 1920s through the 1950s, such actions were sanctioned by the larger community—from public officials and interest groups, such as real estate agencies and white supremacy organizations, to more implicit "block improvement" or other associations.[6]

Post World War II, as rights discourse was becoming more prevalent, residents started utilizing the discourse of homeowners' rights, especially around the "right to choose," in racially coded or at times explicit manners, depending on the area and era. Some cities even passed homeowners' rights ordinances to protect themselves from the desegregation, or "open housing," movement. Such ordinances stated that homeowners have the right to choose their friends and associations as well as the right to choose their brokers, real estate agents, or buyers. For instance, as Thomas Sugrue chronicles in relation to Detroit, between 1943 and 1965 whites founded at least 192 neighborhood organizations, such as "improvement associations," "civic or protective associations," and homeowner's associations.[7] Their stated goals were to guard the investment of residents as homeowners; to improve the neighborhood, aesthetically and otherwise; and to protect and defend the neighborhood and its residents, especially women and children, from disorderly external elements.[8] These homeowner's associations' underlying purpose, however, was to protect the "possessive investment in Whiteness," to borrow from George Lipsitz.[9]

Homeownership and the concept of NIMBY is important to understand as part of the *longue durée* of property and land ownership of what came to be known as the United States (i.e., who can even have a backyard and own land). The idea of property rights is formulated upon the construction of borders, the nation-state, and indigenous land theft. The assumption that one can become a homeowner is based on the erasure of native peoples and their claims to ancestral lands. It presumes that one can own something like land (as opposed to being a guardian and protector of land and the environment, as espoused by indigenous practices) and assumes that this land is ripe for the taking, that it is just there for capitalist consumption and not as a result of genocidal and settler violence. Taken from this stance, the "right" to be a homeowner a priori assumes "rights" as a framework for violence.

The history of property ownership in the United States is also entangled with, if not derived from, the history and praxis of slavery as legal ownership of people as property. It was the intersection between race and property, and not each on its own, that created and maintained racial oppression and established white supremacy in the United States, as Cheryl Harris writes.[10] This interweaving of race and property enshrined itself in law and legal claims to property, what today we might call property rights at large, as well as whiteness and race as property of identity, as Harris elaborates. This was done through various mechanisms, such as the violence of designating and treating racialized people, especially black, as property and assigning property rights to white males but not to Native Americans. Thus property ownership is not a neutral discourse but is only perceived as such. To quote Harris, "Whiteness and property share a common premise—a conceptual nucleus—of a right to exclude."[11] That everyone has a right to own property really betrays the history of colonialism, slavery and heteropatriarchy and masks privilege as a matter of fact as opposed to a matter of violence.

Outward violence was not the only means of dispossession and resisting desegregation, however. Political economy and government interests played a key role in creating de facto racial housing segregation from the 1920s onward. Realtors convinced white home owners that their property value would depreciate if people of color were to move into their neighborhoods, lenders refused to provide mortgages to black people moving into white neighborhoods, and restrictive zoning laws were enacted, partially to quell white protest. Richard Rothstein also shows that racial segregation in housing was the result of government policies in which local and federal guidelines defined and maintained where whites and blacks could live.[12] Without such policies, other factors, such as bias and individual racism, white flight, class differences, and redlining, in which banks and lenders don't provide mortgages in areas considered for people of color, would still play a role, but not as much as they were allowed to play in the absence of state sanctions. Ultimately, and I agree with Rothstein here, such policies, formal and informal, were rooted in systemic racism. They were sanctioned by the state and its actors. For example, the role of the police in maintaining and instigating these acts of vandalism, arson, and other violence against desegregation should not be underestimated. But the state also resides within people. This systemic racism manifested in homeowners' actions, who felt entitled to live with mostly Christian and white peers, although sometimes these desires were couched in color-neutral terms such as fear of "crime" or "safety," of rights and choice, as will be demonstrated later.[13]

An intersectional analysis attuned to race-ability and gender/sexuality is instructive here, as the discourse of racial criminal pathologization was at the heart of fears of housing integration. The battle over the fate of the (white normative) neighborhood was a thoroughly community affair. Women, mostly married and presumably heterosexual, played a crucial role in maintaining the boundaries of who did and did not belong in the neighborhood. Gender also offered a point of security during anti-desegregation protests, as police were more reluctant to arrest white women and children.[14] As Sugrue shows, women were the forerunners of neighborhood associations and utilized much of their time to maintain the status quo in their neighborhoods. Women have also had much tighter connection to the neighborhood through formal (such as parent–teacher meetings) and informal (neighborhood potlucks) networks, which they then could utilize if they felt threatened. This was related to the cult of domesticity cultivated after World War II, in which women were taught to see their homes and families as sacred spaces and their role was to keep the home and children *safe* and *healthy*. This imperative, connecting "danger" with disability, is part of racial criminal pathologization. This manifested in fear grounded in racism and ableism of the different raced/disabled body (and mind) moving in next door, which presented the antithesis of a healthy and safe family and community.

Moral panics of people of color moving into predominantly white blocks or neighborhoods, I suggest, were also founded on beliefs of what a "black neighborhood" looks like—stereotypically and metaphorically. The nightmare image of the idyllic (white) neighborhood was projected into stereotypes of the so-called black ghetto or inner city, from fearing noise and lack of space to shabby appearance of the houses or yards.[15] This imagery and its affective economies led, at least in part, to failed policies like broken windows policing. For example, Robert Taylor Homes ("the projects") in Chicago became synonymous with the discourse of urban crime, which was centered and blamed mostly on poor black men. But as Rashad Shabazz meticulously demonstrates in *Spatializing Blackness*, buildings elicit affective reactions; they are not mere structures but represent social and political ideas. Since black people, especially men, were already perceived as criminally inclined, the objective of urban public housing was to contain and surveil their every step.[16]

Criminal pathologization and race-ability was thus foundational to these fears of integration. The racist imagery of dis-order (crime) and dis-ease as inherent in black populations and locales, as the two were often conflated, formed the basis of the fear of integration as well as legitimation for it. The black urban neighborhood itself seemed plagued, sick, pathological, which conflated fears of disability (as deficit) and antiblack racism into a moral panic over the "new neighbors." I therefore contend that much resistance to racial integration was constructed through ableist imagery of the black urban neighborhood as a plague, a blight, a contagion.[17] The fear is that the "new neighbors" (who are of color) would bring with them whatever contagion plagued their residence of origin and that this would spread and contaminate the new neighborhood, ultimately causing it to look and be the same. To racial majority publics (especially whites),[18] this seemed like the inherent nature of life in black urban communities, rather than stemming from their own racist assumptions or being the result of deliberate state violence and neglect. As a result, some neighborhoods or communities were seen as diseased and in need of fixing or rehabilitation, but others were deemed "terminally ill" and in need of state killing. Such was the case during the euphemistically called "urban renewal," in which certain areas and housing complexes were flattened by city and state officials, to uproot the problem from the ground (and raise in its stead either nothing or unaffordable high-rises, i.e., gentrification). If such fears seem like mere metaphors grounded in race-ableism and not directly about fear of disabled people, I find it important to note that the fear of the "new neighbors," NIMBY attitudes, in the context of race or disability, were also not based on real people but on ideas of "them" and what "they" might do.

Mobilizing against Group Homes and the Case of Cleburne

In examining the history of housing desegregation an important and over-looked connection should be made with the fact that potential and actual homes of people with disabilities (often regardless of but sometimes in addition to their race/ethnicity) were also subject to fierce and violent resistance to community integration.[19] My intent here is not to claim that resisting housing integration based on race was exactly the same as in the disability arena or that people with disabilities are not raced, or vice versa; rather, it is to point to the ways in which both forms of virulent exclusion also brought to bear the connections between racism and ableism and the conflation of criminalization with pathologization. As one potential proprietor of a group home said in 1978 after withdrawing her house following immense pressure: "It's like the Ku Klux Klan . . . and this came from people who used to be my neighbors and friends."[20]

Resistance to community living, especially the construction of group homes for people with intellectual or psychiatric disabilities, was prevalent in acts ranging from the mundane and implicit to the visible and life threatening. Common tactics were similar to those of racial segregation and took the form of circulating petitions, suing the city or group home proprietor, convening town hall meetings, initiating media campaigns, threatening those who were selling their property or land to be built on, demonstrating in front of the home in question, or lobbying and making political dealings with local politicians, among other tactics.

Group homes for those with intellectual disabilities were even firebombed on several occasions, in Staten Island, Washington, D.C., and Michigan, among other locales.[21] For example, in 1978 in Long Island, an arsonist entered a home in which ten adults with labels of intellectual disability lived and poured gasoline throughout the first floor. The family lost their house and their dog in the fire.[22] According to legal scholar Laura C. Bornstein, arson was a common tactic used by opponents of group homes. In 1985, arsonists burned down a group home for those with intellectual disabilities near Tallahassee, Florida, before it was scheduled to open.[23]

I want to turn now to an instructive case that anchors much of the argument against disability-based integration: the first legal challenge to resisting the construction of group homes, *City of Cleburne (Texas) v. Cleburne Living Center.* In 1980, Cleburne Living Center (CLC) purchased a large, four-bedroom, two-bath house for the purpose of establishing the first group home in Cleburne, to house about thirteen people with labels of intellectual disabilities and staff. The city refused to approve the group home because of its interpretation of zoning laws. Basically, the city of Cleburne required CLC to acquire a special permit, which was needed in that area for the operation of "hospitals for the insane or feeble-minded, or alcoholic or drug addicts, or penal or correctional institutions." Even though this was a residential house, the city classified CLC as a "hospital for the insane or feebleminded," and then denied giving the home this special permit use.[24] CLC then sued the city, both on the merits of the case and because it discriminated against so-called mentally retarded persons in violation of the equal protection clause.

The use of the Fourteenth Amendment, which contains the equal protection clause, is what makes this case unique and well known in legal discourse. As one legal commentator describes, *Cleburne* was the "largest constitutional 'moment' for disability law."[25] The city won the case in the district court, but CLC appealed to the Fifth Circuit, which ultimately reprimanded the city for the outlandish claims it had put forth in trying to prevent the home from opening. The court of appeals reversed the district court ruling. The U.S. Supreme Court then disagreed that "the mentally retarded" should be regarded as a quasi-suspect class. Quasi-suspect classification would have enabled "the mentally retarded," as a group of people, to receive higher or closer scrutiny by the courts when bringing claims of discrimination under the equal protection clause. However, the Supreme Court did agree that the zoning ordinance was invalid in the ways the city of Cleburne applied it. The case is therefore considered an immense missed opportunity for anti-discrimination litigation and protection for people with disabilities, especially mental disabilities, but a success on the level of understanding the legal difference between an institution and a group home.

The assertions put forth by the defendants, the city of Cleburne, will come to repeat in many other cases of NIMBY attitudes regarding the establishment of group homes nationally. Many of the claims upon which the city objected to the operation of the home had to do with a fear of change in the makeup of the neighborhood due to increased traffic and noise, population change, safety concerns (for the residents of the "new neighbors"), and co-location fears (the house being near a school, residential neighborhood, children, or the elderly).

The city's claims demonstrated not the exception of a few outliers in the state of Texas but more lucidly the "banality of evil," to borrow from Hannah Arendt,[26] at the core of NIMBY discourse. The judges' pushback against these claims is instructive. The court turned down the city's assertion that the creation of the home would lead to an undue population density or that it would cause traffic congestion since the same house with the same number of occupants would be permitted to be built if the residents were not disabled. In addition, the proposed residents themselves did not drive. The city council claimed that residents of the home could be bullied by the local junior high students, but the court discovered that the school had thirty students who were themselves intellectually disabled. The last claim the city put forth, that the house was sitting on a five-hundred-year floodplain, was not even addressed by the court. The court most meaningfully asserted that the prejudices and fears of the citizenry were not of legitimate governmental interest.

Another lesson from the *Cleburne* case and others like it is that much like homeownership, zoning regulations are not neutral enterprises. From their outset in the 1920s, zoning rules were ways to turn explicit racist ideology as well as policies coded as color neutral (it's only bureaucracy, it's just about geography) into de facto racial segregation, as Rothstein shows in *The Color of Law*.[27] These regulations came about as a means to create and maintain segregation and homogenous communities by designating certain areas as inappropriate for the creation of multiunit homes, in order to exclude people of color and/or disabled people, and on the other hand, designate certain areas as wholly appropriate for such functions as discarding industrial waste, which is an example of environmental racism that is also part of the biopolitics of debilitation.[28]

What are we to make of such appeals? I want to caution us against simply characterizing such NIMBY sentiments as cold manipulation on behalf of privileged stakeholders, although such affective usage certainly had its role to play here. In *The Emotional Politics of Racism,* Paula Ioanide demonstrates that people are not just duped into superficial solutions based on false promises, but instead, in this analysis, they are given responses to situations that genuinely worry them.[29] Instead of constructing a dichotomy of false consciousness (people just don't know any better) or sheer evil and hate (although, again, these registers play out in NIMBY wars), Ioanide suggests that people reap affective rewards from investing in the state and its punitive, and I would add normalizing, apparatuses—wars, policing, putting away bad/strange people, and so on. It also provides people in less privileged positions the ability to feel, and often be, superior to others— undocumented people, the welfare queen, those imprisoned, the disabled. My aim is to shift the discourse away from sorting out "the racists" or specific "evildoers" in this NIMBY phenomenon and toward analyzing affective economies of exclusion.

Affective and Material Economies of Inclusion and Exclusion

A useful approach to analyzing the discourse of resistance around housing integration and the construction of group homes is by utilizing the work of theorist Sarah Ahmed.[30] Ahmed, like other theorists in the "affective turn," challenges the assumption that emotions are individual matters that come from "within"; instead, she suggests that they create the boundaries of bodies, collectives, and discourses. These affective forces construct those who are the bearers of negative attachments as Others and as not part of the collective. It is the emotional reading of fear and hatred that binds the community together and indeed constructs it as "a community." Therefore Ahmed refers to these forces as affective economies.

Ahmed demonstrates that these attachments work best when the "ordinary citizen" is perceived to be in crisis and under attack. In the case of the struggle against the construction of group homes and the production of NIMBY attitudes, it is not so much the "ordinary citizen" but normalcy itself that is seen as being under attack.[31] Normativity and the American, either imagined or felt, way of life (the American Dream, historically white segregated communities of "like-minded people," and so on) are seen as coming under attack. Such affective discourses shift the locus of victimhood from those who are not allowed in to those who oppose their integration as the wounded party. The affective economy of fear creates not only a sense of shared community as a community in crisis struggling to maintain its core values, but also what it is not—the object that is seen as threatening its existence.[32]

One of the pervasive affective registers used to resist disability integration was fear of danger. During deinstitutionalization of those labeled as intellectually disabled and the closure of psychiatric facilities especially, a plethora of editorials and testimonials decried the release of "dangerous" individuals into the community. For example, during the public hearing on Cleburne's permit application, one town resident said, "It's not a very pleasant thought to go to bed and know there's thirteen demented, self-afflicted people across the street from you."[33] In the court proceedings, the city's belief that the home would cause disruption in the neighborhood was backed only by a single anecdote of an intellectually disabled man who had stolen, and later returned, his neighbor's mail and in fact did not live in Cleburne at all.[34] Registers of danger had been stuck to disability, especially psychiatric disability, because of fears that disabled people could cause harm to others, even unknowingly because they "don't know the difference between right and wrong" or they might start a fire or cause damage by mistake, or because they are malicious and can't stop themselves. These sentiments were heard and reproduced in various arenas where potential integration of people with disabilities might occur, including forums held by community members regarding the establishment of group homes as well as in campaigns to stop the closure of a certain facility in a local community.

Danger was not the only affective score used. The other side of the coin was the register of safety, but this time not of the community but of the new residents. For example, in the *Cleburne* case, it was the proximity to a school and the possibility that the new residents would be teased by the students. In this case, the potential residents were scooped under a familiar stereotype of intellectual disability, that of innocence and being childlike. Other examples given by the city are a lack of a yard, the existence of dogs in the neighborhood, and the land sitting on a five-hundred-year floodplain. What all these arguments have in common is that they are described as for the disabled's "own good." These claims, such as in the *Cleburne* case and numerous others, demonstrate the role of exceptionalism and paternalism, which are often hailed as forms of caring or empathy among nondisabled publics, in resisting the construction of such facilities. But this is a double standard, of course; not having a yard on the property or enough light on the street might be a legitimate concern were it not used only against so-called special populations, be they disabled people, substance users, or those exiting prisons.

This register of safety can often be couched in terms of moral superiority, as in the turn to exceptionality, but also in terms of genuine concern for people who are constructed as marginalized and need to be taken care of. For example, Myra Piat conducted an instructive qualitative study on reactions to the construction of three new facilities in Montreal, Canada, in the 1990s.[35] One was for psychiatrized people who had been institutionalized for at least a decade, the second was for children with a variety of disabilities, and the third was a halfway house for women exiting prisons. One of the pervasive themes she found was that the current residents were complaining not so much about the new residents as about the facilities' operation—that in essence, the people who would reside there deserve better. One of the opposers of the group home, for example, even went as far as to say that the so-called group home is just another form of incarceration:

> These kids are being put in a prison. If they would be in an institution there would be no difference at all. It's just because it's a house. But it's not different. In an institution they will be locked in. Here they are locked in too.

Another stated that the home did not provide a family-type atmosphere and concluded that it was an institution based in the community.[36] As I demonstrated in the introduction to this book, it is important to name and analyze the lives of those institutionalized and imprisoned in tandem, as incarceration is a pervasive phenomenon, especially for people with disabilities, recent immigrants, gender nonconforming people, people of color, or people at any intersection of marginality. In this sense, affective responses that compare group homes to prisons are both problematic and important. But these arguments are then used to justify the exclusion of certain populations from secure housing or services. In other words, while it is important to posit the segregated lives of marginalized populations, including people with disabilities, as forms of incarceration and to advocate for better quality of life, it is equally important to examine the exceptionality and moral superiority that underscore such claims and how race-ability supremacy is interlinked therein.

Similar tropes also operated in racial housing desegregation cases. For example, in the 1970s, the Chicago Housing Authority was sued for failing to desegregate housing in the city. The U.S. attorney general at the time defended the decision not to place public housing in white areas by stating, "There will be an enormous practical impact on innocent communities who have to bear the burden of the housing, who will have to house a plaintiff class from Chicago, which they wronged in no way."[37] Housing integration, in this case by race, is seen as a *punishment* inflicted on "the innocent," who do not deserve it because they did not commit any crime or do any harm themselves. Discrimination, purposeful un-distribution of resources and racism, is not seen as ill doing or as posing harm. The mere existence of black people is defended here as an undue burden, and the boundaries of victim–offender, innocence–harm, are drawn even in the absence of an actual "crime."

Connecting these examples to Ahmed's work, it becomes clear that the fear of the Other and fear of integration not only involves the defense of the boundaries of the community but *in affect* creates these borders. By constructing these borders, the "community" creates itself by standing apart from the objects it fears or feels threatened by, that is, people of color, those labeled as developmentally or psychiatrically disabled, people who were imprisoned, and any intersection of these. This helps explain the reasons and the processes by which the "community" constructs itself as qualitatively different from so-called deviant elements, such as those formerly imprisoned or institutionalized, disabled, mad, queer, or substance users, even though such populations have always been part of every community, whether this is acknowledged or not.

One example demonstrating the construction of borders around the "community" is in the practice of *notification*. In many cases, advocates or owners of group homes or treatment facilities, such as for those formerly imprisoned or institutionalized and those dealing with substance use, let the residents of the neighborhood know in advance that such a facility will be built and explain to them the potential implications. Although the 1988 federal Fair Housing Amendments and the 1990 Americans with Disabilities Act gave administrators in the disability/mental health arena the legal authority to forgo the practice of notification when establishing shared supervised houses for disabled people, this practice had been used during the heyday of deinstitutionalization and is still in use today. Although this is done to prevent future opposition to the creation of the homes, in actuality, it does the opposite. As studies show, this practice does not work to qualm the suspicion and opposition of potential neighbors and is more likely to create greater levels of resistance.[38]

However, what I want to focus on here is not the *effectiveness* of the practice of notification, whether it achieves its stated goal of facilitating connections between new and established residents of the neighborhood, but its *affectiveness*. Under the affective economy framework I am proposing here, the practice of notifying current residents of future potential residents can never create a true connection between the two groups because the practice by itself constructs the populations as significantly different. It creates a situation in which residents are warned of the existence of future residents, highlighting only one characteristic of their lives such as that they have a disability or were imprisoned. This, again, comes out of the affective and ideological attachment to exceptionalism, demonstrated previously, such as the *Cleburne* case, which assumes that those criminalized, psychiatrized, disabled, or drug using *should* be dealt with differently, often "for their own good."

The practice of notifications also creates a hierarchy between the groups, in which the current residents have to consent to the presence of the incoming residents. This creates a power imbalance, wherein the incoming residents have no say, although legally they supposedly have the same "right" to reside there. Since notifications make it feel like residing in a diverse neighborhood is somehow a choice and not a social mandate, it should not be surprising that many current residents feel like they can and should fight against it.

Social science research has also contributed to the construction of borders around the "community," I contend, especially by the constant surveying of public attitudes toward community integration. NIMBY surveys ask about attitudes of acceptance of facilities being built next door or new people coming into the neighborhood and whether the individual approves or disapproves, and which populations they most disapprove of. Numerous studies in social science (especially in sociology, social psychology, and geography) have tried to measure these characteristics and determine which is the optimal and the worst population to come in contact with which community.[39] One has to wonder if the creation of panic discourse around community living for formerly incarcerated, imprisoned, and institutionalized populations was further enhanced by the constant need to survey attitudes about this very phenomenon.

The need to continually survey these attitudes cements the idea that these are valid and legitimate questions, and that they are neutral. But the construction of such surveys assumes that there is something fundamentally wrong, or at least qualitatively different, in people who have been imprisoned or have disability labels, and therefore there is a need to ask how people feel about having such Othered groups in their midst. If the perspective was that many disabilities are invisible or undiagnosed and that most of us know people who are psychiatrized or criminalized or are such people ourselves, then such questions would be quite nonsensical. Such surveys, therefore, are not neutral repositories of attitudes but could also be construed as reinforcers of perspectives that further marginalize and Other certain communities, while and by asking about their seeming inclusion.

Both the practice of notifications and NIMBY attitude surveys can be construed as examples of Dis Inc. The discourse of Dis Inc. captures the disabled subject as a commodity for profit in a segregation/incarceration economy, in this case, group homes. At the same time, the disabled subject's appeals for inclusion and incorporation, as the other side of Inc., can only be done under current normative frames (will not be bullied, will not change the neighborhood). Dis Inc., when done through utilizing affective economies of fear and the practice of notifications, for example, creates difference (based on race-ability and connected to gender/sexuality and their normative frames) as foreign and then tries to incorporate it through frameworks that ultimately legitimate its further segregation (they have different needs, it is for their own good, they are qualitatively different and therefore need to be granted permission to enter nonsegregated private and public spaces). Such practices of incorporation by exclusion/inclusion construct and feed the boundaries of belonging in integrated settings. They affectively and discursively construct Others who can only belong through the grace or charity of white nondisabled property owners.

In addition to affective registers of safety/danger, paternalism, and exceptionalism, the other line of argument against housing integration is the fear of decreased property values. The claim of decline in property value following the construction of group homes and other welfare facilities in the area has never been substantiated, as decades' worth of social science research demonstrates.[40] In *There Goes the Neighborhood . . .* , a 1990 meta-analysis of the fifty-eight studies that had been done to that date regarding the effects of group homes and treatment facilities on the neighborhoods in which they are placed, the researchers report, "No studies were found to indicate a negative impact of group home placement upon any aspect of neighborhood life. The studies found that group home placement had not lowered property values or increased turnover, had not increased crime, and had not changed the neighborhood's character. The group homes had not deteriorated or become conspicuous institutional landmarks. The studies did find that all communities had come to accept group homes, and that group home residents have benefited from the access to a wider community life."[41]

Despite the immense evidence to the contrary, the argument around declining property values is still pervasive. But I am equally interested in the reasons why so much energy was given to maintaining the idea that it is financially feasible to include Others in the neighborhood. In other words, what kinds of knowledges, discourses, and questions cannot be calculated in such studies—what does not factor into this economy of abandonment, as Elizabeth Povinelli describes our times?[42] Such discourses invisibilize that property is a product of racism and settler colonialism in the United States, as I was discussing earlier in regard to the creation of homeowner's associations and notions of rights.

In other words, it is the neoliberal calculations of worth that are hidden in these ideas of property values as prices to pay for inclusion. Connecting this to Dis Inc. would show that the price of incorporation is cultural and moral. As I said in earlier chapters, I am using the word incorporation to signal both the cultural and social incorporation of minority difference[43] into the status quo and incorporation as a structure of political economic profit-making impetuses, whether through discourses of cost-effectiveness under neoliberalism or literal corporations raking in profits from incarceration and disposability under plain old capitalism, such as group homes, halfway houses, and prisons. As Lisa Duggan shows, one of the characteristics of neoliberalism as it emerged in the United States in the late 1970s was a new form of "equality," one that does not include redistributive demands, and if it does, it is upward.[44] It was designed for global consumption and a culture of market competitiveness and meritocracy, to cut anything that impedes or could potentially stand in the way of profit making or economic growth, which became the most important value and goal of statecraft. One major way this ascent to neoliberalism took place was by making it value neutral. Who would be against growth, efficiency, effectiveness? Neoliberalism cemented managerial governance over ethical and moral considerations. By so doing, the discourse shifted from public debate and activism to the hands of so-called professionals and economic experts. In this case, it is clear that the discourse of cost-effectiveness took precedence over discussions of the social worth of, or cultural cost to, inclusion of difference. It also became up to such experts literally to measure the cost of integration, in housing, for example.

Segregation in the Community: Reverse Gentrification

Much like their counterparts in the desegregation arena, residents who had the ability to resist or influence decisions regarding the placement of those with disabilities, especially those exiting institutions, psychiatric hospitals, and at times prisons, were mostly families with means who resided in middle- or upper-class dwellings in the city or in "desirable" suburban locales. The result of this resistance was the construction of what geographers Jennifer Wolch and Michael Dear termed "service dependent ghettos" in inner cities in North America,[45] brought forth by exclusion from suburban and affluent communities and in search of affordable housing and access to transportation and services.

What the phenomenon of the construction of shared homes and facilities for those decarcerated shows us is the effects of what I call *reverse gentrification*. In other words, what happens when "undesirable" folk move into an already resource-depleted neighborhood? By undesirable, I am referring again to the consequences of racial criminal pathologization and the moral panics around the figure of the criminal and mentally disabled. As I stated earlier, much had been written in the social science literature about the phenomenon of NIMBY in relation to group homes and deinstitutionalization. But little attention had been paid to the role of race, let alone settler colonialism and white supremacy, in the NIMBY phenomenon in the *disability* arena, with a few exceptions.[46] Nancy Scheper-Hughes's ethnographic work is useful in this lacuna. She looked at discharged mental patients in South Boston in the 1970s and found that they were negatively affected by the exclusionary and racist attitudes of people in the neighborhood.[47] The people there had very rigid notions of what a community is, and they constructed boundaries that kept the patients as outsiders even while they were residing in the community.

In the I/DD field, geographer Robert Wilton's study of community opposition to "special needs" housing in San Pedro, California, is important, as it demonstrates the ways NIMBY reactions facilitated the reproduction of race-ability supremacy.[48] This was done through racializing what Wilton terms "service clients," by linking the rise in service users in the area to more general local demographic change, so that *all* nonwhite residents were now constructed as "special needs" populations. In other words, people of color were pathologized and deemed dependent or "special needs," regardless of their actual diagnosis or label. Dependency, pathology, and race were thus linked through this NIMBY discourse in an attempt to maintain what Wilton terms the socio-spatial privileges of whiteness.[49] Wilton also shows how NIMBY proponents used a romanticized and "whitened" discourse of community to mark "special needs" clients as out of place. This demonstrates the seemingly color-neutral ideology discussed earlier in relation to housing segregation, by which populations are racialized and penalized, but without any explicit mention of race; instead, there are allusions to increases in crime, increases in noise, or decreases in property values, which are coded terms.

The general lack of intersectional analysis of race and disability in relation to deinstitutionalization and NIMBY, especially in the field of intellectual disability, can be observed further in policy reports of the era, warning of the effects of reverse gentrification mostly on people with intellectual and psychiatric disabilities. For instance, a 1981 study of deinstitutionalization in Los Angeles worryingly pointed out that many residents of boarding homes had little contact with their communities because they were isolated in poor neighborhoods with high crime rates, as a result of NIMBY resistance excluding them from more resourced areas.[50] Moreover, they stated that "many of the mentally disabled residents were a racial minority in the immediate neighborhood, further stigmatizing them and opening them up to victimization." Again, the assumption is that people with disabilities, I/DD in particular, are white and innocent (i.e., not dangerous), that poor neighborhoods are not, and that such locales cause inherent danger by simple association. Criminalization (coded for black, poor, "urban") and disability (white, asexual, innocent) are seen here as distinct.

Such advocates also state that living in such "service ghettos" compromises the principle of normalization (discussed in chapter 2 as the need to live as much as possible like one's nondisabled peers) and the ability for rehabilitation and living a normal life for people with disabilities.[51] What I want to pause and elaborate on is the idea of the so-called normal neighborhood. Assuming this is not a normal living environment for those deinstitutionalized and disabled assumes that there is a monolithic criterion as to what comprises a "normal" living environment. If it is not clear by now, I am suggesting here that such criteria are based on colonialism, racism, and orientalism, each combined with heteropatriarchy (what Smith referred to as the three pillars of white supremacy[52]), as is the principle of normalization to begin with. You may recall that one of the critiques of normalization, discussed in chapter 2, is that it is based on white, settler, middle-class, nondisabled, heteronormative assumptions about what constitutes being on par with one's nondisabled peers (for example, peers on what level? And how do race, class, gender, sexuality, or nationality play into these figurations?). Because of the assumption that rehabilitation cannot be achieved in such an abnormal environment, and because such neighborhoods often lack opportunities for affordable recreational activities, diverse amenities, stores, and so on, policy makers in the disability arena advocate for the construction of group homes and other facilities in more affluent, and presumably white, areas. Such policy and analysis miss an important opportunity for creating coalitions to improve these resource-depleted areas and neighborhoods, for the benefit of everyBody. This is also a direct consequence of reverse gentrification, the power of NIMBY, and the lack of intersectional analysis.

One problematic tactic used by advocates for those with developmental disabilities, to resist the creation of what they called "group home ghettos," was to compare them to the plight of African Americans. Such analogies obscure the ways in which race and disability intersect in policy and historically, as well as within the lives of disabled people of color. This can be seen, for example, in the 1986 analysis and recommendations of some in the American Planning Association, who stated that

> ostensibly, these measures are promoted to prevent the establishment of group home "ghettos"—concentrations of facilities in certain locations that may interfere with the process of normalization and integration of the developmentally disabled individual into society. . . . The harshness and unacceptability of these measures becomes apparent if one substitutes another group that has been subject to discrimination—blacks—for developmentally disabled persons in these anticoncentration provisions. . . . The traditional response to segregation has been the adoption of fair housing ordinances that promote freedom of choice in selecting suitable housing in appropriate neighborhoods, and we believe that the same ideological stance should be taken to address housing discrimination against individuals with developmental disabilities.[53]

I quote this at length to demonstrate and then unpack prevailing wisdom and policy at that time. A few things are of note here regarding race-ability in the construction of and resistance to NIMBY. First, the embedded assumption is that integration should be sought based on analogy to, but not intersection with, racial desegregation. Second, it is implied that housing desegregation based on race was successful and was achieved—an assumption that has no merit. Although the Fair Housing Act was indeed passed, through the 1968 Civil Rights Act, the attitudes around racial segregation did not necessarily change with its introduction. Acts of intimidation and violence continued throughout the twentieth century. In the late 1970s, several counties in New York State saw varied turbulence after black families moved into predominantly white blocks or neighborhoods. In one instance, a house was torched in Long Island and a cross was burned in the front yard. In 1982, protests arose and firebombing occurred after three African American residents moved into a predominantly white apartment building in Boston. Patterns of racial segregation in housing, in cities like Chicago and Detroit, actually worsened during the 1970s and 1980s to create segregated neighborhoods that exist to this day.[54] The Southern Poverty Law Center documented 130 cases of resistance to moving in by residents of color in 1989 alone.[55]

The analogy to "group home ghettos" also makes it appear as if race-based discrimination at that time, the mid-1980s, was now unthinkable due to laws and housing policies, while discrimination in the disability arena was an open field. And although it is true that housing discrimination based on disability is still pervasive, even after the Americans with Disabilities Act (ADA) was passed in 1990, so is racial housing segregation. My point is not to encourage this oppression Olympics—which group is more oppressed?—but to point to ways analogies create obstacles to coalition building around issues like housing discrimination and NIMBY.

Fighting Back: Dis Inc. and Race-ability in Resisting NIMBY

I want to end with a discussion of some of the, problematic, tactics that excluded subjects and their allies used to (re)claim the right to live in the community. To combat their characterization as Other, especially the "white Other,"[56] advocates supporting community living tried to distance their charges from affective registers such as fear of danger or changes in property values. By doing so, they unfortunately often fell into racist and ableist tropes of who belongs in the community and who does not. One such example is a 1970 pamphlet titled *New Neighbors* created by the "Community Association for the Retarded."[57] In it, advocates for people with I/DD labels are trying to persuade community residents, presumably white middle or working class, that they (people with intellectual disabilities) "mean no harm" and should pose no danger when moving into the neighborhood. I want to describe the pamphlet in some detail to analyze its affective registers, which try to counter racial criminal pathologization.

New Neighbors is a sixteen-page brochure of sorts; each page (other than the cover and credits) begins with a statement in large type and is accompanied by a photograph. The first page announces, "Some new people will be moving into your neighborhood," and then it goes on to say that one might be concerned, but that there is nothing to worry about, and that the pamphlet is made to dispel common myths about the new neighbors. First (again, on a full page with an image) is the assurance that "they are not dangerous." The myth that people with I/DD labels are dangerous is supposedly dispelled by saying that "some people believe that mentally retarded people are dangerous. This is a myth. People who are mentally retarded are no more dangerous than anyone else. This myth is partly the result of the fact that some people think that mental retardation and mental illness are the same. They are not." Furthermore, "they have no impact on crime."

I want to pause here and point to the rhetorical use of Othering and distancing, first between different disabilities—mental illness and I/DD—and second from so-called criminals. Such distancing reproduces the idea that people with labels of mental illness *are* dangerous, while those with I/DD are not, which not only deepens the construction of those with I/DD labels as innocent and childlike but at the same time paints those who are mad as harmful and dangerous. Second, danger itself is coded here. It is something affiliated with criminals—those who are guilty—who obviously do not belong in the neighborhood, while those with I/DD do. One of the outcomes of such discourses, much like the practices of notification and NIMBY surveying, is to create and maintain the borders of who should belong and who should not belong in the community and what the norms of such community are. By including one population, others must be thrown under the bus, so to speak. But the effects are also felt among those with developmental disabilities, whom the pamphlet is trying to recuperate. In the next pages, the reader is assured that "they will not lower property values," "they will not loiter and disrupt the neighborhood," and finally, "they will fit in." The burden is then placed on those with disabilities to follow these normative claims. Each of these statements is then supported by further details as well as pictures of adults or kids with disabilities who are shown playing sports, swimming, working, or volunteering.[58]

Such advocacy not only combats affective economies of fear or danger but (re)produces them as well. Capitalizing on tropes of innocence and likeness is the major strategy in such campaigns.[59] Innocence works well, as it builds on and reproduces most nondisabled people's notions of people, especially children as pictured here, with intellectual disabilities as childlike and angelic; it also combats fears of disabled people as dangerous. As I discuss in the next chapter, social recognition is only conferred on those who are deemed as normative and nonthreatening, that is, as whitewashed and productive. While easing the feelings regarding the "new neighbors," as they are called in the pamphlet, these tropes also work to distance people with intellectual disabilities from people with psychiatric disabilities ("we are not mentally ill") as well as those criminalized, and they foreclose any strategic path for coalition building in terms of desegregation and community living for the variety of people exiting carceral spaces.

While distancing those with I/DD labels from "criminals," this pamphlet and those like it simultaneously reproduce this coupling of criminal pathologization. If that coupling didn't already exist, nothing would need to be explained away and countered ("we are not criminals, only disabled"). It thus reproduces the idea that those who are criminalized and psychiatrized are indeed dangerous and to be feared, but not so people with intellectual disabilities, who will "fit in." The trope of "we are just like you" is also embedded with racial and heteronormative subtext and does not work as well if people with intellectual disabilities are prototypically thought of as queer, sexual, and nonwhite. In other words, the appeal to likeness only works if one already has an image of a person with a disability as heteronormative, white, and settler and therefore innocent, and having at least the semblance of rights. As a result, this strategy also furthers the plight of those in the disability community who are criminalized, queer, psychiatrized, multiply disabled, undocumented, or nonwhite.[60]

The last set of claims in the pamphlet, and many inclusion campaigns like it, connects likeness to a particular form of citizenship—that of white, middle-class, heteronormative suburbia. The claims that people with disabilities moving into the neighborhood "will not lower property values" and will not "disrupt the neighborhood," and that "they will fit in," play into the kind of racial disability advocacy that actually fits into, as opposed to disrupting, Dis Inc. On the surface, the goal of (white) disability rights and community living is to advocate for nonsegregation for people with disabilities.

They Will Fit In

Some people think that people who have handicaps just won't fit into their neighborhood. This is another myth. In a way, you can understand why the myth still persists.

For years, people who were handicapped were locked away. They were kept at home, out of sight of the neighbors, or in large, overcrowded institutions located away from ordinary communities. Many people have grown up without ever knowing a person who was handicapped, and as a result myths and misconceptions have developed.

In recent years, treatment of handicapped and disabled people has changed dramatically. They are becoming as much a part of the community as they are able.

When people who are disabled move into a neighborhood, they are provided with the means to live as normal a life as possible. They will use community recreational facilities, shopping and entertainment, health care, and other services. They will use the same community services you use. This is their right.

As your neighbors begin to use community facilities, hopefully you will get to know them. When you do, you may be surprised to find they don't fit preconceived notions. You will find that in many ways, people who are disabled are more like you than they are unlike you. Their handicaps do make them different, sometimes physically as well as mentally. But you will find that they are individuals with the same wants and needs you have.

You will also find they can fit into your neighborhood. And, they will be good neighbors.

Images and text from the *New Neighbors* pamphlet created by the Community Association for the Retarded in 1970. Courtesy of the Minnesota Governor's Council on Developmental Disabilities.

They Will Not Loiter And Disrupt The Neighborhood

Some people believe that if disabled people move into a neighborhood they will "hang around," loiter, or otherwise disrupt the neighborhood. This is yet another myth.

People with disabilities have things to do during the day just as you and your children do. They have various responsibilities related to their individual abilities.

If they are children, they attend school just as your kids do. Commonly the children will ride a bus to the local public school to attend special classes. If the children are too young for school, they will attend special programs designed to help them develop skills. The programs are similar to the nursery school or day care center your child may attend, but the activities are designed for children with handicaps and learning problems.

If the disabled people in your neighborhood are adults, they will be involved in a variety of activities. Like the adults in your family, some may have jobs. Others may be in vocational programs preparing them for jobs.

Some of your neighbors may be too handicapped for employment at this time. These individuals participate in programs where they develop the skills they need for daily living. The programs may teach them how to feed themselves, how to count change, or how to use public transportation. Usually such programs are held away from the home, and transportation is provided to and from the programs.

Your new neighbor's days will be as full as your days are. They have responsibilities to fulfill just as you do.

Therefore such advocacy seems to counter, both financially/materially and ideologically, discourses of Dis Inc., which posit disability as unable to be integrated, except as a commodity in carceral spaces like nursing homes and institutions. And while community living is indeed against one set of discourses of Dis Inc. (the "incarcerated" part), it is at the price of being perceived as disruptive to any normative frame, including discourses that legitimate segregation. This is the other side of Dis Inc.—the incorporation of the "disabled" as a legitimate citizen, while erasing her uniqueness and difference. To translate that into praxis, people with disabilities should be welcomed into the community, as long as they don't act or look transgressive, whether by race, class, sexuality, or disability.

To conclude, I want to point to some of the consequences of affective economies of racial pathologization. The backlash against deinstitutionalization and decarceration has taken many forms, including rejection of integration in housing for those criminalized and disabled. The affective economies at the core of NIMBY led not just to exclusion but to de facto segregation in housing and the services that come with undesirable geographical residence based on race and criminalization as well as ability and pathologization. In other words, this resistance led to an increased lack of equal opportunities for those exiting carceral spaces such as prisons, psych hospitals, and institutions. This created the reproduction of class hierarchies based on race-ability, leading to geographical segregation because of processes of reverse gentrification.

In addition to these material consequences of resistance to residential desegregation, NIMBY affectively, and effectively, led to the reproduction of boundaries between "normative" (white, settler, middle class, heteropatriarchical, citizen, and innocent) and "Other" (people of color, immigrants, the dangerous, some disabled, criminals, and the pathological). Thus such heightened affective economies of exceptionalism led not only to housing segregation post deinstitutionalization but to the ideological and material expansion of carceral institutions. In her book, Ioanide shows how emotional attachments to what Lipsitz called "the possessive investment in Whiteness" in increasingly racially integrated neighborhoods ended up expanding military–carceral logics.[61] Even while harmful activities, such as property destruction and other so-called criminal activities, were for the most part far removed from white suburbia, suburban publics felt imminent fear of the spread of criminality and urban decay. Anticipating loss of property value and other emotional investments, they turned to the presence of people of color (and I would also add other "dependent or special needs" populations) in the neighborhood as a culprit. Their reaction fostered and legitimated more surveillance and more punitive approaches to crime and policing, contributing to the expansion of the carceral state more broadly. In this sense, Ionide's work can aid in demonstrating one conduit to the entanglement of racial criminal pathologization, as she shows how NIMBY not only created the active exclusion of people of color from affluent neighborhoods but also advanced the growth of the prison–industrial complex, ideologically and materially, in areas left behind by white flight and in those that were already resource deprived.

This emotional attachment to exceptionalism and boundary making played out similarly in the deinstitutionalization and decarceration arena. NIMBY in relation to deinstitutionalized disabled folks was claimed on many grounds, including on the premise that community living was unsafe, not only for the current residents but also for the incoming ones, the "new neighbors." The sentiment that "this is for their own good" helped to create boundaries between who not only *should* live in the community but who *can* live in the community. According to many detractors of group homes, and even some supporters, many people with disabilities cannot make it "on the outside." They will never be able to be normalized or live independently and they therefore don't belong in community settings. Disabled people in these debates were construed as exceptional—an external threat or dependent charges in need of "special" help or services. They were thus constructed as outside of the community, even though, of course, we have always been a part of every community. Such affective economies and lack of intersectional analysis not only resulted in resistance to desegregation; the same retrenchment of racist and ableist attitudes that led to carceral expansion manifested in resistance to the closure of carceral locales. It is this form of resistance to decarceration and deinstitutionalization that I now turn to discussing.

6

Political and Affective Economies of Closing Carceral Enclosures

In 2012, then governor of Illinois Pat Quinn announced the closure of a variety of carceral facilities in the state: two developmental centers, Jacksonville and Murray; the psych hospitals in Tinley Park and Singer; two juvenile correctional facilities, Joliet and Murphysboro; Dwight, a women's prison; and Tamms, the only supermax prison in Illinois. Although this was part of a larger policy driven by budgetary concerns, the plan to close down these facilities also came as a result of the long and targeted organizing of deinstitutionalization and anti-prison activists in the state and nationally. To my knowledge, however, activists in the prison arena had only cursory knowledge about the efforts of deinstitutionalization activists, and vice versa. Therefore I analyze in this chapter the merits of looking at the suggested closure of these carceral enclosures, and especially the *resistance* to such closures, in tandem. By *carceral (en)closures,* I refer to the need to simultaneously understand various locales of confinement, such as prisons, residential institutions, and psych facilities, as spaces of internment and carcerality and examine the logics that sustain them and prevent their closure. This chapter is therefore about who supports carceral enclosures, why others advocate for their closure, and how the rationalities embedded in such efforts are part of a political and affective economy related to both deinstitutionalization and prison abolition and decarceration.

The prevalent approach to resistance to the closure of carceral enclosures repeats itself across settings, namely, the alliance between employees of the facilities (often discussing safety, for them and those incarcerated) and unions (decrying unsafety, danger, and the economic burden of job loss).

In the arena of institutions (especially for those with intellectual and/or developmental disability [I/DD] labels), some of the fiercest resistance to deinstitutionalization also comes from (some) parents of institutionalized individuals, often evoking rights discourses. For example, in and leading to closure hearings, the Murray Parents Association and the American Federation of State, County, and Municipal Employees (AFSCME), the union representing the employees at Murray Developmental Center, staged rallies and protests. A typical scene looked something like this: people wearing single-color shirts with "Save Murray Center," many of whom are holding signs with slogans such as "We love Murray," "Support choice," "Respect Illinois Unions," and "AFSCME keeps the individuals safe." In addition to safety, some signs or chants utilize the rhetoric of "choice" or "home." For example, traveling from Chicago to Centralia, a giant billboard reads "Please don't close my home! Murray Center Centralia IL," accompanied by a huge photograph of a seemingly disabled woman, perhaps a resident.

This resistance to closure is quite diverse in its rationalities, but I suggest that it is often embedded in the discourse of rights/choice, care/work/labor, and innocence/safety. As the stories of Murray and Tamms will show, much of the struggle is also entangled in changing political economies. Even though these carceral spaces are not a panacea for economic boon, I will show how the discourse of cost-effectiveness is tied with moral, ethical, and affective considerations. I highlight the use of "choice" and "care" as mechanisms to resist carceral enclosures and their potential closure. I show that such rhetoric is not a facade but part and parcel of post-1970s political economy tangled with affective economies of care: choice became a prominent idea in a neo-liberal context at the same time that resources to housing, welfare, and health care were eroding. I further demonstrate that the carceral logics of the prison and institutional–industrial complexes and their political economies are intertwined with gendered and racial divisions of labor, ableist assumptions about who gets to be in the community, and notions of care and caring.

I analyze such resistance to closure of carceral enclosures, especially developmental disability centers and prisons, through the prism of labor: the unpaid labor of families (parenting/mothering) of those imprisoned and institutionalized that shows the porous boundaries between the institution, community, and family, and labor unions resisting closure due to many factors, including the political economy of incarceration and decarceration. I contend that emotional and material labor is paramount in keeping these edifices open in the case of employees, unions, and parents, which plays on registers of safety, innocence, and danger, affective responses that are racialized, gendered, and ableist. Finally, there is the labor of those incarcerated, their allies and loved ones, to push for abolition and closure and in essence resist the resistance to decarceration.

Parents against Institutional Closure and the Construction of Innocent Children

To better understand why some parents and family members so fiercely resist deinstitutionalization and facility closure, while others support it with fervor, it is important to analyze how the range of affective response to the idea of deinstitutionalization, from anger and fear to resignation and guilt, plays out, in ways that differ from reactions to other carceral sites, especially penal ones. In the arena of I/DD institutionalization, which is the focus of this section, I suggest that the construction of innocence and childhood to justify institutionalization is paramount.

Traditionally, parents' attitudes toward deinstitutionalization in I/DD have been split between those who push for better institutions, at times referred to as "institutional parents," and those who advocate for community living for their children.[1] Canadian social scientist Melanie Panitch, for example, shows how the campaign to close down institutions for those labeled as I/DD in Canada was propelled by mothers who were active in the (later named) Canadian Association for Community Living.[2] These were mothers to children diagnosed as developmentally disabled in the 1950s who resented the so-called choice between keeping the kids at home with no support or institutionalizing them in a residential school. This would become the core of the neoliberal dilemma—as the welfare state was dismantled (and, in the United States, increasingly privatized), families were left more with the *idea* of free choice than with the actuality of it.

Constructing services based on a market economy meant that, in theory, people with disabilities and their guardians would be able to select the best course of action for themselves and their children, respectively. But the lack of any available options meant that people with disabilities and their families had to either fend for themselves, which meant mostly relying on women's unpaid care/work at home, or get sent into whatever public facility was available at that time. During deinstitutionalization, parents (mostly mothers) originally sought alternatives to institutionalization because they would improve overcrowding and other conditions in the institutions, not because of a discursive shift regarding human value or quality of life of those labeled as I/DD. In other words, parents who advocated for reform within institutions or for more support for living outside of institutions did not necessarily do so because they perceived the institution to be defunct but because they found it to be unsuitable for *their* children (although some did shift toward institutional abolition, as I discuss later).³

I want to use a story about one family's activism against the closure of an I/DD facility to illustrate the mobilization of the trope of the eternal child as justification for institutionalization. In 2015, the *New York Times* published an article that detailed, as many like it over the last thirty years, the pain and fear some parents feel over the fate of their institutionalized child now that the institutional option for those with I/DD and psychiatric labels is dwindling.⁴ The article discussed the impending closure of the Brooklyn Developmental Center as seen through the critical eyes of the parents of one of the residents, John Cosentino. The article detailed, "Once, New York State had 22 institutions serving more than 27,000 people. By 2017, when the Bernard Fineson Developmental Center in Queens closes, only two institutions—both far from New York City—will remain open, serving a total of 150 people. The Brooklyn Center, which housed 614 residents in 1984, is down to 58 spread across five buildings on a 35-acre campus. For some families of the highest-need residents left there, the policy has caused anger and anxiety." The article went on to tell about the battle (spearheaded and at times fought single-handedly by Mr. Cosentino) to keep the institution open; this is despite the family suing the center for negligence and winning in years past. "We've lived this for 36 years here," Mr. Cosentino said one Sunday after a visit with his son. "This is not a perfect place. What this place gives us, it gives us staffing, it gives us nursing, 24/7. Here, we know what we're dealing with." The sentiments expressed by the Cosentino family in the article are representative of other so-called institutional families who do not see community integration as a realistic option for their family member. Anger and anxiety are mixed here with advocating for the "devil you know." The institution is not necessarily painted as utopian, but it is seen as sufficient and, most of all, familiar.

As the *New York Times* article detailed, John Cosentino had been at the Brooklyn Developmental Center for thirty-six years, which is not unusual.

Many of the people who are currently in large state institutions were institutionalized as children or teenagers, during the heyday of institutionalization and hospitalization. For both them and their parents, there were hardly any viable alternatives at the time. Now that they have been in segregated residential settings for many years, many for decades, any discussion of an alternative seems unrealistic. *Unimaginable* is perhaps a better descriptor. For many of these families, the institution is the only reality they know. Some might psychologize such parents' staunch resistance and say that current distrust of community living and noninstitutional options comes from trying to legitimate and rationalize the choice to institutionalize their disabled child to begin with, which must have been a very difficult decision for the family to make. The last thing such families would want to deal with is questioning the viability of that decision long ago, and now suggesting such institutionalization was not necessary after all.

In public hearings and discussions of closures of institutions, parents would often raise questions like "what will happen to my child?" even though the child in question is often someone in his or her fifties or older. Parents' concern for their disabled child's welfare is understandable, since many parents are getting to an age at which they worry what will happen to their adult child after they are gone. In most current facilities, the average age of the residents had risen, since such facilities don't have many new admissions or younger people coming through (although the case is different in private nursing homes). This perhaps is the best indicator that the era of state institutionalization en masse is over. But for those still incarcerated, this realization is not much relief.

In the (so far successful) attempt to keep Murray Developmental Center in Illinois open, the Murray Parents Association reiterated many of these claims. In a video on their website discussing the need for this institution to stay open, the core parents in the association are interviewed. All the parents are white-appearing; one of the parents also works in the center. Most of the "kids" have been there for decades. The parents narrate their fears as an "inability of any other agency or placement to get the level of care, or love," as one parent says, as they get at Murray. Some have tried a community center or group home previously, and one characterizes it as "a nightmare." In Murray, her daughter thrives, the mother says. "This is their home, it's all they got," says one of the dads at the end. The parents see the decision to close the facility as an attempt to balance the state's budget on the backs of "innocent people," as another parent says in a different video. In that video, at a press conference, their representative states that the closure (of Jacksonville Developmental Center, in this case) is "the elimination of their [the parents'] choice, and that their choice is what really should matter, they are the ones who know their family members best." The last claim heard in the videos and throughout the Murray Parents Association's claims is that their children, and all those with I/DD labels, are entitled to an institutional setting, if that is the level of care they require and their guardians desire.

One of the most pervasive arguments against deinstitutionalization, as evidenced in the video, is the widespread belief that certain people will always require some custodial care. This is especially the case for people with cognitive, psychiatric, and intellectual/developmental disabilities—especially for those whose labels are on the "severe or profound" side of the spectrum. Many professionals, and parents, believe that the best interests of "these people" will always be better served in residential settings, and although others can benefit from programs and therapies, they cannot. As parents, they use affective registers of exceptionalism to designate their cases as special and use their affect as families or parents to elicit an appropriate reaction. If taken from this exceptionalistic and parentalistic perspective,[5] some of the parents' concerns could be better understood, as they view community living to be akin to child abandonment, leaving the helpless to fend for themselves.

Such discourses reproduce tropes of some disabled people as innocent and eternal children. Under the discourse of innocence, social, political, and legal recognition is only inferred on those who are deemed as normative and nonthreatening, which are racialized and gendered constructs. In the prison activism arena, this can be seen through the figure of what Marie Gottschalk called non non nons (nonserious, nonviolent, non-sex-related) and what is discussed in chapter 3 as oppositional to the "dangerous few" (the "real danger"—serial killers, rapists, and so on).[6] Much prison reform is centered on this figure of the "non" but also on the more insidious, and more harmful for movement building for abolition, figure of the innocent. The problem with the discourse of innocence (those who should not be executed like Troy Davis or should not be institutionalized because they are not "really cognitively disabled" or not disabled enough) is that then we are left with the carceral logic intact. Carcerality is viable and justifiable, just not for those who are innocent or should not really be there.[7] As Jackie Wang suggests, "using 'innocence' as the foundation to address anti-black violence is an appeal to the white imaginary."⁸ By doing so, blackness itself is criminalized (and, I would add, pathologized).

Childhood is strongly linked with notions of innocence, lack of reason, lack of ability to consent, both in legal discourses and cultural norms in Western nation-states, as feminist abolitionist Erica Meiners demonstrates.⁹ This notion of childhood, though, is afforded only to a certain subject, that is, white, abled, and nonindigenous. More broadly, the categories of children, disabled, indigenous, and racialized Others (especially black and brown) are then constructed as not quite citizen or civil, but some can be rehabilitated to approximate citizenship. Correcting (rehabilitating) individuals is a modern liberal project—the need to become a good and respectable citizen as well as achieving healthy citizenry on a biopolitical level.¹⁰ This is related to what Naomi Murakawa and Katherine Beckett term *penology of racial innocence,* which treats penal policies and institutions as race neutral and thus naturalizes them.¹¹ Such notions paved the way to the creation of indigenous boarding schools to which native children were scooped up to be assimilated and dis-appeared, as well as to the rise of institutionalization and incarceration more broadly.¹²

When I discuss deinstitutionalization in relation to prison abolition, some are offended by putting the two populations in the same plane especially when it comes to people with intellectual disabilities, who are socially and cultur-ally viewed as "eternal children," angelic and innocent (and as discussed in the previous chapter, they are also presumed white, not "mentally ill," and often asexual). That is often the critique I encounter—that of course we should decarcerate people with disabilities from institutions, they are innocent; unlike those (who are also often people with disability, a fact lost in these discus-sions) who are imprisoned, who are guilty. This trope of innocence is then mobilized problematically in the service of abolition in both the disability and the penal arenas.

In *For the Children,* Meiners discusses the utilization of childhood as a discursive trope both for and against prison abolition. In one of the chap-ters she focuses on the closure of Murphysboro, the juvenile facility men-tioned at the beginning of this chapter. In the rallies against the closure of the Illinois youth prison, children were carrying signs decrying the loss of jobs for their family if the facility were to shutter. The harm done to the families of those incarcerated in these facilities was not seen in this appeal to protect childhood, as Meiners poignantly analyzes. In the rallies and hearings regarding the closure of I/DD facilities, at least the ones I encountered, childhood was used not so much as a signifier of economic contestation as it was a signifier of innocence of those institutionalized in these facilities. People with I/DD labels are often constructed as eternal children, in need of special services and specialized care—of course, with exceptions, as the figure of the menacing or inappropriately sexual person with I/DD and the fearmongering around it will attest to, and as suggested in the previous chapter in relation to the *Cleburne* case. This is connected to general NIMBY attitudes based on fear of the menacing "mentally ill" and "mentally unfit" moving into residential neighborhoods. As I showed in the previous chapter, innocence had to be reinscribed into people with I/DD labels in order to differentiate them from "the mentally ill" or "dangerous," which only contributed to the construction of racial criminal pathologization of others. Add the reality that many of these carceral spaces (prisons and residential institutions) are increasingly in white rural areas, and the racial dynamics of "innocence" become clearer.

Relying on and mobilizing under the affective registers of eternal children, and especially of innocence, is therefore tied to white notions of citizenship and belonging that reproduce carceral logics. Many prison abolitionists are scornful about mobilizing even for abolition, not just reform, purposes around the trope of "innocence," as this only reproduces hierarchies of who deserves to be free and who "belongs" in carceral spaces and technologies, as Ruth Wilson Gilmore, Mariame Kaba, and others suggest.[13] Abolitionists (who are grounded in black radical traditions) claim that by refusing this trope of innocence, abolitionist organizing can be broadened and based on more ethical grounding that does not leave others behind—what I referred to in chapter 3 as maroon knowledges.

Choice, (Least) Restrictive Environments, and Parents' Activism

Neoliberalism could be understood in several ways—as an economic and political-economic measure;[14] as a shift in cultural understanding of worth and the public good;[15] and as a change in state functions.[16] Facility closure is certainly resisted by appealing to economic factors like job loss (which I discuss later in relation to employees and unions), but I want to focus for a moment on the cultural modality of neoliberalism, which is especially prevalent in the disability arena. Neoliberalism brought to the fore the discourse and imperative of personal responsibility, cost-effectiveness, and the need to look at economic considerations above all else (happiness, morality, ethics, equality). In relation to the discourse of disability, or Dis Inc., it is related to increased forms of inclusion via commodification and the notion of consumerism and choice.

Such sentiments against closures under the rubric of "choice" and "right to choose," as seen in the case of Murray Developmental Center and the Brooklyn Developmental Center, had been widespread since the beginning of the deinstitutionalization movement and can be discursively located around the concept of the least restrictive environment (LRE) or continuum approach.[17] The residential continuum is perceived as a spectrum of services ranging from public institutions or state schools (for people with disabilities) to living in the community in a residential neighborhood. In between these poles are nursing homes and other types of institutions, including intermediate-care facilities, group homes, and foster care.[18] In these battles against closures of institutions, parents' groups often hang on to the LRE as a legal concept that is anchored in rights and choice and grounds their belief that residential facilities should always be an option, at least for *their* child.

But many disability advocates, including self-advocates and family members who are proponents of deinstitutionalization, are opposed to the whole discourse of LRE or the residential continuum. At its heart, as Steve Taylor aptly puts it, "the question implied by the LRE is not whether the rights of people with developmental disabilities should be restricted, but to what extent."[19] The concept of the continuum is based on a framework in which people with disabilities are qualitatively different and move progressively from one pole to the other, from segregated settings to living independently. Related to this argument is the assumption that people with disabilities cannot move into the community or live in the community in which they are already residing without being "ready" for the next step in the continuum. Thus, under the continuum approach, one cannot just go get a job but needs to work in sheltered or supervised placements first to gain permission to get unsupervised employment.[20] Similarly, one needs to graduate from living in a group home or foster home to living in an apartment of one's own and not move straight from the institution into living independently with supports.

This disability exceptionalism is rooted in the discourse of Dis Inc., discussed throughout the book. It points to the ways the incorporation or inclusion of disability is only made possible within the status quo, which often legitimates the actual segregation (exclusion) of disability in spaces of incarceration (psych hospitals and developmental centers, in this case). Both sides of the "inc." are therefore at play—either total assimilation/incorporation or incarceration. Relatedly, concepts like the LRE showcase disability yet again as "special" and therefore in need of so-called special services, such as group homes or sheltered workshops. Disability rights advocates denounce such discourses and state that there is nothing special about needing things like education, housing, appropriate health care, and so on. Furthermore, they query why such standards are not used on everyone to see if each person is ready to live in the community or live on her own (with support, as needed). For instance, why are such tests used only on those with disability labels and not on others (such as nondisabled teenagers) who want to live on their own to see if they are ready for community living? Why does the notion of the "community" already assume that people with disabilities are not in it? Why, when standards and tests are used on people with disabilities, is this seen not as discrimination but instead as progress? And of course, who determines when someone is "ready" to live in the community? Thus, for those who critique the institutional mind-set, the concept of the LRE seems to promote professional intervention over self-determination of disabled people and becomes another form of control.

Under the flag of the LRE, several national organizations committed to supporting residential treatments and placements for people with disabilities were created by parents over the years. They were often started by mothers of children with I/DD labels who could not find the right support to get their children's needs met. In the 1950s, The Arc (then the Association for Retarded Children) formed, and by the 1960s, it had more than six hundred chapters nationally. Its members were (and are) mostly white parents of school-age children, although they did represent a variety of economic classes. Despite the class diversity, and perhaps because of the lack of racial one, The Arc mostly focuses on issues of concern to middle-class families, as Anne Parsons shows.[21]

When they felt their needs were finally being met in the institutional context, parents started to fight to keep institutions open, at all costs. The Congress of Advocates was established in 1979 by the mother of a child with cerebral palsy and mental retardation labels; Voice of the Retarded (VOR) was established in 1983 by the mother of an institutionalized child and is still going strong today; it is an active organization with which many smaller parents' organizations consult when creating their campaigns against institutional closures. Both organizations oppose institutional closures and believe that the most appropriate services for some people with developmental disabilities will always be in institutions of some sort.[22]

Although the critique against such an organization as VOR may be obvious, I want to point out a few issues with the rhetoric and affective economies they utilize. Throughout their campaigns, website, and literature, they refer to the LRE as a professional and legal standard that mandates that people should live in placements that suit their needs on a case-by-case basis, including residential options. In regard to who decides these needs, the name of the organization is very telling. Until very recently (2018 or so), they were still named Voice of the Retarded, despite a massive push from self-advocates (people with intellectual disabilities who advocate for disability rights) to abolish the R word and replace it with a nonjudgmental term like "intellectual disability," their own names, and so on.[23] VOR claims to speak for people with intellectual disabilities but does not reflect that in name or ideology. VOR recently changed its acronym to the Voice of Reason, implying that advocates for community living (including other parents) are irrational and that reason should be taken above all else, even though the terms of the debate are clearly waged on affective and moral grounds.

The position of organizations such as VOR and members from the National Alliance for the Mentally Ill (NAMI) is to lobby for increasing "options" and "choices," such as involuntary hospitalizations and medication or residential living options.[24] As an advocacy group, NAMI members want to promote what they perceive as effective treatment of mental illness, including research to find causes and cures for specific disorders. As such, this discourse is light-years away from the philosophy, which is embodied by many survivor and antipsychiatry organizations, that looks at mental health difference not as a disorder but as a difference and an identity. It is not surprising, then, that NAMI aligned itself over the years with the American Psychological Association and conceived of those who did not align with its rhetoric as dangerous and in denial of their "true condition."[25]

As is the case with other realms of disability advocacy, some parents' concerns over deinstitutionalization do not match the desires of people with disabilities themselves. One of the major differences lies in the fact that parents often do not have the same opinions as their children, especially when the children are adults. In the disability rights movement, the slogan "Nothing about us without us" comes to represent this very paradox, to state that people with disabilities should control their own lives and decisions in relation to their lives. It is also understandable that many parents have concerns about their children and disagree with their choices, including not taking psychiatric drugs or refusing treatment. The problem comes to bear when these are not perceived as choices but as representing the inability of the person to govern her own life and, as such, often lead to forced hospitalization or forced institutionalization.

I want to be clear here that I am not critiquing VOR or other anti-deinstitutionalization organizations for only creating a facade that uses the language of rights as a rhetorical tool while denying the rights of disabled people. As long as life in a congregate institution seems like a valid option, and as long as people with (mostly "severe" disabilities) are seen as qualitatively different (childlike, special), the institution will always seem like a rational "choice." I want to suggest instead that this entanglement of rights and choice is the basis of liberal apparatuses (human rights) and neoliberal governance (free market). In other words, this white and liberal framework is not a facade of rights but the problematic and exclusionary consequences of using rights as a framework; it makes all demands appear equal (being in an institution is as valid as living in the community) without being attentive to power dynamics and inequity at play.

What is especially interesting about parents' activism against deinstitutionalization, such as VOR, is that these organizations use rights and choice as discourses to protect people with disabilities from the harms *of the community*. In their view, people with "mental retardation" labels who are placed in community settings are forced to modify and be "normalized" to fit a norm they cannot and should not be asked to uphold. From a disability culture stance, this may seem like quite a progressive view, proposing that norms are socially constructed and that people should not be expected to change themselves to fit societal norms not of their creation, as people have value just as they are. But a second look at these organizations' platforms does not yield itself to such an interpretation. What they seem to strive for is a life in segregated congregate spaces in which people have the right to be "retarded" or disabled. This is again where the other side of discourses of Dis Inc. comes into play, in which incarceration in segregated institutions is justified not by discourses of inclusion but actually by seemingly progressive rights discourses. The right to be different legitimates segregation and incarceration, again, for safety reasons and "for their own good."

Unions and the Utilization of Labor against Closure

In addition to the affective mobilization of innocence and childhood, and the discourse of choice and rights, financial reasoning is one of the most pervasive discourses to maintain carceral spaces. In public hearings and protests regarding the closures of residential institutions (or developmental centers, as they are often called), the power of workers and their unions cannot be denied, as they are the ones who most often do the labor of organizing (such as sending out calls for action, buying airtime for media campaigns, purchasing signs and shirts to be used at rallies). During closure hearings, many people come dressed in their local union T-shirts or hold signs representing the union. In the case of the fight to keep the Brooklyn Developmental Center open, participants in protests held signs that read "Show some respect" and "We do our jobs, you do yours" (referring to the legislature) and "Stop the dumping, lives are at stake." They are all signed "CSEA" or Civil Service Employees Association, which is the local union. To fully understand who resists closure of carceral spaces, on what grounds, and how to combat it, I turn now to discussing unions' and employees' involvement in the battle for and against decarceration and deinstitutionalization and the political and affective economy that surrounds this involvement.

The proposed facility closures in Illinois came as part of a rebalancing initiative. These rebalancing plans have become rather common in recent years of austerity, especially in states with a budget deficit, such as Illinois. As part of neoliberal and (neo)conservative efforts to lower budgets, social services had been shrinking since the 1980s. Neoliberalism and transformations in the economy are intimately tied to logics and political economies of incarceration and decarceration. As suggested in the introduction to the book, the prison–industrial complex is a framework that helps to account for the state's investment in punishment, which grows in sharp contrast to the cuts in other areas of social policies, including health care, education, and housing. As Ruth Wilson Gilmore shows regarding California's vast expansion of incarceration, changes in the economy and the making of surplus land, populations, capital, and state capacity have led to the creation of the prison as a profitable industry.[26] The creation of the penal system as an industrial complex appropriated this surplus unemployed/underemployed population as well as undeveloped depreciated land during deindustrialization. Under this new configuration, men of color in particular have turned into commodities in high demand for the growing prison industry, while controlling them from rising up against their conditions of being.[27]

Scholars show how in an era of austerity measures, the corrections industry has ballooned, creating a trade-off between the right hand of the state (punishment, corrections, incarceration, militarization, policing) and the left hand (welfare, social safety net, housing). Budgets shifted from one area to the other without shrinking overall.[28] This shift from the left to the right arm of the state is more nuanced in the case of disability-based incarceration. Massive disability-based institutions indeed closed—partially as an attempt to save money. But this led to the rise of a decarceration–industrial complex, based on both for-profit entities like nursing homes and group homes and also on waivers and reimbursement from state entities very much part of the left hand of the state (Medicaid and Medicare, for example).

Disability and deinstitutionalization advocates show that, although costs vary by state and place of confinement (state funded, private, veteran run), it is cheaper to financially sustain a disabled person, with support, in the community than it is to institutionalize her.[29] But, in postindustrial times, disablement has become big business. As Russell and Stewart painstakingly demonstrated in 2001, from the point of view of the institution–industrial complex, disabled people are worth more to the gross domestic product when they occupy institutional "beds" than they are in their own homes.[30] This is the logic of *handicapitalism,* as Russell refers to it.[31] These cost estimates raise an ongoing debate, as it is hard to compare community placement with minimal support, as it is now, to institutions which have an array of services embedded within their budgets. What is clear, though, from looking at governmental policies is that the institutional bias (i.e., the impetus to institutionalize people with disabilities instead of providing them with support to live in the community with the same funds) is embedded in U.S. policy—Medicaid, for example—and represented in current legislation and lobbying efforts.[32] This institutional bias means that federal and state funds go to alternative types of institutions, such as nursing homes or group homes, but not to the beneficiaries of disability benefits or waivers. This deprives disabled people who receive Medicaid or other disability benefits of the ability to receive alternative care (peer, family, or in-home supports).

Under this political-economic framework of the institution– and prison–industrial complex, it is easy to understand how they are used, materially and rhetorically, as profit-making enterprises. To keep their jobs secure in economically insecure times, unions had historically and contemporarily resisted closures of prisons and disability institutions. Despite the opportunity for coalition building between progressive social movements such as labor/workers' rights, disability rights, and prison abolition, it is most often the case that unions represent the fiercest opposition to the abolition and closure of prisons and institutions. This leads to a quandary aptly presented by James Kilgore in his overview of the confluence of unions, labor, and the carceral state[33]—is the task of a union only to represent the interests of its members or of the working class more generally, who comprise many of those incarcerated and their families?

Even though such resistance comes (at least in large part) from economic investment in wanting to keep these carceral spaces open as sources of employment, the argument is often couched in terms of care (especially in the disability arena) and safety (in the case of prisons, psych facilities, and I/DD institutions). Often such resistance in the disability arena is expressed as benevolent and representing "the best interests of the residents," as we saw in the previous chapter in relation to the phenomenon of NIMBY and group homes. Employees coalesce with others (in the disability arena, with some parents of those institutionalized; in the prison arena, with so-called victim's groups) in an organized effort to persuade the public that some people are not suitable for community living and that such people will be better served by staying in the institution, hospital, or prison.

There is debate in the literature about the level of influence guard unions have on penal policy in reality, including facility closure. This is especially the case for larger unions like AFSCME, who represent many workers, not only those within corrections.[34] It does seem clear that unions did not cause the explosion in mass incarceration, but unions and correctional workers grew alongside the prison boom, and at least in some states, so did their influence. As Gottschalk points out, correctional officers' unions have sometimes pointed attention to overcrowding or conditions within prisons, especially as they jeopardize staff, and therefore led to changes that reduced incarceration and its scope.[35] Historian Heather Ann Thompson argues that most guard unions opposed closing prisons, because such closures meant the transfer of those incarcerated to other facilities, making them even more crowded and harder to work in.[36]

In the cases on which this chapter focuses, unions were a central and integral part of opposition to closing down carceral facilities, which does not mean they are successful or effective agents in doing so. There is also a vast difference within correction guard unions. The New York State Correctional Officers and Police Benevolent Association is one of only two powerful unions to break away from AFSCME to represent only prison guards or correctional officers. The other one is the California Correctional Peace Officers Association, analyzed in depth by Joshua Page.[37] He shows that this association was atypical in this regard and defined itself from its inception in opposition to the labor movement, opposed rehabilitation, and supported punitive segregation. As he demonstrates, the California Correctional Peace Officers Association represented its members well and secured for them better working conditions and salaries, but often on the backs of those incarcerated, especially by portraying the latter as manipulative, violent, dangerous, and irredeemable. Even when its campaigns did not bear fruit, the California Correctional Peace Officers Association strengthened carceral logics and the idea that those incarcerated are qualitatively different, or worse, than those outside prison walls.

For instance, in 2010, in response to then New York State governor Paterson's proposal to close three prisons, the New York State Correctional Officers and Police Benevolent Association ran an advertising campaign criticizing the New York State Department of Corrections for closing prisons and not making administrative cuts, calling these actions a "dangerous choice" and "a difference between life and death." These ads ran on TV and on radio, in addition to the call being taken up at rallies, at protests, and in lobbying efforts, and urged the public to take action. It was not mentioned that this was a campaign related to employment issues; instead, it emphasized "public safety." There are, of course, also heterogendered and racialized aspects to such campaigns. In the TV ads, a white girl symbolizes the idea of who is to be kept safe. One ad ends with an image of a white woman holding a white baby and comforting him, supposedly from the "danger" that will occur if prisons close. The implication pits this cishetero-patriarchal white family against the imagined danger of those imprisoned, presumably men of color from New York City.[38]

In my experience, there is no debate regarding the impact of unions on the closure of disability-based carceral institutions and their significant role in preventing and actively protesting the closure of disability-based carceral spaces. For example, in 1975 at the height of deinstitutionalization, AFSCME, which represents 250,000 employees in the public health sector, authored a report titled *Out of Their Beds and into the Streets*. The report presented deinstitutionalization as a failing practice that will leave the indigent uncared for or, worse yet, will move the care from public entities into for-profit sectors that will decrease state budgets and will not truly care for and about the disabled.[39] In 1978, the Civil Service Employee Association sponsored a public relations campaign to show the public and politicians that deinstitutionalization means dumping populations into the streets, a claim that became axiomatic in the discourse of backlash against deinstitutionalization and which was problematized in chapter 4. Generally speaking, this was also the case in regard to closure of psychiatric hospitals and I/DD institutions.[40]

Recent closure hearings and campaigns (especially after the 2008 recession) make it clear that at least some local unions present their cases very simply—we can't afford to lose jobs in this economic downturn. This is especially the case in rural and poor districts. Appeals to safety become, then, only secondary. That was the case in the fight to close down Tamms supermax in Illinois.[41] The prison opened in 1998 in Tamms, a rural community of about one thousand people in downstate Illinois. The prison was built in Tamms, at least in part, because of "courting" from the people who live there. With the prison boom in the 1980s onward, state and federal authorities often offer incentives for towns to build prisons so that today many towns compete for the chance to have a prison in their jurisdiction. To compete, some towns offer the land for free or provide housing subsidies for the guards. The prison is promoted as a recession-proof, no-fail industry that is nonpolluting and will bring job opportunities, especially to areas damaged by agribusiness or where other blue-collar unionized jobs have moved elsewhere.[42] Much like the siting of early asylums, most new prisons, at least 350 since the 1980s, have ended up in rural communities with overwhelmingly white populations.[43] This tendency is due to failed development, outmigration trends, and other factors[44] like deindustrialization, monopolies in agribusiness, and other trends leading to persistent poverty in rural and small towns.[45]

But in general, prisons are not a good economic development tool for small towns because they do not contribute to growth in the local economy. Mosher, Hooks, and Wood conducted comprehensive statistical analysis on the thirty-one hundred U.S. counties in which a prison (or several prisons) had been built. They hypothesize that one of the main reasons for this lack of growth (economically and in terms of employment) in prison towns is that the communities try to attract prisons by supplying infrastructure (such as electricity and roads), which diverts necessary resources from already impoverished towns into the business of corrections. The new employees also show little interest in purchasing a home in the area. Food and supplies for the sustenance of the prison are often ordered from centralized state locations.[46] Prisons also facilitate the opening of national chain stores around them (fast food, retail chains, etc.) and drive local shops out of business.[47] In addition, prison sites often cause environmental (in addition to social and potential economic) harm.[48] Most jobs are not taken up by local residents, whether as guards or construction workers.[49] The majority of guards do not live in the county in which the prison resides, as these jobs usually require seniority, and many of the guards transfer to and from various facilities.[50] And yet, prisons are often still discussed as an economic engine, and the resistance to their closure is often couched in pure economic terms. This was the case in Tamms, as well.[51]

But those working in carceral facilities are not always paid employees; neither are they volunteers. Over the course of the twentieth century in residential institutions and asylums,[52] and in prisons into the twenty-first century, those incarcerated fill many of the low-wage jobs that keep these carceral enclosures operating, from custodial work, cleaning, and laundry to operating the kitchen. If workers are paid, as is the case for some jobs in prisons, it is for pennies on the dollar.[53] The situation of inmate labor was especially egregious in the arena of those with I/DD labels. As Ruthie-Marie Beckwith carefully documents, by 1972, forty-seven thousand workers in institutions for individuals with intellectual disabilities were inmates who were not paid and did not receive benefits for their labor. This practice had been halted only recently and brought to the public's attention through a chain of lawsuits filed in the 1970s and 1980s. Most of these lawsuits used the Thirteenth Amendment to contest the practice of involuntary servitude.[54] They also tried to show that Fair Labor Standards apply to institutional settings, which became a sticking point in the courts. In most cases, instead of paying incarcerated laborers their fair wages (and to some, back wages), most facilities decided simply to discontinue the work of institutionalized people and hire nondisabled, paid employees for low wage.

Surprisingly, unions representing employees in institutional settings were also players in these battles over the labor practices of those incarcerated. In the formidable lawsuit in the case of institutional peonage, *Souder v. Brennan*, which would determine how and whether Fair Labor Standards apply to institutional settings, both AFSCME and the American Federation of Labor and Congress of Industrial Organizations (AFL-CIO) joined the plaintiffs in the suit. Beckwith discusses the reasoning as such: "In 1976, Tarr-Whelan, an AFSCME union spokesperson responded to the question as to why the union had sought to intervene in *Souder v. Brennan*: 'There are two reasons for this change of position. One is a philosophical reason that unions are in the business to see that everyone gets paid adequately. A minimum wage is the right of anyone who works. The second reason is philosophical, but is more pragmatic. AFSCME feels that many of the fears among workers regarding the payment of residents in institutions—*fears that their jobs will disappear or that there will be no place for them*—are misplaced. Our position now is that the employee and the resident have many of the same problems'" (emphasis mine).[55]

As this example shows in the disability arena, although most contemporary unions are against closure of prisons and institutions, there are potentials for coalition and solidarity to form among workers, including those who work inside, that is, between labor movements, unions, and those who are incarcerated, for both pragmatic economic and ethical reasons.[56] If those incarcerated are not thought of only as "natural resources" or surplus people, and thought of as people at all, it becomes harder to couch resistance to decarceration and facility closure in purely economic terms.

Carceral Care/Work and Employees' Resistance to Facility Closure

To understand the triad of resistance to closure of carceral enclosures (by unions, employees, and some parents of those incarcerated/institutionalized), it is important to understand the differences and similarities between employees who work in penal carceral enclosures versus disability-based carceral enclosures. It is also imperative to keep in mind the political-economic shifts that led to changes in employees' demographics over time and space. While currently (according to the Bureau of Labor Statistics in 2018 for Illinois) correctional officers make an average of $27.46 per hour, home health aides, psychiatric aides, nursing assistants, and orderlies make between $11 and $14 an hour. The benefit for keeping institutions and prisons open, therefore, is surely economic for its employees, but the stakes are not the same in the penal and disability carceral arenas. This is due to the demographics of workers in these carceral settings (and community-based ones) based on differences in race/ethnicity and gender.

Many discussions about resistance to closure (especially in the context of prisons) focus on unions as amorphous entities made of self-interested people who only care about the economic bottom line. But much less discussion is devoted to the workers in these facilities from a feminist perspective that focuses on race-ability and its relation to those who work and (are forced to) live in these places. In addition, a discussion of the oppositional role of unions in relation to prison and institutional closure simultaneously, as I offer here, complicates the connections between labor, care, and work (paid and unpaid)—what I refer to, when applicable, as care/work as shorthand to denote not only the coupling of the work of care (i.e., carework) as often unpaid labor discussed in feminist literature but the disjuncture of care/caring and labor/work more broadly.

The discussion about unions' and employees' resistance to the closure of carceral enclosures often paints "workers" in very masculine terms (guards, union leaders), although that is not the reality in all carceral settings, especially disability-based ones. Within penal settings, the image and reality are that the majority of workers are men and that these are very masculine jobs. I want to elicit a more nuanced and feminist analysis of labor (and in the disability arena, care/work) that happens in these settings. Working in corrections, in this case, as prison guards, assumes a willingness and ability to use force, physical or otherwise, and be "manly." This is pervasive in disability-type facilities[57] but is especially pronounced across penal institutions.[58] This is also due to the penalization and criminalization of disability carceral spaces, which is tied to the reproduction of heteropatriarchy and cisheteronormativity in these settings.[59] As Dana Britton writes about prison guards, "simply by virtue of being male, they are perceived by supervisors, coworkers, and administrators (and perhaps by themselves as well) as more capable of doing their jobs, as 'real officers' and thus, by definition, 'real men.'"[60] This masculine approach also applies to nonmen or nonmasculine people who become prison guards, in men's and women's carceral settings. Women who work in prisons, especially as guards or supervisors, are subject to humiliation and harassment by colleagues and the administration.[61] This is exacerbated for women of color and gender-nonconforming people.

Because many prisons are in rural white areas, for reasons discussed earlier, they attract (by design) a predominantly white workforce. The (slowly) changing racial demographics of prison guards has been named the *Attica effect*, after the 1971 uprising at Attica prison, which held predominantly people of color, especially black and Spanish speaking, but where the guards were almost entirely white, leading to even more animosity and a saturated racist environment. Since Attica, there has been a concerted effort to hire more staff of color in prisons in order to control and decrease future uprisings. As a result, the percentage of nonwhite correctional workers in prisons has more than doubled, but they are still a minority nationally.[62]

If jobs in penal enclosures (especially prisons) are white and masculine, the case in disability settings is more complex and today would be the mirror image, as most workers are women and of color. That is a result of changes over time, much of which had to do with deinstitutionalization, resulting in a different workforce within current institutional settings as well as within community settings in which paid carework is more prevalent. Large state institutions and asylums were often in rural or suburban areas, and in their heyday, many were major employers in their area.[63] With deinstitutionalization (as I defined it: as closure of disability-based carceral facilities, the transition of disabled people to smaller and community-based services and facilities, and deinstitutionalization as a nonsegregationist logic), the role and demographic of disability careworkers began to change. Today, disability support staff work in more geographically varied and increasingly urban environments, which is where disabled people are located and receive services. For example, in the area of I/DD (for which there are more consistent and longitudinal national data available and in which deinstitutionalization and its resistance are still very much ongoing), there is a dramatic shift from receiving services in residential versus community settings. By the end of the 1970s, more than two hundred thousand people with labels of I/DD receiving government services lived in large state institutions. Today, they number fewer than seventy thousand.[64]

Instead of working in institutional settings in more rural areas, direct support workers now work in community-based services, which are often private. Deinstitutionalization led to an exponential increase in community-based settings in which people with I/DD labels receive services, increasing from 11,006 in 1977 to 152,322 in 2005.[65] In 2007, 501,489 individuals with I/DD labels received support through the Medicaid Home and Community-Based Waiver program, compared to 96,527 living in institutional settings and 26,013 living in nursing homes.[66] As a result, disability support staff now work primarily within the private sector for companies who hire them to work directly in the homes of disabled people or in private facilities such as group homes or nursing homes. In the past, these were overwhelmingly public-sector jobs with clear benefit packages and strong unions.

Because of these changing demographics and political-economic dynamics in disability carceral settings, it is paramount when discussing resistance to closure to keep in mind the complex structural differences and lived experiences of those who work there, especially through an intersectional feminist frame anchored in race-ability. In her upcoming book, Akemi Nishida engages in relational analysis of circumstances disability care/workers are put into with those of disabled Medicaid beneficiaries. She does so as she acknowledges and "highlights how their circumstances are interwoven and co-experienced in the political climate [of neoliberalism]." As Nishida highlights, "care is a racialized, gendered, and im/migration-, disability-, age-, and class-based and queer matter. In other words, care is structured in the entanglement of racial and cis-heteropatriarchal capitalism as well as neocolonial, global, and ableist economy."[67]

Intimate care/work in nursing homes, group homes, and psych facilities is deeply gendered and racialized in the United States. To be clear, when discussing employees or workers within institutions, and now more community settings, I am referring to a myriad of occupations that do direct care/work, such as nursing aides, orderlies, and attendants; home health aides; personal and home care aides; and psychiatric aides. This diffusion makes it hard to decipher national trends over time, as these differ by role, state, and disability type (which determines where the service originates and which agency pays for and keeps track of it—psych, I/DD, physical disability, or aging sector). Such work has been and still is considered feminine and is predominantly done by women (ranging from 65 percent to over 90 percent, depending on the setting) who are in their late twenties to late forties.[68] Over the years, and certainly post deinstitutionalization, with its geographical dispersal of such jobs and its increased demands for lower pay in the private sector, direct support, or care workers, increased in terms of racial diversity and immigration status. This varies across sectors, where paid care/work in the aging and physical disability sectors is seeing an even higher proportion of newly migrated workers and workers of color, whose percentage of postsecondary degree holders is lower than in the I/DD and psych sectors.[69] Across the board, direct support work is done by newly migrated or first-generation Americans whose first language is not English. Some of these workers worked as health practitioners previously (at times as doctors or nurses). For some, working in these jobs is a pathway to gaining credentials and experiences in the health care industry in the United States. This process of racialization of the care/work force is also a continuation of tropes like the mammy and the work that women of color had done and are doing as domestics.[70] For immigrant women, doing care/work for children, older people, and disabled people is often seen as a substitution for families in their origin country.

Because employees of developmental centers and hospitals are often women of color and newly migrated, their resistance to closure emanates from a desire to maintain employment but also to continue literally to care. Many employees of developmental centers and psych facilities truly believe that "their clients" are better served in the institution. It is important to remember that some worked in a single institution for many years, sometimes for decades, and developed strong bonds with "clients," who had also often been there for years. For some of those institutionalized, it is one of the only human bonds they have, especially if they are estranged from their origin families.

Their resistance to closing such facilities is therefore different than among prison employees, but some of the rationales are similar, especially in times of austerity. Employees in carceral enclosures, and their unions, fear losing stable jobs to more precarious ones in the private sector, in more dispersed geographical areas, or in arenas that are not unionized. They both often use the lens of safety to resist carceral closures, but in the prison arena, it is often the safety of the workers and the community, whereas in disability settings, it is the safety of those incarcerated as well. Even though the tactics used by employees and their unions are similar, the stakes are not the same, due to the dynamics of race and gender of the employees and the difference between these sites of incarceration. Although I suggested in previous chapters that both institutions and prisons are sites of correction, penal and treatment-based confinements carry different rationalities. Therefore the ideology of the carceral facility as caring and its employees as family is a discourse that is pervasive in disability-based institutions but not in prisons, where employees might see each other as connected or kin (and, as I stated earlier, this also varies due to racial and gender/sexuality inequalities) but not those who are incarcerated.

The Institution as Community and Family

The political-economic transmission of care (from "home" to "group home" or "nursing home," and vice versa) has to be acknowledged when discussing any prospects of deinstitutionalization or reentry or community living, because within the patriarchal social arrangements we have now, women (broadly defined) would be expected to informally take up even more roles as caregivers and shoulder up the responsibility vacated by these carceral institutions, especially psychiatric facilities and I/DD institutions. This is not to suggest that these carceral institutions and their rationales do not need to be done away with, but as alternatives are conjured, I want to stress the need to ensure they are feminist (broadly defined) and ones that take intersectionality of oppressions into account.

In feminist disability studies literature, there is much discussion about the politics of care, in ways that create but sometimes critique binaries between so-called caregivers and those with disabilities. This binary implies that people with disabilities do not provide care to others, including other disabled people and children, as well as reciprocal care to those who care for them, or that so-called care/workers are not disabled themselves.[71] This mutual exclusivity also implies that those with disabilities are not also raced, gendered, or sexual. Feminists have critiqued the state for cutting its services and dismantling the social safety net on the backs of women, as they are now expected to provide care/work within the institution of the family. But feminist disability studies, especially by those insisting on global political-economic analysis, complicates this argument. As Nirmala Erevelles claims, pointing out the carework provided within the family for no pay as exploitative, does not mitigate the political-economic conditions that create the exploitative work of women who *are paid* to provide care, in nursing homes, for example. It only reproduces the sexual division of labor, which rests on the construction of disability, but shifting it outside the home.[72]

In other words, the fear is that any (feminist or other) critique of the politics of care and the connection and differences between paid and unpaid carework will result in halting processes of deinstitutionalization/decarceration, because the implications would be that women would then need to add on to their already full load of providing care. As Erevelles summarized the debate in 1996, "feminists have argued that 'community care' relocates the burden of informal care on women. . . . Disability activists on the other hand claim that such arguments by feminists would undermine the right of disabled persons to live meaningful lives within the community by continuing to relegate them to the oppressive confines of institutional settings."[73] I want to show that this is not necessarily a binary.

A queer of color analysis demonstrates how racialized gender and sexual practices antagonize the normative frames of state and capital, often through the frame of home and family, as Ferguson shows.[74] A crip/mad of color analysis would add to this the destabilization of the boundary between home and family, in this case, through the lens of care and labor. Under neoliberalism and its demands, careworkers and family are not oppositional but are often one and the same. This ideology of "family" care is not only encouraged but often mandated, whether in the "family home" (which is not necessarily a safe space or place of quality care for disabled or queer children) or state-sanctioned "home," such as a nursing home or group home. For example, Lisa Dodson and Rebekah Zincavage provide fascinating ethnographic research of certified nursing assistants who work in nursing homes taking care of elderly residents.[75] As one of their participants recounts, "one manager described how, 'In order to work in a long-term care setting or in a healthcare setting such as this, you have to be part of the family.'"[76] The workers, the vast majority of whom were migrant women and women of color, were expected to provide care to those institutionalized as they would to their own families. But they were not afforded any of the emotional, economic, or other benefits of doing so, such as being able to grieve over those who passed away or getting paid for overtime, which was frequent and expected. One nurse assistant said, "We don't have good benefits but . . . you come every day, it's like family."[77] These women are interpolated into the discourse of the institution as community, and group homes and nursing homes in the community as family, and one can see the appeal of this—for the workers and also the residents.

In a different context, but through a related logic, Erevelles describes the conundrum of women in India who come to work in disability residential institutions. The "choice" to work in these disability service organizations and institutions is often the only option open to these lower-caste women. But, as Erevelles describes, they talk about it not as a last resort but as a calling. They are therefore perceived, by others and themselves, as philanthropic and fitting into a version of neoliberal subjecthood as altruistic and doing good. The reliance on this discourse of choice, altruism, and family for paid care/workers justifies and reproduces abjection, of the workers and of those incarcerated.

Who has access to choice and who is interpolated as a participant in the economy of choice (white, settler, nondisabled, and so on) should therefore be the guiding question. Erevelles provides what I would characterize as a crip of color critique and emphasizes the need to question the historical and political-economic conditions that create this discourse of choice, not to engage with it uncritically or demand to be included therein. As these feminist scholars show, "the institutional use of a family ideology creates a workplace culture ripe for the exploitation of the lowest-paid direct care workers."[78] This ideology of so-called choice and the impetus not only to work but to care, to be a family, does not just uphold a monetary system of exploitation. It also maintains the logic of inclusion via direct exclusion of others, or Dis Inc. This includes economic exploitation but also needing to disregard on-the-job racism and sexism[79] to maintain the idea of the institution as family, and as community.

In other words, the carceral institution is seen as community, and post-institutional settings (like group homes and nursing homes) as family, and the people, most of whom are women, who work in these facilities are allies with parents and others who want to keep the facility open for complex reasons. As I demonstrated, these jobs create a leaky boundary between public and private, family, care, and work.[80] Those supporting institutionalization paint the *community*, not the institution or those living in it, as dangerous. They simultaneously also paint the institution *as community*, and not as something exterior to it.

As the Murray Parents Association says on their website, "We believe that Murray Center is the least restrictive setting for our loved ones and that they are part of a community. Many of our residents have received care from multiple generations in Centralia and the surrounding area over the past 50 years. They go into the community and are well accepted by community members. Placing our loved ones in small settings scattered throughout the state places them at risk for abuse and neglect and will not result in an improved quality of life. We must continue to fight the misguided ideology of the powerful advocate groups. It's time to listen to the families."

Within the debate over living arrangements and services for those with developmental disabilities, the "community" is often seen as negation: that which is not the institution, as Allison Carey shows.[81] In such discourses, "community" is an entity that can be symbolically marked as being out-side the walls of the institution, the prison, or other carceral enclosures.[82] But in reality, imprisoned and institutionalized people are still a part of their communities, especially via their families, and have tremendous effect on the communities from which they came, even if they are physically absent, or especially because of that reason. Their notions of community go well beyond geographical boundaries,[83] especially when meaningful community relationships are hard to come by, because of the types of NIMBY and resis-tance based on race-ability discussed in the previous chapter.[84]

Some of those institutionalized also see fellow incarcerated people as fam-ily and community, which sometimes leads them to resist the closure of the facility.[85] Especially for those psychiatrized or institutionalized at an early age, some never experienced a different living arrangement. Many made mean-ingful friendships in the institutions, with both residents and staff members, and did not want to see these relations severed. Their genuine sense of loss, combined often with feelings of anxiety and excitement about moving into the community, was often not dealt with effectively by advocates of institutional closure.[86] Such opposition needs to be better understood and addressed, as opposed to dismissed, by those who are committed to abolition. False con-sciousness is not a satisfactory analysis in my opinion, because it can become a knee-jerk reaction about resistance to any kind of change. In this case in particular, it leads back to regressive arguments about the ability of people with disabilities (especially with intellectual or psychiatric disability labels) to make decisions about their own lives. What interests me here, however, is the way these affective attachments to institution as community and home were utilized in debates around closure of carceral locales. Testimonies of those with disabilities, or their families as proxies, who discussed their places of living (institutions) as useful, neat, and friendly and their fear of moving into uncaring communities, were used as a battle cry against closure. In some closure hearings and videos done by opponents of institutional closure, those institutionalized are pitted against professional opinion and presented, per-haps for the first time ever, as people with expert opinions who have a right and ability to make decisions about their own lives. And then, after closure, or if the facility stays open, they are not often publicly consulted with again.

On the other hand, following the initial steps of deinstitutionalization, people with developmental disabilities sought others who shared their expe-riences of learning to (re)live in the community.[87] These were the sprouts of many developing self-advocacy groups and associations. In turn, these groups advocated for the closure of more (or all) institutions and the move of all their peers into community-living settings. As they were most affected by institutional closure, self-advocates became the most vocal and insistent voices in the fight for the abolition of institutions and psych facilities, as opposed to calls to reform such institutions and make them more livable.[88] Such examples again destabilize the binary that posits people with disabilities as passive receivers of care and instead shows the peer and reciprocal nature of care and taking care of, especially in formations that are outside of the state and that came as a result of resisting institutionalization, as a form of state violence.

Parents for Carceral Closures

To understand why some parents resist the closure of segregated residential institutions, it's equally important to recognize the crucial role that parents (often mothers) play in *decarceration* efforts. The thrust behind much of deinstitutionalization and prison decarceration activism came from parent groups. Parents' advocacy was certainly a major engine behind deinstitutionalization, especially for those labeled as intellectually disabled.[89] During the 1960s, when deinstitutionalization in the developmental disability realm took a slower pace than anticipated and desired, parents were often the most vocal in demands to push things along toward community living.[90]

It is not just parents but specifically mothers who find themselves as advocates for institutionalization or decarceration, what Nancy Naples has termed in a different context *activist mothering*.[91] Panitch describes the work of such mothers as "accidental activists" and demonstrates how their experience of caring for their disabled children was a major source of knowledge and activism around deinstitutionalization in Canada. Panitch's description of the parents', and mostly mothers', advocacy efforts should resonate with those familiar with prison decarceration and abolition. For example, in *The Golden Gulag*, Gilmore describes the desire of mothers of those imprisoned to create an organization that would help them understand their sons' incarceration and ultimately aid in decarcerating them.[92] The organization Gilmore describes, later named Mothers Reclaiming Our Children, was driven by outrage over the murder of a young black man by the police in Los Angeles in 1991. His aunt started organizing small discussion groups for mothers to encourage them to talk more about police and gang violence. These women then came to each other's hearings and monitored courtroom practices. They learned how the criminal (in)justice system works from the inside. By studying and researching various laws and procedures, and the structures that sustain them, the mothers learned about the conditions that kept them and their children in subordinate positions.[93]

I want to foreground here the ways that Gilmore, Panitch, and others identify motherhood as political and show how using it as a tool of resistance conflates the traditional boundaries between public and private spheres.[94] As feminists have pointed out for decades, while motherhood is seen as a matter of the home, a private affair, political activism is seen as related to the public sphere, the arena of work, of goods, and since women are associated with the private sphere, often their roles in political organizing and activism have gone unacknowledged. I will also add that in these battles for decarceration (and also the right to institutionalization), the boundaries between parenting–home–private and community–public–labor–political are not so clear-cut.

My intent in mentioning these two brief examples of mothers' activism to decarcerate their children, however, is not to imply that these "accidental activists," as Panitch refers to them, came from the same background and shared similar experiences. It is quite clear that many groups of activist mothers, such as Moms against Gun Violence, for example, or the coalition to close Tamms prison, are fierce women of color and that their form of resistance is part of a long history of black liberation struggle against the state and its violence. The same cannot be said for mothers' activism in the deinstitutionalization arena, whose lineage to this activism was different, as many were white and/or had class privilege. They used this privilege primarily to make demands of the state that would serve the needs of their families better. Because they did not view institutionalization as a form of debilitation and state violence, they have fewer qualms seeking relief from the state and its apparatuses for ills of its own creation. This is not to discount the immense activism done by mostly white mothers for establishing state supports and safeguards historically (such as fighting for pensions and anti–child labor laws[95]) but to connect this to an understanding of the lineage of mothers' activism as also connected to different understandings of, critiques of, and engagements with the state.

Their call for the inclusion of their disabled family member in the status quo is what I called Dis Inc. throughout this book to specifically connect the nexus of inclusion to that of incarceration. I am using the word *incorporation* here to signal both *cultural and social inclusion* into the status quo and *incorporation as a structure of* political-economic profit-making impetuses (in sites of enclosure, for example). Dis Inc. is a discourse that calls for inclusion by assimilation, so in essence, the erasure of difference/disability is the price to pay for life outside the institution through the reproduction specific discourses and subject positions (whiteness, class, heteronormativity, and so on). As demonstrated in previous chapters, and as others document in relation to other struggles (LGBT rights, rights under neoliberal regimes, able-nationalism[96]), this inclusion legitimates further segregation of other bodies and minds.

Thus these differences between parents' activism in decarceration are important, especially since, as Puar shows, they demonstrate how some (through white heteropatriarchy, racial capitalism, settler colonialism) are folded into life precisely because others become available for injury. Puar expands Foucault's conceptualization of biopolitics to notions of debility. For Foucault, biopolitical discourses, as opposed to disciplinary ones, work on a population level, not just of the body but of the body politic. The life (ability to live, not to die) of some is predicated on the death (slow death, social death, premature death) of others so that it is not just life itself but the quality of this life in terms of societies and populations that is of import here. In this case, the inclusion of some (through white settler middle-class norms) is then used to reproduce the sense of the "good life" everyBody/mind must strive for or be entitled to. By so doing, the state presents itself as progressive, while it perpetuates the debilitation of others or susceptibility to premature death (i.e., racism, in the words of Ruthie Gilmore).

Under neoliberal frameworks, one group may have a facade of choice (to institutionalize or not), but they are made to fight over intentionally depleting resources through the reality and discourse of scarcity constructed through hierarchies and oppression. In other words, inclusion (via Dis Inc.) solidifies liberal notions of choice and rights while affirming the status quo.

As discussed at the beginning of this chapter, in 2012, Quinn, then governor of Illinois, proposed to close Tamms supermax. He proposed the closure because of many factors, primarily his desire to rebalance the budget, but as is the case with every closure described in this book, it also arose out of the valiant and concerted efforts of devoted activists, including family members of those incarcerated. Originally conceived as an art and culture project by local Chicago artists, such as Lori Jo Reynolds, who spearheaded the project, Tamms Year Ten began in 1998 as a more widespread campaign. As an arts-based social project, Tamms Year Ten created a remarkable exhibit of what they called *Photo Requests from Solitary,* in which local artists, photographers, and later the public would take or create images or pictures that an individual in Tamms would like to see.[97] Because of the extreme conditions of solitary confinement, those incarcerated in Tamms have not been outside in years or seen the sun, let alone their families. The aim was to humanize those incarcerated and highlight the horrific conditions in this supermax facility, in which people were locked up in solitary in tiny cells with human and sensory deprivation, sometimes for decades. These violations were later substantiated by the ACLU, Amnesty International, and a court ruling. The end goal of the campaign was to abolish the facility and, with it, the practice of solitary confinement.

As Quinn announced the closure of the facility, a coalition formed to resist it. It was quite different than the one that resisted the closure of Murray, however. This time, parents, especially mothers, were strong proponents of the plan. The makeup of these parents was quite different, as well. As mothers of those incarcerated in Tamms, most were women of color—the majority were black and a few Latina—which represented the makeup of those in Tamms. This was in stark contrast to the Murray Parents Association, which was majority white, even though Centralia (where Murray is) and Tamms are less than two hours apart and equally rely on an economy of incarceration. What was similar was the mobilization of the local union against the closure of each facility. In the case of Tamms, AFSCME went as far as to file a lawsuit to prevent the closure.

Mothers of those incarcerated, with the initiative and backing of Tamms Year Ten, decided to confront the union, as Kilgore documents: to demand that the union "acknowledge the human rights catastrophe that has taken place at Tamms" and "honor their own progressive past and remember that mass incarceration is the civil rights issue of our time."[98] The results brought race, class, and gender to coalesce with the union and its past head-on. Women, especially mothers of those incarcerated in Tamms, marched to AFSCME offices in Chicago carrying signs stating "I am a Mom" and "My son is not a paycheck." These signs alluded, of course, to the famous placards held by black men who were sanitation workers in Memphis in 1968, made famous by the fact that it was the last protest in which Martin Luther King Jr. participated before his assassination. The differences between the two protests are striking: one was organized mostly by men, who saw the conditions of poor black men as both a civil rights issue and a pertinent labor issue; the second was an attempt to utilize the trope of motherhood to bring to light another "civil rights issue of our time"—mass incarceration and its relation to racism and capitalism. By the powerful use of gendered registrars of motherhood, the protesters tried to show AFSCME, as the guards' representative, that it was on the wrong side of history—what one journalist unequivocally called "Unionizing the New Jim Crow."[99]

As Tamms Year Ten was trying to appeal to people's morals (do what is right, this is torture, no human being can live in sensory deprivation and without human contact), the union representatives, local politicians, and legislators couched their claims in pure economic terms. Or as the signs protesters held stated, "Torture is a crime, not a career." Today, in many states, closure of carceral enclosures is a trend, one that is likely to increase.[100] The question for unions and workers who care is how to respond to changing economic and social realities in ways that get their economic and emotional

I Am a Mom demonstration, part of the Tamms Year Ten campaign, held at the James R. Thompson Center in Chicago, 2012. Photograph attributed to Adrianne Dues. Courtesy of Lori Jo Reynolds and the Tamms Year Ten campaign.

needs met without holding on to defunct industries, including the industry of human warehousing for care, profit, or both.

Seizing on Safety and Danger: Potential for Anticarceral Coalitions

Among the many factors that keep places like Murray Developmental Center open is the appeal of the idea that "it will keep the individuals safe," as the AFSCME sign at its rallies states. Evoking notions of danger and safety (which, as we have seen, are afforded to some at the expense of others) is one of the most pervasive tropes keeping the carceral logic alive. In relation to closure of prisons and jails, objections are constructed around cries that those incarcerated are dangerous and that the only way to maintain the safety of the larger community (and often of the employees) is to keep the facility as it is. As discussed in chapter 5, these appeals (often appearing in NIMBY sentiments) both reproduce and construct an imagined community of caring and its borders. These borders then maintain processes of social abandonment upon which the "good life" can thrive.[101] In the case of carceral spaces, these borders are easy to see (the walls of institutions and prisons), but in their logics, these borders between abandonment and caring are much more blurry.

Let me end with a brief illustration of how this discourse of safety is mobilized in carceral closures through the pendulum of abandonment and caring, and how it connects criminalization to pathologization as well as decarceration to deinstitutionalization. In March 2016, Broome Developmental Center in upstate New York had closed its gates for good, after much opposition from the usual triad—parents/family members, employees, and union members. Their campaign was rooted firmly in the language of safety. Their flyers read "Closing Broome DC is unsafe for . . . people with DDs," that closure is unsafe for "our communities," and that it is unsafe for "BDC workers." But this time, this turn to safety and danger came with a twist. In a fact sheet opponents to the closure of Broome Developmental Center authored, they noted that "part of BDC is the Local Intensive Treatment center, which houses people with developmental disabilities who have either been placed by court order or voluntarily admitted because they may have committed offenses that (if they weren't developmentally disabled) would have given them a sexual offender designation."

These cause-and-effect argumentations that sexual harms should lead to exile and punishment, and then surveillance via "sex offender registries," are heavily critiqued by abolitionists. Erica Meiners meticulously breaks down the problem with such registries and shows how they promise more safety but deliver more precarity and violence instead.[102] First, they mask violence that is not encompassed by the "stranger danger" narrative, specifically harm from family and acquaintances, which is more than 90 percent of child sexual assault. Second, they fail survivors of sexual violence, as opposed to supporting them or decreasing their pain or the occurrence of sexual violence. Third, they expand the carceral state. In relation, they also expand new surveillance technologies. Lastly, the category of sexual assault, especially in regard to minors, is so loose that it can encompass almost anything.

In the same "fact sheet," the Broome coalition immediately informed the reader that "now some of them have already been placed into our neighborhoods with virtually no notification to law enforcement or the community, and without the proper supervision that could keep them from potentially re-offending." This kind of panic discourse relies on the nexus of criminal pathologization discussed in previous chapters, which transforms even the "most vulnerable" populations of people with I/DD into being disposable and dangerous. Once they are criminalized, the public outcry becomes about the safety of the community that has to be exposed to the likes of so-called sex offenders. Because of the lack of accountability and realization that sexual harm occurs from so-called loved ones and not strangers, the accompanying solution espoused here used the practice of notification, which I critiqued in the previous chapter.

This nexus of criminal pathologization in the case of Broome Developmental Center could be a great opportunity for coalition building between disability rights or advocacy groups and anti-prison or criminal justice reform groups. The discursive frame of sexual dereliction comes from eugenic notions of defectiveness, deeply tied to the construction of feeblemindedness as well as gendered notions of sexual excess. This had been one of the rationales behind segregation and confinement historically, justifying these populations as derelict and not quite human.[103]

The one organization that seized this challenge as a teaching and advocacy opportunity to the disability community more broadly was the Southern Tier Independence Center (the center for independent living serving Broome County in New York), which picked up the glove and provided a scathing critique of prevalent discourse around sex offenders and their registries. In response to the panic discourse induced by the coalition against the closure of the center, they wrote that "all of us share our communities with criminals. None of us knows whether our neighbors, disabled or not, have committed assaults, murders, kidnappings, armed robbery, or arson, or whether they are likely to do it again. People are very nervous about sex crimes. But is there a rational explanation for why we publicize the location of people who inappropriately touch someone, but do not tell everybody where all the drunk drivers who have killed children live? A federal Department of Justice study found that strangers were the offenders in fewer than 5% of sexual assaults against pre-teen children. Over 95% of these acts were committed by people known to the children and, most likely, to their families. Did knowing those people and where they live protect the children? No, it did not. But it's easier for people to hate and hound and ostracize strangers than it is for them to take responsible action to make sure their spouses, siblings, and friends don't molest their kids."[104]

By mobilizing a counter-discourse to the hegemonic "stranger danger" narrative offered by Broome Developmental Center proponents, the Southern Tier Independence Center statement offers a different response to harm that does not rely on panic and fear of an unknown Other. This offers a powerful corrective that can ground solidarity politics between populations often described through the trope of danger—people with I/DD or psych disabilities (especially "hypersexual men") and those imprisoned, especially for violence. More broadly, as Meiners and other feminists suggest, vulnerability is metaphorically and materially assigned to women, children, and those with disabilities, who are often infantilized as in need of protection. This can offer an opportunity to band around and offer a different interpretation of harm and violence, as the preceding statement suggests.

The main sticking point and the reason such moments of solidarity are so rare is that often this protection from vulnerability and violence is sought from and comes from the state. This masks the violence of the state and the ability of state apparatuses to define what violence means. Incarceration and institutionalization are then not considered violence against a person or group of people (whether in the case of boarding schools for indigenous people or detention centers), which creates the paradox seen here in which one group can be in favor of protection from the danger of vulnerable people but see their segregation and incarceration as the solution instead of the problem. This leads to absurdities in which resistance within and to carceral settings (like refusing to eat or spitting on guards or attendants) is considered an act of violence but the rationale for incarcerating people in the first place is not.

If sites of carceral enclosures were understood as sites of debilitation (physical, mental, etc.), then labor and disability movements might be able to coalesce and facilitate their closure. The disabled–careworker binary is also simplistic when considering the demands of the job and its disabling nature. According to the U.S. Bureau of Labor Statistics, the injury rate for nursing assistants is among the highest of all occupations in the country.[105] Put differently, many of the people who work in these facilities, especially those who do it for prolonged periods, often in second and third shifts, are also disabled. Perhaps debilitated would be a better descriptor of the slow rundown that occurs among this population, especially taking into account the juncture of race-ability and gender. Jasbir Puar offers the triangulation of debility, capacity, and disability to discuss how disability "is about bodily exclusion that is endemic rather than epidemic."[106] Disability and debility in this formulation do not counter each other but are in fact interdependent— the discourse of rights and empowerment relies on the same economy (i.e., neoliberalism, colonialism, and racial capitalism) that capacitates certain bodies (makes them available for identification) and makes others available for injury. Some might be one and the same, of course (such as disabled and caregiver, debilitated paid and unpaid laborers). It might not be the same disability (e.g., intellectual), but debility is normative in these carceral settings and spaces of care, even though it is often unacknowledged.[107]

This solidarity with disability from employees should be especially appealing in a supermax facility, in which people are deprived of human contact and lose their mental capacities frequently as a result. However, to try to stop the closure of Tamms, AFSCME sued the governor and the state by using debilitation as a strategy not for closure but for its prevention.[108] In the suit, the union stated that their members (employees at the facility) could face potential harm, injury, and death if Tamms were to close and those incarcerated were to be moved to various other facilities less equipped to deal with them. Because debilitation and disability are understood only negatively, this strategy reproduces ableism, which further punishes those already disabled in carceral systems. In other words, those already disabled behind bars are not seen as allies to workers in this web of state violence and debilitation, but quite the opposite. This attempt at prevention of debilitation is therefore done on the backs of those who are disabled by the same system that makes incarceration legitimate and profitable.

Despite AFSCME's and politicians' concerted efforts, which resulted in the Illinois legislature voting against the closure, Governor Quinn vetoed the vote and closed down Tamms supermax in 2013. A campaign led by artists and family members, and later by some of those decarcerated out of Tamms, led to the closure of one of only a few supermax facilities in the nation. As with many other cases of prison closures, the vast majority of those incarcerated in Tamms were transferred out not to freedom but to other facilities. As an incarcerated individual wrote after Tamms closed, small victories are still worth celebrating: "Being in Tamms felt like being held underwater and drowning, not being able to breathe. Leaving that place was as if you suddenly came up for air. You're gulping in air. You feel alive and real again. Every step of the journey of transitioning from Tamms has been a revelation of things both big and small. Our natural human senses, having been so repressed at Tamms, were suddenly and shockingly activated simply by boarding the IDOC bus . . . the waist and leg shackles severely hindered our movement and were as uncomfortable as they were difficult, yet every prisoner from the first to the last man had the biggest smiles on their faces."[109]

As the stories of Murray and Tamms show, deinstitutionalization and prison abolition are much more than about closure of specific locales; as I discussed previously in relation to abolition as dis-epistemology, abolition is about erasing carceral logics and creating a society without the need for or footprint of such logics, logics entangled in discourses of innocence and danger, care and cost-effectiveness. What is needed is a shift in the discourse that constructs certain populations as financial capital (or drain, as people with disabilities and people of color are seen as superfluous populations unless they are in cages or institutional beds) within battles over carceral closures. As I have shown in relation to the continuum approach, for example, while institutionalization remains one option out of many, it makes it as legitimate as any other "choice." Only when it is no longer presented as a legitimate option can this neoliberal discourse of choice under a so-called free market be abolished.

In short, what many activists are attempting to do is to shift the discourse to ethical and moral imperatives for inclusion and nonpunitive responses to harm and away from discourses that need to prove or disprove people's worth to the national (political) economy. In many hearings regarding the potential closures of institutions or prisons, one of the most pervasive arguments to keep them open (second only to "safety") is about the facilities being major economic engines for their surrounding areas and the loss of jobs their closures will entail. But the ethical questions that come from this neoliberal assessment are hardly ever discussed. Just because something is potentially profitable (and many of these facilities are not even that) does not mean it is desirable, ethical, or necessary. Incarcerating people for so-called treatment, rehabilitation, warehousing, or incapacitation is a social goal. These are (white) man-made priorities. Employment cannot triumph over people's freedom. One cannot and should not profit from oppression.[110]

What labor unions could be doing, for example—and some have already begun this transition—is advocating for better wages and opportunities for their employees to work in community noncarceral settings, for example, advocating for legislation that ensures good pay for personal care attendants outside of institutions and using the experience of such devoted institutional employees to work with (and sometimes for) disabled people in the homes in which they reside. This will require more than a policy shift, though; it will require an epistemic one. Such employees, and all of us, will need to understand disability not as devalued and deficit driven and people with even complex disabilities as agents of their own lives.

As I suggested in chapter 3, abolition as an ethic and epistemology demands that we let go of attachments to hegemonic narratives of danger but also of safety. As Meiners and Jackson suggest, "to effectively dismantle our investments in incarceration and not simply transfer those old fears (of the drug dealer, serial killer, or home invader) to new bodies (fundamentalist terrorist, sex offender, welfare queen) requires ... rethinking how we are taught to feel safe and protected and excavating how White supremacy, heteronormativity, and other oppressions are central to our fears."[111] Perhaps then, as Butler,[112] Meiners, and others suggest, the push should not be to do away with vulnerability but to reframe it. As I suggested in chapter 3, embracing abolition as a dis-epistemology, a space of not knowing, can provide a useful entry point into the politics of the utopian, the unrealistic—in short, a praxis of abolition. Instead of conceiving of safety–danger, family–workers–unions, and institution–community as oppositional, it might be fruitful to imagine what kinds of communities we want to be in and build infrastructure that supports it. Disability and the value of vulnerability, as well as reframing innocence and danger, could be an entry point into the complex battles surrounding the closure of carceral enclosures and the labor and care involved therein.

7

Decarcerating through the Courts

Past, Present, and Future of Institutional and Prison Litigation

One of the most mentioned and debated tactics of deinstitutionalization and decarceration is class action lawsuits. Did such litigation make meaningful improvements in the quality of life of those incarcerated? And more centrally in relation to the vexed relation between reform and abolition, did such litigation taint the presence and legitimacy of carcerality in ways that are abolitionary? What were the effects of such litigation, on those incarcerated but also on the continuity and legitimacy of carceral logics? I therefore investigate here the role class action litigation played in the closure of carceral enclosures (prisons and institutions) and the consequences of utilizing it as a technique of decarceration and abolition.

Years before Tamms supermax, discussed in the previous chapter, would be shuttered, another supermax was ordered to shut down, this time by legal means. In 1977, *Ramos v. Lamm* was filed against Colorado's supermax prison due to its conditions of confinement.[1] At the end, the district court held that conditions at the prison were unconstitutional, including an inadequate physical environment, lack of prisoner safety, idleness and lack of exercise, inadequate medical attention, broad visitation restrictions, and other violations. As a result, the court ordered to *close down the entire prison* and declared it unfit for human habitation. Those imprisoned in this facility were not freed, however, but much like in the case of Tamms supermax, they were transferred to other carceral facilities.

In the same year, 1977, another infamous lawsuit was under way, *Halderman v. Pennhurst State School and Hospital,* regarding a different carceral enclosure. By 1987, Pennhurst State School in Pennsylvania finally closed its gates. At its height, Pennhurst held three thousand people with I/DD labels.[2] It was a notorious institution, both in Pennsylvania and nationally.[3] Pennhurst closed owing to many factors, most significant of which was a court order issued in 1977, when Pennhurst confined twelve hundred people in despicable conditions. One of the main arguments put forth by the plaintiffs was that the "school" (if there ever was a euphemism, state "schools" are surely one of the worst) was actually making its charges *more* disabled. In other words, the people incarcerated there deteriorated in their mental and physical capacities while being deprived of their liberty and freedom in the process. Their incarceration therefore became unjustifiable. Those exiting Pennhurst were transferred to "less restrictive environment[s]," mostly group homes in the community.

Ramos and *Pennhurst* are two out of numerous landmark cases of that era that resulted in important changes in prisons, psychiatric hospitals, and residential institutions for those with intellectual and/or developmental disability (I/DD) labels. This chapter provides an analysis of prison and institutional reform litigation as an important tactic in the push for decarceration and for abolition more broadly. Litigation was an often used mechanism of decarceration and closure of carceral facilities, especially in the late 1960s and throughout the 1970s, ushering in and reliant on prisoners' and disability rights movements and discourses of the era. As I show, advocating for changes in conditions of confinement and decarceration through prison reform litigation did not stop there, however, but continued after the 1960s and 1970s by taking up gender (especially in women's facilities) and disability (especially the mental health of those incarcerated) as new tactics. Institutional reform litigation also extended in the 1990s to focus more on increasing community-based living options for those with disability labels.

This chapter is also devoted to connecting litigation in the prison arena and the institutional arena through the lens of race-ability and especially criminal pathologization. As I suggested in the book's introduction, by race-ability, I mean the ways that constructions of race and criminalization are interwoven with disability (and pathologization) without subsuming one into the other, analogizing them, or competing in "oppression Olympics." Much has been written about prison rights/prison reform litigation in the 1960s to the 1980s (which is when litigation was at its highest, and therefore the focus of this chapter).[4] Even more had been written and discussed in relation to institutional reform litigation, but surprisingly, the two had not been discussed in tandem.[5] The coalitional work I am proposing throughout this book intersected in remarkable ways in the arena of institutional reform litigation. Although racial criminal pathologization undergirds much of these cases, it is important also to discuss the *differences* between prison litigation and lawsuits in the institutional arena. The differences and continuities are important both for the short-term goal of litigation (getting specific individuals out of specific carceral settings or getting specific facilities or units to close down) and the long-term goals of abolition of carceral enclosures. What I hope this analysis does, in addition to learning from each arena to inform the other, is also to move from simplistic questions of whether certain lawsuits were successful to more wide-reaching questions about what reform litigation did, cumulatively. I show that in addition to a politicizing effect, it ushered in more effective ways to incarcerate, and those two effects do not necessarily negate each other.

I begin with the foundational era of reform litigation and discuss a few landmark cases, such as *Wyatt, Willowbrook, Holt,* and especially *Pennhurst,* which I describe as a form of abolition litigation.[6] I then analyze the effects of these cases from a broader sociopolitical frame, such as their politicization and mobilization potential and their unintended consequences, which led to more effective systems of incarceration. The rest of the chapter shifts to the 1980s and 1990s, which withstood numerous changes in reform litigation—especially if examined through the prism of gender-related litigation and the rise of carceral feminism. It was also the era of legal restrictions on litigation, state repression, and co-optation. In an effort to combat this repression, I analyze how disability, as a material reality and legal category, might be and indeed was used to abolitionary ends. Through an intersectional disability analysis, I show and critique the effects of utilizing disability as a tactic for decarceration, which composes the third portion of this chapter. I argue that reform litigation is not a zero-sum game in which players move from one arena (prisoners' rights) to another (disability and deinstitutionalization) but instead I show how current prison litigation increasingly relies on disability, often uncritically. I end with a broader queer of color critique of the utilization of litigation done through a liberal rights discourse.

Context and Landmark Cases in Institutional Reform Litigation

Institutional reform litigation (or public law litigation) refers to legal actions, in the form of lawsuits, that sought to reform or improve conditions of public facilities or desegregate them, especially on the basis of race or disability. This form of litigation was most pervasive, as a tool of decarceration and deinstitutionalization, in the mid-1960s and 1970s. It had its roots in the *Brown v. Board* decision.[7] The first group of prison litigation cases in the early 1960s was tied directly to the project of desegregating public facilities that began with *Brown*, including prisons and other correctional facilities.

The second form of reform litigation was an attempt to have the courts recognize the First Amendment (freedom of religion, speech, press, and assembly) and Fourteenth Amendment (equal protection and due process) rights of those imprisoned. Black Muslim groups especially were gaining legal successes, particularly regarding freedom of religion. Between 1961 and 1978, sixty-six lawsuits were brought forth by Black Muslim organizations.[8] But it was only from the mid-1960s that the courts began entertaining plaintiffs' claims regarding the violation of the Eighth Amendment, or the cruel and unusual guarantee, regarding imprisonment.[9] The first such cases involved challenging prison discipline, specifically corporeal punishment.

The mid-1960s to the 1970s was also a time of disability rights advocacy, especially the spread of the normalization principle, which advocated for community, as opposed to institutional, living in the field of "mental retardation"[10] and the growth of antipsychiatry, which fought for the closure of psych facilities.[11] Here, too, as was the case with decarceration, the legal arena was a major battleground in which deinstitutionalization, desegregation, and rights for people with disabilities started to be implemented de facto.[12] Most deinstitutionalization litigation was brought as class action lawsuits, and the plaintiffs were usually institutionalized people, affiliates of Arc, advocacy organizations including those of self-advocates, and parent groups. Much like other avenues of pushing for decarceration in prisons and institutions, parents were instrumental here,[13] in combination with employees of the facilities.[14]

I turn now to analyzing key court cases in institutional reform litigation. One of my aims here is to show how cases in prison reform and deinstitutionalization litigation illuminate the differences and connections between various forms of confinement and their logics and rationales. In addition, I bring up these specific cases because they are the ones often cited by legal scholars and advocates but also by critics of deinstitutionalization and de-carceration, the latter to show that such ligation is costly and ineffective and therefore should be halted. I also chose to focus on a few cases that to me come close to abolition litigation, and not just reform, in both prisons and institutions.

One of the first legal challenges to confinement in psychiatric and "mental retardation" institutions was *Wyatt v. Stickney,* in Alabama. It was filed initially on behalf of employees of Bryce Hospital for people with mental illness in 1970, asserting that because of inadequate staffing, so-called patients at the facility could not receive treatment. At the time the suit was filed, Bryce had just one clinical psychologist, three medical doctors, and two social workers to provide therapy and treatment to fifty-two hundred institutionalized people.[15] It was later decided to add a patient, Ricky Wyatt, to the lawsuit to strengthen the case. The class action expanded in 1971 to include Searcy Psychiatric Hospital as well as Partlow State School for people with "mental retardation."

The *Wyatt* case is important to the analysis I am foregrounding here not only because it was the first legal case to clarify the right to treatment as a constitutional right, or because it is the longest and one of the most notorious litigations in the history of mental health litigation (staggeringly, the case was litigated for longer than three decades and was finally dismissed in 2003). But this case also demonstrates the important slippages between criminalization and pathologization, as the plaintiff was placed at Bryce Hospital through a criminal justice pathway and then psychiatrized and incarcerated indefinitely as a result. Ricky Wyatt was a fifteen-year-old "juvenile delinquent" with no label of mental illness who had been court ordered to be confined in the psych facility in an attempt to "improve his behavior." In addition, in his ruling, U.S. District Court judge Frank Johnson said that so-called patients at Bryce were "involuntarily committed through noncriminal procedures and without the constitutional protections that are afforded defendants in criminal proceedings," thus comparing criminal pathways to psychiatrization in his decision. He continued, "Adequate and effective treatment is constitutionally required because, absent treatment, the hospital is transformed 'into a penitentiary where one could be held indefinitely for no convicted offense.'"[16] The case makes the connection and differences between the rights of those incarcerated in psych hospitals, residential institutions, and prisons clear. Without quality treatment, a hospital is a prison.

One of the other famous cases and a turning point in deinstitutionalization history and litigation was *New York State Association for Retarded Children v. Rockefeller in New York,* aka the *Willowbrook* case, filed in 1973. One of the reasons this became such a landmark case was that at its peak, in 1969, Willowbrook was the largest institution for people with mental retardation labels in the world, holding sixty-two hundred people. Another reason was Geraldo Rivera's famous exposé of the institution in 1972.[17] Although Willowbrook and its lawsuit were the subject of several monographs and countless research and journalistic articles, a neglected aspect about the case is that it too connected the legal status and fate of those incarcerated in institutions to those in prisons.[18] Noting that federal courts had ruled that prisoners had a right to be free from cruel and unusual punishment, the judge in the *Willowbrook* case, Orrin Judd, reasoned that those confined to Willowbrook must be entitled to at least the same rights as prisoners. This connection is important for legal reasons but also for the kind of potential coalitional politics I am forwarding in this book, one that can connect the liberation of those incarcerated in a variety of locales, instead of freeing one group to be re-incarcerated in another way.

Judge Judd was no stranger to reform litigation,[19] as he also ruled in several prison reform cases.[20] But Judd did not think of the prison cases and the *Willowbrook* case as alike, as he did not perceive those institutionalized in Willowbrook to be *incarcerated.* Although most were institutionalized without their consent, and were committed by either their parents or court order, they were legally free to leave, in Judd's opinion. Therefore cruel and unusual punishment under the Eighth Amendment would not be applicable, even though those institutionalized had no means, support, or capacity for leaving and in fact had nowhere to go, in large part because the state had not invested in suitable community-based living. Here, as in other examples throughout this book, we can see the importance of understanding the ways different carceral locales are viewed in terms of their perceived goals and rationalities. In this case, the judge relied on common distinctions between the ethics and legality of custody of those whose incarceration is legitimated by "care" versus "punishment."

Because of Judd's, and others', narrow interpretation of incarceration, the legal team had to abandon Eighth Amendment protections (cruel and unusual). Instead, they decided to expand the legal scope of the right to protection from harm in institutions. The lawyers decided to utilize newer theories in the field of I/DD that called for the integration of those with disabilities into nonsegregated residential and educational settings. Specifically, the lawyers in the *Willowbrook* case utilized the principle of normalization, which meant that people with disabilities should be given the opportunity to live and be treated as much as possible like their nondisabled peers.[21] These theories made the claim that the only environment conducive to rehabilitation and education is a nonsegregated one. Since institutions were seen as the antithesis of inclusive settings and as inherently harmful, the lawyers argued that the only way to protect residents from harm, which is caused by living in abnormal settings, is to release them to live in the community. In his ruling, Judd upheld the right of those institutionalized to protection from harm. The ruling, like those following it, did not result in the immediate closure of the facility but instead led to a lengthy consent decree. However, the legal strategy used in this case was novel and approximates, in my mind, abolitionary instead of reformist strategy. In other words, the goal was to show that the only quality care that people with disabilities could ever obtain would be outside of the institution.

At the same time, a groundbreaking lawsuit in the prison litigation arena was developing, the ruling of which can be read as contributing to an abolitionary logic. *Holt v. Sarver* was initiated in 1969 when a group of prisoners held at Cummings Prison Farm and in Tucker Penitentiary filed a class action lawsuit that accused the entire prison system of being unconstitutional. At the time, the 1960s and early 1970s, the penal system in Arkansas comprised only two prisons, which were segregated by race. The Arkansas prison system was identified as a national disgrace after unmarked graves of murdered prisoners were found on the grounds of Cummins Prison Farm in 1968. As a result, the court found that "the totality of conditions" in the Arkansas system was unconstitutional. After finding out about the deplorable conditions and intense violence to which the prisoners were subjected, Judge Henley held that conditions and practices throughout the Arkansas penitentiary system, including the open barracks system, conditions in isolation cells, and the absence of a meaningful rehabilitation program, amounted to a violation of the Eighth Amendment's prohibition against cruel and unusual punishment.[22] Also, the state had failed to provide sufficient protection to those incarcerated (besides solitary confinement) who lived in constant fear for their lives. Therefore the district court in Arkansas ruled that the *entire* prison could be a form of cruel and unusual punishment.

Holt v. Sarver would open up the golden age of prisoners' rights litigation. Immediately after, federal judges elsewhere began issuing similar orders. The most expansive cases occurred in the South, where prisons were explicitly modeled after slave plantations and were expected to operate at low or no cost to the state. However, prisoners' rights judgments were handed down against prisons and jails not just in the South but in virtually all fifty states.[23] By 1984, almost one-quarter of the nation's 903 state prisons were operating under a court order.[24]

But even what some might describe as successful reform litigation, which in this case went as far as necessitating the *closure,* and not just reform, of specific facilities, actually led to increasing the scope of the carceral state. In the *Ramos* case described at the beginning of the chapter, the court declared the prison to be unfit for human habilitation, and it had to close down (after appeals). But in its place, Colorado erected not one but *three* new correctional facilities.[25] What we can learn from this case and others is that *closure on its own is not enough.* Much like the exposés discussed in chapter 2, conditions of confinement provided an entryway into public outrage and legal measures that might result in closing a specific facility (although most of the time they result in no significant action) or lead into reforming a facility (via a lengthy court ruling or a consent decree). The Colorado example, among many others, shows that closure of a facility does not necessarily bring about an epistemic shift in breaking down the rationality and legitimacy of confinement as a practice. As I argue here, following many abolitionists, closure of carceral institutions, such as mental hospitals and prisons, is a necessary but not sufficient action on the road to abolition.[26]

The most remarkable case in the history of decarceration litigation and one founded on what I call abolition litigation was in the disability arena. It was not until the *Halderman v. Pennhurst State School and Hospital* case, filed in 1974, that the *institutional/carceral logic* itself was placed on trial.[27] According to David Ferleger, the lawyer who handled the case, the case began when a high-level administrator urged the mother of an institutionalized woman (Terri Lee Halderman) to file suit on behalf of all residents of the institution and sent her to Ferleger, who was then the director of the Mental Patient Civil Liberties Project in Philadelphia. The lawyers did not just seek reparation for or change in the conditions of institutions but sought to prove that these carceral locales are inherently unnecessary and unconstitutional, and therefore need to be closed altogether.[28]

The rights to habilitation, protection from harm, and the least restrictive environment merge in the *Pennhurst* case into a direct challenge to the very concept of institutionalization, especially of those with intellectual disabilities. The right to protection from harm was understood by the legal team and the court as encompassing the right to be without the harms of institutionalization itself—resulting in loss of skills and dehumanization. The institution as such became legally and morally unjustifiable.[29] The connection with civil rights cases regarding desegregation was made clear in the ruling when Judge Broderick opined that "the confinement and isolation of the retarded in the institution called Pennhurst is segregation in a facility that clearly is separate and not equal."[30] Judge Broderick's decision was upheld by the Third Circuit Court, but the Supreme Court twice overturned it on narrow legal grounds and never engaged with the profound questions raised by this case and its implications for other institutions.

The *Pennhurst* case is unique and important for several reasons. Unlike the court's opinion in cases like *Willowbrook*, Judge Broderick understood the catch-22 of institutionalization and the inaccuracy of the claim of "free will" while incarcerated. As he explained it, "if the residents state that they wish to leave the institution and the staff determines that there is no place for them in the community, or believes that the individuals are not ready to go into the community, the staff will petition the courts to have the individuals committed to the institution by a court. Furthermore, those residents who either do not understand their alternatives, or are physically unable to indicate that they wish to leave Pennhurst, will be deemed to have consented to their continued placement at the institution."[31] Either route leads to the legitimation of confinement under the guise of voluntary treatment.

The plaintiffs and lawyers in the *Pennhurst* case were able to present, and win, a case against the merits, and not only conditions, of disability-based confinement. How were they able to do so? First, the professional tide was moving toward deinstitutionalization and community living.[32] The trial was filled with expert testimonies, all of which agreed that institutionalization of those with intellectual disabilities, regardless of the "severity" of their disability, is no longer the prevailing professional opinion. Instead, they discussed the importance of normalization, education, and habilitation. Former inmates of Pennhurst also made compelling testimonies to that effect. This put the *institutional logic* on trial. Second, Pennsylvania already had community-living arrangements for those with intellectual disabilities; therefore it was possible to show the success of this model and contrast it with the awful and abusive living conditions prevailing in Pennhurst. Finally, there is no doubt that in this era of the "hero judge," as Margo Schlanger calls it,[33] Judge Broderick played a significant role in advancing the strategy of abolition litigation.[34] In the sixth week of the trial, Broderick asked an expert witness, "Would you agree with the other witnesses I've heard that it is time to sound the death knell for institutions for the retarded?" These aspects led to a perfect storm that led to what I call *abolition litigation*.

What made this case most unique is that it showed the difference between litigation based on conditions of confinement versus whether confinement or segregation is justifiable to begin with. As Ferleger eloquently describes it, "legal efforts for the mentally disabled first emphasized commitment procedures (how you get in). Gradually, intra-institutional issues, including the right to treatment, began to receive attention (what happens once you are in). The newest inquiry in the law is whether there is justification for institutionalization (whether anyone should be in at all)."[35] Therefore, to me, *Pennhurst* signifies the first, and to date only, deinstitutionalization case that was about abolition as opposed to institutional reform. It did not call for reforming the institution—making it less crowded, improving staffing, offering more programming for those incarcerated—but instead marked a legal course showing the facility as inherently and fundamentally unjustifiable.

What can be learned from the Pennhurst case, as an abolition litigation? First, rejecting conditions of confinement as the primary legal strategy led the judge and legal counsel to reach the broad condemnation of institutionalization provided in this case. Second, and perhaps most important, despite the conditions I outlined above making *Pennhurst* a perfect case study, these only made for a perfect case in hindsight as none of those factors was understood at the time the case was pursued. This represents taking up what I call abolition dis-epistemology, letting go of attachments to ways of knowing what to do and embracing a utopian positionality, one that is centered on bringing about a noncarceral future while living in the here and now.[36] As Ferleger suggests about the case, "it was May 1974, and, no matter what one's personal views toward institutions, there was no reason to believe that any court in the United States would embrace an 'anti-institutionalization' position." But that is exactly what happened.

The Pennhurst case also crystalizes some of the stakeholders and those at the helm of litigation in this era of institution/prison reform. As was common, the suit was brought forth by "activist lawyers" and incarcerated plaintiffs. In deinstitutionalization, the forefront was the Mental Health Law Project, formed by some of the lawyers and mental health professionals who worked on early cases (later renamed the Bazelon Center), such as *Pennhurst, Willowbrook,* and *Wyatt.* In prisoners' rights litigation, there was much affinity with the civil rights movement at the time, which both depended on and spurred litigation as an engine of social change.[37] The major players in the prisoners' litigation arena, the NAACP Legal Defense and Education Fund and the ACLU, demonstrate the close relation between civil rights and prisoner rights struggles in that era.[38] Some lawyers who were involved in the civil rights movement simply followed their clients into prisons and got involved in penal reform that way. Although deinstitutionalization activists certainly took pages from the civil rights playbook, they were generally not officially connected to any black power or civil rights groups.

Legal scholar James Jacobs goes further to suggest that "many lawyers began to see themselves no longer as technicians but instead as prisoners' rights advocates working for the reform or abolition of the prison system."[39] It is important to note Jacobs's use of both abolition and reform as simultaneous goals for activist lawyers trying to effect change in prisons in that era, a point to which I return at the end of this chapter. For now, I will just point out that reform itself can come in different forms, including non-reformist reforms, such as reducing disablement and torturous conditions in prisons and institutions via litigation. Non-reformist reforms are the ones that create changes within the system, but without contributing to its expansion or legitimization, and are often a part of the abolitionary arsenal.

It was not only activist lawyers outside the walls but those inside as well that contributed to the prominence and relative success of prison reform litigation. Imprisoned intellectual Mumia Abu-Jamal also chronicles the contributions of "jailhouse lawyers" to establishing current penal codes regarding prisoners' rights as well as the repression that results from this advocacy.[40] For instance, it was jailhouse lawyers who exposed the deplorable conditions in the Texas prison system in the early 1970s, which eventually led to legal decrees that led to reforms. In general, Abu-Jamal demonstrates that it was jailhouse lawyers in many states who pioneered and advanced the practice of "prison law" and prisoners' rights.[41] An important example is the *Ruiz v. Estelle* case.

Ruiz v. Estelle was the most massive and potentially longest running prisoners' rights suit, which targeted and eventually led to many changes to the

Texas correctional system. It is important because it was filed by so-called jailhouse lawyers and also because of the disgraceful practices of many southern prisons, which dated back to eras that relied on convict leasing. The suit concerned prison conditions and the violation of the Eighth Amendment (cruel and unusual). It was filed in 1972 by David Ruiz, who was incarcerated in Texas, as a handwritten writ and became a class action suit with seven other imprisoned men. Specifically, the suit cited violations related to overcrowding, inadequate health care, unsafe working conditions, lack of safety, and severe and arbitrary disciplinary practices. What made the case and the Texas system unique in its monstrosity was the practice of making prisoners work in the field or serve essentially as guards (or trusty or tenders, as these were called), inflicting punishment on others who were incarcerated.

This practice was derived from the lineage of slavery to the convict lease system to modern-day prison farms. But it was not only the inhumane practice of using those incarcerated to surveil and corporally punish others but the resulting abuse, including sexual abuse, that resulted from such practices. As Robert Chase documents, "it constructed a vicious sex trade in which building tenders were given the prison administration's tacit approval to use their power to rape other inmates and engage in the buying and selling of inmate bodies as a sexual commodity that signified cultural standing and societal power."[42] The court ruled in the plaintiffs' favor, citing numerous instances of mistreatment and ordering sweeping changes throughout the Texas system. The state, however, continues to fight the ruling on appeals and in unimplemented consent decrees.

In the institutional litigation arena, especially for I/DD institutions, it was not jailhouse lawyers per se that brought on such class action suits but the persuasiveness of disabled plaintiffs and their insistence that they should not be forced to live in these places. In the *Pennhurst* case, for example, those formerly institutionalized described how their new lives in the community, with spaces of their own, support, and friends, were the opposite of the kind of segregation and isolation they'd felt while incarcerated.[43] In another example, in the famous *Olmstead* case, which I discuss later, the judge said of the plaintiffs' testimonies, "I was amazed. They were both so articulate. At a party after the hearing, they gave a talk about how it felt to take care of themselves and what a wonderful life they were leading. I went up on the podium and hugged each one of them. I'd never done that before."[44] Although this could be read as a compliment, within disability culture circuits such "praise" is described as "inspiration porn," which is the other side and companion to pitying people with disabilities.[45] Both are touted in low expectations the public and nondisabled professionals have of people with disabilities and self-advocates so that when they perform ordinary tasks (speaking in public, having sex, riding a bike), these are seen as extraordinary and inspirational acts for the nondisabled person to learn from. Even so, there is no doubt that those incarcerated or formerly incarcerated in institutions made a huge impact on deinstitutionalization litigation.

Effects of Prison and Institutional Reform Litigation

At this juncture, I want to offer a response to the question I posed at the beginning of the chapter: can class action litigation make meaningful improvement in the quality of life of those incarcerated? There is no doubt that some cases led to incremental changes in some facilities. In the aforementioned cases, some tried to use litigation to critique or halt specific carceral locales or practices (as in the *Ruiz* case), but even for those who tried to charge the whole system *(Holt)* or the rationale for incarceration itself *(Pennhurst)*, the results were reformist at best. In putting forth this question, my intent is not to paint a bleak picture of "failure" of institutional reform litigation. In fact, this strategy of sounding off alarms and characterizing institutional reform litigation as inherently unsuccessful has been used as a deliberate tactic by opponents of decarceration and deinstitutionalization that wanted to portray them as unrealistic and wasteful. This kind of critique would usher in legislation like the PLRA, which I discuss later. In other words, many critics have based their opinion on the success of litigation for prison and institutional reform on a few worst cases, among them Partlow and Bryce (the *Wyatt* case) and the prison farms in Arkansas (the *Holt* case).[46] These litigations indeed lasted for decades, and the court orders that called for closure or complete overhaul of the facilities were never quite adhered to, resulting in more litigation.

But I am not bringing forth these cases to question the efficacy of the legal strategy in quite the same way as its opponents. The questions that I want to put forward here are—What counts as "success" in such legal cases? Does ruling in favor of the plaintiffs and complying with subsequent court orders count as success? What is the goal of such litigation? As a nationwide study of prisoners' civil rights suits from 1973 to 1977 reports, "nearly everyone we interviewed believed that the cases have had great impact. Many have pointed out that even losing cases have resulted in reform."[47] But then again, what does reform in this context mean?

As Rachel Herzig suggests in her aptly titled article "Tweaking Armageddon" regarding campaigns to reform prison conditions, "improved conditions allow imprisoned people to resist that inhumanity more effectively and vigorously, challenging the systems and regimes in which they are confined. They also make it possible to stay alive while living in a cage." However, "it can further entrench the popularly held assumption that imprisonment is a necessary evil."[48] As I discussed in relation to exposés in the context of deinstitutionalization, such focus on "shock and awe" and deplorable conditions ends at best at reforming these facilities but not in abolishing them or their rationale.

Nonetheless, should we not celebrate the real improvements such lawsuits made in the lives of those incarcerated, even if they were not abolitionary, perhaps as a non-reformist reform? I suggest that there were various effects for institution and prison reform litigation that were both powerful and troubling; because they politicized those incarcerated and aided in forming resistance movements, they simultaneously brought on the creation of a more effective prison.

Politicization through Litigation

The significance of institutional reform litigation was not just in the specific outcome of the legal cases (who won, how well the case was implemented, how long it lasted, and so on) but in the broader sociolegal and political implications such lawsuits brought to bear as part of a larger arsenal of activist struggles for radical social change. The value of many of these cases was to bring attention to the conditions in prisons and in psychiatric and mental institutions, to which the general population was oblivious.[49] Ultimately, as Dean Spade suggests, law reform and legal advocacy can also expose the system and show the inherent contradiction it holds.[50] The symbolic value of institutional reform litigation was much bigger than its effect on the plaintiffs who brought the cases.

One such effect of reform litigation was that it constructed and reified the groups these suits were brought on behalf of as people deserving of rights and protection from the state. Although I critique, following many others, the rights framework throughout the book, it is important to note that obtaining rights as incarcerated people was not a small or obvious feat. Without perceiving those imprisoned and those with psychiatric and intellectual disabilities as groups deserving of constitutional rights, no litigation could have come from them or their behalf. On the most fundamental level, they had to be perceived, by the court and the public, as people, and not as property of the state. Of interest, then, is that the era of prisoners' rights litigation had to begin with granting prisoners, not rights, but selfhood.[51] This was not possible before the 1960s, as up until then, the courts only legally recognized prisoners as "slaves of the state."[52] The perception of prisoners as property of the state and as objects (of punishment, rehabilitation, labor, or experimentation) was not questioned in the courts in a sustained fashion before the era of reform litigation and black power. As I discussed in earlier chapters, prison abolitionists often position slavery, the convict lease system, and imprisonment on a continuum, as sites of warehousing and exploitation of the racialized underclass, hence the lineage of the concept of abolition.[53] According to Orlando Patterson, the slave doesn't enter into a relation of value exchange; she has no symbolic value and can only enter by relation of force and irrationality, through social death, violence, and/or familial discontinuity, a point expanded on by Hortense Spillers. For Saidiya Hartman, the ontological position of the slave is bound in nonexistence, in fungibility. Thus she is by definition nonhuman. Such theorizations would cast the project of seeking redemption through appeals to human rights as impossible.[54]

It was a somewhat related struggle in terms of the rights of those institutionalized who were not seen as subjects, but more as objects, often without an exchange value. Treating people with intellectual disabilities and other institutionalized populations as objects to be warehoused, profited off of, and considered fungible was the prevailing attitude throughout much of the twentieth century.[55] It is this assumption of absolute difference that mandated the segregation of disabled people and rationalized their institutionalization. Seeing those with disabilities, especially intellectual/cognitive and psychiatric, as "people first"[56] and as individuals with a claim to their own lives started to seep into new professional opinion in the 1970s and ultimately appeared in the courts as well.

In these ways, publicized court cases went beyond the narrow scope of the rights of those incarcerated. One of the great achievements of such litigation was that it brought more visibility to carceral sites and specific issues of those incarcerated within them to the courts' and the public's attention.

From being "out of sight, out of mind," the lawsuits acted much like earlier exposés did in questioning the efficacy, the legality, and, to some extent, the legitimacy of American carceral institutions, whether for punishment or for rehabilitation.[57]

Prisoners' rights, and reform litigation, made the prison a topic of public discussion. It made those incarcerated visible on a national scale.[58] As James Jacobs puts it, "prison litigation may be the peaceful equivalent of a riot."[59] But there were also nonmetaphorical uprisings in this era, which ushered in changes, including legal ones, in carceral enclosures. Dan Berger and Toussaint Losier discuss this era, especially 1968–72, as "the prison rebellion years," in which prisons produced publicly recognized revolutionary figures and witnessed an unprecedented scale of protests, including strikes, hostage taking, popular books, and newsletters.[60] As they suggest, the courtroom allowed incarcerated people in the 1960s not only their rights but a public platform and a vehicle to garner and construct a revolutionary agenda.

Therefore litigation became a powerful pedagogical and mobilization tool. The prisoners' rights movement, antipsychiatry, and self-advocacy movement galvanized and politicized those inside, as well as those not incarcerated, to understand incarceration and institutionalization as social and not just individual issues.[61] Within prisons, Black Muslims and the Nation of Islam were the earliest organizers for prisoners' rights in the 1960s, as Liz Samuels describes in her important genealogy of radicalism and prisoners' rights.[62] They shifted the thinking of many black prisoners to understand their situation as linked to racism via colonialism and therefore as a form of collective oppression. They were the first to bring forth lawsuits that established themselves as a group, and then a protected group demanding rights and freedoms. Such organizing by those imprisoned led to the creation of study groups, peer support regarding sexual assault or, later on, HIV, newsletters, unions, and revolutionary organizations.[63] Prison organizing was class based (like the United Prisoners Union, which was formed in 1970 and sought to organize prisoners as a protected class), antiracist and/or racially based (black power, Puerto Rican liberation), and, sometimes, nationalistic (Afrikanist). These uprisings as well as litigation led by and for prisoners had brought together incarcerated people across social distinctions into one "convict class."

In a similar analysis, Emily Thuma discusses campaigns to free women political prisoners in the 1970s as part of an undercurrent of anticarceral feminism in the era. They were mobilizing tools for freeing the individual person but also political building blocks for movements. These campaigns helped to change the discourse around who is a political prisoner to include noncisgendered men. The momentum helped build solidarity with incarcerated women and brought feminist antiracist organizers into the prison. Lastly, it was a feminist anticarceral approach in the sense that it shifted from "Free Joan Little" to "free them all." It became a call for abolition.[64]

In the deinstitutionalization arena, self-advocacy groups, people with intellectual or developmental disabilities who advocate for social change, became ubiquitous in the 1970s. Much like their prisoner counterparts, many self-advocates became politicized while incarcerated in residential institutions, and action within self-advocacy groups arose out of a desire to help their friends get out. Many self-advocates also testified in hearings about institutional closure and are still filing lawsuits on behalf of those institutionalized. This resistance did not go unnoticed by the powers that be. For example, to this day, self-advocates are often denied visitation to their peers in nursing homes and institutions for the fear of "influencing them" with an anti-institutional ideology.[65]

In short, the symbolic effects of lawsuits, beyond the specific individual or institution involved in the suit, extended to educating the public regarding institutionalization and imprisonment, or advancing a new or alternative ideology such as normalization, least restrictive environment, or imprisonment as cruel and unusual punishment.[66] It questioned not just the efficacy of incarceration but in some cases also its rationale. These court cases, much like exposés, also aided in raising awareness about the conditions in prisons and institutions, which were mostly unknown or not discussed in a public way. In addition to collectivizing those incarcerated, class action suits offered the possibility to create policies that stretch beyond the individual case. Unfortunately, and because of the repression that came from the success of such inside organizing, some of these changes resulted in increased carceral capacity and techniques.

The Rise of the Governable Cage

Institutional reform litigation led not only to incremental changes in the conditions of the prison and institution but also to a more effective way to govern these carceral spaces. What Schlanger calls "the lawful prison" ushered by litigation reform is certainly a step up from the "wild west" version in which those incarcerated were truly out of sight and out of mind, as well as out of legal reach. But as Feeley and Rubin suggest, "the modern constitutional prison is a mixed blessing.... Conditions and practices are much improved and the constitutionalization of the process assures that these improvements are likely to be permanent. But the mission of prisons and jails remains safety and security by means of a tight system of control. Judicial reform has, on balance, enhanced the ability of officials to pursue this mission."[67]

Institutional reform litigation therefore also ushered in the growth of these edifices not just as cages but as "iron cages," as sociologist Max Weber described the coming age of bureaucratic management in 1905.[68] Applying Weber's theory to incarceration, I suggest that instead of autocratic super-intendents and wardens, we now have forms and ways that, instead of setting people free, increasingly legitimate and neutralize their captivity. Such ongoing and expansive litigation brought in the technocratic era[69] in carceral enclosures. Instead, or mostly in addition to, indifference or abuse, post the era of litigation, those incarcerated were and are treated with bureaucratic measures. People's captivity was not enough, and neither was disciplining or self-disciplining, as Foucault proposes.[70] I suggest that the governable iron cage indicates seemingly more humane ways of capture, ways that need constant administrative oversight as a result of litigation or consent decrees in specific facilities or states. The result is forms piling on forms, increased administrative staff, and a growing prison– and institutional–industrial complex—as well as a decarceration–industrial complex.[71]

This is also part of Dis Inc., the ways that disability is both incarcerated and incorporated. By incorporation, I mean both the inclusion of disability and disabled people in education, housing, and so on, and incorporation by literal corporations as part of the institutional–, prison–, and decarceration–industrial complex. The administrative grip and oversight that came as a result of some of these suits did not lead to the liberation of people but to more effective ways to ensure their confinement. Even with the closure of institutions, other sites and forms of incarceration and incorporation emerged, such as group homes and halfway homes, in which those in the human service industry are now in charge of measuring and surveilling that life is carried out according to all rules and regulations. This historical process further ensures that those deinstitutionalized and decarcerated are incorporated into community settings according to even more rules and regulations.

This is an aspect discussed frequently regarding the success of deinstitu-tionalization. Between 1977 and 2009, the total number of residential settings in which people with developmental disability labels received residential ser-vices grew from 11,008 to an estimated 173,042 (an increase of 1,472 percent), while total service recipients increased from about 247,780 to an estimated 439,515 individuals (77.4 percent).[72] Because most of these newer settings are much smaller than the massive institutions of previous decades, they are not typically counted as "institutional" placements. But the number of people housed therein as well as daily routines and other aspects of life in these set-tings lead many people with disabilities, family members, and advocates to view them as smaller institution-like settings within the community.

Even if one lives in the community with support (especially those with I/DD labels), the iron cage of governmentality looms large. For example, as discussed in chapter 2 regarding the principle of normalization, or social role valorization, we now have not the empowerment of people with dis-abilities to live independently but checklists by a managerial class to ensure that they act "as normal as possible" as their peer group. This includes check-ing up to ensure people "act as expected" by waking up at specific hours, brushing their teeth, using a fork instead of a spoon, and other daily activities that actually constrain people's lives and create new subjectivities, as Drink-water demonstrates,[73] as part of the decarceration–industrial complex.

In many cases, what some might describe as successful reform litigation, which improved overcrowding or conditions in a specific site of enclosure or necessitated its closure, resulted in increased carceral capacity. Joshua Guetzkow and Eric Schoon examined the unintended effect of prison over-crowding litigation on incarceration in forty-nine states from 1972 to 1996. They show that on average, prison overcrowding litigation had no discern-ible impact on prison crowding itself, which remained unchanged after an overcrowding litigation action occurred. And while they indicate that prison overcrowding litigation, as well as prison crowding itself, does not result directly in an increase in the incarceration rate, indirectly, it has a small effect by boosting prison capacity, which has a direct effect on the incarcera-tion rate.[74]

If we stretch this argument to more recent litigation and advocacy to improve prison conditions, the case becomes even clearer, for example, the framework of gender-responsive justice, which came to replace or compete with the idea of equal treatment, punishment, and sentencing for women, also known as the parity model, within the criminal justice system. Because advocacy, including by self-proclaimed feminists, turned to focus on women's unacceptable conditions of confinement in dilapidated facilities designed for men, the response was building new prisons and sites of incarceration just for women (which would sometimes also include transgender women and gender-nonconforming people). Thus litigation and advocacy led to further retrenchment of carcerality. With increased oversight and fear of litigation came increased capacity for incarceration.

Present and Future of Institutional Reform Litigation

The 1970s were a turning point in reform litigation, especially regarding prisons. In September 1971, an uprising erupted in Attica prison in upstate New York and became a five-day takeover of the facility by about a thousand prisoners. By the time it ended, thirty-nine people, ten of whom were guards, had been killed by state troopers on the order of Governor Rockefeller. The revolt came days after the murder of radical black prison activist George Jackson in San Quentin prison in California. But prisoners who took over Attica did not attribute the revolt only to his murder, which some saw as a political assassination, but also to the conditions within the prison at the time and of their incarceration overall.

After Attica, some reforms were initiated in prisons in New York, which allowed for more religious freedom and more recreation time and addressed some other issues that were brought up by those incarcerated in Attica. In the public consciousness, though, Attica became a symbol of both the need for reform and, more importantly, of state repression in its extreme. For many people of that generation, especially young, white, and middle class, Attica was the first time they got a glimpse of what goes on in U.S. prisons, as well as the way the state handles political unrest, and the incident ended up politicizing a whole generation of activists, some of whom became more involved in prisoners' rights movements or other social justice causes of the era as a result.

As some got politicized, some got radicalized, others became disillusioned. As Liz Samuels discusses in her comprehensive analysis of the roots of prison abolition in the 1970s, "the 'Attica rebellion' ... also marked the beginning of the end of the revolutionary prisoners' movement—at least as an item of national attention."[75] Attica made some of those already politicized become so disappointed with the push and pull of prison reform that they came to believe that the only reform could be the abolition of imprisonment and the conditions leading to it. But some claim that these uprisings actually led to the demise of the prisoners' rights era, not to its strengthening. I suggest that, contrary to many accounts declaring the demise of reform litigation, it did not end in the 1970s but shifted focus and strategies.

In *The Rise and Fall of California's Radical Prison Movement*, Eric Cummins suggests that activists and groups on the left, which were mostly young, white, educated activists, romanticized the prison as a hothouse for breeding radical politics. They were also infatuated with individual prisoners, especially well-spoken political prisoners, and started thinking that all those incarcerated are potential political leaders and soldiers of the revolution. In his polemic book, Cummins essentially blames this revolutionary fervor for the demise of effective prison activism after 1970.[76]

Taken from a broader analytic, I suggest that it would be dismissive to declare the demise of litigation as a tool of decarceration or even "the fall of the prisoners' rights movement." It is true that the image of the revolutionary prisoner, à la George Jackson, has subsided, but it is equally important to remember the gendered dynamics of that image. If the image of *the* prisoner in the 1970s was that of (mostly black) revolutionary zealots, and in the 1980s, it was the frivolous complainers (the image that led to the creation of the Prison Litigation Reform Act, as I describe later), the image of the prisoner in the 2000s is that of the overcrowded, mentally and physically injured incarcerated individual, as Jonathan Simon suggests.[77] In other words, the earlier image of prisoners' rights (freedom fighter, mostly black, mostly man) came as a result of state repression, which both led to an influx of political prisoners and politicized those incarcerated. In the 2000s onward, with the ascent of mass or hyperincarceration,[78] state violence manifested not just in incarceration and its conditions but in its quantity, the mass character of it. This is part of what Puar refers to as the biopolitics of debilitation.[79]

The image, tactics, and populations targeted by prison litigation had shifted, but it did not die; it only became less masculine and therefore less known or discussed. I therefore turn now to chart the present and possible futures of institutional reform litigation by analyzing how gender/sexuality and disablement became renewed avenues for prison reform litigation from the 1970s onward.

Litigation in Women's Prisons

As legal activist Ellen Barry aptly puts it, "something happened to the prisoner's rights movement from 1975 to the 1990s. Women happened."[80] Some may perceive "women's issues" in prisons, or gender, to be a specific and minute aspect of the growing carceral state. But as feminist abolitionists point out, a feminist analysis of the prison–industrial complex can shed light not only on those incarcerated who identify as women or gender nonconforming but on the entire rationale of segregation, punishment, and incarceration.[81] This illumination in turn helps organizing, litigation, and scholarship that try to chip away at carceral spaces and ultimately aids all those who are incarcerated and their loved ones. Andrea Ritchie describes her own important project, as it "emphasized police violence against black women and women of color . . . and asks what these experiences teach us about manifestations of structural racism. Finally, it pushes us to consider what it would mean for women to no longer be invisible in discourses of racial profiling, police brutality, mass incarceration, violence and safety."[82]

Anti-prison activism has always been characterized by a kind of "women's work." Whether as partners, mothers, or family of incarcerated or formerly incarcerated loved ones or as radical attorneys, women (broadly defined) have been the core of anti-prison organizing.[83] Even though black power movements, especially the Black Panther Party, understood the need for strong programming for families and children, this understanding did not necessarily translate into a major focus of their organizing within prison walls. It was mainly those incarcerated in women's prisons who have historically organized to fight against a different set of prison conditions, mainly the ones that separate those incarcerated from their families and communities on the outside (such as draconian visitation policies). These issues, particularly around parenting, medical care, and birthing behind bars, had become sources of litigation in several states, especially during the 1980s. By 1988, at least fifteen states had gender-based equal protection suits pending for their prisons.[84]

The most litigated aspect in women's facilities had been brought as part of equal protection, mainly whether those incarcerated in women's facilities get access to the same or similar services as those incarcerated in men's prisons.[85] Feminist criminologist Nicole Rafter discusses the often inferior conditions or programs received in women's facilities as rationalized as being due to "numbers" (the smaller proportion of those incarcerated in such facilities) and "nature" (women are innately nurturing or promiscuous or other beliefs about women's character as a class).[86] The "parity movement," seen in the 1970s and 1980s, also aimed at making sure those incarcerated in women's prisons got equal treatment and adequate access to services, some on par with men and some specifically tailored to their own needs (around reproductive health, for example).

There is no doubt that litigation was a useful mobilization tool, and some lawsuits resulted in real material changes for those imprisoned in women's prisons, for example, regarding visitation rights, access to rehabilitation and reentry programs. As Rafter mentions, most equal protection suits do not even go to trial, but they have been used as tools to ensure those in women's prisons have access to specific programming and services not otherwise afforded to them.[87] In addition, much like the larger prisoners' rights movement, lawsuits galvanized women and feminists inside and outside carceral spaces to raise awareness of the plight of incarcerated women as well as the issue of mass incarceration more broadly.

But equality with men's prisons can be achieved in a variety of ways, including importing punitive measures that already exist in men's facilities into women's facilities. It can also be achieved by the opposite tactic—showing that there are no adequate programming or services in men's facilities and therefore they don't have to provide them in women's facilities either.[88] But the broader critique in terms of reform as well as carceral abolition is whether this type of litigation also helped to expand incarceration (building more women's facilities, harsher treatments and punishments, etc.) to seemingly accommodate demands for gender equality.

In other words, litigation regarding prison conditions and gender parity can often fall under the discourse of carceral feminism, adding to the expansion of the carceral state instead of chipping away at it. For example, Elizabeth Whalley and Colleen Hackett show how rape crisis centers and gender-responsive programming for criminalized women ended up advancing mainstream, white liberal feminist agendas, or "dominating feminisms."[89] They define *dominating feminisms* as "a version of feminism that seeks to leverage formal institutional powers—including the carceral state—vis-à-vis a white supremacist state order with the hope of securing equality between (cis-gendered) men and women." This nexus of gendered racial criminal pathologization is painfully clear in the lives of women and gender-nonconforming people, especially indigenous and black.

Therefore many abolitionist feminists refer to this type of advocacy as "carceral feminism,"[90] the belief that the state and especially the criminal justice system can alleviate violence or abuse against women. Anticarceral feminists[91] or abolition feminists[92] contest this approach for several reasons. One is because they maintain that prisons *are* a form of violence against women[93] and gender-nonconforming or trans folks. Prisons don't protect women from violence, as mainstream anti–domestic violence campaigns make it appear, but instead unleash state violence (in the form of increased policing, surveillance, and incarceration, to name a few) onto women, gender-nonconforming people, and their families.[94] Second, such approaches end up expanding the scope of the carceral state, with the most detrimental effects being felt by women, gender-nonconforming, and trans folks in communities of color.[95]

It is therefore important to understand that appeals to gender equality in corrections or gender-responsive programming always intertwine gender, race-ability, sexuality, and class in a version of respectability politics that is antithetical to liberation and freedom more broadly. In the context of prison litigation, the consequences of carceral feminism are clear in relation to its function as expanding the carceral state. Class action suits at times led to establishing separate programs or units for women prisoners, and even led to the court advocating for the establishment of new prisons that will serve only women, as was the case in *Fiandaca v. Cunningham* (1987).[96]

Expanding this analysis of prison reform litigation to the 1980s and 1990s, I would go further to say that it wasn't just "women" who happened to prison litigation but *gender* that became a primary target of legal activism, and especially the intersection of gender, race, and sexuality.[97] For example, Regina Kunzel discusses the abandonment of incarcerated LGBTQ people by the larger LGBT movement/s in the 1980s due to the shift of the gay rights movement from solidarity-based politics to a liberal politics focused on rights and respectability, such as gay marriage.[98] This orchestrated forgetting privileged particular subjects as deserving and indeed as the focus of LGBT activism, which merged heteropatriarchy and gender normativity with class and whiteness.

In the 1990s, LGBT activists were active fighting against homophobic and transphobic violence. Just like the anti–domestic violence movement, however, this activism, which often took the form of legal campaigns and lobbying, helped in creating hate crime legislation, which entailed giving harsher sentences for those convicted of violence due to discrimination, especially race and sexuality. This is what Sarah Lamble calls "queer investments in punishment."[99] These legislative campaigns, again, increase the scope of incarceration and the reach of the carceral state without actually address-ing the needs and safety of queer people, especially those of color and gen-der nonconforming. Bassichis, Lee, and Spade ask in their scathing critique of movements for trans and queer liberation that we remember that LGBT movements came from activism of those most marginalized, such as Sylvia Rivera and Marsha P. Johnson, and they further ask us to keep that legacy alive: "What would it mean to *embrace*, rather than *shy away from*, the impos-sibility of our ways of living as well as our political visions? . . . Could these groundbreaking and often unsung activists have imagined that only forty years later the 'official' gay rights agenda would be largely pro-police, pro-prisons, and pro-war—exactly the forces they worked so hard to resist?"[100] In other words, (some) queer and trans activists see the State itself, with its violent apparatuses (the police, the military, the courts, and confinement), as mech-anisms we should fight to abolish, not beg to reform or be included within.

Increased awareness of gender/sexuality in sites of incarceration (women, queer, trans, gender nonconforming) made it appear like prison activism as a whole had subsided since the 1970s and that the prisoners' rights move-ment and legal activism in regard to incarceration had died down instead of changed, in terms of eras, targets, and strategies. But the activist fire of those incarcerated had certainly refused to die, despite much effort by the state to extinguish it.

Olmstead and New Institutional Reform Litigation

Even though the heyday of deinstitutionalization and decarceration litiga-tion had been halted by the state and the courts, it had not vanished, as we have seen with women- and gender-specific litigation; but it did change from earlier institutional litigation in the 1970s. In the disability arena, the case that became the litmus test of what can be termed "new institutional reform litigation" is *Olmstead v. L.C.* (1999). The case involved two develop-mentally disabled women—Lois Curtis, who teamed up with a lawyer, Sue Jamieson, at Atlanta Legal Services, and Elaine Wilson, who joined the suit after. By then, Curtis had spent half her life in one institution or another. Jamieson recounts how Curtis would periodically pick up the phone and call her, always asking the same question: "When can I get out of here?"[101]

Both Wilson and Curtis were admitted to a psychiatric unit in a Georgia hospital and were confined to it for years, even after medical professionals said they were ready to move to a community-based setting. But because the state of Georgia claimed they didn't have such placements available, the women stayed confined. The suit utilized the 1990 Americans with Disabilities Act (ADA), which was not available in earlier reform litigation. Eventually, the Supreme Court upheld the Eleventh Circuit decision that Georgia had indeed violated the ADA by forcing the two women to remain in a state mental hospital after they were deemed ready for discharge and ruled that a state is required under the ADA to provide community-based treatment for those with mental disabilities, if certain conditions are met.[102] By the time the case reached the Supreme Court in 1999, both plaintiffs were already living in the community; however, *Olmstead* would still become a landmark case for contemporary disability rights and deinstitutionalization.

The case was followed by a wave of new or renewed litigation challenging the unlawful incarceration of people with intellectual and psychiatric disabilities in residential institutions and psychiatric facilities. By 2012, the Department of Justice had filed or joined *Olmstead*-related suits in at least twenty-one states. But as disability legal scholar Samuel Bagenstos suggests, the legal arguments used in these lawsuits were quite different from the ones used in previous institutional reform litigation. The litigation used in the 1970s and 1980s relied heavily on due process. Instead, current litigation relied on the ADA. The implication is that the legal challenge had moved from protesting the loss of liberty due to institutionalization (and the need to justify this confinement with rehabilitation, for example) into an *antidiscrimination* argument.[103]

The critical decision to shift litigation into an antidiscrimination claim, and the ability to do so once the ADA was passed in 1990, was what made the *Olmstead* case significant.[104] This new legal strategy would push "new institutional reform" forward. If, in the 1960s up until the 1980s, litigation sought to improve living conditions in institutions and in some cases to close down certain facilities, because they were inhumane or inhabitable, the strategy post *Olmstead* is to increase community-based living. In other words, the fight is not so much about the institution and its conditions as about what comes *after or even instead of* the institution. The goal is to expand budgets that states spend on community-based services and placements and to ensure that these are quality services.[105]

The change in immediate goals could in part be attributed to the success of early reform litigation. The general trend in most states had been to decrease institutionalized populations, but now the fight needed to shift to what happens post deinstitutionalization, once people are discharged. In abolitionary terms, the strategy had shifted from decarceration to focusing on building alternative services and structures and making sure people are not reincarcerated. This is not done in an either/or approach but instead it is a both/and, as one strategy cannot prevail without the other.

Olmstead signaled a meaningful turn for the legal rights of those with disabilities to live in a noncarceral setting that is not segregated (with qualifications to this right). But much like earlier deinstitutionalization litigation, it did not actually lead to the desired changes hoped for. In 2009, on the tenth anniversary of *Olmstead,* the grassroots organization ADAPT descended on Atlanta in an effort to make *Olmstead* a reality. Much like in earlier institutional litigation, a decade after the landmark case, the state of Georgia had not complied with its basic tenets. ADAPT's trip to Georgia was significant for another reason, as ADAPT is a direct-action disability rights organization (focusing in the past few decades on ensuring community living as opposed to institutional or nursing home living for people with disabilities) that uses nonviolent resistance as its main tactic. As such, it was important for ADAPT activists to visit the Martin Luther King Jr. Center for Nonviolent Social Change in Atlanta, as a symbol and inspiration for the tactics used in their activism. In the rose garden in front of the MLK national historical site, ADAPT members gathered to hear from Georgia advocates, including Lois Curtis and Sue Jamieson, who had spurred the *Olmstead* lawsuit.[106]

The ADAPT newsletter documents the 2009 actions in Georgia with a full-page description of the trip to the MLK Jr. Center under the title "ADAPT makes a pilgrimage to the King Center," which denotes the importance and symbolism of this trip. Following the description appears a striking photograph of an unnamed man. It's a color photograph of a black man from his waist up who looks to be in his sixties. He is sitting, seemingly staring into space, behind a fence overlaid with what looks like barbed wire. The photo is striking because, as explained in the newsletter, "in stark contrast to the beautiful rose garden in front of the King Center a barbed wire fence separated us from the Parkview Manor Nursing Facility next door. Having one symbol of liberty juxtaposed next to that symbol of oppression reminded us all of how easily people with disabilities in this country can lose their freedom because of the institutional bias in long term care."[107] The juxtaposition that ADAPT alludes to and is aware of is between the MLK Jr. Center, which symbolizes freedom struggles, and the incarceration happening in the facility next door.[108] ADAPT's decades-long activism brought to the forefront the idea that what happens in such nursing homes and group homes is indeed (disability based) incarceration, and their actions popularized this view.

These connections between incarceration and race-ability are important for understanding the interrelatedness of various sites of incarceration and the kinds of coalitional work needed to counter them. Many hailed *Olmstead* as the "civil rights case of disability." As disability advocate Mark Johnson said of Elaine Wilson (the second *Olmstead* plaintiff) after her passing, "to people with disabilities, this case is as significant as Brown v. Board of Education was to people of color."[109] This analogy makes sense, as many deinstitutionalization strategies, especially in the legal or antidiscrimination arena, such as *Olmstead*, took a page out of the civil rights playbook. But from an intersectional perspective, such statements only further assume, and then actively construct, disability rights and disability movements as white. In this case, such proclamations are even more disturbing, because the original plaintiff in the *Olmstead* case, Lois Curtis, is a black woman. For her, it is not a choice between civil rights and disability rights—her positionality necessitates both. This is the essence of an intersectional approach, which was developed as a legal framework by critical legal scholar Kimberlé Crenshaw.[110]

The term *intersectionality* in its original context produced by Crenshaw came about from a similar context to the one used here under the ADA, that is, in the context of antidiscrimination law. Crenshaw wanted to apply the race/class/gender analysis of black feminism to laws that did not and at the time could not (legally) acknowledge these connections. Specifically, under the interpretation of discrimination in the eyes of the law, black women could not show gender-based discrimination (because not all women were discriminated against, only black women) or race-based discrimination (because not all black people were discriminated against, only women). Intersectionality, then, came about not as a new framework in feminism (as others, including Crenshaw, detail, this analytic can be traced back to long before the twentieth century among black feminists) but as a new feminist legal conceptualization that can account for black women's oppression legally.

The kind of attention to race-ability and criminal pathologization I am trying to advance here asks, what if ADAPT were to position themselves as an abolitionary organization in a variety of carceral settings for disabled people, including disabled people of color, which include nursing homes but also prisons? And what if prisoners' rights litigation and desegregation was not just an analogy but an actual intersectional analytic? And what if this intersectional analytic also extended to disability?[111] As I now turn to showing, disability became a major trope in prisoners' rights litigation, but not necessarily from a critical or intersectional positioning.

Disabling Prisoners' Rights Litigation

When funding and support for prison reform litigation started to subside beginning in the early 1980s, some claimed that lawyers moved on to pursue institutional reform in other arenas, particularly in relation to mental disabilities, which became a prominent area of litigation. For example, Jacobs remarks in his broad survey of the prisoners' rights movement in 1980, "The luster of the prisoners' rights movement seems to be fading. The image of the prisoner as hero, revolutionary, and victim is disappearing. Other minority rights movements, such as that associated with the handicapped, are increasingly attracting resources and the energies of young attorneys."[112]

But I want to suggest that this is not a zero-sum game in which players moved from one arena (prisoners' rights) to another (disability and deinstitutionalization). As I have demonstrated throughout the book, disability, imprisonment, and deinstitutionalization are intimately connected, and incarceration does not happen only in prisons. Litigation continued in the prison and institutional arena in ways that constantly intersect: disablement became an even bigger rallying cry in prisons, and placement in residential or treatment facilities was beginning to be seen as a form of incarceration. Despite common belief, deinstitutionalization was not pursued at the expense of, nor did it take the spotlight away from, prison litigation, as Jacobs suggests in the preceding quote. Such assumptions not only pit one group (disabled, considered non-incarcerated, and mostly white) against another (those imprisoned, not discussed as disabled and mostly of color and men) but also fuel the discourse of prisons as the new asylums, as I have deconstructed in chapter 4.

Indeed, what strikes me in recent prison litigation is the immense degree of *reliance* on disablement, the ways that sites of incarceration are disabling, as potential conduits to decarceration, as I explain in the following pages in relation to *Plata* litigation. I therefore suggest that it is more useful to discuss the ways prisoners' rights and disability rights intersected and morphed over time, as related to decarceration, than it is to paint a progress narrative in which one (deinstitutionalization and disability rights) subsumed the other (prison litigation). An important case in point for such intersectional analysis is the passage of the Prison Litigation Reform Act (PLRA).

Owing to the partial successes of reform litigation, it may not be surprising to learn that such efforts were soon curtailed by the State. The PLRA was passed in 1996 with a stated purpose, backed up by a conservative agenda, to combat seemingly frivolous and costly litigation by prisoners. The act was passed with no actual evidence demonstrating any substantial problems with so-called frivolous litigation, but the rhetoric of pampered prisoners who were abusing the system with their minor complaints ultimately won the day. As feminist legal scholar Beth Ribet summarizes, "the PLRA's various components have essentially devastated the prospects for using the federal courts in the service of prisoner advocacy or progressive prison reform, as collectively they restrict types and duration of relief and remedy, place barriers in the way of prisoner's ability to file suit at all, and mediate against the prospects of finding legal representation."[113]

Mumia Abu-Jamal discusses the crucial context of the passage of the PLRA in 1996, at a time of massive attack on the practice of advocacy and litigation by public interest lawyers and especially jailhouse lawyers. The passage of the PLRA with larger reforms does not escape Abu-Jamal, as it was the same time that Temporary Assistance for Needy Families had changed and welfare was curtailed by the same administration (Clinton's). Abu-Jamal connects these policy changes to media portrayals that showcased poor people, especially those of color, as lazy and deceiving the taxpayers into getting welfare instead of going to work. At the same time, the same media accounts constructed prisoners as trying to deceive the system by over-complaining and litigating and therefore requiring restrictions on their right to sue from prison.

If we look at the PLRA from a further intersectional lens, it is clear that this act poses challenges to any prisoner or advocacy group attempting to use the law to reform or challenge the system, but it represents an even greater barrier to disabled prisoners as prospective plaintiffs. The PLRA seems to be in direct conflict with the ADA, diluting an already weak piece of legislation to a point at which it is made meaningless in a prison context. Put simply, if the aim of the ADA was to eliminate barriers to equitable participation of people with disabilities in various arenas of life (as to mitigate discrimination), the aim of the PLRA is the outright creation of barriers so that prisoners (including disabled prisoners and their advocates) will have less access to seek relief from the courts. But, as Ribet suggests, advocacy groups and imprisoned people can and should attempt to use the ADA to neutralize or minimize the effects of the PLRA as much as possible.[114] Ribet claims that since disability in prisons is not the exception but in fact the norm, most of those incarcerated (and/or their advocates) can use the ADA to circumvent the PLRA. Like other abolitionists, Ribet is not proposing that disabled prisoners be made into a distinct group that will then be exempt from a particular legislation (in this case, the PLRA) but instead that the *prevalence of disability be used to eradicate* this legislation and essentially make it meaningless.

Thus disablement or debilitation might be used to abolitionary ends and provide some relief from the tightening restrictions on litigation reform. In fact, much of the new litigation around prison conditions has to do with disabled people (and, as discussed earlier, women or gender-nonconforming folks) who are incarcerated.[115] Nothing highlights this more than recent cases in the California prison system, chronicled in Jonathan Simon's *Mass Incarceration on Trial*. These cases show that institutional reform litigation is not just alive and well but has become a major decarceration engine, mostly by using the cases of disabled prisoners to bring to light the deplorable conditions those incarcerated have to endure on a daily basis. The most recent and best known case, *Coleman-Plata v. Schwarzenegger,* filed in 2009, was a consolidation of two cases, both of which had to do with disablement in prisons. *Coleman v. Wilson* was a case from 1995 ordering comprehensive reform in mental health delivery in California's prisons, and *Plata v. Davis* was a 2002 agreement in which California was required to provide better health care in prisons.

The *Coleman* suit charged that the presence of so-called mentally ill people in prisons was not an aberration but an integral part of the current prison system. Because of this, the lack of mental health services in prisons becomes a human rights violation. The underlying claim was therefore that mass incarceration itself is the source of unconstitutional conditions. It showed that incarceration en masse with its overcrowding and the high presence of prisoners with mental and physical ill health is not a temporary condition of the system but its very foundation. *Plata,* therefore, put mass incarceration itself on trial, according to Simon.[116]

The three judges in the *Coleman-Plata v. Schwarzenegger* case ruled that California's chronic overcrowding has persisted despite two decades of lawsuits to prevent it, and this condition prevents any possibility of providing adequate mental health and general health care in California prisons, as instructed in earlier lawsuits by the court. The judges therefore ordered California to reduce the number of prisoners to 137 percent capacity in two years (a reduction of approximately forty thousand prisoners).[117] *Coleman-Plata* is made even more remarkable since the federal court challenged the very rationale of mass incarceration, which had become a de facto forty-year policy of overcrowding and lack of provisions, in an era of extreme court deference because of PLRA. This was a major victory for prison reform and institutional reform litigation, and much has been written about the case and its effects. But little has been said about the vehicle by which decarceration was sought—the way disability was front and center; how ableism permeates such cases; and the ways it wasn't just mass incarceration that was put on trial but *disablement* in prisons.

Coleman-Plata v. Schwarzenegger also carries on the legacy of institutional and prison litigation of the past, especially in their heyday. Simon shows how the suit humanized those incarcerated by showing the inhuman conditions they had to live in everyday and indicting the system for their indignities. Simon contends, or hopes, that the stories in *Plata* change the image of prisoners in the twenty-first century. Through such legal exposés, Simon suggests, the image of those incarcerated will therefore shift from a population of violent perpetrators or dissidents to a vulnerable population at risk of debilitation or death from incarceration itself.

Thanks in part to the reduction of those incarcerated in California, the number of those incarcerated in prisons in the United States is starting to fall. Simon contends therefore that as a result of this suit, *mass* incarceration, as a penal policy leading to overcrowding and abominable conditions, was severely undermined and was "put on trial." But is that the case? It seems that legal victories of the past should warrant us to be cautious of such statements. Using the terrible conditions of confinement and lack of health care in carceral spaces for institutional reform is not a new strategy, as shown earlier.

Both deinstitutionalization and prison reform litigation used strategies of decarceration through appealing for habilitation and mental and other health care provisions in carceral enclosures as ways to either force the closure of these facilities or decarcerate those who reside in them. Even if it is true that *Plata v. Schwarzenegger* put *mass* incarceration on trial, it did not critique confinement itself and the legitimacy of these carceral edifices. Unlike the *Pennhurst* decision, the need for segregation was not questioned by the courts, only the conditions by which people are segregated. Will such court decisions lead to a more effective governable iron cage or to liberation? In other words, will cases reliant on disablement lead to a rethinking of mass incarceration, or will they instead lead to incarceration by means that comply with the courts' vision of "humane" incarceration, for example, the opening of more jails and prisons so they are less overcrowded or provide more psychopharmaceuticals (the most common "treatment" of mental crisis in prisons), what Kilgore referred to as carceral humanism?[118] Or maybe the opening of new facilities, but this time with better health care, or perhaps with separate mental health facilities, a form of carceral sanism? Will that be a victory of prison litigation? Of reform? What does reform mean when the carceral state is in constant flux?[119] Therefore carceral feminism (the belief that the criminal justice system can alleviate violence against women) is today compounded with carceral ableism/sanism, as explained in the introduction and conclusion of this book. I want to add here, though, that carceral ableism, and especially sanism (the oppression of people with mental health differences), also plays a role in the ways *decarceration,* and not just incarceration, is done and discussed.

Individual Decarceration Cases and Carceral Ableism/Sanism

Even seemingly benevolent attempts by the courts to reinstate the human rights of prisoners and those institutionalized reinforce instances of ableism if done under a view of the prison or institution as a place that can contain justice. It then reinforces ableism because of the need to emphasize vulnerability and abjection to secure any kind of relief from the courts.

In the groundbreaking *Olmstead* case, for example, the court seems to follow a framework of antidiscrimination and even rights for people with disabilities, supporting their right to live in the community. However, the actual text of the summary judgment renders analysis more complex. In the summary, Judge Kennedy states, "It must be remembered that for the person with severe mental illness who has no treatment the most dreaded of confinements can be the *imprisonment inflicted by his own mind,* which shuts reality out and subjects him to the torment of voices and images beyond our own powers to describe."[120] Such interpretation of disability as its own form of confinement is ostensibly offensive to people with disabilities, who do not (at least not necessarily or a priori) feel they are "incarcerated in their own body/mind" but is often the way nondisabled publics perceive disabilities. Yet, this ableist assumption about the lives of those with disabilities is what ultimately led the judges to grant the seemingly victorious decision in *Olmstead*. Put differently, what led the judges in this decision is entrenched ableism and not a belief in the full competency of people with psychiatric and cognitive disabilities that should grant them the right to live with their peers and chosen families in the community.

Another example of ableism by the court leading to a ruling in favor of the disabled plaintiff is demonstrated in the 1995 *Clarkson v. Coughlin* case. Doris Clarkson was a Deaf inmate in the state of New York. While in prison, she and other prisoners were routinely denied sign language interpreters, thus limiting their ability to participate in or understand parole hearings, prison activities, and medical or psychiatric appointments. They sued under the ADA. The federal judge in the case ruled in the plaintiff's favor that the prison in fact violated the ADA by not providing them accommodations while in prison. But one can also interpret the decision as coming from an ableist stance. The judge wrote, "The absence of these critical elements of the ADA scheme at the Reception Facilities has truly sentenced class members to a 'prison within a prison.'"

There are two ways to interpret this decision. One is that the judge is pointing to processes of disablement that occur in the prison and are inflicted unequally on those who come to the prison as Deaf or disabled. In other words, the judge could be pointing to systemic oppression and the segregation that results from imprisonment for Deaf and disabled prisoners. But another more likely interpretation is that the judge and the courts see disabled prisoners (in prisons or institutions) as a priori defective, inferior, incompetent, and so on, and therefore see them as vulnerable and in need of protection from the court. The problem with such an interpretation of being disabled, mad, or Deaf as a "prison within a prison" is that it reproduces ableism, sanism, and audism, a view that sees disability or Deafness as equating incompetence (not hearing as a prison), instead of focusing on the disabling features of imprisonment and its debilitating features. Therefore it is a continuation and reinforcement of racial criminal pathologization, which ultimately restricts the lives of people with disabilities, in and out of carceral spaces, and helps to send them into these spaces. In other words, as I argue here, the same logic that prepares people to be captured by systems of incarceration cannot be the framework that will set us free.

Disability and debility are understood under these legal cases only as traits to overcome or fixed attributes attached to specific people's bodies or minds and not as the result of socio-politico-economic processes. And disablement and debility are certainly not discussed as emanating from state violence such as incarceration, racism, or lack of affordable health care as disabling. Alternatively, when disablement is discussed in relation to sites of confinement, as in the *Plata* case, disability is not understood as an identity or a site of resistance but only as a deficit. Just like the legal cases that preceded them, disability and mental difference are still seen as abject.

This line of thinking, that is, ableism or sanism as a decarceration legal tactic, often as reconstructed versions of charitable or philanthropic attitudes of "pity the vulnerable populations," can also be seen in the practice of compassionate release or medical pardon cases. The strategy of seeking early release based on diminishing mental or physical capacities of those incarcerated is a crucial legal strategy at the intersection of disability justice and decarceration legislation. Some activist lawyers, including in abolitionist organizations, are utilizing early compassionate release, mostly for individuals with degenerative disabilities or who have incurable diseases, as means to get people out and have them spend at least their last months or days outside of a prison setting. The problem is that there is a fine line between diseases and permanent impairments, and some of these cases clearly blur such distinctions intentionally. For instance, in the case of people who have full-blown AIDS symptoms or such conditions as Lou Gehrig's disease, it is hard to determine if they are dying or have disabilities.[121]

Some advocates and organizations are well aware of the problems implicit in using such tactics but still maintain that they improve the lives of individual prisoners who they are petitioning for, who have no other recourse and would otherwise languish and die in prison. Some also see it as a nonreformist reform that chips away at the prison–industrial complex by releasing as many people as possible, even if only a few at a time. Such interpretation is aligned with the model of abolition by attrition, first discussed in the 1970s handbook *Instead of Prisons*. According to the attrition model, the function and power of prisons will be slowly worn down by decarcerating as many people as possible as well as excarcerating (creating alternatives to incarceration).[122] There are quite a few critics of this strategy, however. For example, Canadian abolitionist Ruth Morris critiqued the attrition model by asserting that it is indeed an aggressive reform effort, but a reform nonetheless. The point is to decarcerate prison populations one by one—first the young, then the mentally ill, and so on. The problem of chipping at the margins of the system is that the center, the logic of incarceration itself as neutral and essentially benign (as long as those incarcerated are healthy and not mistreated), remains intact.[123]

The issue with using such tactics from a disability culture and disability justice stance is that they often evoke disabling sentiments either by the petitioning parties or the judges, as we have seen. In other words, you have to claim that these incarcerated individuals have no life ahead of them and no quality of life to speak of for judges to grant them early release. This critique is often heard from disability rights organizations and activists such as Not Dead Yet and ADAPT, who try to resist such practices. Not Dead Yet, for example, is a grassroots disability rights organization that rejects and protests assisted suicide and euthanasia of disabled people. They do so because they believe that support for such policies is based on ableism and discrimination as it builds on the assumption that disabled lives are worthless and worth less, often based on intersections with race, gender, class, and so on. If disabled people would have been as worthy as, or seen as being as competent as, nondisabled people, then any idea of "mercy killing" would have looked a lot like "killing" and necessitated a very different response (most likely criminalization or pathologization). The other problem with this tactic of compassionate release and relying on debilitation as deficit is that it very rarely succeeds. Even the most outrageous and debilitating conditions do not grant the right for medical parole in the eyes of the courts. When they do, it is often too late, as can be seen in the tragic case of Herman Wallace,[124] who died a few days after his release from prison, after being in solitary confinement for forty-one years.

Assessing Institutional Reform Litigation

Institutional reform litigation is an important case study that connects advocacy in prisons and institutions for those labeled as intellectually and psychiatrically disabled. It offers a glimpse into the ways race-ability and incarceration were perceived by courts and legal advocates, especially in the 1970s. Even though not all saw those incarcerated in institutions in the same manner as those in prisons, the tactics for decarceration were similar and interrelated. As I demonstrated, one cannot understand this era of decarceration without attending to both arenas and their connections.

Since class action lawsuits were seen as the major engine for deinstitutionalization, they are especially helpful for current-day abolitionists to learn from, including from their shortcoming as a tactic. As I showed, the problem with consent decrees and court-mandated changes is that then money and energy is devoted to compliance instead of ensuring the freedom and equality of those who appealed for justice. It then becomes a bureaucratic game of shifting money and responsibility instead of an epistemic and societal shift in how to deal with harm and difference among us. Attempts to use litigation to delegitimate the *necessity* of confinement, especially in the disability arena, were especially useful as one out of many tools in the abolitionary arsenal that ultimately led to deinstitutionalization.

As I asked at the beginning of this chapter, what were the effects of such litigation, on those incarcerated, but also on the continuity and legitimacy of carcerality? Despite the wins gained by plaintiffs in this era of reform in certain aspects of their living conditions (be it black Muslims or those in Attica winning rights to religious freedom and programming or institutionalized folks gaining right to habilitation), the main gains of litigation were not in its outcome. It is the pedagogical and political education advanced by reform litigation that would turn out to have the most lasting influence over the discourse of decarceration and its effects. Despite some proclamations, I argue that prison reform litigation persisted beyond the 1970s, but it shifted its locales and tactics. Much of it had centered on women's prisons and legal activism related to sexuality/gender. After the passage of the ADA, prison litigation focused on disablement and mental health care as legal tools to change the material conditions within prisons and to decarcerate specific individuals and facilities.

This recent focus on imprisonment as a state mechanism of debilitation and its ensuing lawsuits should attest to the need to understand both disability and debilitation as part and parcel of prison activism. The cries that institutional reform litigation had moved from prisons into disability-based institutions, therefore, mask the making of prisons as sites of debilitation. It also obscures the connections between recent legal challenges to imprisonment and new institutional reform litigation (such as the *Olmstead* decision) that focuses on ensuring quality services and housing after deinstitutionalization, which is a direction that anti-prison activists can learn from as well.

Such legal recourse and the whole enterprise of reform litigation and trying to change the conditions inherent in prisons (overcrowding, the need to build specific enclosures for specific populations) have led to prison expansion and the rise of the governable cage and gender-responsive, gay-affirmative, and accessible types of incarceration. By insisting on changes within the prison or institution, these tactics reinforce the system and its logic, so that positive change in the daily lives of those incarcerated actually perpetuates the power structure that keeps carceral spaces as legitimate and benign.[125] The logic of segregation and incarceration remain unchanged when we whittle away at the system one component at a time through reform or attrition measures.

Therefore an equally important question raised by reform litigation is, even if such lawsuits are successful, do the ends justify the means and the consequences? One area I exemplified is the ableism and sanism produced in some prison litigation that was decided on the side of the disabled plaintiffs. This is my critique of pushing for decarceration by critiquing what Puar describes as the biopolitics of debilitation[126]—it falls into discourses that see disability as deficit driven and therefore would consider it a useful engine from which to protest slow death and debilitation via state violence. But to end this violence through this strategy also increases ableism and sanism, which are of course also forms of violence. In addition, such arguments end up reproducing the notion that disabled people are defective and live in a prison within a prison, as if one prison is not enough to legitimate decarceration, let alone abolition. It further asserts that commonplace debilitation via incarceration is not enough, but only the excesses of it could be litigated. What I suggested we need is coalitional and intersectional analysis and organizing instead.

As I suggested in the introduction to this book, anti-prison movements can learn from deinstitutionalization and disability rights and justice movements how to understand disability as an analytic, a lens from which to view the world and not only through ableist frameworks. Equally important, abolitionist and fugitive knowledges in the prison arena can inform disability rights activism about the dangers of seeking relief through the state, and the need to grapple with state violence. It is clear that litigation reform resulted in increased politicization of those incarcerated (prisoners' rights movements, self-advocacy) and the legal notion that these are populations deserving of rights at all. On the other hand, such seemingly progressive measures also led to the strengthening of the carceral state. Penal expansion and the bureaucratic management of both incarceration and *decarceration* soon followed as a result of litigation reform.

For example, after the *Olmstead* decision, states had to create policies by which people with disabilities can be integrated into community-living arrangements instead of living in restrictive settings. But the rate of decrease in the number of institutionalized people actually slowed considerably in the post-*Olmstead* period.[127] A similar slowdown was found in a comparable study examining the deinstitutionalization of individuals with I/DD labels more broadly.[128] What can explain this deceleration in rates of deinstitutionalization in light of legal decisions found in favor of the disabled plaintiffs that affirm their right to live in the community?

Put differently, what I am interested in here is whether rights were a mechanism used and resulting in attempts to pacify systemic change, quell dissent, and instead embrace reform under the status quo, that is, through the doctrine of inclusion, or Dis Inc., as I characterized it throughout the book. The ADA can be perceived as a reform measure that seemingly provides equality under the law, thus pacifying more radical opposition (from groups like ADAPT, which use direct action to protest the capture of people with disabilities in nursing homes). If we look at rates of unemployment of people with disabilities, which have not declined since the enactment of the ADA, we can begin to analyze such laws as a form of neoliberal governance. As Spade asks us to contemplate, "various social movements have had to contend with why legal change in the form of rights has not brought the deep transformation they were seeking, why disparities in life chances have increased during a period when we have seen the elimination of formal segregation and the advent of policies prohibiting discrimination on the basis of sex, race, and disability."[129]

The narrative of the State that is being reinforced by going to the law for protection is that the state itself is a level playing field from which to seek monetary compensation, protection, and legal rights. This conjoining of state-sanctioned violence with demands for social emancipation is what Chandan Reddy terms "freedom with violence."[130] Even when activism is critical of the state and its apparatuses, its politics remain reformist, as Reddy explains, because the liberal state embodies and constitutes that upon which the claims for equality are demanded. The modern nation-state has taken up a monopoly over "legitimate" forms of violence and acts as protector from "arbitrary" individual violence. Freedom with violence is the freedom enjoyed by the citizenry, predicated on heteropatriarchy, settler, and other forms of colonialism, as well as on racism and capitalism. Under this view, using the law to create change assumes that the law is just and is a fruitful arena through which change can come to harmed populations. Litigation and rights discourse draw on the state in fixing social ills of its own creation.

Can litigation be a successful strategy for social change, then? Well, what constitutes success, for whom, and under which circumstances are all contextual, as is the definition of change—change in the specific conditions of the carceral enclosure, change in discourse, change in the lives of those incarcerated, then, now, or in the future? I suggested previously that deinstitutionalization should not be seen as merely a process but as a form of activism, a goal of a movement, a logic. The prisoners' rights movement can also be construed as a significant social movement, by itself or as part of larger liberation movements, civil rights, and/or black liberation struggles more generally.[131] As such, the question of the efficacy of institutional reform litigation becomes much broader, one more about the ability to build capacity for such movements, than the narrow legal grounds upon which much of these suits were brought—did such and such prison or institution improve its conditions in regard to a specific aspect or another? Cementing the governable iron cage should therefore lead not just to rethinking strategies such as litigation but also to actively building coalitional techniques of resistance that take into account the changing nature of carceral logics.

Epilogue

Abolition Now

In 1976, Fay Honey Knopp and members of Prison Research Education Action Project (PREAP) published *Instead of Prisons,* the first English-language comprehensive guide to prison abolition.[1] In it they summarized the praxis of prison abolition through five interrelated components, which together compose the attrition model for abolition: *decarceration* of those already incarcerated (through parole, for example, or releasing the old, the young, women, and the mentally ill); *excarceration* of those not (yet) incarcerated through diversion, decriminalization, and alternatives to incarceration; *moratoria* on new jails/prisons; "restraint of the few" as the necessity to limit movement for a small number of cases; and *building a caring community* as the "real" alternative to a society that currently has prisons is building one in which prisons would be nonsensical. To conclude this book, I want to activate and critique the components outlined by PREAP as wisdom from an era of deinstitutionalization and decarceration—the 1970s—to reassess our present circumstances and infrastructure for abolition in relation to imprisonment, disability, and deinstitutionalization.

Deinstitutionalization in the field of mental health began toward the end of the 1950s and in the field of intellectual and/or developmental disabilities (I/DD) about fifteen years later. Some states in the United States had yet to close their large residential institutions for people with disabilities, especially I/DD. For other states in which deinstitutionalization had taken place, enough time had gone by to take stock. What happened in the aftermath of the closure of disability carceral enclosures? Has deinstitutionalization brought liberation to people with disabilities? And how do disability and decarceration intersect today, decades after the heyday of deinstitutionalization?

The eras in which deinstitutionalization and its backlash took place co-incided with the ascent of neoliberalism. The decimation of the social safety net accompanied and furthered investments (material, political economies, affective economies, and cultural investments) in corrections as economic and ideological structures. Throughout the book, I used Dis Inc. as a concept to question the incorporation of disability on both counts: through capitalist accumulation (on the backs of those labeled as disabled) in the disability- and prison–industrial complexes and through erasure of the transgressive aspects of race-ability in order to gain inclusion to the nation-state. I inter-rogated the cost of incorporation, of inclusion under the (racial, settler hetero-normative ableist) status quo. I end, then, with caution: What happens when we "win," once deinstitutionalization becomes institutionalized? What new forms of subjugation and confinement came to replace and intersect with institutionalization? And what can decarceration and abolitionary move-ments in the prison arena learn from deinstitutionalization? In what follows, I offer a brief assessment of our current conditions by assessing deinstitu-tionalization through PREAP's road map for prison abolition.

Decarceration

Was deinstitutionalization abolitionary? I defined *deinstitutionalization* in three ways: the movement of people with psychiatric and intellectual or devel-opmental disabilities from state institutions and hospitals into community liv-ing, and the accompanying closure of large (mostly state-sponsored/funded) institutions and hospitals. But deinstitutionalization is not only moving people from one place to another but the social movements that resisted and still resist segregationist logic. One can certainly see deinstitutionalization as a form of decarceration of disabled people and the closure of disability-based carceral settings.

Was deinstitutionalization as an act of *desegregation* a success? What hap-pened to people with disabilities after deinstitutionalization? There are no comprehensive figures in the field of mental health, but in the field of I/DD, is it clear that today, most people with I/DD labels no longer reside in insti-tutions. As of 2013, 71 percent resided with a family member. This is to the credit of so many who fought for deinstitutionalization and are very much still fighting for it. But in terms of political economy, the policy and financial picture has not changed much from the heyday of institutionalization. Since little profit can be generated by investing in homecare performed by a family member (especially women), it should not be surprising that less than o.5 percent of families who support a loved one with an I/DD label get paid for their labor.[2] The likelihood of strong financial support for family caregivers recedes further when one considers the gendered and racialized dynamics of caregiving and the ways in which women's work (and what is considered to be the "women's domain") in the private sphere remains devalued.

In addition, funding for care for those institutionalized still goes to the institution or facility and not the disabled or senior person. There is an inherent bias in federal programs like Medicaid, which requires states to provide care in nursing homes but makes home- and community-based services optional in terms of funding. This bias means that money (in the form of benefits or waivers) goes directly toward institutions, nursing homes, or group homes but not to the person who benefits from these state supports directly. In addition, such funding is lacking in covering services like nonhospitalization long-term treatment, day and vocational habilitation, and advocacy and support for living in the community, which means that programs like Money Follows the Person (in which Medicaid funding goes directly to seniors and disabled adults to live in noncongregate settings) are still on voluntary bases for states to opt into and are willfully lacking.

I further defined *abolition of psychiatric incarceration* in three ways: the act and process of closing down psychiatric hospitals; abolition of the rationale for long hospitalization; and finally, abolition of biopsychiatry. It is certainly the case that psychiatric hospitals closed en masse in almost all U.S. states. But as a consequence, other spaces of confinement proliferated, such as psych wards in regular hospitals, halfway homes, and nursing homes for those exiting carceral spaces, those in recovery, and those with disabilities more generally. In addition, the placement of these recovery settings, halfway homes, and mental health clinics in locales with depreciated resources is related to the NIMBY phenomenon and the constructions of borders around who belongs "in the community," as I detailed in chapter 5.

Living in group homes, halfway homes, and smaller community-based settings is different than living in large residential institutions to be sure, but is it better?[3] New forms of subjugation came as a prerequisite to living in these "community"-based settings. As discussed throughout the book, with inclusion came the need and requirement to assimilate. As Lovell and Scheper-Hughes suggest, "American deinstitutionalization, then, neither modified psychiatry's function as an 'agent of the state' nor threatened professional power. Instead, it expanded the range of possibilities for professional and psychiatric power over deviant individuals."[4] Psychiatric commitment was abolished en masse but is still being practiced alongside new technologies of psy governance, such as imperatives to be productive and the advent of psychopharmaceuticals.[5] The literal cage of the congregate institution and hospital was extended through an iron cage of bureaucratic surveillance and mandates. Normalization, which was meant to push policy in which people with disability live and learn with their peers in the community, and community living more broadly are being implemented by technocratic measures and checklists, as I showed in chapter 2. To get state and federal aid, people have to perform race-able heteronormative expectations of living and swallow the pill (often literally, as Erick Fabris describes in relation to community treatment orders[6]).

In addition, deinstitutionalization in mental health also led to different criteria for psychiatric hospitalization. Today, there are many more controls and barriers to hospitalization as a first course of action when someone is in mental distress, which is what many psychiatric survivors fought for. These heightened protections had effects that did not necessarily increase the scope of confinement, which is helpful, but it did have other consequences, especially for people of color. Because of the forces of racial criminal pathologization, once "danger" was added as the main rationale for psych hospitalization, the population in psych hospitals during and right after deinstitutionalization had changed, and those who are institutionalized today tend to be poorer and more people of color.

Deinstitutionalization influenced prison reform as well. As Anne Parsons documents in relation to Pennsylvania, during the 1960s, correctional policy makers created community-based alternatives to institutions, such as furloughs, halfway houses, and work-release programs. They took inspiration in new community-based ideologies within psychiatry and within community-based models during deinstitutionalization. By the early 1970s, the numbers of people in prisons and jails across many states reached their lowest point in decades, despite uprisings and expanding police forces.[7] As Parsons further shows, though, this was short-lived. In the 1970s, politicians on the right and left started to critique social welfare policies as wasteful or not effective, which resulted in critique of the rehabilitation function of incarceration, both in prisons and in psych hospitals. The tide shifted to warehousing, law and order, and incarceration due to danger.[8]

In the first chapter, I asked whether we can call the deinstitutionalization that resulted from neoliberal ideologies that show no concern for quality of life and life itself a win. Is it abolition if the closure is done through neoliberal racist ideology? The answer to these questions is not just theoretical. Many of the closures of disability-based enclosures happened due to fiscal crises of states and the desire to shift costs to the federal government, as well as the desire to cut mental health treatment and any social supports altogether. As a result, a growing industry of privately run nursing homes and board and care facilities began to emerge with the phase-out of the hospitals and in some cases gained a lobby that advocated proactively for closure to increase their profits. In the prison arena, closures and decarceration measures motivated by carceral logics end up increasing the scope of the carceral state.[9]

There is disagreement among scholars and activists about the influence of the 2008 financial crisis in the United States on decarceration trends. Some believe that states will start, and others continue to be, closing carceral locales like jails and prisons because they are too costly to maintain, just like in the heyday of institutionalization. Bernard Harcourt suggests that the growth of the private prison sector resembles other "bubble economies," especially the housing market and the real estate bubble, which some blame for the current economic crisis. In essence, Harcourt argues that prison building (which is a form of real estate itself) seems to have exploded in the 1990s but is now starting to accumulate massive debts instead of profits.[10] Like the housing bubble, the prison sector also grew out of speculative prices and growth beyond its capacity, which might also lead to its eventual crash. Activists from groups like Californians United for a Responsible Budget (CURB), Critical Resistance, and ADAPT are cleverly mobilizing the recent financial crisis as an impetus to push state budgets into reducing their reliance on incarceration and institutionalization and engage in discussions on the financial cost-saving merits of such abolitionist propositions.

The strategy of pushing for decarceration through financial crisis can also backfire, especially if it is not utilized in an abolitionary way. Marie Gottschalk, for example, argues that in the face of financial crisis, legislators and policy makers usually go for more punitive measures.[11] This tactic serves to distract an anxious public from growing financial disparities and provides a useful scapegoat for the causes and consequences of economic decline. Therefore advocates of decarceration should tread with caution when framing the issue as primarily relying on economic justification over social, moral, and ethical reasonings.[12] Discourses relying solely on cost-effectiveness are part of neo-liberal and carceral logics. As such, they further empower a professional class of economic and other "experts" as having power/knowledge over those with direct experience of incarceration and decarceration.

Deinstitutionalization can further teach us that there is a strong affinity between closure of carceral locales and abolition, but they are by no means the same thing. As I argue throughout the book, closure of carceral institutions, such as mental hospitals and prisons, is a necessary but not sufficient action on the road to abolition. Currently most deinstitutionalization in the field of I/DD focuses on closing state-run institutions, but it is important to recognize that a substantial number of people with I/DD labels live in other institutional settings, including 26,695 in large (more than sixteen residents) nonstate I/DD facilities and 29,608 in nursing homes.[13] In the ethnography *Deinstitutionalizing Women,* Kelley Johnson describes the lives of women in a locked ward within an institution for people with developmental and intellectual disabilities. When a decision to close the institution was made, most of the women studied asked to be placed with family or their advocates. For the most part, their requests were ignored, and out of twenty-one women, one-third were moved to other institutions, and the remaining were placed in group homes. As a result, Johnson contends that although the institution finally closed, its deinstitutionalization was a failure.[14]

Excarceration

What of alternatives to incarceration, then, or in the words of PREAP, excarceration? Often what we hear about people with various mental differences and disabilities, and substance users who are caught in the criminal injustice system, is that they need medical help and treatment and not incarceration and punishment. Relatedly, those who find the living conditions of disabled prisoners deplorable often call for the creation of more hospital beds in prisons, the reform of psychiatric hospitals, or the creation of more accessible prisons.

In the early 1990s, Gilles Deleuze suggested that disciplinary societies, whose main characteristic is the organization of vast spaces of enclosure and in which the individual merely passes from one to the other, are being replaced by societies of control, in which less focus is given to the location in which social control is prescribed. One only need look at some suggested alternatives to incarceration at present to understand Deleuze's proclamation. Activists who fight and resist incarceration should be wary of (and are today quite savvy about) this "progressive and dispersed installation of a new system of domination."[15] Seemingly progressive steps under the rubric of alternatives to incarceration such as psychiatric care clinics in the community are seen by many antipsychiatry activists as measures to increase surveillance on those psychiatrized, especially in relation to compliance with the psychopharmaceutical regimen that has become an order and not a choice, contributing to what Fabris described as "chemical incarceration."[16] In addition, measures such as electronic monitoring bracelets that seemingly aid in the release of more prisoners are perceived by prison abolitionists as increasing the net of incarceration and punitiveness at large and not adding to the freedom of those who had been criminalized.[17]

These investments, as Sarah Lamble calls them,[18] in carcerality and their so-called alternatives are not just ideological but monetary as well. It is clear that today incarceration (especially of people with disabilities, people of color, and their intersection) is profitable. But apparently, so is *decarceration*. As lifelong activist Jean Stewart remarked in 2016, "if capitalism found a clever way to profit from disabled people by placing them in institutional beds . . . in 2015 it has also found a way of turning a profit by releasing disabled people from said beds!" As Stewart and I further show, deinstitutionalization created a need, and later a market, for the placement of disabled people in settings outside the walls of institutions and hospitals. While deinstitutionalization activists and people with disabilities advocate for supported living at home, considerable money is now being spent on placing disabled people in smaller "community" settings. Rehabilitation programs, day habitation, treatment facilities, and supervised residential settings are often perceived as alternatives to incarceration and institutionalization, though in fact they represent a back-door expansion of incarceration for profit.[19]

In the prison arena, this expansion can be seen quite clearly. Private corrections companies now diversify their portfolios by expanding into probation, parole, reentry, and other so-called community areas. The Right on Crime campaign, the American Legislative Exchange Council, and the for-profit bail industry have all become major advocates for privatizing probation and parole, as a solution to the problem of overcrowded prisons and abysmal conditions for confinement. The United States is one of only two countries that permit for-profit bail bonds.[20] A report titled *Treatment Industrial Complex,* written by the American Friends Service Committee and Grassroots Leadership, shows in detail how the incarceration industry moved into areas such as forensic mental hospitals, halfway homes, home arrests, and civil commitments. In addition, because of lawsuits regarding horrific conditions related to negligent health care, private prison companies have also moved into the arena of prison medical care.[21] In other words, to address the disabling effects of incarceration, "corrections" departments and states have begun contracting out medical care delivery to private companies, thus further profiting off the bodies of sick and disabled prisoners, which, as shown earlier, compose a large segment of the incarcerated population.

As one example, the report cites the GEO group, the second largest private prison company in the United States, as a trendsetter in terms of this pivot toward the marketing of so-called alternatives to incarceration. In 2012, GEO created a subsidiary euphemistically called GEO Care, which provides mental health services in prison, in addition to operating state psychiatric hospitals with forensic units. The irony and audacity of a for-profit company providing mental health services to counter the disabling effects of its own prisons should not be lost here. The report also mentions that in 2013, a private company in Connecticut was contracted to create a nursing home specifically for aging and disabled state prisoners.[22] GEO calls this the "correctional lifecycle," including addiction and mental health treatment and electronic monitoring.[23] In 2010, GEO acquired Behavioral Interventions Inc., the company that makes ankle bracelets. But, as many activists who protest the prison–industrial complex point out, technologies like electronic monitoring, house arrest, and forced psychotropic drugs are alternatives to *prison* without providing a meaningful alternative to *incarceration*.

Moratoria and No New Jails

Understanding the connections among disability/mental health, abolition, and imprisonment cannot be more urgent. Although new prison construction has been halted in several states, the prison–industrial complex continues its growth through other means, and many of its current rationalities are deeply entangled with disability, debility, and madness. At the time of writing this, many counties and cities across the United States are proposing the construction of new jail facilities as benefiting not the larger society (through incapacitation and segregation) but rather those who are and will be incarcerated therein. The proposed new jails are promised to provide services related to addiction, mental health, and recovery. This is what James Kilgore referred to as carceral humanism.[24] In speaking with abolitionist comrades nationally engaged in struggles to oppose new jail construction, it has become clear that almost all the facilities are promoted under the rubric of mental health in some shape or form. This is what I mean by carceral ableism or carceral sanism.

For example, in Toledo, Ohio (where much of this book was written), there was a recent ballot initiative to finance the construction a new jail, to replace the old, outdated jail. Lucas County was seeking a $1.37 million levy over thirty-seven years for the construction of a new, $185 million jail. The ballot was defeated in the local election in November 2018 mostly because people in the county did not want a new tax and could not afford it, not because of abolitionist organizing or frameworks. The county had since then purchased land where it is saying the new jail will be built no matter what. Although the construction plans for the jails had been halted for now, time and massive organizing will tell the outcome. Most important for the kind of thinking I hope this book incites, the jail was not even discussed as such. The campaign that the county put out prior to the elections included flyers that encouraged voters to "Vote yes on issue 10, A Better Way." In the flyers, they describe the need to build a "Solution Center" in which they would provide "less expensive treatment for people with addiction issues instead of costly jail time."[25] In a state like Ohio, where the opioid crisis is raging, this is very alluring. Many friends told me after the election that they didn't understand that the measure was about building a new jail but instead thought it was about helping those with mental health and addiction. Indeed, in election materials, the facility or "Solution Center" was never mentioned as a jail.

As this book has shown, today carceral humanism is compounded with carceral feminism and carceral ableism/sanism to expand the net of the carceral state and of carceral logics. As anticarceral feminists advise, appeals to gender equality in corrections (from "gender-responsive prisons" to violence against women or hate crime legislation) often lead to the expanding and retrenchment of the carceral state, not the protection of vulnerable populations, especially women of color as well as gender-variant people.[26] In conjunction with this framework, I want to underscore the usage of disability and mental health as justification for prison and jail expansion. This intersection manifesting in carceral sanism is an excellent opportunity for mad and disability activists to declare "not in our name" to the construction of new jails and join others (antipoverty, antiracist, feminists, and prison abolitionists) who are engaged in these struggles for the prevention of incarceration and the further buildup of the U.S. prison nation.[27]

In addition, mental health jails as carceral sanism show us the need to coalesce with disability and mad activists to fight not only carceral expansion via prisons and jails but also so-called treatment—and not just treatment behind bars but in general. Biopsychiatry is often the only form of so-called treatment, but mad studies and experiences push us to think beyond this framework, as I show throughout this book. Therefore it is crucial to provide a crip/ mad of color critique of incarceration and decarceration: to center the experiences of disablement and ableism in criminal, racial, and social justice movements—to understand trauma and disabling effects of detention and incarceration but also alternatives to incarceration that are proposed and their net effect on increasing ableism/sanism, especially through race-ability, and carceral logics simultaneously.

Restraint of the "Dangerous Few"

The authors of the 1976 *Instead of Prisons* add "restraint of the few" as part of the attrition model that they propose in their manual for abolition. This is the suggestion that I, and many deinstitutionalization and abolition activists, diverge from the most. Prison abolition is a diverse affair, of course, in terms of praxis and political mission. Many prison abolitionists advocate for transformative justice and healing practices in which no one will be restrained or segregated, while some, like PREAP, believe that there will always be a small percentage of those whose behavior is so unacceptable or harmful that they will need to be incapacitated, socially exiled, or restrained, and that this should be done humanely, temporarily, and not in a carceral or punitive manner.

In the field of developmental disabilities and antipsychiatry, a similar debate arose alongside early discussions of deinstitutionalization. The equivalent of the "dangerous few" needing restraint are debates around the need for institutionalization or segregation of the "severely disabled." As I discussed in chapter 3, a key starting point to decarceration as an abolitionist practice, or as a dis-epistemology, is to start decarceration from the position of the seemingly toughest cases (most medically in need, severe cases) and not what in the prison reform arena are called the "non non nons" (nonviolent, nonserious, nonsexual "offenses"). People who are considered "radical inclusionists" in the disability arena advocate that no one should be segregated in schooling, housing, or other life activity, regardless of their label or "severity." In other words, there should be no "restraint of the few." For proponents of this attitude, segregation is never a viable response, even for those whose behavior is challenging and "disturbing" to others. The goal is to make people with and without disabilities aware of social norms (such as touching others without consent) but simultaneously challenge social views and attitudes that construct normalcy in particular ways (for instance, having to regulate one's body and behavior to fit specific cultural expectations). It also entails changing the education system, housing, and other infrastructure to make them accessible, affordable, and inclusive to all.[28] In the field of antipsychiatry, such attitudes also involve opposition to psychiatric hospitalization, even of those labeled "psychotic," in favor of support in the community, by and among one's peers, and without coercion.

There are of course many critiques of this idea of no institutionalization or segregation in the disability arena, especially from those who support the continuum approach. As discussed in chapters 2 and 6, this approach views the residential, and educational, placement of disabled people as a continuum, with segregated congregate facilities, that is, institutions, on one side and supported living in one's home on the other. In other words, it supports the idea that a segregated facility should be one of myriad options in which people with disability can and should reside. This is another important lesson from deinstitutionalization as a logic of desegregation: the neoliberal choice model of the free market makes it appear as if all choices on the continuum are equally valid. Within battles over the abolition of carceral facilities, what needs to shift is the discourse that constructs certain populations as financial capital, or drain, as people with disabilities and people of color are seen as superfluous populations unless they are in cages or institutional beds. Positioning deinstitutionalization and prison closures as economic saving measures uncritically can backfire, as suggested earlier, as the discourse of cost-effectiveness is tied to carceral logics.

Only when the institutional model is no longer a viable option for anyone can new alternatives grow, get traction (and funding), and gain legitimacy. This, then, is the deepest lesson from deinstitutionalization—the only way to do it effectively is to not institutionalize people in the first place. As one man wrote to the Tamms Year Ten committee after the successful campaign to close down the Tamms supermax prison in Illinois, which I discussed in chapter 6, "Sadly, I believe the ones to benefit the most from this will be those who will never have to go to Tamms. For those who spent time there, they are damaged on some level, to some degree. While none of us will ever be the same, some are broken beyond repair."[29] As the writer recognizes, the disabling and maddening nature of incarceration needs to be addressed, not by fixing people, but by stopping it at the source—closing these facilities but also preventing new "admissions" and, most importantly, logics of incarceration. In this sense, prevention of incarceration is a formidable abolitionary goal, one that seemed impossible at the time the campaign to close Tamms began. This is the value of abolition as a dis-epistemology, bringing the desired future in the here and now through sustained nonreformist collective action and imagination without knowing what the future entails.

In other words, decarceration could be closer to abolition as a measure of not just harm reduction but prevention, creating a noncarceral world through preventing new admissions and any new carceral facility construction. The people who benefit the most, as the preceding letter details, are those who will never have to experience the horror of such locales. In this specific sense, deinstitutionalization was successful, as the rates of new admission have gone down substantially in psych hospitals and institutions for people with I/DD. Most people who are in these I/DD institutions are older; those in psych hospitals are there for shorter durations. Institutionalization and hospitalizations are now mostly reserved as a last resort rather than the first or even second line of action. Doctors do not recommend institutionalization for children born with disabilities, as was the prevalent attitude until the 1970s. Abolition had been endorsed by many mainstream organizations and become a mandate and policy. From utopia, it became a reality. The question now is what to do this with this "win."

Building Noncarceral Societies

An accompanying shift must also occur in mind-set—a nonsegregationist logic, a radically different approach to dealing with harm and difference, has to take hold for these changes to be not just reformist but abolitionary and sustained. Ultimately, institutionalization should not be a choice, not for workers of carceral facilities, not for parents of disabled people, and not for our collective imagination. Institutionalization is state-sponsored violence against people with disabilities, many of whom are currently people of color and elderly. Therefore what disability rights activism can learn from the arena of abolition is the importance of anchoring struggles in an analysis of state violence, as well as the need to understand abolition as dis-epistemology rooted in race-ability.

Therefore we must understand abolition as dis-epistemology and as *non-alternative*. In their analysis of antipsychiatry in the United States and Italy, Lovell and Scheper-Hughes weigh the influence that deinstitutionalization had on psychiatry, in practice and prestige.[30] During the 1960s especially, the legitimacy of psychiatry, especially psychiatric confinement, was cracking and parallel therapies and alternatives were being established, as a field. Nonetheless, psychiatry came out intact. I suggest that one of the problems, as critics of "consumer" choice in psychiatry note, is that biopsychiatry and its alternatives were on parallel tracks. According to Judi Chamberlin, antipsychiatry, from the patient perspective, views psychiatry as a mechanism to normalize some and discard and confine the ones that cannot be normalized.[31] Giuseppe Bucalo, an antipsychiatry activist in Italy, further states that "antipsychiatry is not a theory, but a set of practical and daily actions that human beings put into effect in order to defend themselves from psychiatric violence and to manage their own existence."[32] Bucalo does not perceive the actions that he and his comrades are taking as "alternatives to psychiatry," because alternatives to torture and oppression should not exist. What should exist is living up to people's potential and abolishing oppression and torture. According to Bucalo and other antipsychiatry activists, the only way to abolish psychiatry is not to utilize it as a referent—not to use its discourse, its language, and its assumptions. The strategy of mad movements and those against psychiatry is not to fight against psychiatry or create alternatives to it but to legitimize other modes of being or refuse to adopt "normal" behavior. This does not negate the need to hold others and be accountable in peer, collective, and noncoercive ways.

The organizing and "self-help" groups that ex-patients established started as ways to respond to lacks and failures within the mental health system, and at times in defiance to that system, is a case in point. One can also look at these initiatives for their intrinsic merit, not in comparison to the established system, that is, not as alternatives, but as ways of dealing with crisis, mental difference, and issues of mental pain. As organized strategies and initiatives,

these are collective responses, which are vastly different than the individualized responses given out by modern medicine.

The knowledge of decarceration and abolition gained since the 1970s,
when PREAP wrote its manual for abolition, is immense. And so are new
forms of carcerality. What these examples, such as new and improved jails
as a form of carceral sanism, as well as chemical and e-carceration, show is
that "the win" of decarceration and deinstitutionalization should be cele-
brated but also studied and understood under the vestiges of the shifting
contours of the carceral state.[33] I don't raise this in order to end the book
with a kind of "the more things change, the more they stay the same" attitude. I am not claiming that group homes are the same as institutions, much
like I did not claim that prisons are like asylums. The point is that the logics
of capture and carcerality are related, and my more specific point is that
so are forms of resisting incarceration. As Foucault suggested, new subjuga-
tions and subjectivities also bring with them new forms of resistance. Today,
as opposed to 1976, there's much more emphasis on the intersectional nature
of oppression, with decades of feminist queer antiracist analysis and praxis
at our disposal.

The consequences of Dis Inc. as forms of inclusion of minority difference via assimilation and commodification are also bringing new forms,
strategies, and analysis for liberation. As the title of this book suggests, decarceration in the form of deinstitutionalization and prison abolition should be
thought of as linked. As I suggested, there is an urgent need to understand
the disabling and maddening effect of carceral sites, including jails and prisons, as not only segregating and incarcerating disability/madness (as asylums or "the new asylums") but as sites of disablement and, more so, sites
of targeted debilitation, which is a biopolitical form of state violence. As
I further urged, however, this targeted debilitation needs to be countered
in a nonableist and intersectional way, one that understands lived forms of
disablement that is, disability, as political. The goal, then, would be not only
to capture disability as biopolitical (i.e., when it is weaponized by the state)
but to mobilize disability collectives and movements for the service of abolition. For those who are already invested in projects of prison abolition and
radical liberation struggles, I hope that an immersion in mad and disabled
histories and knowledges, like the ones I provided here regarding deinstitutionalization, will facilitate a greater coalitional struggle and more nuanced
tactics and analysis.

Throughout the book, I have tried to avoid definitive and prescriptive answers ("tell us what to do"), not because I am not immersed in these struggles but for quite the opposite reason. I understand abolition as dis-epistemology, letting go of certain ways of knowing in order to gain others, unlearning in order to learn.[34] In Deaf studies and culture, there is a critique of the term *hearing loss,* which is perceived as deficit driven and one that comes from hearing norms and supremacy; instead, there is a discussion of "Deaf gain."[35] I hope that this book provides and leads to an understanding of madness and disability gain, not (or not only) on a corporeal level but by gaining perspective and knowledge, which can then be utilized in freedom struggles.

What is clear is that abolition is not an alternative, and neither were de-institutionalization and antipsychiatry. It's a project of building, an imperative to push aside discourses of cost-effectiveness and measurements of exclusion or inclusion. It's an ethical commitment, one that calls on us to embrace vulnerability and uncertainty; to treat difference and harm, but not through corrections; to undertake collective and community account-ability—a call to foreground care while understanding its gendered and racial implications in relation to disability, madness, and life without carceral enclo-sures and their logics. It is a collective resolve for coalition building through dis-epistemology, through centering the dangerous, the severe, the fierce and ungovernable, in the long and hard work for collective liberation.

Notes

Introduction

1. Michelle Alexander, *The New Jim Crow: Mass Incarceration in the Age of Color-blindness* (New York: New Press, 2012); Marie Gottschalk, *Caught: The Prison State and the Lockdown of American Politics,* rev. ed. (Princeton, N.J.: Princeton University Press, 2016); and for a discussion of the difference between mass incarceration and hyperincarceration, Loïc Wacquant, "Class, Race and Hyperincarceration in Revanchist America," *Daedalus* 139, no. 3 (2010): 74–90.

2. When I use the term *disability* throughout the book, I mean to encompass a variety of identities, fields of scholarships, and social movements under this umbrella, including Deaf/deaf/hard of hearing, mad/psychiatrized, intellectual/developmental/cognitive disabilities, neurodiversity, those with nonvisible disabilities, and so on. I do this heuristically, to encompass the broad range of diagnosis or lived experience that can fall under the "disability" label, although of course there are vast differences between these categorizations. Many under the above grouping do not necessarily politically identify as disabled, and when applicable I make this division explicit.

3. Liat Ben-Moshe, "Disabling Incarceration: Connecting Disability to Divergent Confinements in the USA," *Critical Sociology* 39, no. 3 (2013): 385–403, https://doi.org/10.1177/0896920511430864; Liat Ben-Moshe, Chris Chapman, and Allison C. Carey, eds., *Disability Incarcerated: Imprisonment and Disability in the United States and Canada* (New York: Palgrave Macmillan, 2014).

4. Michelle Brown and Judah Schept, "New Abolition, Criminology and a Critical Carceral Studies," *Punishment and Society* 19, no. 4 (2017): 440–62.

5. Crip of color critique is an extension of Roderick Ferguson's queer of color critique to disability studies and crip theory. It was separately and simultaneously discussed by me, in relation to incarceration, and Jina Kim, and first published in Jina B. Kim, "Anatomy of the City: Race, Infrastructure, and U.S. Fictions of Dependency" (PhD diss., University of Michigan, Ann Arbor, 2016). "Crip" refers to a politicized disability identity and disability as an analytic. In relation to queer theory, see Robert McRuer, *Crip Theory: Cultural Signs of Queerness and Disability* (New York: NYU Press, 2006).

6. Monographs on incarceration, such as Marie Gottschalk, *The Prison and the Gallows: The Politics of Mass Incarceration in America* (New York: Cambridge University Press, 2006), and Loïc Wacquant, *Punishing the Poor: The Neoliberal Government of Social Insecurity* (Durham, N.C.: Duke University Press, 2009), mention deinstitutionalization briefly, but often only to blame it for the rise in imprisonment.

7. David L. Braddock, Richard E. Hemp, Emily S. Tanis, Jiang Wu, and Laura Haffer, *State of the States in Intellectual and Developmental Disabilities*, 11th ed. (Washington, D.C.: American Association on Intellectual and Developmental Disabilities, 2017).

8. The figures are for people who are identified as I/DD and who receive support and services from a state I/DD agency. James Houseworth, Renáta Tichá, John Smith, and Roqayah Ajaj, *Developments in Living Arrangements and Choice for Persons with Intellectual and Developmental Disabilities*, Policy Research Brief 27, no. 1 (Minneapolis: University of Minnesota, Institute on Community Integration, 2018).

9. Houseworth et al.

10. Bernard E. Harcourt, "Reducing Mass Incarceration: Lessons from the Deinstitutionalization of Mental Hospitals in the 1960s," *Ohio State Journal of Criminal Law* 9 (2011): 53.

11. Cathy Cohen, "Death and Rebirth of a Movement: Queering Critical Ethnic Studies," *Social Justice* 37, no. 4 (2011): 126–32; Dean Spade, *Normal Life: Administrative Violence, Critical Trans Politics, and the Limits of Law*, rev. and exp. ed. (Durham, N.C.: Duke University Press, 2015); Roderick A. Ferguson, *Aberrations in Black: Toward a Queer of Color Critique* (Minneapolis: University of Minnesota Press, 2003).

12. Jina B. Kim, "Toward a Crip-of-Color Critique: Thinking with Minich's 'Enabling Whom?,'" *Lateral* (blog), May 15, 2017, https://csalateral.org/issue/6-1/forum -alt-humanities-critical-disability-studies-crip-of-color-critique-kim/.

13. bell hooks, "Choosing the Margin as Space of Radical Openness," *Framework* 36 (1989): 15.

14. Michel Foucault, *Madness and Civilization: A History of Insanity in the Age of Reason* (New York: Pantheon Books, 1965); Foucault, *Mental Illness and Psychology* (Oakland: University of California Press, 2008); Foucault, *Discipline and Punish: The Birth of the Prison*, 2nd ed. (New York: Vintage Books, 1995).

15. Wendy Brown, *Politics Out of History* (Princeton, N.J.: Princeton University Press, 2001).

16. Shelley Tremain, *Foucault and the Government of Disability* (Ann Arbor: University of Michigan Press, 2015); Nikolas S. Rose, *Governing the Soul: The Shaping of the Private Self*, 2nd ed. (London: Free Association Books, 1999).

17. In mad studies and movements, *psy* is shorthand for discourses like psychology, psychiatry, social work, and similar others.

18. Michel Foucault, "Nietzsche, Genealogy, History," in *Language, Counter-memory, Practice: Selected Essays and Interviews by Michel Foucault*, ed. D. F. Bouchard, 139–64 (Ithaca, N.Y.: Cornell University Press, 1980).

19. Michel Foucault, *The Birth of the Clinic* (New York: Vintage Books, 1994).

20. John Gramlich, "America's Incarceration Rate Is at a Two-Decade Low," Pew Research Center, May 2, 2018, https://www.pewresearch.org/fact-tank/2018/05/02/americas-incarceration-rate-is-at-a-two-decade-low/.

21. Bureau of Justice Statistics, *Annual Probation Survey, Annual Parole Survey, Annual Survey of Jails, and National Prisoner Statistics Program, 2006–2016*, April 2018. Summary can be found at https://www.bjs.gov/content/pub/pdf/cpus16.pdf.

22. Jean Stewart and Marta Russell, "Disablement, Prison, and Historical Segregation," *Monthly Review*, July 1, 2001, https://monthlyreview.org/2001/07/01/disablement-prison-and-historical-segregation/.

23. Liat Ben-Moshe and Jean Stewart, "Disablement, Prison and Historical Segregation: 15 Years Later," in *Disability Politics in a Global Economy: Essays in Honor of Marta Russell*, ed. Ravi Malhotra, 87–104 (London: Routledge, 2017); Rose Braz and Craig Gilmore, "Joining Forces: Prisons and Environmental Justice in Recent California Organizing," *Radical History Review* no. 96 (2006): 95–111.

24. Stewart and Russell, "Disablement."

25. Angela Y. Davis, *Are Prisons Obsolete?* (New York: Seven Stories Press, 2003); Justice Now, https://www.justicenow.org/; INCITE! Women of Color against Violence, ed., *Color of Violence: The INCITE! Anthology* (Durham, N.C.: Duke University Press, 2016),

26. Patricia Erickson and Steven Erickson, *Crime, Punishment, and Mental Illness: Law and the Behavioral Sciences in Conflict* (New Brunswick, N.J.: Rutgers University Press, 2008).

27. Human Rights Watch, "U.S.: Number of Mentally Ill in Prisons Quadrupled," September 5, 2006, https://www.hrw.org/news/2006/09/05/us-number-mentally-ill-prisons-quadrupled.

28. For more information on the plight of Deaf prisoners, refer to https://behearddc.org/.

29. Dylan Rodriguez, *Forced Passages: Imprisoned Radical Intellectuals and the U.S. Prison Regime* (Minneapolis: University of Minnesota Press, 2006).

30. By *settler*, I am referring to a system of settler colonialism, prevalent in nations like the United States and Canada, and in this case how education is related to it. For example, Eve Tuck and K. Wayne Yang, "Decolonization Is Not a Metaphor," *Decolonization: Indigeneity, Education, and Society* 1, no. 1 (2012).

31. A masterful example of the centrality of gender/sexuality (and race) to any critical analysis of imprisonment can be found in the classic Davis, *Are Prisons Obsolete?*, and in Beth E. Richie, *Arrested Justice: Black Women, Violence, and America's Prison Nation* (New York: NYU Press, 2012).

32. Refer to note 2 on page 285.

33. Simi Linton, *Claiming Disability: Knowledge and Identity* (New York: NYU Press, 1998), 2.

34. Peter Beresford, "What Have Madness and Psychiatric System Survivors Got to Do with Disability and Disability Studies?," *Disability and Society* 15 (January 1,

2000): 167–72; Elizabeth J. Donaldson and Catherine Prendergast, "Introduction: Disability and Emotion:'There's No Crying in Disability Studies,'" *Journal of Literary and Cultural Disability Studies* 5, no. 2 (2011): 129–35; Bradley Lewis, "A Mad Fight: Psychiatry and Disability Activism," in *The Disability Studies Reader*, ed. Lennard J. Davis, 331–54 (New York: Routledge, 2006); Margaret Price, *Mad at School: Rhetorics of Mental Disability and Academic Life* (Ann Arbor: University of Michigan Press, 2011); Nev Jones and Robyn Brown, "The Absence of Psychiatric C/S/X Perspectives in Academic Discourse: Consequences and Implications," *Disability Studies Quarterly* 33, no. 1 (2012).

35. Robert Bogdan and Douglas Biklen, "Handicapism," *Social Policy* 7, no. 5 (1977): 14–19; Thomas S. Szasz, *The Myth of Mental Illness: Foundations of a Theory of Personal Conduct* (New York: Harper Perennial, 1974).

36. Steven J. Taylor, "Before It Had a Name: Exploring the Historical Roots of Disability Studies in Education," in *Vital Questions Facing Disability Studies in Education*, vol. 2, 289–306 (New York: Peter Lang, 2016).

37. David Harvey, *A Brief History of Neoliberalism* (Oxford: Oxford University Press, 2007).

38. Lisa Duggan, *The Twilight of Equality? Neoliberalism, Cultural Politics, and the Attack on Democracy* (Boston: Beacon Press, 2004); Grace Kyungwon Hong, *Death beyond Disavowal: The Impossible Politics of Difference* (Minneapolis: University of Minnesota Press, 2015).

39. Gottschalk, *Caught*; Wacquant, *Punishing the Poor*; Wacquant, *Prisons of Poverty* (Minneapolis: University of Minnesota Press, 2009).

40. Julia Chinyere Oparah (formerly Sudbury), "A World without Prisons: Resisting Militarism, Globalized Punishment, and Empire," *Social Justice* 31, no. 1/2 (2004): 11–12; Linda Evans and Eve Goldberg, *The Prison Industrial Complex and the Global Economy* (Montreal, Quebec: Kersplebedeb, 1998).

41. Oparah, "World without Prisons."

42. Ruth Wilson Gilmore, *Golden Gulag: Prisons, Surplus, Crisis, and Opposition in Globalizing California* (Berkeley: University of California Press, 2007).

43. Elizabeth A. Povinelli, *Economies of Abandonment: Social Belonging and Endurance in Late Liberalism* (Durham, N.C.: Duke University Press, 2011); Craig Willse, *The Value of Homelessness: Managing Surplus Life in the United States*, 1st ed. (Minneapolis: University of Minnesota Press, 2015).

44. Some of the major corporations in the institution/hospital industry in North America are Res-Care; Beverly Enterprises of Fort Smith, which employs more people than the entire automobile industry; Healthsouth Rehabilitation Corporation; the Columbia/HCA hospital chain; Humana; and Summit Health.

45. Michael Oliver, *The Politics of Disablement: A Sociological Approach* (New York: St. Martin's Press, 1990); James I. Charlton, *Nothing about Us without Us: Disability, Oppression, and Empowerment* (Berkeley: University of California Press, 2000); Wolf Wolfensberger, "Human Service Policies: The Rhetoric versus the Reality," in *Disability and Dependency*, ed. Len Barton, 23–41 (Lewes, U.K.: Falmer Press, 1989).

46. Deborah Stone, *The Disabled State* (Philadelphia: Temple University Press, 1994); Liat Ben-Moshe, "Disabling Incarceration: Connecting Disability to Divergent Confinements in the USA," *Critical Sociology* 39, no. 3 (2013): 385–403.

47. Hong, *Death beyond Disavowal*.

48. Hong, *Death beyond Disavowal*, 19.

49. Ruth Wilson Gilmore, "Fatal Couplings of Power and Difference: Notes on Racism and Geography," *Professional Geographer* 54, no. 1 (2002): 21.

50. Ferguson, *Aberrations in Black*.

51. Sharon Snyder and David Mitchell, "Introduction: Ablenationalism and the Geo-politics of Disability," *Journal of Literary and Cultural Disability Studies* 4, no. 2 (2010): 113–25.

52. Gilmore, *Fatal Coupling*.

53. Ben-Moshe, "Tension between Abolition and Reform"; Kaba, "Prison Reform's in Vogue."

54. https://www.alternet.org/2016/10/electronic-monitoring-restrictive-and -wrong/; also the project https://www.challengingecarceration.org/about-project/.

55. Erick Fabris, *Tranquil Prisons: Chemical Incarceration under Community Treatment Orders* (Toronto: University of Toronto Press, 2011).

56. James Kilgore, "Repackaging Mass Incarceration," *Counterpunch*, June 6, 2014, https://www.counterpunch.org/2014/06/06/repackaging-mass-incarceration/.

57. Michael L. Perlin, "On Sanism," *SMU Law Review* 46 (1993): 373–407.

58. Richie, as well as the work of INCITE! Women of Color against Violence, offers a critique of this kind of "feminism" that calls for equality in the results in punitive measures. Victoria Law discusses the term *carceral feminism* in her 2014 article in *Jacobin*: https://www.jacobinmag.com/2014/10/against-carceral-feminism/.

59. Mariame Kaba, "Free Us All: Participatory Defense Campaigns as Abolitionist Organizing," *New Inquiry*, May 8, 2017, https://thenewinquiry.com/free-us-all/.

60. Angela Y. Davis, "Racialized Punishment and Prison Abolition," in *The Angela Y. Davis Reader*, ed. Joy James, 96–107 (Malden, Mass.: Blackwell, 1998); Kim Gilmore, "Slavery and Prison—Understanding the Connections," *Social Justice* 27, no. 3 (2000): 95; Joy James, ed., *The New Abolitionists: (Neo) Slave Narratives and Contemporary Prison Writings* (Albany: SUNY Press, 2005).

61. Angela Y. Davis, "From the Convict Lease System to the Super-Max Prison," in *States of Confinement*, 60–74 (New York: Palgrave Macmillan, 2000); Matthew J. Mancini, *One Dies, Get Another: Convict Leasing in the American South, 1866–1928* (Columbia: University of South Carolina Press, 1996); Douglas A. Blackmon, *Slavery by Another Name: The Re-enslavement of Black Americans from the Civil War to World War II* (New York: Anchor Books, 2008).

62. Robert T. Chase, "We Are Not Slaves: Rethinking the Rise of Carceral States through the Lens of the Prisoners' Rights Movement," *Journal of American History* 102, no. 1 (2015): 73–86.

63. Gottschalk, *The Prison and the Gallows*.

64. Wacquant, *Punishing the Poor*.

65. James, *New Abolitionists*; Dylan Rodriguez, *Forced Passages*; Julia Oparah (formerly Sudbury), "A World without Prisons: Resisting Militarism, Globalized Punishment, and Empire," *Social Justice* 31, no. 1/2 (2004): 9–30; Sudbury, "Maroon Abolitionists: Black Gender-Oppressed Activists in the Anti-prison Movement in the U.S. and Canada," *Meridians* 9, no. 1 (2009): 1–29.

66. Gilmore, "Slavery and Prison," 95.

67. Christian Parenti, *Lockdown America: Police and Prisons in the Age of Crisis* (New York: Verso, 1999); Gilmore, *Golden Gulag*.

68. Cedric Robinson, *Black Marxism: The Making of the Black Radical Tradition* (Chapel Hill: University of North Carolina Press, 1983); Gilmore, "Fatal Couplings of Power and Difference."

69. Saidiya V. Hartman, *Scenes of Subjection: Terror, Slavery, and Self-Making in Nineteenth-Century America* (New York: Oxford University Press, 1997); Orlando Patterson, *Slavery and Social Death: A Comparative Study* (Cambridge, Mass.: Harvard University Press, 1982).

70. Steve Martinot and Jared Sexton, "The Avant-Garde of White Supremacy," *Social Identities* 9, no. 2 (2003): 169–81.

71. Frank Wilderson, "The Prison Slave as Hegemony's (Silent) Scandal," *Social Justice* 30, no. 2 (2003): 18–27.

72. Alexander, *New Jim Crow*.

73. I use the term *race neutral* as opposed to *color-blind*, which I find to be a confusing and ableist term.

74. Regarding class, legal scholar James Forman Jr. shows that for African American men with some college education, the probability of being imprisoned actually decreased slightly between 1979 and 1999. So the issue is not only antiblack racism but its deadly coupling (to paraphrase Stuart Hall) with class and capitalism. Forman, "Racial Critiques of Mass Incarceration: Beyond the New Jim Crow," *New York University Law Review* 87, no. 21 (2012): 101–46.

75. Andrea Ritchie, *Invisible No More: Police Violence against Black Women and Women of Color* (Boston: Beacon Press, 2017).

76. Forman, "Racial Critiques," for example.

77. Chase, "We Are Not Slaves."

78. Sudbury, "Maroon Abolitionists."

79. *Maroon* refers to the communities of runaway slaves and indigenous people that have formed in the Americas since the seventeenth century.

80. Not intentionally using the term abolition in deinstitutionalization is perhaps not surprising since race and racial capitalism were not central in these liberation struggles, as discussed in chapters 2, 3, and 5. For current examples of psychiatric abolition refer to Bonnie Burstow, Brenda A. LeFrançois, and Shaindl Diamond, eds., *Psychiatry Disrupted: Theorizing Resistance and Crafting the (R)evolution* (Montreal, Quebec: McGill-Queen's University Press, 2014).

81. In 1979, for example, self-advocates in Nebraska held a press conference stating that all institutions should be closed. B. Shoultz and P. Williams, "We Can Speak for Ourselves," 1982. Also refer to https://www.sabeusa.org/meet-sabe/policy-statements/closing-institutions/.

82. Leroy F. Moore Jr., "CAGED, Goddamn Philadelphia," SoundCloud, March 27, 2013, https://soundcloud.com/blackkrip/caged-goddamn-philadelphia.

83. For more information, visit https://kriphopnation.com/, https://harriettubmancollective.tumblr.com/, and https://www.sinsinvalid.org/.

84. Chris Bell, "Introducing White Disability Studies: A Modest Proposal," in *Disability Studies Reader*, ed. Lennard J. Davis, 2nd ed., 275–82 (New York: Routledge, 2006).

85. Liat Ben-Moshe, "'The Institution Yet to Come': Analyzing Incarceration through a Disability Lens," in *The Disability Studies Reader* 4th. ed., ed. Lennard J. Davis, 132–43 (New York: Routledge, 2013).

86. Bell, "Introducing White"; Beth A. Ferri and David J. Connor, *Reading Resistance: Discourses of Exclusion in Desegregation and Inclusion Debates* (Bern, Switzerland: Peter Lang, 2006); Nirmala Erevelles, *Disability and Difference in Global Contexts: Enabling a Transformative Body Politic* (New York: Palgrave Macmillan, 2011). Also Jasbir K. Puar, *The Right to Maim: Debility, Capacity, Disability* (Durham, N.C.: Duke University Press, 2017), for further critiques on this gap.

87. Michel Foucault, *"Society Must Be Defended": Lectures at the Collège de France, 1975–1976*, trans. David Macey, 1st ed. (New York: Picador, 2003).

88. Subini A. Annamma, David Connor, and Beth Ferri, "Dis/ability Critical Race Studies (DisCrit): Theorizing at the Intersections of Race and Dis/ability," *Race, Ethnicity, and Education* 16, no. 1 (2013): 1–31; Annamma, *Pedagogy of Pathologization*.

89. Beth Harry and Janette K. Klingner, *Why Are So Many Minority Students in Special Education? Understanding Race and Disability in Schools* (New York: Teachers College Press, 2005); Audrey Trainor, book review of *Why Are So Many Minority Students in Special Education? Understanding Race and Disability in Schools* by B. Harry and J. Klingner, *Remedial and Special Education* 29, no. 1 (2008): 58–59; Robin M. Smith and Nirmala Erevelles, "Towards an Enabling Education: The Difference That Disability Makes," *Educational Researcher* 33, no. 8 (2004): 31–36.

90. D. L. Adams and Erica Meiners, "Who Wants to Be Special? Pathologization and the Preparation of Bodies for Prison," in *Critical Urban Education: Dismantling the School to Prison Pipeline,* ed. A. Nocella, P. Parmar, and D. Stovall, 145–64 (New York: Peter Lang, 2014).

91. Ferri and Connor, *Reading Resistance*.

92. Jelani Exum, "The Death Penalty on the Streets: What the Eighth Amendment Can Teach about Regulating Police Use of Force," *Missouri Law Review* 80, no. 987 (2015), https://ssrn.com/abstract=2881511.

93. Ritchie, *Invisible No More*, 89.

94. Jin Haritaworn, "Beyond 'Hate': Queer Metonymies of Crime, Pathology and Anti/violence," *Global Jindal Law Review* 4, no. 2 (2014): 44–78.

95. Nirmala Erevelles and Andrea Minear, "Unspeakable Offenses: Untangling Race and Disability in Discourses of Intersectionality," *Journal of Literary and Cultural Disability Studies* 4, no. 2 (2010): 127–45; Annamma, *Pedagogy of Pathologization*; Ashley Taylor, "The Discourse of Pathology: Reproducing the Able Mind through Bodies of Color," *Hypatia* 30, no. 1 (2014): 181–98.

96. "Mom of Autistic Man at Center of Charles Kinsey Shooting: My Son Is Traumatized," *Miami Herald,* July 23, 2016, https://www.miamiherald.com/news/local/community/miami-dade/north-miami/article91472342.html.

97. For a brief analysis of the case, refer to Tanja Aho, Liat Ben-Moshe, and Leon J. Hilton, "Mad Futures: Affect/Theory/Violence," *American Quarterly* 69, no. 2 (2017): 291–302.

98. Talila A. Lewis, "Honoring Arnaldo Rios-Soto and Charles Kinsey: Achieving Liberation through Disability Solidarity," *Talila A. Lewis* (blog), July 22, 2016, https://www.talilalewis.com/blog/achieving-liberation-through-disability-solidarity.

99. I am using the broad term *policing* here, as opposed to *police brutality,* which implies that there is policing that is not violent or brutal.

100. Cathy Cohen, "Death and Rebirth of a Movement: Queering Critical Ethnic Studies," *Social Justice* 37, no. 4 (2011): 126–32; Spade, *Normal Life*; Ferguson, *Aberrations in Black.*

101. Patty Berne, "Disability Justice—a Working Draft," *Sins Invalid* (blog), June 10, 2015, http://sinsinvalid.org/blog/disability-justice-a-working-draft-by-patty-berne.

102. "The state-sanctioned or extralegal production and exploitation of group-differentiated vulnerability to premature death." Gilmore, *Golden Gulag.*

103. E.g., Leroy Moore's critique of sensitivity training in regard to the Rios case, "Yes, It Goes Deeper than Training, Police Shooting Arnaldo Rios Soto Interview with Matthew Dietz, Attorney for the Family of Arnaldo Rios Soto," *Poor Magazine,* July 9, 2016, http://poormagazine.org/node/5564.

104. Mia Mingus, "Changing the Framework: Disability Justice, How Our Communities Can Move beyond Access to Wholeness," 2011, https://leavingevidence.wordpress.com/2011/02/12/changing-the-framework-disability-justice/.

105. Liat Ben-Moshe and Sandy Magaña, "An Introduction to Race, Gender, and Disability: Intersectionality, Disability Studies, and Families of Color," *Women, Gender, and Families of Color* 2, no. 2 (2014): 105–14.

106. In the I/DD context, for example, refer to Sandra Magaña et al., "Racial and Ethnic Disparities in Quality of Health Care among Children with Autism and Other Developmental Disabilities," *Intellectual and Developmental Disabilities* 50, no. 4 (n.d.): 287–99.

107. Puar, *Right to Maim,* xii.

108. Lauren Berlant, *Cruel Optimism* (Durham, N.C.: Duke University Press, 2011).

109. Helen Meekosha, "Decolonising Disability: Thinking and Acting Globally," *Disability and Society* 26, no. 6 (2011): 667–82.

110. Puar, *Right to Maim,* 110.

111. Puar, xvii.

112. Angela Y. Davis, "From the Convict Lease System to the Super-Max Prison," in *States of Confinement: Policing, Detention, and Prisons*, ed. Joy James, 60–74 (New York: Palgrave Macmillan, 2000).

113. "Response of the Harriet Tubman Collective to the THE RUDERMAN WHITE PAPER ON MEDIA COVERAGE OF LAW ENFORCEMENT USE OF FORCE AND DISABILITY: The Harriet Tubman Collective," Harriet Tubman Collective, https://harriettubman collective.tumblr.com/post/174479075753/accountable-reporting-on-disability -race-and.

1. The Perfect Storm

1. Dae-Young Kim, "Psychiatric Deinstitutionalization and Prison Population Growth: A Critical Literature Review and Its Implications," *Criminal Justice Policy Review* 27, no. 1 (2016): 3–21.

2. Michel Foucault, "Nietzsche, Genealogy, History" (1977), in Bouchard, *Language, Counter-memory, Practice*, 139–64.

3. Foucault, 140.

4. Gavin Kendall and Gary Wickham, *Using Foucault's Methods* (London: Sage, 1999).

5. Paul Di Georgio describes the role of necessity and contingency in Nietzsche's genealogy as "anything could have happened (contingency), but only certain things did happen, and these things that did happen are necessary." Paul di Georgio, "Contingency and Necessity in the Genealogy of Morality," *Telos* 162 (2013): 97–111.

6. Marie Gottschalk, "Cell Blocks and Red Ink: Mass Incarceration, the Great Recession and Penal Reform," *Daedalus* 139, no. 3 (2010): 62–73; Bernard E. Harcourt, "Reducing Mass Incarceration: Lessons from the Deinstitutionalization of Mental Hospitals in the 1960s," *Ohio State Journal of Criminal Law* 9 (2011): 53.

7. David L. Braddock, Richard E. Hemp, Emily S. Tanis, Jiang Wu, and Laura Haffer, *State of the States in Intellectual and Developmental Disabilities*, 11th ed. (Washington, D.C.: American Association on Intellectual and Developmental Disabilities, 2017).

8. David L. Braddock, Richard Hemp, Mary C. Rizzolo, Emily Shea Tanis, Laura Haffer, and Jiang Wu, *The State of the States in Intellectual and Developmental Disabilities: Emerging from the Great Recession* (Washington, D.C.: American Association on Intellectual and Developmental Disabilities, 2015).

9. Liat Ben-Moshe, Chris Chapman, and Allison C. Carey, eds., *Disability Incarcerated: Imprisonment and Disability in the United States and Canada* (New York: Palgrave Macmillan, 2014).

10. Bernard Harcourt, "From the Asylum to the Prison: Rethinking the Incarceration Revolution," *Texas Law Review* 84 (2006): 1751–86.

11. Harcourt.

12. Goodey credits Locke with establishing the dichotomy between mental illness and intellectual disability (although there is some disagreement about it). D. Braddock and L. Parish, "An Institutional History of Disability," in *Handbook of Disability*

Studies, ed. G. Albrecht, K. Seelman, and M. Bury, 11–68 (Thousand Oaks, Calif.: Sage, 2003).

13. James W. Trent Jr., *Inventing the Feeble Mind: A History of Mental Retardation in the United States* (Berkeley: University of California Press, 1994).

14. Wolf Wolfensberger, *The Origin and Nature of Our Institutional Models* (Syracuse, N.Y.: Center on Human Policy, Syracuse University Division of Special Education and Rehabilitation, 1974), 66.

15. Chapman et al., *"Reconsidering Confinement"*; Trent, *Inventing the Feeble Mind*.

16. It is unclear what the exact nature of her disability was prior to the lobotomy, and one can only speculate if the lobotomy was also due to the different gendered expectations given to Rosemary Kennedy as opposed to her siblings.

17. President's Panel on Mental Retardation.

18. Parsons provides a historical exploration of how this was operationalized in Pennsylvania. Anne E. Parsons, *From Asylum to Prison: Deinstitutionalization and the Rise of Mass Incarceration after 1945* (Chapel Hill: University of North Carolina Press, 2018).

19. Paul Lerman, "Deinstitutionalization and Welfare Policies," *Annals of the American Academy of Political and Social Science* 479 (1985): 132–55.

20. Lerman shows that deinstitutionalization didn't become fully realized until new funding sources were in place and could be used by those advocating for non-institutional placements. Prior to 1974, for example, certain mental health issues could only be reimbursed if treated in a hospital.

21. Ann Braden Johnson, *Out of Bedlam: The Truth about Deinstitutionalization* (New York: Basic Books, 1990).

22. Panel members had strong differences of opinion on basic matters, as some favored a focus only on individuals with chronic conditions, while others wanted to focus on all mental health problems as well as their prevention.

23. Johnson.

24. Although not an exposé in the traditional sense, the Attica uprising in 1971 could be seen as a form of exposé that led to reform and discussions regarding prison conditions.

25. I am using the term U.S. publics, following Paula Ioanide, *The Emotional Politics of Racism: How Feelings Trump Facts in an Era of Colorblindness* (Stanford, Calif.: Stanford University Press, 2015).

26. I am indebted here to the work of Steve Taylor for pointing how these cycles of reform, as he calls them, operated in the 1940s and 1950s. Taylor, *Acts of Conscience: World War II, Mental Institutions, and Religious Objectors* (Syracuse, N.Y.: Syracuse University Press, 2009).

27. Taylor.

28. Parsons, *From Asylum to Prison*.

29. Parsons.

30. Michel Foucault, *History of Madness* (New York: Routledge, 2013).

31. *New York Times*, September 10, 1965.

32. Burton Blatt and Fred Kaplan, *Christmas in Purgatory: A Photographic Essay on Mental Retardation* (Boston: Allen and Bacon, 1966), v.

33. *Christmas in Purgatory* can still be viewed online today, but a warning: it is very disturbing, with depictions of nudity, neglect, and abounding institutional violence.

34. Blatt and Kaplan, xx.

35. David Goode, Darryl B. Hill, Jean Reiss, and William Bronston, *A History and Sociology of the Willowbrook State School* (Washington, D.C.: American Association on Intellectual and Developmental Disabilities, 2013), 139.

36. Burton Blatt, Andrejs Ozolins, and Joe McNally, *The Family Papers: A Return to Purgatory* (New York: Longman, 1979), vi.

37. Taylor, *Acts of Conscience*, 380.

38. Lisa Merri Johnson and Robert McRuer, "Cripistemologies: Introduction," *Journal of Literary and Cultural Disability Studies* 8, no. 2 (2014): 127–48.

39. Rachel Herzig, "'Tweaking Armageddon': The Potential and Limits of Conditions of Confinement Campaigns," *Social Justice* 41, no. 3 (2015): 190–95.

40. Syrus Ware, Joan Ruzsa, and Giselle Dias, "It Can't Be Fixed Because It's Not Broken: Racism and Disability in the Prison Industrial Complex," in Ben-Moshe et al., *Disability Incarcerated*, 163–84.

41. Judith Gran, "Deinstitutionalization Litigation: Experiences and Outcomes," *IMPACT* 9, no. 1 (1995–96): 8–9.

42. Gran.

43. Steve J. Taylor provides an excellent overview of this case and many other deinstitutionalization cases regarding people with intellectual disabilities in "Institutions and the Law," in *Encyclopedia of American Disability History*, ed. S. Burch, 485–89 (New York: Facts on File, 2009).

44. https://disabilityjustice.org/wyatt-v-stickney/.

45. Cited in Taylor, "Institutions and the Law."

46. For more on the legal battle over Willowbrook, refer to the fascinating book by David J. Rothman and Sheila M. Rothman, *The Willowbrook Wars: Bringing the Mentally Disabled into the Community* (Piscataway, N.J.: Transaction, 1984).

47. Cited in Taylor, "Institutions and the Law."

48. David Ferleger and Penelope A. Boyd, "Anti-institutionalization: The Promise of the Pennhurst Case," *Stanford Law Review* 31, no. 4 (1979): 720.

49. Laura C. Bornstein, "Contextualizing Cleburne," *Golden Gate University Law Review* 41 (2010): 91–119.

50. Bornstein.

51. S. J. Taylor and S. J. Searl, "Disability in America: A History of Policies and Trends," in *Significant Disability: Issues Affecting People with Significant Disabilities from a Historical, Policy, Leadership, and Systems Perspective*, ed. E. D. Martin, 16–63 (Springfield, Ill.: Charles C. Thomas, 2001).

52. In *Willowbrook Wars*, Rothman and Rothman provide a full account of the consent decree and its contradictions.

53. Johnson goes as far as to state that in the field of mental health, one of the immediate consequences of deinstitutionalization in the 1970s was that more patients were treated in institutions than before the program began, and more money was going to institutional care than to community mental health. Johnson, *Out of Bedlam*.

54. Lerman, "Deinstitutionalization and Welfare Policies."

55. A. Bagnall and G. Eyal, "'Forever Children' and Autonomous Citizens: Comparing the Deinstitutionalizations of Psychiatric Patients and Developmentally Disabled Individuals in the United States," in *50 Years after Deinstitutionalization: Mental Illness in Contemporary Communities*, 27–61 (Bingley, U.K.: Emerald Group, 2016).

56. Lerman, "Deinstitutionalization and Welfare Policies."

57. In Jerome G. Miller, *Last One over the Wall: The Massachusetts Experiment in Closing Reform Schools* (Columbus: Ohio State University Press, 1991).

58. Ruthie-Marie Beckwith, *Disability Servitude* (New York: Palgrave Macmillan, 2016).

59. I discuss this more in chapter 6.

60. Trent, *Inventing the Feeble Mind*.

61. Reagan's tactics as governor to decrease the number of admissions to mental hospitals in California were twofold: the first was called a "county bounty," by which districts would get extra money from the state to spend on whatever they chose if their admissions fell below a certain level predicted by state calculations; the second was to use progressive legislation to create stringent admission criteria and decrease involuntary commitments. For example, the passage of the Lanterman–Petris–Short Act limited involuntary hospitalization. Johnson, *Out of Bedlam*; P. Ahmed and S. Plog, *State Mental Hospitals: What Happens When They Close* (New York: Plenum Medical Books, 1976).

62. Paul R. Dingman, "The Alternative Care Is Not There," in Ahmed and Plog, *State Mental Hospitals*, 45–61. Gronfein empirically assessed the timing of deinstitutionalization associated with the introduction of psychotropic drugs and demonstrated that the introduction of drugs did not initiate deinstitutionalization and instead only facilitated the deinstitutionalization process in the 1960s. William Gronfein, "Incentives and Intentions in Mental Health Policy: A Comparison of the Medicaid and Community Mental Health Programs," *Journal of Health and Social Behavior* 26 (1985): 192–206.

63. For commentary about its use in Willowbrook and Fernald, see David Goode, Darryl B. Hill, Jean Reiss, and William Bronston, *A History and Sociology of the Willowbrook State School* (Washington, D.C.: American Association on Intellectual and Developmental Disabilities, 2013).

64. Bagnall and Eyal, "Forever Children."

65. Johnson, *Out of Bedlam*.

66. Judith P. Swazey, *Chlorpromazine in Psychiatry: A Study of Therapeutic Innovation* (Cambridge, Mass.: MIT Press, 1974).

67. Quoted in Johnson, *Out of Bedlam*, 46.

68. Foucault, *History of Madness*.

69. As Bagnall and Eyal, "Forever Children," also suggest.

70. Johnson, *Out of Bedlam*, 34. Also, Michael E. Staub, *Madness Is Civilization: When the Diagnosis Was Social, 1948–1980* (Chicago: University of Chicago Press, 2011).

71. Bagnall and Eyal, "Forever Children."

72. Meghann O'Leary and Liat Ben-Moshe, "Homage to Lucas: The Politics of 'Treatment' and 'Choice' in Neoliberal Times," in *Madness, Violence, and Power*, ed. Andrea Daley, Lucy Costa and Peter Beresford (Toronto: University of Toronto Press, 2019).

73. In a sense, Willowbrook was the price that needed to be paid for scientific advancements in the fields of I/DD and mental health. Refer to D. J. Rothman and S. M. Rothman, *The Willowbrook Wars*, 1st ed. (New York: Harper and Row, 1984).

74. Price, *Mad at School*; Shaista Patel, "Racing Madness: The Terrorizing Madness of the Post-9/11 Terrorist Body," in Ben-Moshe et al., *Disability Incarcerated*, 201–15.

75. Jasbir K. Puar, *Terrorist Assemblages: Homonationalism in Queer Times* (Durham, N.C.: Duke University Press, 2017).

76. Lerman, "Deinstitutionalization and Welfare Policies."

77. Steven J. Taylor, "The Institutions Are Dying, but Are Not Dead Yet," in *Deinstitutionalization and People with Intellectual Disabilities: In and out of Institutions*, ed. K. Johnson and R. Traustadottir, 93–107 (London: Jessica Kingsley, 2005).

2. Abolition in Deinstitutionalization

1. Foucault, "Society Must Be Defended," 7.

2. Foucault, "Society Must Be Defended," 7.

3. Foucault, 8.

4. Hong, *Death beyond Disavowal*.

5. Sara Ahmed, *On Being Included: Racism and Diversity in Institutional Life* (Durham, N.C.: Duke University Press, 2012); Duggan, *Twilight of Equality?*; Wahneema Lubiano, "Like Being Mugged by a Metaphor: Multiculturalism and State Narratives," in *Mapping Multiculturalism*, ed. Avery F. Gordon and Christopher Newfield, 64–75 (Minneapolis: University of Minnesota Press, 1996).

6. Ferri and Connor, *Reading Resistance*.

7. Paula Kluth, Diana M. Straut, and Douglas P. Biklen, *Access to Academics for All Students: Critical Approaches to Inclusive Curriculum, Instruction, and Policy* (New York: Routledge, 2003).

8. "There Is No Place Called Inclusion," https://www.iidc.indiana.edu/pages/There-is-No-Place-Called-Inclusion.

9. Ferguson, *Aberrations in Black*.

10. Maxwell Jones, "The Concept of a Therapeutic Community," *American Journal of Psychiatry* 112, no. 8 (1956): 647–50.

11. Harold Garfinkel, "Conditions of Successful Degradation Ceremonies," *American Journal of Sociology* 61, no. 5 (1956): 420–24.

12. Erving Goffman, *Asylums: Essays on the Social Situation of Mental Patients and Other Inmates* (New York: Doubleday, 1961).

13. David J. Vail, *Dehumanization and the Institutional Career* (Springfield: C. C. Thomas, 1966).

14. Nirje defined *normalization* as "the formula 'to let the mentally retarded obtain an existence as close to the normal as possible.' Thus, as I see it, the normalization principle means making available to the mentally retarded patterns and conditions of everyday life, which are as close as possible to the norms and patterns of the mainstream of society." Bengt Nirje, "The Normalization Principle and Its Human Management Implications," in *Changing Patterns in Residential Services for the Mentally Retarded,* ed. Robert B. Kugel and Wolf Wolfensberger (Washington, D.C.: President's Committee on Mental Retardation, 1969), 181.

15. Bengt Nirje was influenced greatly by volunteering with the Swedish Red Cross in refugee camps in Austria as a young man. His insights on the devastating consequences of camp life were later applied to his work with children with cerebral palsy and cognitive disabilities in Sweden. "Bengt Nirje on Normalization," http://mn.gov/mnddc/bengtNirje/index.html.

16. Kugel and Wolfensberger, *Changing Patterns in Residential Services.*

17. Nirje, "Normalization Principle."

18. This comes out from conversations I had with Wolf Wolfensberger and those who knew him, especially Steven J. Taylor.

19. Kim E. Nielsen, *A Disability History of the United States* (Boston: Beacon Press, 2012).

20. Robert Prouty, G. Smith, and K. Charlie Lakin, eds., *Residential Services for Persons with Developmental Disabilities: Status and Trends through 2004* (Minneapolis: University of Minnesota, Institute on Community Integration, Research and Training Center on Community Living, 2005).

21. Wolf Wolfensberger, *The Origin and Nature of Our Institutional Models* (New York: Human Policy Press, 1975).

22. Steven J. Taylor, "Before It Had a Name: Exploring the Historical Roots of Disability Studies in Education," *Vital Questions Facing Disability Studies in Education* 2 (2006): 289–306.

23. Gil Eyal, Brendan Hart, Emine Onculer, Neta Oren, and Natasha Rossi, *The Autism Matrix* (Cambridge: Polity Press, 2010).

24. For example, some applied normalization through reform frameworks such as creating routines in the institution, emphasizing age-appropriate behaviors in an abnormal setting. The early theorists of the principle of normalization, such as Nirje, advocated for change in institutions, but if the institutions were "homelike," these placements would follow the rules of the normalization principle. But the goal of normalization was to move away from the institutional model, not to create smaller institutions in the community, even if it matched other characteristics (daily routines resembling those of peers, age appropriateness, culturally appropriate, etc.).

25. That is also his critique of the inclusion movement, in which, in his opinion, kids are put together in the same setting, but their roles are not changed and not valued. Although Wolfensberger calls this process *inclusion,* others characterize it as

mainstreaming, which is a different process and ideology. As I stated earlier, mainstreaming would be more akin to bringing disabled students into regular classrooms without modifying the system of education (curriculum, how it is delivered, class size, adequate staffing, etc.). *Inclusion* is a philosophy that ensures that everyone can learn and appreciates the benefits of diversity in education. Refer to the work of educator Douglas Biklen for more on this distinction.

26. Wolf Wolfensberger, *A Brief Introduction to Social Role Valorization as a High-Order Concept for Structuring Human Services* (Syracuse, N.Y.: Syracuse University Training Institute, 1991); Wolfensberger, *A Brief Introduction to Social Role Valorization: A High-Order Concept for Addressing the Plight of Societally Devalued People, and for Structuring Human Services* (Syracuse, N.Y.: Training Institute for Human Service Planning, Leadership and Change Agentry, Syracuse University, 1998).

27. Wolfensberger, *A Brief Introduction to Social Role Valorization: A High-Order Concept.*

28. Training Institute for Human Service Planning, Leadership, and Change Agentry and Wolf Wolfensberger, *Program Analysis of Service Systems (PASS)* (Syracuse, N.Y.: Syracuse University, 1976). I would be remiss not to mention here his longtime collaborator in workshops, training, and writing Susan Thomas, who was instrumental in conceptualizing SRV and PASS but is much less known than Wolf.

29. Even though Wolfensberger's theories add to the technocratic management and surveillance of people with disability by health care professionals, it is ironic but important to add here that Wolfensberger had his own critique of health professions, one that is much less known than Oliver's. Wolfensberger critiqued the notion of "special needs" for disabled people, stating, "They may be said to 'need' to be institutionalized. They may be said to 'need' bizarre and injurious treatments. It may be said that it is in their best interests if they died, and that they have the 'need' to be killed." Wolfensberger, *A Brief Introduction to Social Role Valorization as a High-Order Concept,* 29. Human services have traditionally been regarded as moral enterprises that service and assist people in need. However, according to Wolfensberger and Marxist analysts, the latent function of such industry is self-preservation and expansion—oftentimes at the expense of the users of these services, as he shows at length, using nursing homes as an example.

30. Max Weber suggested in 1905 that there was a change in social life brought forth by capitalism and consequently by bureaucratic mechanisms that uphold it. He referred to it as an "iron cage." This technocratic regime (what Foucault would call discourse or episteme) not only sustains capitalism as an effective economic system but also upholds the values and worldview emanating from it.

31. Kugel and Wolfensberger, *Changing Patterns in Residential Services.*

32. As theorist Fiona Kumari Campbell further explains, "the introduction of 'SRV' has not only been instrumental in the development of new methods for the 'management' of disability, the very discourse of 'SRV' has effected the constitution of the 'disablised body' within social policy and legislative reforms." Campbell, "Social

Role Valorisation Theory as Discourse: Bio-medical Transgression or Recuperation?," http://fionacampbell.tripod.com/srv.htm.

33. Chris Drinkwater, "Supported Living and the Production of Individuals," in *Foucault and the Government of Disability,* ed. Shelley Lynn Tremain (Ann Arbor: University of Michigan Press, 2015).

34. Mike Oliver, "The Social Model of Disability: Thirty Years On," *Disability and Society* 28, no. 7 (2013): 1024–26.

35. Mike Oliver, "Capitalism, Disability and Ideology: A Materialist Critique of the Normalization Principle," 1994, http://www.leeds.ac.uk/disability-studies/archiveuk/; Campbell, "Social Role Valorisation Theory"; Jim Overboe, "'Difference in Itself': Validating Disabled People's Lived Experience," *Body and Society* 5, no. 4 (1999): 17–29.

36. Quoted in Oliver, "Capitalism, Disability and Ideology."

37. Oliver.

38. For more on the institutional–industrial complex, refer to chapter 1 of Ben-Moshe et al., *Disability Incarcerated*; Marta Russell, *Beyond Ramps: Disability at the End of the Social Contract* (Monroe, Maine: Common Courage Press, 2002); Ben-Moshe and Stewart, "Disablement."

39. Lennard J. Davis, *Bending Over Backwards: Disability, Dismodernism, and Other Difficult Positions* (New York: New York University Press, 2002).

40. In a different context (responding to debates around whether normativity is inherently bad in certain strands of feminist and queer theory), Alexis Shotwell defines *normalization* as policing or disciplinary processes that enforce (certain) norms. Shotwell, *Against Purity: Living Ethically in Compromised Times* (Minneapolis: University of Minnesota Press, 2016).

41. Sylvia Wynter, "Unsettling the Coloniality of Being/Power/Truth/Freedom: Towards the Human, after Man, Its Overrepresentation—an Argument," *New Centennial Review* 3, no. 3 (2003): 257–337.

42. Campbell, "Social Role Valorisation Theory."

43. Michael Gill, *Already Doing It: Intellectual Disability and Sexual Agency* (Minneapolis: University of Minnesota Press, 2015), xii–xiii.

44. Phil Smith and Christine Routel, "Transition Failure: The Cultural Bias of Self-Determination and the Journey to Adulthood for People with Disabilities," *Disability Studies Quarterly* 30, no. 1 (2009), https://doi.org/10.18061/dsq.v30i1.1012.

45. Dina Gilio-Whitaker, "Indian Self-Determination and Sovereignty," Jan 17, 2013, https://newsmaven.io/indiancountrytoday/archive/indian-self-determination-and -sovereignty-BwLXMp7gtkuOmKZfVr3Sfw.

46. Liat Ben-Moshe, "'The Institution Yet to Come': Analysing Incarceration through a Disability Lens," in Davis, *Disability Studies Reader,* 132–43.

47. Erving Goffman, *Stigma: Notes on the Management of Spoiled Identity* (New York: Prentice Hall, 1963).

48. Nick Walker, "Neurodiversity: Some Basic Terms and Definitions," *Neurocosmopolitanism* (blog), September 27, 2014, http://neurocosmopolitanism.com/neuro diversity-some-basic-terms-definitions/.

49. Carol Gill, "A Psychological View of Disability Culture," *Disability: The Social, Political, and Ethical Debate* (1995): 163–69; Paul K. Longmore, "The Second Phase: From Disability Rights to Disability Culture," *Disability Rag and Resource* 16, no. 5 (1995): 4–11.

50. Elizabeth J. (Ibby) Grace, "NeuroQueer: Are You Neuroqueer?," *NeuroQueer* (blog), September 18, 2013, https://neuroqueer.blogspot.com/2013/09/are-you-neu roqueer.html; Melanie Yergeau and Michael Scott Monje, "NeuroQueer: Melanie Yergeau and Michael Scott Monje Jr at #CRCon 2014," *NeuroQueer* (blog), October 31, 2014, https://neuroqueer.blogspot.com/2014/10/melanie-yergeau-and-michael-scott -monje.html.

51. Fiona A. Campbell, "Exploring Internalized Ableism Using Critical Race Theory," *Disability and Society* 23, no. 2 (2008): 151–62.

52. Allison C. Carey, *On the Margins of Citizenship: Intellectual Disability and Civil Rights in Twentieth-Century America* (Philadelphia: Temple University Press, 2009).

53. Roland Johnson and Karl Williams, *Lost in a Desert World: An Autobiography* (Philadelphia: Speaking for Ourselves, 1999).

54. Bonnie Shoultz served as an advisor to people first in Nebraska for many years. Paul Williams and Bonnie Shoultz, *We Can Speak for Ourselves: Self-Advocacy by Mentally Handicapped People* (London: Souvenir Press, 1982).

55. Ray died unexpectedly in 1979. His wife, Nancy Loomis, became a leader in the group after his passing. Another active ally to Project Two, in addition to Shoultz, was Shirley Dean.

56. Williams and Shoultz, *We Can Speak for Ourselves,* discusses that this is potentially the first time that those with I/DD spoke for themselves publicly in front of stakeholders such as businesspeople, policy makers, politicians, and parents and in support of deinstitutionalization. Later that year, a scandal broke out when a boy died in Beatrice as a result of abuse. Project Two held a press conference in which they demanded that all residents of Beatrice be brought to live in the community and no new admissions to the institution occur, essentially necessitating the closure of Beatrice. Their support of the ideology of community living was unequivocal and unique.

57. During the 1960s, the Swedish government would sponsor courses for those with I/DD to learn about voting, self-management, decision-making, and so on. People in these courses would often meet in regional conferences until they decided to host a national conference in 1968, focusing on recreational clubs and activities.

58. Williams and Shoultz, *We Can Speak for Ourselves.*

59. As Shoultz and Williams discuss, such groups have been meeting in the United States since the 1950s, but without the title and cohesion of "self-advocacy." Most of the groups focused on recreational activities and were often run by professionals.

60. Allison C. Carey and Lucy Gu, "Walking the Line between the Past and the Future: Parents' Resistance and Commitment to Institutionalization," in Ben-Moshe et al., *Disability Incarcerated,* 101–19.

61. Williams and Shoultz, *We Can Speak for Ourselves*; Carey, *On the Margins of Citizenship*.

62. Steven J. Taylor, "The Institutions Are Dying, but Are Not Dead Yet," in *Deinstitutionalization and People with Intellectual Disabilities: In and out of Institutions*, ed. Kelley Johnson and Rannveig Traustadottir, 93–107 (London: Jessica Kingsley, 2005).

63. Burton Blatt and Fred Kaplan, *Christmas in Purgatory: A Photographic Essay on Mental Retardation* (Boston: Allyn and Bacon, 1966).

64. Burton Blatt, Andrejs Ozolins, and Joe McNally, *The Family Papers: A Return to Purgatory* (New York: Longman, 1979), 143. Emphasis mine.

65. Steven Taylor, *Acts of Conscience: World War II, Mental Institutions, and Religious Objectors* (Syracuse, N.Y.: Syracuse University Press, 2009).

66. Jerome G. Miller, who closed down all the juvenile detention facilities in Massachusetts in the 1970s, mentions the Center on Human Policy as one of the only progressive organizations to write reports and do policy analysis that realized that institutionalization is big business and that the road to change is hampered by professionals who would like nothing more than to maintain the status quo. Miller, *Last One over the Wall: The Massachusetts Experiment in Closing Reform Schools* (Columbus: Ohio State University Press, 1991).

67. "The Community Imperative," Syracuse University, Center on Human Policy, http://thechp.syr.edu/resources/position-statements/the-community-imperative/.

68. Wolf Wolfensberger, "Will There Always Be an Institution?," *Mental Retardation* 9, no. 5 (1978): 14–20.

69. Wolfensberger, 13.

70. I thank Sue Schweik for this point and for pointing me to Wolfensberger's article on Nebraska values.

71. As he writes about the Nebraska model, "it was innovative in that it: (a) was based on those seven values just discussed … (b) ejected the institutional model; (c) endorsed dispersed specialized residences and (d) emphasized programs rather than buildings." Wolf Wolfensberger, "Why Nebraska?," in *Out of the Darkness and into the Light: Nebraska's Experience with Mental Retardation,* ed. Robert L. Schalock and David L. Braddock, 23–52 (Washington, D.C.: AAMR, 2002). These Nebraskan values include, according to Wolfensberger, attachment to law and order, constitutionalism, middle-church Protestantism, Protestant ethic, nonduplication of services, rugged individualism and mutual assistance, private enterprise, frontier pragmatism (which led to the success of citizen advocacy), local initiative and control, and fiscal conservatism. I want to focus for a moment on the latter, as I think it poses interesting lessons for abolitionists. Wolfensberger writes, reflecting on challenges in the 1960s and 1970s, "*all* they had heard in the past had been *simply* 'more!' and vague and/or sentimental mish-mash and perhaps an accusatory admonition, 'How dare you put a dollar price on human misery?' … In the liberal service mentality, one is virtually indoctrinated to ignore costs and to reflexively ask for 'more.' There *is* merit in the stance, but it had never been an effective one." Therefore Wolfensberger contemplates

the combination of appealing to fiscal conservatism (the idea that institutionalization is indeed expensive) in asking for their dissolution—an argument that can be heard today among deinstitutionalization activists and prison abolitionists.

72. Corbett J. O'Toole, "The Sexist Inheritance of the Disability Movement," in *Rethinking Normalcy: A Disability Studies Reader,* ed. Rod Michalko and Tanya Titchkosky (Toronto: Canadian Scholars Press, 2009); Adrienne Asch et al., *Gendering Disability* (New Brunswick, N.J.: Rutgers University Press, 2004).

73. Carey, *On the Margins of Citizenship.*

74. Douglas C. Baynton, "Disability and the Justification of Inequality in American History," *Disability Studies Reader,* ed. Lennard J. Davis, 17–33 (New York: Routledge, 2013).

75. Eyal et al., *Autism Matrix.*

76. Staub, *Madness Is Civilization.*

77. *Action for Mental Health: Final Report of the Joint Commission on Mental Illness and Health 1961,* https://www.apa.org/pubs/books/4320366; American Bar Foundation, Frank T. Lindman, and Donald M. McIntyre, *The Mentally Disabled and the Law: The Report on the Rights of the Mentally Ill* (Chicago: University of Chicago Press, 1961); Goffman, *Asylums.*

78. Michel Foucault, *Folie et Déraison: Histoire de la folie à l'âge classique* (Paris: Librairie Plon, 1961). Shortened version originally translated to English as Michel Foucault, *Madness and Civilization: A History of Insanity in the Age of Reason* (New York: Pantheon Books, 1965).

79. Szasz, *Myth of Mental Illness,* 1961; R. D. Laing, *The Divided Self: An Existential Study in Sanity and Madness,* rev. ed. (New York: Penguin Books, 1965). The premise behind Laing's approach (which was quite controversial in its time) is that people with mental illness diagnoses are not that different from those who were not labeled as such, in the basic sense that they are human beings with interesting perceptions that are worth listening to. Therefore, the solution is not to change the patient/person but to treat him or her as an equal and develop effective communication.

80. Ken Kesey, *One Flew over the Cuckoo's Nest* (New York: Berkley, 1963).

81. Although *One Flew over the Cuckoo's Nest* offers important critiques of settler colonialism ECT, and the power of psychiatry, it was written by and from the perspective of a former male attendant, not a mad identified person. One of the only women figures in the novel is the villain Nurse Ratched and, as Caminero-Santangelo posits, it generally lacks gendered analysis. Marta Caminero-Santangelo, *The Madwoman Can't Speak; or, Why Insanity Is Not Subversive* (Ithaca, N.Y.: Cornell University Press, 1998).

82. Frederick Wiseman, *Titicut Follies* (Cambridge, Mass: Production Zipporah Films, 1967). Wiseman would later make documentaries in other institutions, such as schools and hospitals.

83. Roger Ebert, "Titicut Follies Movie Review and Film Summary," October 8, 1968, https://www.rogerebert.com/reviews/titicut-follies-1968.

84. Sylvia Plath, *The Bell Jar* (New York: Faber and Faber, 1963). There were other influential feminist figures such as Kate Millet and Phyllis Chesler, whose works came out in the 1970s and 1980s, after the peak of deinstitutionalization and therefore outside the frame of this chapter. In these accounts by mad women writers, madness is not necessarily celebratory (and is often perceived as a burden, challenge, or break from life), nor is it a rejection of patriarchal constraints and norms (like in the *Yellow Wallpaper*). These women, if one can generalize, are neither active rebels nor do they view their madness as social punishment, as Caminero-Santangelo's analysis of these texts argues. Caminero-Santangelo, *The Madwoman Can't Speak*.

85. Thomas J. Scheff, *Being Mentally Ill: A Sociological Theory* (Piscataway, N.J.: Transaction, 1971).

86. Dorothy E. Smith, "'K Is Mentally Ill': The Anatomy of a Factual Account," *Sociology* 12, no. 1 (1978): 23–53.

87. For more on that time frame, refer to Peter Sedgwick, *Psycho Politics: Laing, Foucault, Goffman, Szasz, and the Future of Mass Psychiatry* (New York: Harper and Row, 1982).

88. For example, Anne Parsons discusses the organizing done in Holmesburg Prison in Philadelphia in the 1980s. The prison was notorious for dermatological and psychopharmacological testing on prisoners and was discussed in Allen M. Hornblum's book *Acres of Skin: Human Experiments at Holmesburg Prison*. The prison at the time was 85 percent black. Parsons, *From Asylum to Prison*.

89. As Sue Schweik and Steve Taylor reminded me, the same can be said of deinstitutionalization in I/DD with antiwar activists like William Bronston, who is the doctor that exposed Willowbrook in the 1970s and conscientious objectors in World War II.

90. Regina Kunzel, "Queer History, Mad History, and the Politics of Health," *American Quarterly* 69, no. 2 (2017): 315–19; A. J. Withers, "Definitions and Divisions: Disability, Anti-Psychiatry and Disableism" Paper given in PsychOut: A Conference for Organizing Resistance against Psychiatry, OISE, Toronto, 2010, http://individual.uto ronto.ca/psychout/papers/withers_paper.pdf.

91. Phil Brown, *The Transfer of Care: Psychiatric Deinstitutionalization and Its Aftermath* (New York: Routledge, 1985).

92. In my current research I am looking at historical cases that combined black power, feminist organizing, and a critique of psychiatry such as the coalition that successfully challenged the creation of the Center for the Study and Reduction of Violence at UCLA in the early 1970s.

93. Stephen Dillon, *Fugitive Life: The Queer Politics of the Prison State* (Durham, N.C.: Duke University Press, 2018).

94. Emily Thuma, "'Against the Prison/Psychiatric State': Anti-violence Feminisms and the Politics of Confinement in the 1970s," *Feminist Formations* 26, no. 2 (2014): 26–51.

95. Burstow et al., *Psychiatry Disrupted*.

96. GIP refers to Le Groupe d'information sur les prisons (The Prisons Information Group), in which Foucault was involved in the 1970s. See note 68 in chapter 3 for more.

97. Dylan Rodríguez, "Disrupted Foucault: Los Angeles' Coalition against Police Abuse (CAPA) and the Obsolescence of White Academic Raciality," in *Active Intolerance: Michel Foucault, the Prisons Information Group, and the Future of Abolition,* ed. Perry Zurn and Andrew Dilts (New York: Palgrave Macmillan, 2016), 147.

98. Such as Sedgwick, *Psycho Politics*; and *Women's Madness: Misogyny or Mental Illness?,* ed. Jane M. Ussher (Boston: University of Massachusetts Press, 1991).

99. The official and active directors of the AAAIMH were George Alexander, Ronald Leifer, and Thomas Szasz. Leifer trained in psychiatry under Szasz and became a Buddhist practitioner in 1980, eventually founding the Ithaca Dharma Society in Ithaca, NY. Alexander was involved in the organization from its inception but did not have the celebrity status afforded to Goffman and Szasz. Alexander was then a young dean of the law school at Santa Clara University, where he remained in various positions until his death in 2013. Alexander specialized in antitrust and elder law as well as psychiatry and law. His official bio can be found at https://law.scu.edu/faculty/pro file/alexander-george/.

100. Szasz goes as far as to say that it is this term that undermined his own critiques of psychiatry. As he states, "the word 'antipsychiatry' proved to be an effective weapon in the hands of psychiatrists to collectively stigmatize and dismiss critics, regardless of the content of the criticism." He further asserts that his fellows "Cooper, Laing, Foucault, and the French intellectual fakes associated with the antipsychiatry movement were power-hungry left-wing statists who were interested in taking over psychiatry, not destroying its intellectual foundations and scientistic pretensions." Thomas Szasz, "Debunking Antipsychiatry: Laing, Law, and Largactil," *Current Psychology* 27, no. 2 (2008): 79–101.

101. Szasz, *Myth of Mental Illness.*

102. Szasz.

103. Jeffrey A. Schaler, ed., *Szasz under Fire: The Psychiatric Abolitionist Faces His Critics* (Chicago: Open Court, 2004), 18.

104. Sedgwick, *Psycho Politics.*

105. Personal conversation with the author. Szasz saw other disabilities as real, even though "mental retardation" is the ultimate metaphor turned diagnosis! There is no virus that causes "retardation," as retardation or slowness is measured in relation to norms, to others, not in relation to any objective criteria. It's an umbrella term; to borrow from Szasz himself, it is a pure metaphor.

106. Disability and antipoverty activist A. J. Withers details how antipsychiatry activists often use ableist rhetoric to confront the ill effects of psychiatrization (the effects of pharmaceuticals or electroshocks on the brain as disabling): "One commonly heard affirmation by psychiatric system survivors is something like 'I am not disabled, I was targeted by an oppressive system, and there is nothing wrong with

me.' As a disabled person, when I hear statements like that, I hear, 'There is nothing wrong with me, but there is something wrong with you, and I do not want to be associated with that.' Positions like this actually work to legitimize medicalization." Withers, "Definitions and Divisions."

107. In conversation with the author.

108. In *Outsiders*, originally published in 1963, Howard Becker proposes that "deviance is not a quality of the act a person commits, but rather a consequence of the application by others of rules and sanctions to an 'offender.' The deviant is one to whom the label was successfully applied." Becker, *Outsiders: Studies in the Sociology of Deviance* (New York: Free Press, 1973), 9.

109. Goffman, *Stigma*.

110. For more critiques and engagement with Goffman's stigma theory within disability studies, refer to Jeffrey Brune, Rosemarie Garland-Thomson, Susan Schweik, Tanya Titchkosky, and Heather Love, "Forum: Reflections on the Fiftieth Anniversary of Erving Goffman's Stigma," *Disability Studies Quarterly* 34, no. 1 (2014).

111. For more on this critique, Tanya Titchkosky, "Disability Studies: The Old and the New," *Canadian Journal of Sociology/Cahiers Canadiens de Sociologie* 25, no. 2 (2000): 197–224.

112. Erving Goffman, *Asylums: Essays on the Social Situation of Mental Patients and Other Inmates* (Garden City, N.Y.: Anchor Books, 1961).

113. Goffman, xviii.

114. Goffman, 6.

115. And it does not seem to matter to Goffman what in-group differences may exist (such as varied positions based on race, class, or gender) in each group or subgroup.

116. Steven J. Taylor and Robert Bogdan, "Defending Illusions: The Institution's Struggle for Survival," *Human Organization* 39, no. 3 (1980): 209–18.

117. Thomas Szasz, *Liberation by Oppression: A Comparative Study of Slavery and Psychiatry* (Piscataway, N.J.: Transaction, 2003), 30.

118. Goffman, *Asylums*, 384.

119. Susan Schweik, "Stigma Management," *Disability Studies Quarterly* 34, no. 1 (2014). I discuss the *Wyatt* case briefly in the previous chapter and analyze it more fully in chapter 7.

120. Schweik.

121. Gerald N. Grob, *From Asylum to Community: Mental Health Policy in Modern America* (Princeton, N.J.: Princeton University Press, 1991), 284.

122. Membership in the AAAIMH was both a badge of honor and a way to identify dissenters to coercive psychiatry, and band them together. In the first issue of the *Abolitionist* in 1971, the explicit goals of the group are laid out: "To create and promote an understanding of the dehumanizing effects of involuntary psychiatric interventions, especially involuntary mental hospitalization; to foster a desire for the abolition of involuntary psychiatric interventions, especially involuntary mental hospitalization; to promote the movement to obtain legislative and judicial action making such involuntary psychiatric interventions, especially involuntary mental hospitalization, unlawful;

to aid individuals who seek assistance in avoiding involuntary psychiatric interventions, especially involuntary mental hospitalization, by all lawful means; to establish centers for the members in order to coordinate efforts at abolition, exchange information and provide opportunities for further study and dissemination of information concerning involuntary psychiatric interventions, especially involuntary mental hospitalization; and to do such other lawful things as the members shall approve to further the end of such abolition." http://www.szasz.com/abolitionist.html.

123. The title of the newsletter is also the name of a current circular issued by one of the most important contemporary prison abolition groups in the United States, Critical Resistance, to its supporters and incarcerated members. As I discuss further in the following chapter, the similarity is not purely linguistic but a deliberate choosing of the terminology and tactics associated with *abolition* instead of reform or improvement of coercive institutions that restrict people's freedom.

124. A typical newsletter had excerpts from Szasz's speeches; recent writing or reviews of his work; a recap of any court cases related to involuntary commitments or any other aspects of coercive psychiatry; a section titled "The Therapeutic State," which included critique and commentary on such topics as new mental "illnesses" and psychiatric diagnoses (such as "transvestitism" or "cultism") that were "discovered" (i.e., invented and reified); psychiatric testimony in criminal trials, and more; and a section titled "The Freedom Train" that included short news about people, organizations, and entities that resist psychiatry, including mental patients, Szasz, other physicians, and lawyers.

125. *Abolitionist.*

126. Both of which are the major tenets of the National Alliance on Mental Illness, or NAMI, activism, discussed more in chapters 4 and 6.

127. Judi Chamberlin, *On Our Own: Patient-Controlled Alternatives to the Mental Health System* (New York: McGraw-Hill, 1978).

128. For example, Jonathan Metzl, *The Protest Psychosis: How Schizophrenia Became a Black Disease,* 1st ed. (Boston: Beacon Press, 2010).

129. Abram J. Lewis, "'We Are Certain of Our Own Insanity': Antipsychiatry and the Gay Liberation Movement, 1968–1980," *Journal of the History of Sexuality* 25, no. 1 (2016): 83–113.

130. Lewis.

131. Phyllis Chesler is a feminist psychologist that is most famous for her 1972 study on women and madness and her critique of psychology. For his part, Szasz did not address in his work the sexist nature of psychology, which he saw as benevolent, nor did he repudiate the sexual assault and harassment that women experience in therapy, which became the hallmark of Chesler's work.

132. Fay Honey Knopp and Prison Research Education Action Project, *Instead of Prisons: A Handbook for Abolitionists* (Syracuse, N.Y.: Prison Research Education Action Project, 1976).

133. Bonnie Burstow, "The Withering Away of Psychiatry," in Burstow et al., *Psychiatry Disrupted,* 34–51.

134. Ruth Morris, *Penal Abolition, the Practical Choice: A Practical Manual on Penal Abolition* (Toronto: Canadian Scholars' Press, 1995).

135. Backlash to these antipsychiatry theories came not only from their proponents but also from their early supporters. Psychiatrist E. Fuller Torrey, for example, became known in the early 1970s as a supporter of antipsychiatry, especially as theorized by Thomas Szasz. However, during the period of deinstitutionalization in mental health, he became one of the most vocal critics of Szasz, antipsychiatry, and deinstitutionalization. He made a very successful career out of these critiques, as can be seen in the slew of publications devoted to discrediting deinstitutionalization activists and antipsychiatry. See Torrey, *Nowhere to Go: The Tragic Odyssey of the Homeless Mentally Ill* (New York: HarperCollins, 1988); Torrey, *Out of the Shadows: Confronting America's Mental Illness Crisis* (New York: John Wiley, 1997); Torrey, *The Insanity Offense: How America's Failure to Treat the Seriously Mentally Ill Endangers Its Citizens* (New York: W. W. Norton, 2008). He is also one of the most popularized professionals working for and with NAMI.

136. Harcourt discusses this trend more generally in "Reducing Mass Incarceration." Parsons, *From Asylum to Prison*, discusses this trend of racialization in relation to Pennsylvania, and Metzl, *Protest Psychosis*, in relation to Ionia Hospital in Michigan.

137. Parsons, *From Asylum to Prison*.

138. This argumentation was especially prevalent in the 1975 case of O'Connor v. Donaldson, 422 U.S. 563 (Supreme Court 74–8), to which Szasz devotes much of his 1997 book *Psychiatric Slavery*.

139. As discussed in chapter 7.

140. Foucault, *Madness and Civilization*.

141. Dori Spivak, "Can the Mad Speak? The Mental Patients' Liberation Movement and the Problem of Representation," PhD diss., Harvard Law School, 2000. This idea of having those most directly affected at the forefront of knowledge production and policy debates (what in the disability rights movement created the motto of "nothing about us without us") can also be turned against the likes of Foucault and Szasz. As Rodriguez claims in his critique of the Group Information of Prisons (GIP) with which Foucault was affiliated in the 1970s, their motto of "giving prisoners the floor" might not be as noble as it looks. Rodriguez asserts that there was no consideration that "to give prisoners the floor" is a colonial move; perhaps they already have a floor, but it is not known to the likes of Foucault and other white academics who have not been incarcerated.

142. Linda Morrison, *Talking Back to Psychiatry: The Consumer/Survivor/Ex-Patient Movement* (New York: Routledge, 2009).

143. For a more nuanced account of how this dichotomy played out in later years, refer to Jijian Voronka, "The Politics of 'People with Lived Experience': Experiential Authority and the Risks of Strategic Essentialism," *Philosophy, Psychiatry, and Psychology* 23, no. 3/4 (2016): 189–201.

144. Spivak, "Can the Mad Speak?"

145. Morrison, *Talking Back to Psychiatry*.

146. Nancy Tomes, "Patients or Health-Care Consumers? Why the History of Contested Terms Matters," in *History and Health Policy in the United States*, ed. Rosemary A. Stevens, Charles E. Rosenberg, and Lawton R. Burns, 83–110 (New Brunswick, N.J.: Rutgers University Press, 2006).

147. Morrison, *Talking Back to Psychiatry*; Spivak, "Can the Mad Speak?"

148. Hong, *Death beyond Disavowal*; Duggan, *Twilight of Equality?*; Ferguson, *Aberrations in Black*.

149. Hong, *Death beyond Disavowal*, 7.

150. Spivak, "Can the Mad Speak?"

151. Chamberlin, *On Our Own*.

152. Liat Ben-Moshe, Anthony J. Nocella, and A. J. Withers, "Queer-Cripping Anarchism: Intersections and Reflections on Anarchism, Queer-Ness, and Dis-Ability," in *Queering Anarchism*, ed. C. B. Daring, J. Rogue, Deric Shannon, and Abbey Volcano, 207–20 (Oakland, Calif.: AK Press, 2013).

153. Szasz, *Liberation by Oppression*, 8. But I want to be careful here not to paint Szasz as "not caring" about psych survivors/patients. In his seminal book, when discussing the differences between Goffman and Szasz toward suffering, Staub writes that for Szasz, "seeing the pain of the mentally ill did not cause him to acknowledge that pain but rather to question its legitimacy" (103) and that "he had little use for the actual experiences of the mentally ill" (114), Michael E. Staub, *Madness Is Civilization*. It's important to point out that in addition to other complexities (or contradictions) in his biography, Szasz was a practicing therapist trained in psychoanalysis and psychiatry (when he began his training, these were closely related). He practiced what he called "listening and talking" (i.e., psychotherapy) throughout his vast career, from 1948 to 1996, when he retired. His critique of the biomedical approach that psychiatry vehemently espoused did not negate his belief in human suffering and the need to alleviate it, if and when possible. He did object to this suffering being called an illness and critiqued those who did so, whether they were fellow psychiatrists or patients themselves, which to some seemed rigid, self-serving, and counter to the self-determination approach that is grounded in the leadership of those who are most affected.

154. Szasz, *Psychiatric Slavery*; Szasz, *Liberation by Oppression*.

155. Szasz, 5.

156. Brenda A. LeFrançois, Robert Menzies, and Geoffrey Reaume, *Mad Matters: A Critical Reader in Canadian Mad Studies* (Toronto: Canadian Scholars' Press, 2013).

157. It is interesting and unfortunate to note that many of the accounts of the c/s/x and antipsychiatry movements, such as Morrison, *Talking Back to Psychiatry*, or Staub, *Madness Is Civilization*, do not mention race or colonialism, and these are not central to their description and analysis.

158. Rachel Gorman, "Mad Nation? Thinking through Race, Class, and Mad Identity Politics," in LeFrançois et al., *Mad Matters*, 269–80.

159. Puar, *Right to Maim*; Puar, *Terrorist Assemblages*.

160. Louise Tam, "Whither Indigenizing the Mad Movement? Theorizing the Social Relations of Race and Madness through Conviviality," in LeFrançois et al., *Mad Matters*, 281–97.

161. Gorman, "Mad Nation?"

162. Gorman, 272.

163. This can be witnessed by the fact that by 2004, 183 organizations had signed the Community Imperative. See also Carey, *On the Margins of Citizenship*.

164. Spivak, "Can the Mad Speak?"

165. For example, Schaler, *Szasz under Fire*.

166. As a recent study suggests in relation to youth incarceration, "We trace four themes challenging the divide between residential placement as social welfare and care and juvenile detention as retribution and punishment. First, many of the children we interviewed experienced group homes as inherently insecure places that often subjected them to greater violence and uncertainty than on the 'outs' or in juvenile hall. Second, youth saw group homes as industries built on making money from their misfortune. Third, our research participants were often placed far from family and friends. Finally, many experienced group home placement as greater punishment than time in juvenile hall." Elizabeth Brown and Amy Smith, "Challenging Mass Incarceration in the City of Care: Punishment, Community, and Residential Placement," *Theoretical Criminology* 22, no. 1 (2018): 4–21.

167. Erick Fabris, *Tranquil Prisons: Chemical Incarceration under Community Treatment Orders* (Toronto: University of Toronto Press, 2011).

168. Burstow et al., *Psychiatry Disrupted*.

169. Burstow characterizes prison abolition as a movement that seeks to end the prison system but does not mention the antiracist and anticapitalist roots and tenets of the movement. Furthermore, she states that one similarity is that "in their case too, albeit to a lesser extent, some inmates voluntarily seek out prison 'services,' with people, indeed, committing crimes precisely to get back behind bars," which is a simplistic, inaccurate, and dangerous claim.

3. Abolition as Knowledge and Ways of Unknowing

1. For more on fugitive abolitionary knowledges, see Rodriguez, *Forced Passages*; Fred Moten and Stefano Harney, *The Undercommons: Fugitive Planning and Black Study* (Wivenhoe, U.K.: Minor Compositions, 2013); Dillon, *Fugitive Life*; James, *New Abolitionists*; Michael Hames-Garcia, *Fugitive Thought: Prison Movements, Race, and the Meaning of Justice* (Minneapolis: University of Minnesota Press, 2004).

2. Although I do draw here on conceptualizations from some European or diasporic theorists, my research and claims are grounded in the North American context, particularly carceral abolition movements in the United States, and should be read from this specific geographical and historical context.

3. Omar Wasow, "How to Go from #BlackLivesMatter to #BlackPolicyMatters," *Root*, July 16, 2016, https://www.theroot.com/how-to-go-from-blacklivesmatter-to-blackpolicymatter-1790856042.

4. Robert Fanuzzi, "Abolition," in *Keywords for American Cultural Studies*, ed. B. Burgett and G. Hendler, 7–10 (New York: NYU Press, 2014).

5. Fanuzzi.

6. Vivian Saleh-Hanna, "Black Feminist Hauntology: Rememory the Ghosts of Abolition?," *Champ pénal/Penal field* 12 (2015), http://journals.openedition.org/champpenal/9168.

7. *Beloved* is of course also a disability-related novel with madness as a running theme throughout. See Caminero-Santangelo, *The Madwoman Can't Speak.*

8. Saleh-Hanna, *Black Feminist Hauntology.*

9. This is also directly linked to the lineage of abolition of slavery. As Kim Gilmore explains, "the connections between slavery and imprisonment have been used by abolitionists as a historical explanation and as part of a radical political strategy that questions the feasibility of 'reform' as an appropriate response to prison expansion." Gilmore, "Slavery and Prison—Understanding the Connections," *Social Justice* 27, no. 3 (2000): 195–205.

10. Oparah, "Maroon Abolitionists."

11. Rodriguez, *Forced Passages.*

12. Avery F. Gordon, *Keeping Good Time: Reflections on Knowledge, Power and People* (Boulder, Colo.: Paradigm, 2004).

13. Gordon, 8.

14. Liat Ben-Moshe, "The Tension between Abolition and Reform," in *The End of Prisons: Reflections from the Decarceration Movement,* ed. M. Nagel and A. J. Nocella II, 83–92 (New York: Rodopi Press, 2012).

15. Emily Thuma, "'Against the Prison/Psychiatric State': Anti-violence Feminisms and the Politics of Confinement in the 1970s," *Feminist Formations* 26, no. 2 (2014): 26–51.

16. Thuma.

17. Richie, *Arrested Justice.*

18. Ben-Moshe, "Tension between Abolition and Reform."

19. See the insightful work of Erica Meiners on the topic of "stranger danger" and sex offender registries.

20. Priya Kandaswamy, "Innocent Victims and Brave New Laws," in *Nobody Passes: Rejecting the Rules of Gender and Conformity,* ed. M. B. Sycamore, 83–94 (Emeryville, Calif.: Seal Press, 2006).

21. Puar, *Right to Maim.*

22. Rodriguez, *Forced Passages.*

23. Davis, *Are Prisons Obsolete?,* 107.

24. Davis, "From the Convict Lease System to the Super-Max Prison."

25. Morris, *Penal Abolition.*

26. Morris.

27. Yves Bourque, "Prison Abolition," *Journal of Prisoners on Prisons* 1, no. 1 (1988): 23–38.

28. Rashad Shabazz, *Spatializing Blackness: Architectures of Confinement and Black Masculinity in Chicago* (Champaign: University of Illinois Press, 2015).

29. Assata Shakur, *Assata: An Autobiography* (Westport, Conn.: Lawrence Hill, 1974); Angela Y. Davis, *If They Come in the Morning . . . : Voices of Resistance* (New York: Signet, 1971).

30. Dylan Rodríguez, "The Disorientation of the Teaching Act: Abolition as Pedagogical Position," *Radical Teacher* 88, no. 1 (2010): 7–19.

31. Zayd Shakur, "America Is the Prison," in *Off the Pigs! The History and Literature of the Black Panther Party,* 247–80 (Metuchen, N.J.: Scarecrow, 1976).

32. Luana Ross, *Inventing the Savage: The Social Construction of Native American Criminality* (Austin: University of Texas Press, 1998).

33. Ritchie, *Invisible No More*; Katherine Beckett and Naomi Murakawa, "Mapping the Shadow Carceral State: Toward an Institutionally Capacious Approach to Punishment," *Theoretical Criminology* 16, no. 2 (2012): 221–44.

34. Alexander, *New Jim Crow*.

35. Knopp and Prison Research Education Action Project, *Instead of Prisons*; INCITE! Women of Color against Violence, ed., *Color of Violence: The INCITE! Anthology* (Cambridge, Mass.: South End Press, 2006); Erica Meiners, "Never Innocent: Feminist Trouble with Sex Offender Registries and Protection in a Prison Nation," *Meridians: Feminism, Race, Transnationalism* 9, no. 2 (2009): 31–62.

36. Brady T. Heiner and Sarah K. Tyson, "Feminism and the Carceral State: Gender-Responsive Justice, Community Accountability, and the Epistemology of Antiviolence," *Feminist Philosophy Quarterly* 3, no. 1 (2017): 16.

37. Ann Russo, *Feminist Accountability* (New York: NYU Press, 2018); Rojas Durazo, Ana Clarissa, Alisa Bierria, and Mimi Kim, "Community Accountability: Emerging Movements to Transform Violence," *Social Justice* 37, no. 4 (2011): 44–57; "Creative Interventions Toolkit: An Invitation and Practical Guide for Everyone to Stop Violence," 2012, http://www.creative-interventions.org/tools/toolkit/.

38. Ana Clarissa Rojas Durazo, "In Our Hands: Community Accountability as Pedagogical Strategy," *Social Justice* 37, no. 4 (2011): 76–100.

39. For example, tool kits and resources created by Generation Five, http://www.generationfive.org/; Alisa Bierria, Onion Carrillo, Eboni Colbert, Xandra Ibarra, Theryn Kigvamasud'Vashti, and Shale Maulana, "Taking Risks: Implementing Grassroots Community Accountability Strategies," in INCITE!, Color of Violence. Women of Color against Violence resources on community accountability: https://incite-national.org/community-accountability/.

40. See writings by Susan Wendell, *The Rejected Body: Feminist Philosophical Reflections on Disability* (New York: Routledge, 1996); Jenny Morris, "Impairment and Disability: Constructing an Ethics of Care That Promotes Human Rights," *Hypatia* 16, no. 4 (2001): 1–16; J. Price and M. Shildrick, "Uncertain Thoughts on the Dis/Abled Body," in *Feminist Reconfigurations of the Bio/logical Body,* ed. M. Shildrick and J. Price, 224–49 (Edinburgh: Edinburgh University Press, 1998); Alison Kafer, *Feminist, Queer, Crip* (Bloomington: Indiana University Press, 2013).

41. Knopp and Prison Research Education Action Project, *Instead of Prisons*; Morris, *Penal Abolition*.

42. Foucault, *Discipline and Punish*.

43. Applied behavior analysis is based on operant conditioning (behaviorism, training behavior based on rewards and negative reinforcement). It is frequently used on

people on the autism spectrum and resisted by them, as can be viewed in a plethora of blog and social media posts. Also Melanie Yergeau, *Authoring Autism: On Rhetoric and Neurological Queerness* (Durham, N.C.: Duke University Press, 2017).

44. Ross, *Inventing the Savage*; Sarah Deer, *The Beginning and End of Rape: Confronting Sexual Violence in Native America* (Minneapolis: University of Minnesota Press, 2015); Andrea Smith, *Conquest: Sexual Violence and American Indian Genocide* (Durham, N.C.: Duke University Press, 2005).

45. Ross, *Inventing the Savage*.

46. Lennard Davis, *Enforcing Normalcy: Disability, Deafness, and the Body* (London: Verso, 1995).

47. Carey et al., *Disability Incarcerated*.

48. Elizabeth Whalley and Coleen Hackett, "Carceral Feminisms: The Abolitionist Project and Undoing Dominant Feminisms," *Contemporary Justice Review* 20, no. 4 (2017): 456–73.

49. Eric A. Stanley, Dean Spade, and Queer (in)Justice, "Queering Prison Abolition, Now?," *American Quarterly* 64, no. 1 (2012): 115–27.

50. Joe Sim, *Punishment and Prisons: Power and the Carceral State* (Los Angeles, Calif.: Sage, 2009).

51. Yves Bourque, "Prison Abolition," *Journal of Prisoners on Prisons* 1, no. 1 (1998).

52. Refer to Kafer's political/relational model of disability in *Feminist Queer Crip* and Aimi Hamraie, *Building Access: Universal Design and the Politics of Disability* (Minneapolis: University of Minnesota Press, 2017).

53. Henri-Jacque Stiker, *A History of Disability*, trans. W. Sayers (Ann Arbor: University of Michigan Press, 1999), 128.

54. Some professionals, and parents, believe that the best interests of "these people" will always be better served in residential settings, and although others can benefit from programs and therapies, they cannot. This is the position of organizations such as Voice of the Retarded and members from the National Alliance on Mental Illness (NAMI), which I elaborate on in chapter 6.

55. Mariame Kaba, "Prison Reform's in Vogue and Other Strange Things," *Truth-Out*, March 21, 2014, https://truthout.org/articles/prison-reforms-in-vogue-and-other-strange-things/; Ruth Wilson Gilmore, "The Worrying State of the Anti-prison Movement," *Social Justice*, February 23, 2015, http://www.socialjusticejournal.org/the-worrying-state-of-the-anti-prison-movement/; Gottschalk, *Caught*.

56. Saleh-Hanna, *Black Feminist Hauntology*.

57. Robert McRuer, *Crip Theory: Cultural Signs of Queerness and Disability* (New York: NYU Press, 2006). Also refer to Carrie Sandahl, "Queering the Crip or Cripping the Queer? Intersections of Queer and Crip Identities in Solo Autobiographical Performance," *GLQ: A Journal of Lesbian and Gay Studies* 9, no. 1 (2003): 25–56.

58. McRuer, *Crip Theory*, 4.

59. Miller, *Last One over the Wall*.

60. Robin D. G. Kelley, *Freedom Dreams: The Black Radical Imagination* (Boston: Beacon Press, 2002).

61. Mariame Kaba, "Free Us All: Participatory Defense Campaigns as Abolitionist Organizing," *New Inquiry,* May 8, 2017, https://thenewinquiry.com/free-us-all/.

62. Emily L. Thuma, *All Our Trials: Prisons, Policing, and the Feminist Fight to End Violence* (Urbana: University of Illinois Press, 2019). A current important example is the work of the organization Love and Protect, which grew out of the Free Marissa Alexander Chicago campaign.

63. Thomas Mathiesen, *The Politics of Abolition* (New York: Halsted Press, 1974).

64. Ami Harbin, *Disorientation and Moral Life* (Oxford: Oxford University Press, 2016), 2.

65. Richie, *Arrested Justice.*

66. Mathiesen, *Politics of Abolition.*

67. Moten and Harney, *Undercommons.*

68. The Prisons Information Group (GIP) was a French activist collective in the early 1970s with which Foucault was involved. It emerged at a moment of what they saw as a crisis, and their sense of urgency (related to the etiology of abolition) came from leftists (mostly white) being imprisoned. The prison regime here is therefore understood as exceptional (despite Foucault's best efforts at times). Foucault's desire for "no prescription, no recipe and no prophecy" in the GIP contrasts with organizations like CAPA that were concerned with praxis, with liberation. CAPA (Los Angeles's Coalition against Police Abuse), as an extension of the LA chapter of the Black Panther Party, prioritized the knowledge of racially criminalized people, not "activists." It emerged as part of the black radical tradition of political education, self and legal defense, and mobilizations against racist state terror, including police brutality. CAPA was thus addressing state (carceral) violence in ways that were both "political" and mundane, normal. Dylan Rodríguez, "Disrupted Foucault: Los Angeles' Coalition against Police Abuse (CAPA) and the Obsolescence of White Academic Raciality," in *Active Intolerance,* 145–68 (New York: Palgrave Macmillan, 2016).

69. Sara Ahmed, "Killing Joy: Feminism and the History of Happiness," *Signs* 35, no. 3 (2010): 581.

70. Ahmed.

71. Ahmed, 583.

72. Davis, *Are Prisons Obsolete?*

73. For more on the usage of prefigurative politics on contemporary movements, refer to Chris Dixon, "Building 'Another Politics': The Contemporary Anti-authoritarian Current in the US and Canada," *Anarchist Studies* 20, no. 1 (2012): 32–60.

74. Kafer, *Feminist, Queer, Crip.*

75. Jasbir K. Puar, "In the Wake of It Gets Better," *Guardian,* November 16, 2010, https://www.theguardian.com/commentisfree/cifamerica/2010/nov/16/wake-it -gets-better-campaign.

76. Judith Halberstam, *The Queer Art of Failure* (Durham, N.C.: Duke University Press, 2011); Ahmed, "Killing Joy," 581.

77. Ahmed.

78. Ahmed, 593.

79. Audre Lorde, *The Cancer Journals: Special Edition* (San Francisco: Aunt Lute, 1997), 76.

80. José Esteban Muñoz, *Cruising Utopia: The Then and There of Queer Futurity* (New York: NYU Press, 2009), 1.

81. Muñoz.

82. Muñoz, 3.

83. Muñoz, 9.

84. Muñoz.

85. James Overboe, "'Difference in Itself': Validating Disabled People's Lived Experience," *Body and Society* 5, no. 4 (1999): 17–29; David T. Mitchell and Sharon L. Snyder, *The Biopolitics of Disability: Neoliberalism, Ablenationalism, and Peripheral Embodiment* (Ann Arbor: University of Michigan Press, 2015). It is important to keep in mind, however, that many of these accounts of disability culture and epistemology do not often provide the kind of intersectional analysis, especially in relation to race, that fugitive knowledges demand. Also refer to Puar, *Right to Maim,* for such critique.

86. Merri Johnson and Robert McRuer, "Cripistemologies: Introduction," *Journal of Literary and Cultural Disability Studies* 8, no. 2 (2014): 127–48.

87. Berne, "Disability Justice."

88. Angela Y. Davis, with Dylan Rodriguez, "The Challenge of Prison Abolition: A Conversation," *Social Justice* 27, no. 3 (2000): 212–18.

89. Davis, 215.

90. Ruth Wilson Gilmore, foreword to *The Struggle Within: Prisons, Political Prisoners, and Mass Movements in the United States,* by D. Berger (Oakland, Calif.: PM Press, 2014), viii.

91. W. E. B. Du Bois, *Black Reconstruction: An Essay toward a History of the Part Which Black Folk Played in the Attempt to Reconstruct Democracy in America, 1860–1880* (New York: Harcourt, Brace, 1935).

92. Davis, *Are Prisons Obsolete?*

93. For the origin of term "black radical tradition" and its meaning, see Cedric Robinson, *Black Marxism: The Making of the Black Radical Tradition* (Chapel Hill: University of North Carolina Press, 1983).

4. Why Prisons Are Not "the New Asylums"

1. Dahlia Lithwick, "Prisons Have Become Warehouses for the Mentally Ill," *Slate,* January 5, 2016, https://slate.com/news-and-politics/2016/01/prisons-have-become-warehouses-for-the-mentally-ill.html.

2. Gary Fields and Erica E. Phillips, "The New Asylums: Jails Swell with Mentally Ill," *Wall Street Journal,* September 26, 2013, sec. U.S., https://www.wsj.com/articles/the-new-asylums-jails-swell-with-mentally-ill-1380161349.

3. Miri Navasky and Karen O'Connor, dirs., *Frontline,* season 23, episode 8, "The New Asylums," aired May 10, 2005.

4. http://www.pbs.org/wgbh/pages/frontline/shows/asylums/special/excerpt.html.

5. http://www.treatmentadvocacycenter.org/about-us.

6. As suggested by a recent editorial and *New York Times* forum: Dominic A. Sisti, Andrea G. Segal, and Ezekiel J. Emanuel, "Improving Long-Term Psychiatric Care: Bring Back the Asylum," *JAMA* 313, no. 3 (2015): 243–44; Dominic Sisti, "Psychiatric Institutions Are a Necessity," *New York Times,* May 9, 2016, http://www.nytimes.com/roomfordebate/2016/05/09/getting-the-mentally-ill-out-of-jail-and-off-the-streets/psychiatric-institutions-are-a-necessity.

7. James D. Wright, "The Mentally Ill Homeless: What Is Myth and What Is Fact?," *Social Problems* 35, no. 2 (1988): 182–91.

8. Johnson, *Out of Bedlam*; Arline Mathieu, "The Medicalization of Homelessness and the Theater of Repression," *Medical Anthropology Quarterly* 7, no. 2 (1993): 170–84.

9. Wright, "Mentally Ill."

10. Martin De Santos, "Fact-Totems and the Statistical Imagination: The Public Life of a Statistic in Argentina 2001," *Sociological Theory* 27, no. 4 (2009): 466–89.

11. Craig Willse, *The Value of Homelessness: Managing Surplus Life in the United States* (Minneapolis: University of Minnesota Press, 2015), 54.

12. Willse.

13. For more on this, refer to Johnson, *Out of Bedlam.*

14. The concept of "mental illness" as an identity and social construction (and not a biological deficit) was further discussed in chapter 2. On the intersections with race and gender, refer to the excellent mad studies anthology LeFrançois et al., *Mad Matters,* as well as Metzl, *Protest Psychosis.*

15. Judi Chamberlin, *On Our Own: Patient-Controlled Alternatives to the Mental Health System* (New York: McGraw-Hill, 1978).

16. Wright, "Mentally Ill."

17. David A. Snow, Susan G. Baker, Leon Anderson, and Michael Martin, "The Myth of Pervasive Mental Illness among the Homeless," *Social Problems* 33, no. 5 (1986): 407–23.

18. Snow et al.

19. Ben-Moshe and Stewart, "Disablement."

20. On the subject, also refer to J. Morrissey and K. Gounis, "Homelessness and Mental Illness in America: Emerging Issues in the Construction of a Social Problem," in *Location and Stigma: Contemporary Perspectives on Mental Health and Mental Health Care,* ed. C. Smith and J. Giggs, 285–303 (Boston: Unwin Hyman, 1988).

21. It is also the focus of the next chapter, dealing with housing desegregation in relation to race-ability.

22. Expanding on Ferguson's queer of color critique *Aberrations in Black.*

23. Stewart and Russell, "Disablement," 61.

24. Povinelli, *Economies of Abandonment.*

25. Ahmed and Plog, *State Mental Hospitals.*

26. Johnson, *Out of Bedlam.*

27. Arline Mathieu, "The Medicalization of Homelessness and the Theater of Repression," *Medical Anthropology Quarterly* 7, no. 2 (1993): 170–84.

28. Staub, *Madness Is Civilization,* 185.

29. Johnson, *Out of Bedlam*; Kim Hopper, *Rethinking the Link between Homelessness and Psychiatric Disorder: A Limited Goods Perspective* (New York: Columbia University, 1985).

30. Cheryl Harris, "Whiteness as Property," *Harvard Law Review* 106, no. 8 (1993): 1707–91; Joanne Passaro, *The Unequal Homeless: Men on the Streets, Women in Their Place* (New York: Routledge, 2014); Keeanga-Yamahtta Taylor, *Race for Profit: How Banks and the Real Estate Industry Undermined Black Homeownership* (Chapel Hill: University of North Carolina Press, 2019).

31. Refer to Susan M. Schweik's excellent discussion of the ugly laws in *The Ugly Laws: Disability in Public* (New York: NYU Press, 2010).

32. Katherine Beckett and Naomi Murakawa, "Mapping the Shadow Carceral State: Toward an Institutionally Capacious Approach to Punishment," *Theoretical Criminology* 16, no. 2 (2012): 221–44.

33. Katherine Beckett and Steve Herbert, *Banished: The New Social Control in Urban America* (Oxford: Oxford University Press, 2011).

34. In New York City, for example, police force was used in combination with medical staff to forcibly and involuntarily hospitalize or send to shelters homeless people during the winter of 1985–86. Mathieu, "Medicalization."

35. Harcourt, "From the Asylum to the Prison."

36. I discuss this more in Ben-Moshe, "Disabling Incarceration."

37. The major hypothesis is that the mental health system reroutes individuals into the criminal justice system via arrests and placement in jails and prisons. Overall, studies suggest that in relation to arrests, this hypothesis may be corroborated, as the percentage of mental patients with prior arrests had increased from the 1940s to the 1970s. But studies of imprisonment seem more inconclusive, suggesting that some inmates end up in jails after being arrested, but not so much in prisons. The research conducted by Liska et al. find no support for the hypothesis that a decrease in hospital capacity would lead to an increase in the capacity of jails and prisons, what they term the *functional-alternative thesis*. They did find, however, some support for the *conduit thesis*, which means that the criminal justice system operates as a conduit to the mental health system, but not vice versa. The movement of some people from jails and prisons and into hospitals could be done by official transfers decided upon by a judge and based on psychiatric evaluations, or it could be based on more unofficial means, such as plea bargains for reduced time or an individual decision that hospital time is better than time in prison. Allen E. Liska, Fred E. Markowitz, Rachel Bridges Whaley, and Paul Bellair, "Modeling the Relationship between the Criminal Justice and Mental Health Systems 1," *American Journal of Sociology* 104, no. 6 (1999): 1744–75. More recently, Raphael and Stoll analyzed census data between 1950 and 2000 and found that many of those who were institutionalized in the 1950s and 1960s, and were subsequently deinstitutionalized, did not experience large increases in incarceration. In particular, this was the case for women (who comprised nearly half the mental hospital population) as well as the elderly (who were nearly 30 percent of the mental hospital inpatient population at its peak). In general, they found

no evidence of transinstitutionalization for the period between 1950 and 1980. However, for the twenty-year period from 1980 to 2000, they found significant transinstitutionalization rates for all groups. They estimate, however, that only between 4 and 7 percent of incarceration growth between 1980 and 2000 can be attributed to deinstitutionalization. Steven Raphael and Michael A. Stoll, "Assessing the Contribution of the Deinstitutionalization of the Mentally Ill to Growth in the US Incarceration Rate," *Journal of Legal Studies* 42, no. 1 (2013): 187–222.

38. Some of those espousing this approach are Wacquant, *Punishing the Poor*; Michael J. Dear and Jennifer R. Wolch, *Landscapes of Despair: From Deinstitutionalization to Homelessness* (Princeton, N.J.: Princeton University Press, 1987); Rael Jean Isaac and Virginia C. Armat, *Madness in the Streets: How Psychiatry and the Law Abandoned the Mentally Ill* (New York: Free Press, 1990).

39. Discussed more fully in Ben-Moshe, "Disabling Incarceration."

40. Harcourt, "From the Asylum to the Prison."

41. Harcourt, "From the Asylum to the Prison."

42. Henry J. Steadman, John Monahan, Barbara Duffee, and Eliot Hartstone, "The Impact of State Mental Hospital Deinstitutionalization on United States Prison Populations, 1968–1978," *Journal of Criminal Law and Criminology* 75 (1984): 474.

43. Harcourt, "From the Asylum to the Prison."

44. It is hard to demonstrate a rise in this population, since we have no reliable baseline from which to measure such rise. In other words, since prison authorities do not provide census data with the number of incarcerated people who are deemed mentally ill over the years, social scientists can't determine if rates had increased or not. In addition, it should be clear that any measurement of something as contested as "mental illness" would be highly suspect to begin with.

45. Ben-Moshe and Stewart, "Disablement."

46. In comparison, in the general nonincarcerated population, suicide is the tenth leading cause of death, according to the National Center of Health Statistics: http://www.cdc.gov/nchs/fastats/leading-causes-of-death.htm.

47. Meredith P. Huey and Thomas L. McNulty, "Institutional Conditions and Prison Suicide: Conditional Effects of Deprivation and Overcrowding," *Prison Journal* 85, no. 4 (2005): 490–514. Huey and McNulty show that it is *prison conditions* that should be examined if we want to have a holistic understanding of the high rates of suicide behind bars. As Liebling adds, this narrow focus on the individual had led to limited and ineffective analysis and prevention policy for suicide in prisons. A. Liebling, "Prison Suicide and Prisoner Coping," in *Prisons*, ed. M. Tonry and J. Petersillia, 283–359 (Chicago: University of Chicago Press, 1999).

48. Jean Stewart, "Life, Death, and Disability Behind Bars," *New Mobility* 9 (June 1998).

49. Ben-Moshe, "Disabling Incarceration."

50. Even though the episode mentions the imprisoned people interviewed by name, I will not mention their last names here because of privacy and ethical concerns.

51. Gilmore, *Golden Gulag*, 28.

52. Terry Kupers, *Prison Madness: The Mental Health Crisis behind Bars and What We Must Do about It*, 1st ed. (San Francisco: Jossey-Bass, 1999).

53. Davis, *Are Prisons Obsolete?*, as well as the organizations Justice Now, based in Oakland, California, and Sisters Inside, based in Brisbane, Australia.

54. For a history of this practice, refer to Lisa Guenther, *Solitary Confinement: Social Death and Its Afterlives*, 1st ed. (Minneapolis: University of Minnesota Press, 2013).

55. On segregation of gay, trans, or gender nonconforming prisoners, refer to Elias Walker Vitulli, "Dangerous Embodiments: Segregating Sexual Perversion as Contagion in US Penal Institutions," *Feminist Formations* 30, no. 1 (2018): 21–45.

56. Haney lists rage, loss of control, hallucinations, and self-mutilations as some of the adverse effects prisoners secluded in supermax and solitary confinement have experienced. Craig Haney, "Mental Health Issues in Long-Term Solitary and 'Supermax' Confinement," *Crime and Delinquency* 49, no. 1 (2003): 124–56.

57. Kathryn D. DeMarco, "Disabled by Solitude: The Convention on the Rights of Persons with Disabilities and Its Impact on the Use of Supermax Solitary Confinement," *University of Miami Law Review* 66, no. 2 (2011): 523–66. It is important to note that the United States had not ratified the convention.

58. Keramet Reiter and Thomas Blair, "Punishing Mental Illness: Transinstitutionalization and Solitary Confinement in the United States," in *Extreme Punishment*, 177–96 (London: Palgrave Macmillan, 2015).

59. Sharon Shalev details the detrimental health effects of solitary confinement, including trauma, nightmares, headaches, hallucinations, and overall emotional and physical breakdown. Shalev, *A Sourcebook on Solitary Confinement* (London: Mannheim Center for Criminology/London School of Economics, 2008), www.solitary confinement.org/ sourcebook.

60. "Locked Up, Alone, and Mentally Ill," American Civil Liberties Union of Ohio, http://www.acluohio.org/locked-up-alone-and-mentally-ill.

61. Staughton Lynd, *Lucasville: The Untold Story of a Prison Uprising* (Oakland, Calif.: PM Press, 2011).

62. The state settled with the inmates for $4.1 million and with the widow of the guard who was killed for another $2 million.

63. Lynd, *Lucasville*.

64. The Lucasville 5, those charged with initiating the rebellion and condemned to death row, were among the first occupants of the new prison. According to Lind, citing the judge and other documents from the lawsuit after the uprising, it was known that a supermax was not needed in Ohio and that it would operate on a "you build it, they will come" mentality. Most of the early prisoners in the Ohio State Penitentiary were transferred there without a hearing or established criteria.

65. The objectives of the decree were "(1) to reduce the disabling effects of serious mental illness and enhance the inmate's ability to function within the prison environment, (2) to reduce or, when possible, eliminate the needless extremes of human suffering caused by serious mental illness, and (3) to maximize the safety of the prison

environment for staff, inmates, volunteers, visitors, and any other persons on prison premises." http://www.clearinghouse.net/detail.php?id=897.

66. The image of the "group therapy" session in a cage is the first image that comes up when one does an internet search for "The New Asylums" *Frontline* episode. Despite it being such a public image of the episode and used in marketing the episode on PBS, I was not given permission to display it here.

67. Reiter and Blair, "Punishing Mental Illness."

68. Chamberlin, *On Our Own*; Fabris, *Tranquil Prisons*; Robert Whittaker, *Anatomy of an Epidemic: Magic Bullets, Psychiatric Drugs, and the Astonishing Rise of Mental Illness in America* (New York: Broadway, 2010).

69. Kupers, *Prison Madness*.

70. See note 6.

71. Sisti, "Psychiatric Institutions Are a Necessity."

72. Harry R. Lamb and Linda E. Weinberger, "Rediscovering the Concept of Asylum for Persons with Serious Mental Illness," *Journal of the American Academy of Psychiatry and the Law* 44, no. 1 (2016): 106–10.

73. For these claims and their rebuttals, see https://truthout.org/articles/reviving -the-asylum-is-not-the-answer-to-gun-violence/.

74. J. Wolch, C. Nelson, and Annette Rubalcaba, "To Back Wards? Prospects for Reinstitutionalization of the Mentally Disabled," in Smith and Giggs, *Location and Stigma*, 264–85.

75. Wolch et al.

5. Resistance to Inclusion and Community Living

1. Clifford D. May, "Homes Serving Mentally Disabled Meet Resistance," *New York Times*, March 24, 1986, sec. N.Y./Region, https://www.nytimes.com/1986/03/24/ nyregion/homes-serving-mentally-disabled-meet-resistance.html. Emphasis mine.

2. A notable exception is Ferri and Connor, *Reading Resistance,* regarding desegregation for race and disability in the education arena.

3. Discussed in chapter 2.

4. These themes were gathered by sifting through countless accounts of lawsuits, demonstrations, town hall meetings, public zoning meetings, and more.

5. City of Cleburne (Texas) v. Cleburne Living Center, 105 S. Ct. 3249 (1985).

6. Stephen Grant Meyer, *As Long as They Don't Move Next Door: Segregation and Racial Conflict in American Neighborhoods* (Lanham, Md.: Rowman and Littlefield, 2001).

7. Thomas J. Sugrue, *The Origins of the Urban Crisis: Race and Inequality in Postwar Detroit*, rev. ed. (Princeton, N.J.: Princeton University Press, 2005).

8. Sugrue.

9. George Lipsitz, *The Possessive Investment in Whiteness: How White People Profit from Identity Politics*, rev. and exp. ed. (Philadelphia: Temple University Press, 2006).

10. Cheryl I. Harris, "Whiteness as Property," *Harvard Law Review* 106, no. 8 (1993): 1707–91.

11. Harris.

12. I say white and black populations here as Rothstein only focuses on African Americans and not Asian, Latinx, etc. Richard Rothstein, *The Color of Law: A Forgotten History of How Our Government Segregated America* (New York: Liveright, 2017).

13. I am using the term *color neutral* as I find the term *color-blind* to be ableist (equating blindness with lack of knowledge) or confusing to people who identify as being color-blind.

14. Sugrue, *Origins*, discusses this intersection of women at the forefront of resisting housing integration in more detail.

15. Sugrue.

16. Rashad Shabazz, *Spatializing Blackness: Architectures of Confinement and Black Masculinity in Chicago* (Urbana: University of Illinois Press, 2015).

17. Kelly Fritsch and Anne McGuire, "Introduction: The Biosocial Politics of Queer/Crip Contagions," *Feminist Formations* 30, no. 1 (2018): vii–xiv.

18. I am again borrowing the term *racial minority* publics from Ioanide, *Emotional Politics of Racism.*

19. May, "Homes Serving Mentally Disabled."

20. Robert Keating, "The War against the Mentally Retarded," *New Yorker,* September 17, 1979.

21. Center on Human Policy, "The Community Imperative: A Refutation of All Arguments in Support of Institutionalizing Anybody Because of Mental Retardation," Syracuse University, http://thechp.syr.edu/wp-content/uploads/2013/02/imperative .pdf; Keating, "War against the Mentally Retarded"; Susan L. Parish, "Deinstitutionalization in Two States: The Impact of Advocacy, Policy, and Other Social Forces on Services for People with Developmental Disabilities," *Research and Practice for Persons with Severe Disabilities* 30, no. 4 (2005): 219–31.

22. Keating, "War against the Mentally Retarded."

23. Laura Bornstein, "Contextualizing Cleburne."

24. E. T. Sharpe, "A House Is Not a Home: City of Cleburne v. Cleburne Living Center," *Pace Law Review,* no. 6 (1985): 267–310.

25. Michael E. Waterstone, "Disability Constitutional Law," *Emory Law Journal* 63 (2013): 527–80. Also discussed in Steven K. Hoge, "Cleburne and the Pursuit of Equal Protection for Individuals with Mental Disorders," *Journal of the American Academy of Psychiatry and the Law* 43, no. 4 (2015): 416–22.

26. In Hannah Arendt, *Eichmann in Jerusalem: A Report on the Banality of Evil,* 1st ed. (New York: Penguin Classics, 2006). Arendt refutes the idea that one has to be "evil" to perform evil acts (in this case, mass genocide). Arendt characterized Eichmann as a cog in the wheel, a follower of orders, murderous as they may be. Other historians and philosophers refuted her claims and showed he was an avid Nazi supporter, or a detached monster, and more. But for my purposes, her claim is of interest here, especially for those who are literal gatekeepers of carceral locales (guards, superintendents, workers) and more symbolic gatekeepers (those upholding the NIMBY attitudes and practices I describe here).

27. Rothstein, *Color of Law.*

28. A term used by Puar, *Right to Maim*.

29. Ioanide, *Emotional Politics*.

30. Of particular interest here is Ahmed's work on affective economies; Sara Ahmed, "Affective Economies," *Social Text* 22, no. 2 (2004): 117–39.

31. Ahmed.

32. Findings suggest that becoming the victim was the result of several crucial factors: (1) a loss of individual rights, (2) destroying a homeowner's dream, and (3) altering the social fabric of the community. Community residents felt their democratic rights were taken away. They explained that as taxpayers, they indirectly financed group homes, and as such, they had the right to decide on whether the group home was implemented in their community. Community residents felt that the group home destroyed the residential nature of their neighborhood. They had chosen to live in a quiet residential community and wanted it to remain that way. Myra Piat, "Becoming the Victim: A Study on Community Reactions towards Group Homes," *Psychiatric Rehabilitation Journal* 24, no. 2 (2000): 108–16.

33. Bornstein, *Contextualizing*.

34. I was instructed here by Michael Green's paper "Fighting for a Place in the Neighborhood: City of Cleburne vs. Cleburne Living Center, Inc." presented at the Society for Disability Studies 2015.

35. Piat, "NIMBY Phenomenon."

36. Piat.

37. Quoted in Rothstein, *Color of Law*, 35.

38. Zippay's study (which included interviews with 169 mental health administrators in seven states and 138 staff members) demonstrates that residences that utilized a notification strategy are likely to experience higher levels of initial opposition from neighbors and that longer-term neighborhood relations may not vary significantly regardless of whether neighbors were notified or whether initial opposition was present. Allison L. Zippay, "Psychiatric Residences: Notification, NIMBY, and Neighborhood Relations," *Psychiatric Services* 58, no. 1 (2007): 109–13.

39. For instance, Segal and Aviram hold that three main factors influence people's attitudes about community acceptance or rejection: the characteristics of the "host" community (socioeconomic status, for example), the characteristics of the residents (formerly incarcerated, dealing with addiction, disabled, etc.), and the characteristics of the facility (open, gated, inviting, etc.). Steven P. Segal and Uri Aviram, *The Mentally Ill in Community-Based Sheltered Care* (New York: John Wiley, 1978).

40. Community Residences Information Services Program, *There Goes the Neighborhood . . .* (White Plains, N.Y.: CRISP, 1990). This is a summary of the fifty-eight studies that have been done of the effects of group homes and treatment facilities on the neighborhoods in which they are placed. No studies were found to indicate a negative impact of group home placement upon any aspect of neighborhood life. The studies found that group home placement had not lowered property values or increased turnover, had not increased crime, and had not changed the neighborhood's character. The group homes had not deteriorated or become conspicuous institutional

landmarks. The studies did find that all communities had come to accept group homes and that group home residents have benefited from the access to a wider community life. Also http://www.disabilityrightsohio.org/; "Opening the Doors: Confronting Housing Discrimination," https://www.disabilityrightsohio.org/opening-doors-con fronting-housing-discrimination; Metropolitan Human Services Commission, "The Non-effect of Group Homes on Neighboring Residential Property Values in Franklin County," August 1979; Michael Dear, "Impact of Mental Health Facilities on Property Values," *Community Mental Health Journal* 13, no. 2 (1977): 150–57; City of Lansing Planning Department, "The Influence of Halfway Houses and Foster Care Facilities upon Property Values," 1976; State University of New York at Brockport, "The Effect of Community Residences for the Mentally Retarded on Real Estate in the Neighbor-hoods in Which They Are Located," 1980 (showing that average home selling price rose 9 percent one year after the group home operated); Princeton University, "The Effect of Siting Group Homes on the Surrounding Environs," 1976 (property values increased in fifteen of sixteen samples); Diana Antos Arens, "What Do the Neighbors Think Now? Community Residences on Long Island, New York," *Community Mental Health Journal* 29, no. 3 (1993): 235–45; Mark L. Silver and Martin Melkonian, eds., *Contested Terrain: Power, Politics, and Participation in Suburbia* (Westport, Conn.: Praeger, 1995).

During the lawsuit over Willowbrook residential facility, discussed in chapter 7, New York State enlisted the help of Julian Wolpert, a renowned urban geographer, to research the validity of such claims, and they were disproved in his study. For more on the case, refer to David J. Rothman, *The Willowbrook Wars: Bringing the Mentally Disabled into the Community,* 1st ed. (New Brunswick, N.J.: Routledge, 2004).

41. CRISP, *There Goes.*

42. Povinelli, *Economies of Abandonment.*

43. Refer to Ferguson, *Aberrations in Black.*

44. Duggan, *Twilight of Equality?*

45. Dear and Wolch assume that most institutions were in urban settings, but in most states, that was not the case in relation to I/DD institutions, or prisons, which were often built in remote areas, requiring family members to travel large distances to visit those incarcerated. Dear and Wolch, *Landscapes of Despair.*

46. Outside the disability arena, race is discussed very frequently in relation to NIMBY sentiments (e.g., in relation to environmental racism). One of the excep-tions to this lacuna is in the area of ecocriticism, which is beginning to grapple with issues of disability, through the framework of eco-ability, for example, but even there, there is often not an emphasis on the intersections of race and disability rights and studies.

47. Nancy Scheper-Hughes, "Dilemmas in Deinstitutionalization: A View from Inner City Boston," *Journal of Operational Psychiatry* 12, no. 2 (1981): 90–99.

48. Robert D. Wilton, "Colouring Special Needs: Locating Whiteness in NIMBY Conflicts," *Social and Cultural Geography* 3, no. 3 (2002): 303–21.

49. Wilton.

50. This study was cited in Martin S. Jaffe and Thomas Patrick Smith, *Siting Group Homes for Developmentally Disabled Persons*, no. 397 (American Planning Association, 1986).

51. As stated in Smith and Jaffe, "presumably, the concentration of such facilities in certain geographic areas has the potential for undercutting normalization by no longer making the neighborhood a normal living environment."

52. Andrea Smith, "Heteropatriarchy and the Three Pillars of White Supremacy: Rethinking Women of Color Organizing," in *Color of Violence*, 66–73.

53. Smith and Jaffe, *Siting Group Homes*.

54. Meyer, *As Long as They Don't Move Next Door*, in relation to neighborhood racial segregation in Detroit.

55. Rothstein, *Color of Law*.

56. Affective economies that led to resistance to the construction of group homes, or NIMBY, could be said to have had their roots in eugenic beliefs. As shown in earlier chapters, in the late nineteenth century, as the eugenics movement gained momentum, it was declared that all feebleminded people were potential criminals, an act which led to their institutionalization. It was therefore this White Other that was targeted as criminal or dangerous, in addition to the person of color or the immigrant (which were targeted heavily by both eugenic science and policies of incarceration and exile).

57. Community Association for the Retarded Inc., *New Neighbors* (Palo Alto, Calif.: 1970), https://mn.gov/mnddc/parallels2/pdf/70s/70/70-NNS-CAR.pdf.

58. Community Association for the Retarded Inc. The pictures in the pamphlet are in black and white and given the photos' age and poor reproduction quality, the subjects' race, gender, and disability in some of the photos are hard to discern.

59. Tropes of innocence are often mobilized in anti-prison and anti–death penalty campaigns, too. See Jackie Wang, *Carceral Capitalism* (Cambridge, Mass.: MIT Press, 2018); Gilmore, "Worrying State."

60. Much like the adage of "*All* the Women Are *White, All* the Blacks Are Men, *but Some of Us Are Brave*," which feminists of color were trying to contest.

61. As Ioanide, *Emotional Politics*, brilliantly shows. See also Lipsitz, *Possessive Investment*.

6. Political and Affective Economies of Closing Carceral Enclosures

1. Steven J. Taylor and Stanford J. Searl, "Disability in America: A History of Policies and Trends," in *Significant Disability: Issues Affecting People with Significant Disabilities from a Historical, Policy, Leadership, and System Perspective*, ed. E. Davis Martin Jr., 16–63 (Springfield, Ill.: Charles C. Thomas, 2001).

2. Melanie Panitch, *Disability, Mothers and Organization: Accidental Activists* (New York: Routledge, 2008).

3. There are of course differences between parents who work on a national/state level (in organizations like The Arc) and parents on the ground, and I do not want to be monolithic here. For an excellent exploration of how parents' activism shifted within The Arc in Pennsylvania from expansion/reform to abolition, refer to Allison C. Carey

and Lucy Gu, "Walking the Line between the Past and the Future: Parents' Resistance and Commitment to Institutionalization," in Ben-Moshe et al., *Disability Incarcerated,* 101–19.

4. Liz Robbins, "For Special-Care Residents, New York State Policy Means Leaving Home," *New York Times,* January 29, 2015, sec. New York, https://www.nytimes.com/2015/02/01/nyregion/as-new-york-moves-people-with-developmental-disabilities-to-group-homes-some-families-struggle.html.

5. *Parentalism* is a term coined by Arlene Kanter at Syracuse University's Law School to indicate that women could also be implicated in "paternalistic" attitudes.

6. Gottschalk, *Caught.*

7. Jenna Loyd, "Race, Capitalist Crisis, and Abolitionist Organizing: An Interview with Ruth Wilson Gilmore," in *Beyond Walls and Cages: Prisons, Borders, and Global Crisis,* ed. Jenna Loyd, Matt Mitchelson, and Andrew Burridge, 42–56 (Athens: University of Georgia Press, 2012).

8. Jackie Wang, "Carceral Capitalism," *Semiotext(e)* 21 (2018): 263.

9. Erica Meiners, *For the Children?* (Minneapolis: University of Minnesota Press, 2016).

10. Alexis Shotwell, *Against Purity: Living Ethically in Compromised Times* (Minneapolis: University of Minnesota Press, 2016).

11. Naomi Murakawa and Katherine Beckett, "The Penology of Racial Innocence: The Erasure of Racism in the Study and Practice of Punishment," *Law and Society Review* 44, no. 3–4 (2010): 695–730.

12. Chris Chapman, Allison C. Carey, and Liat Ben-Moshe, "Reconsidering Confinement: Interlocking Locations and Logics of Incarceration," in Ben-Moshe et al., *Disability Incarcerated,* 3–24.

13. See Gilmore, foreword to *Struggle Within.* Also refer to Mariame Kaba in relation to recent defense campaigns, especially around black women (such as Bresha Meadows and Marissa Alexander), in "Free Us All."

14. Harvey, *A Brief History of Neoliberalism.*

15. Duggan, *The Twilight of Equality?*; Hong, *Death beyond Disavowal.*

16. Gottschalk, *Caught;* Wacquant, *Punishing the Poor;* Loïc Wacquant, *Prisons of Poverty* (Minneapolis: University of Minnesota Press, 2009); "Paradoxes of Neoliberalism," 2013, http://bcrw.barnard.edu/videos/paradoxes-of-neoliberalism/.

17. The concept of the continuum gained prominence in the 1960s, when professionals and parents in the field of special education began to advocate for a wider range of placements for students with disabilities, and was later taken up by legislation and the courts.

18. Taylor, "The Institutions Are Dying."

19. Taylor.

20. Michael J. Kennedy, "The Disability Blanket," *Mental Retardation* 32, no. 1 (1994): 74–76.

21. Parsons, *From Asylum to Prison.*

22. Carey, *On the Margins of Citizenship.*

23. Over the past two decades, self-advocates have contested their represent-ation as inferior. As a means of cultural resymbolization, they had called for the end of the use of the *R* word (referring to the designation of "mentally retarded"). Through lobbying for legislation (the removal of the *R* word from service offices in several states, then federally), petitions, and media campaigns that include disabled and nondisabled celebrities, they have called on mostly nondisabled people to become aware and to stop using what self-advocates perceive to be archaic and oppressive terminology.

24. In 1979, the National Alliance for the Mentally Ill (NAMI) was founded as an advocacy group of family members of those defined as mentally ill. Over the years, it grew also to include representation of those defined as mentally ill, but only those willing to align with NAMI's politics. NAMI began by trying to counteract some of the influential theories, especially during the 1950s, and some to this day, of the causal relation between mental illness and relationships within the family, especially with the mother, which were espoused by psychoanalytic theory (such as in the case of the "refrigerator mother").

25. See the polemic writings of Dr. Fuller Torrey for examples of such argumenta-tions discussed in chapter 4.

26. Gilmore, *Golden Gulag.*

27. Parenti, *Lockdown America.*

28. Wacquant, *Prisons of Poverty;* Wacquant, *Punishing the Poor.*

29. Russell, *Beyond Ramps.* Refer to figures from Braddock et al., *State of the States.*

30. Marta Russell and Jean Stewart, "Disablement."

31. Russell, *Beyond Ramps.*

32. The American Health Care Association, for instance, which represents for-profit nursing homes and care facilities, is one of the biggest financial contributors to the campaigns of political candidates.

33. James Kilgore, "Mass Incarceration and Working Class Interests: Which Side Are the Unions On?," *Labor Studies Journal* 37, no. 4 (2012): 356–72.

34. For more on this debate, see responses to Page's article in *Criminology and Public Policy* 10, no. 3. As historian Heather Ann Thompson further states, "it turns out, when one maps this nationally, that there is little correlation between the presence of guard unions . . . and the fate of a given state's carceral apparatus." But correlation does not mean causation. The guard's unions did not cause the growth of the carceral state, but they are a vocal component in maintaining carceral logics and legitimating it. Heather Ann Thompson, "Downsizing the Carceral State," *Criminology and Public Policy* 10, no. 3 (2011): 771–9.

35. Gottschalk, *Caught.*

36. Thompson, "Downsizing."

37. Joshua Page, "Prison Officer Unions and the Perpetuation of the Penal Status Quo," *Criminology and Public Policy* 10, no. 3 (2011): 735–70.

38. Page.

39. As cited in Taylor and Searl, "Disability in America."

40. As historian Anne Parsons shows in detail in relation to struggles to close Retreat Hospital and Byberry Hospital in Pennsylvania in the 1970s, AFSCME actively resisted the closure and argued that the closure will hurt those with disabilities. However, this concern by unions was not corroborated by other actions, as the AFL-CIO (representing Byberry) simultaneously opposed a bill supporting patients' rights. In fact, despite the fact that deinstitutionalization was becoming a fiscal and policy reality, union workers went on strike and actively resisted the closure of psychiatric hospitals (and ultimately lost).

41. For a good overview, see Kilgore, "Mass Incarceration," and writings and talks by Lori Jo Reynolds, who spearheaded the campaign to close Tamms.

42. Gilmore, *Golden Gulag*; Kevin Pyle and Craig Gilmore, *Prison Town: Paying the Price* (Northampton, Mass.: Real Cost of Prisons Project, 2005), http://www.realcost ofprisons.org/materials/comics/prison_town.pdf.

43. As Kilgore points out in "Mass Incarceration."

44. As Gilmore further details regarding the prison boom in California, it was due to the availability and management of surplus people (as poverty doubled in the 1970s, connected to the ideology of scarcity, leading to racial and other animosity), surplus and depreciated land (because of changes in production and in the importance of agriculture, as well as the need to sell useless and depreciated irrigated land), capital (a shift from investment in plants and equipment to finance capital, e.g., $5 billion bonds for new prison construction), and state capacity. Gilmore, *Golden Gulag*.

45. Ryan S. King, Marc Mauer, and Tracy Huling, *Big Prisons, Small Towns: Prison Economics in Rural America* (Washington, D.C.: Sentencing Project, 2003); Ryan S. King, Marc Mauer, and Tracy Huling, "An Analysis of the Economics of Prison Siting in Rural Communities," *Criminology and Public Policy* 3, no. 3 (2004): 453–80.

46. Clayton Mosher, Gregory Hooks, and Peter B. Wood, "Don't Build It Here: The Hype versus the Reality of Prisons and Local Employment," in *Prison Profiteers: Who Makes Money from Mass Incarceration*, ed. Tara Herivel and Paul Wright, 90–106 (New York: New Press, 2007).

47. Ahrens, "Prison Town"; Kilgore, "Mass Incarceration"; King et al., "Analysis of the Economics," for example, demonstrated that placing prisons in rural counties in New York did not significantly reduce unemployment (much of the prison staff, particularly prison officers, lived elsewhere) or decrease poverty.

48. Rose Braz and Craig Gilmore, "Joining Forces: Prisons and Environmental Justice in Recent California Organizing," *Radical History Review* 2006, no. 96 (2006): 95–111.

49. In actuality, most new prison jobs do not stay in the town housing the prison. For instance, the new prison built in Delano, California, in the mid-1990s generated about sixteen hundred jobs, out of which seventy-nine went to local residents of Delano. Ahrens, "Prison Town."

50. King et al., "Analysis of the Economics."

51. Molly Parker, "Tamms: Forgotten," *Southern Illinoisan*, May 17, 2015, https://thesouthern.com/news/local/tamms-two-years/tamms-forgotten/article_17f0430c-3011-5d07-8dbb-5ab09e6e55cb.html.

52. Beckwith, *Disability Servitude.*

53. King et al., "Analysis of the Economics."

54. Between 1964 and 1988, private public interest lawyers filed a total of eighteen institutional peonage cases in state and federal courts on behalf of individuals with disabilities who performed labor in public institutions (mostly under the Thirteenth Amendment). Beckwith, *Disability Servitude.*

55. Beckwith, 52.

56. An important contemporary example is the formation of IWOC in 2014, the Incarcerated Workers Organizing Committee, which is a part of IWW (Industrial Workers of the World). Its purpose is to unionize those incarcerated in prisons and to end what it calls "prison slavery."

57. Chris Chapman, "Becoming Perpetrator: How I Came to Accept Restraining and Confining Disabled Aboriginal Children," in *Psychiatry Disrupted: Theorizing Resistance and Crafting the (R)evolution,* ed. Bonnie Burstow, Brenda A. LeFrançois, and Shaindl Diamond (Montreal: McGill-Queen's Press, 2014).

58. Dana M. Britton, "Perceptions of the Work Environment among Correctional Officers: Do Race and Sex Matter?," *Criminology* 35, no. 1 (1997): 85–106.

59. Chapman, *Becoming Perpetrator.*

60. Dana M. Britton, "Gendered Organizational Logic: Policy and Practice in Men's and Women's Prisons," *Gender and Society* 11, no. 6 (1997): 813.

61. Marie L. Griffin, Gaylene S. Armstrong, and John R. Hepburn, "Correctional Officers' Perceptions of Equitable Treatment in the Masculinized Prison Environment," *Criminal Justice Review* 30, no. 2 (2005): 189–206.

62. Kevin N. Wright and William G. Saylor, "A Comparison of Perceptions of the Work Environment between Minority and Non-minority Employees of the Federal Prison System," *Journal of Criminal Justice* 20, no. 1 (1992): 63–71.

63. Amy Hewitt and Sheryl Larson, "The Direct Support Workforce in Community Supports to Individuals with Developmental Disabilities: Issues, Implications, and Promising Practices," *Mental Retardation and Developmental Disabilities Research Reviews* 13, no. 2 (2007): 178–87.

64. Braddock et al., *State of the States.*

65. Hewitt and Larson, "Direct Support Workforce."

66. Amy Hewitt, Sheryl Larson, Steve Edelstein, Dorie Seavey, Michael A. Hoge, and John Morris, *A Synthesis of Direct Service Workforce Demographics and Challenges across Intellectual/Developmental Disabilities, Aging, Physical Disabilities, and Behavioral Health* (Minneapolis: University of Minnesota, Institute on Community Integration, Research and Training Center on Community Living, 2008).

67. From the introduction of Akemi Nishida's forthcoming book, tentatively titled *Dare to Care: Affective Living of Disability, Race, and Gender* (Philadelphia: Temple University Press, forthcoming).

68. Hewitt et al., *Synthesis of Direct Service Workforce.*

69. Hewitt et al.

70. Evelyn Nakano Glenn, "From Servitude to Service Work: Historical Continuities in the Racial Division of Paid Reproductive Labor," *Signs* 18, no. 1 (1992): 1–43;

Pierrette Hondagneu-Sotelo, *Domestica: Immigrant Workers Cleaning and Caring in the Shadows of Affluence* (Berkeley: University of California Press, 2001); Mary Romero, *Maid in the USA* (New York: Routledge, 1992).

71. Nishida, *Dare to Care*.

72. Nirmala Erevelles, "Disability and the Dialectics of Difference," *Disability and Society* 11, no. 4 (1996): 519–38.

73. Erevelles, 520.

74. Ferguson, *Aberrations in Black*.

75. Lisa Dodson and Rebekah Zincavage, "'It's Like a Family': Caring Labor, Exploitation, and Race in Nursing Homes," *Gender and Society* 21 (2007): 905–28.

76. Dodson and Zincavage, 912.

77. Dodson and Zincavage, 916.

78. Dodson and Zincavage, 922.

79. Dodson and Zincavage. They show how workers and managers disregard racial insults or perceive them as an inevitable experience for workers of color in nursing homes.

80. Some of these workers came to these jobs because they themselves have disabled children or family members.

81. Allison C. Carey, "The Quest for Community: Intellectual Disability and the Shifting Meaning of Community in Activism," *Research in Social Science and Disability* 6 (2011): 189–213.

82. Liat Ben-Moshe, "The Contested Meaning of 'Community' in Discourses of Deinstitutionalization and Community Living in the Field of Developmental Disability," in *Disability and Community*, ed. Allison C. Carey and Richard K. Scotch, 241–64 (Bingley, U.K.: Emerald, 2011).

83. As Vivienne Saleh-Hanna extrapolates from her interviewees who are involved in prison abolition in "Penal Abolition: An Ideological and Practical Venture against Criminal (In)justice and Victimization," MA thesis, School of Criminology, Simon Fraser University, 2000.

84. Nancy Scheper-Hughes's ethnographic work is instructive in this regard as well. She looked at discharged mental patients in South Boston and found that they were negatively affected by the exclusionary and racist attitudes of people in the neighborhood. The people there had very rigid notions of what a community is, and they constructed boundaries that kept the patients as outsiders even while they were residing there. Nancy Scheper-Hughes, "Dilemmas in Deinstitutionalization: A View from Inner City Boston," *Journal of Operational Psychiatry* 12, no. 2 (1981): 90–99.

85. John Lord and Cheryl Hearn, *Return to the Community: The Process of Closing an Institution* (Kitchener: Centre for Research and Education in Human Services, 1987).

86. Lord and Hearn.

87. Carey, *On the Margins of Citizenship*.

88. For example, in the documentary *Kings Park: Stories from an American Mental Institution* (2011), about the psychiatric hospital in Long Island of that name, former

residents and some staff discuss the facility as a community, a place that "made you be something." It was a place to which people were tied by strong affect—on one hand, a former attendant romanticized it as paradise and a place of romance, and on the other, someone who was incarcerated there discussed the fear of living there—the strong bonds that were formed but also that "people don't need to be abused to find their strength." After the closure of the asylum in 1996 (which had operated since 1885), former residents of Kings Park formed Hands across Long Island as a group meeting space in a coffee shop, which later became a large peer support network in New York State.

89. Allison C. Carey, Pamela Block, and Richard Scotch, *Allies and Obstacles: Disability Activism and Parents of Children with Disabilities* (Philadelphia: Temple University Press, forthcoming).

90. Robinsue Frohboese and Bruce Dennis Sales, "Parental Opposition to Deinstitutionalization: A Challenge in Need of Attention and Resolution," *Law and Human Behavior* 4, no. 1/2 (1980): 1–87; Carey, *On the Margins of Citizenship*.

91. Nancy A. Naples, *Grassroots Warriors: Activist Mothering, Community Work, and the War on Poverty* (New York: Routledge, 2014).

92. Gilmore, *Golden Gulag*.

93. Gilmore. The young man was George Noyes, who was killed by police in South Central Los Angeles.

94. For example, Naples, *Grassroots Warriors*.

95. Theda Skocpol, *Protecting Soldiers and Mothers: The Political Origins of Social Policy in the United States* (Cambridge, Mass.: Belknap Press of Harvard University Press, 1992). I thank Allison Carey for this point and for her helpful comments on this chapter.

96. Spade, *Normal Life*; Mitchell and Snyder, *Biopolitics of Disability*; Ryan Conrad, ed., *Against Equality: Queer Revolution, Not Mere Inclusion* (Oakland, Calif.: AK Press, 2014).

97. For more on the creative arts projects of Tamms Year Ten, refer to Laurie Jo Reynolds and Stephen F. Elsenman, "Tamms Is Torture: The Campaign to Close an Illinois Supermax Prison," *Creative Time Reports,* May 6, 2013, http://creativetimereports.org/2013/05/06/tamms-is-torture-campaign-close-illinois-supermax-prison-solitary-confinement/.

98. Kilgore, *Mass Incarceration*, 365.

99. Brian Tierney, as cited in Kilgore.

100. Kilgore, *Mass Incarceration*. In 2010, fifteen states closed prisons, eliminating more than fifteen thousand beds. In 2012, Florida alone shuttered ten correctional institutions.

101. Povinelli, *Economies of Abandonment*.

102. Meiners, "Never Innocent."

103. Chapman et al., "Reconsidering Confinement."

104. Southern Tier Independence Center, http://www.stic-cil.org/.

105. Dodson and Zincavage.

106. Puar, *Right to Maim*, xvii.

107. Puar, *Right to Maim*.

108. As Kilgore, "Mass Incarceration," quotes in his chronology of events.

109. Reynolds and Elsenman, "Tamms Is Torture."

110. VOR and Murray parents also use experts and facts and the language of choice. Perhaps the best way to counter resistance to decarceration is not with more studies but with interacting with other parents whose kids went through the same battles and transitioned out of restrictive settings, as promoted by the motto of the disability rights movement, "Nothing about us without us." This was also a suggestion posed by prominent researchers in the field of I/DD Heller and Braddock in the 1980s as deinstitutionalization in I/DD was well under way and so was the resistance to it.

111. Jessi Lee Jackson and Erica R. Meiners, "Fear and Loathing: Public Feelings in Antiprison Work," *Women's Studies Quarterly* 39, no. 1/2 (2011): 270–90.

112. Judith Butler, *Precarious Life: The Powers of Mourning and Violence* (New York: Verso, 2004).

7. Decarcerating through the Courts

1. Ramos v. Lamm, 713 F.2d 546 (10th Cir. 1983). A supermaximum security prison is one in which people reside in a single cell (the size of a small bathroom) for twenty-three hours a day for the duration of their incarceration in the facility. It is long-term solitary confinement for all who are incarcerated in the prison.

2. Penelope A. Boyd, "The Aftermath of the DD Act: Is There Life after Pennhurst," *University of Arkansas Little Rock Law Review* 4 (1981): 449.

3. Pennhurst State School and Hospital opened in 1913 as Eastern State School for the Feeble-minded and Epileptic, after the Pennsylvania Commission for the Care of the Feeble-minded issued a statement that so-called feebleminded people were "unfit for citizenship" and "posed a menace to the peace." Based on eugenic beliefs of the time, the commission recommended "a program of custodial care" to "break the endless reproductive chain." This argument of "unfit for citizenship" was the same language used in the *Dred Scott v. Sanford* case sixty years earlier, enshrining African Americans as inferior to whites and as "unfit for citizenship." http://www.preservepennhurst.org/default.aspx?pg=93.

4. For more on prisoner rights and activism of the era, refer to Dan Berger's work, especially *Captive Nation: Black Prison Organizing in the Civil Rights Era* (Chapel Hill: University of North Carolina Press, 2014), and Berger and Toussaint Losier, *Rethinking the American Prison Movement* (New York: Routledge, 2017).

5. A notable exception is the recent work of Anne Parsons, who discusses specific case law connecting prisons and deinstitutionalization.

6. Because the 1970s was an influential era of exposés and changes in the arena of "mental retardation," and because it is a less known story in the genealogy of deinstitutionalization, I focus on litigation in intellectual disabilities and less on mental health facilities.

7. Much of my analysis of the historical context of litigation reform is owed to Margo Schlanger, "Beyond the Hero Judge: Institutional Reform Litigation as Litigation," *Michigan Law Review* 97, no. 6 (1999): 1994–2036.

8. In a series of decisions, federal courts ruled that (black) Muslim inmates should have the same access to religious materials and services that are available to other (Christian) inmates, that Muslims had a right to a pork-free diet, and the like. See Schlanger.

9. The Eighth Amendment to the U.S. Constitution states, "Excessive bail shall not be required, nor excessive fines imposed, nor cruel and unusual punishments inflicted." It therefore prohibits the imposition of punishments that are excessive of the harm or "crime" that has been committed, either while awaiting trial or after conviction.

10. In recognizing that the language of "mental retardation" is archaic and considered by self-advocates to be offensive, I will be using this terminology only to refer to the ways it was used and perceived in this time frame, i.e., the 1960s and 1970s, as written into law, policies, and case law of that era.

11. I discuss the normalization principle and these new theories that led to deinstitutionalization in chapter 2.

12. Academics and scholar-activists also played a central role in the legal arm of the deinstitutionalization and prison abolition movements, as can be viewed in judges' opinions that cite such scholars as Erving Goffman, Greshem Sykes, Wolf Wolfensberger, Gunner Dybwad, and others.

13. As sociologist Allison Carey details, parents of children with developmental disabilities spent about two decades, in the 1950s–1970s, lobbying politicians, fundraising, writing letters, and creating successful noninstitutional alternative living and educational experiments. When they felt that their calls for reform were left unanswered, parents were at the forefront of bringing lawsuits against institutions for those labeled as I/DD to change the living conditions of their children (some of whom were now adults). Carey, *On the Margins of Citizenship*.

14. I discussed this push for and resistance to closure of institutions and prisons by parents, unions, and facility employees in the previous chapter.

15. https://disabilityjustice.org/wyatt-v-stickney/.

16. Wyatt v. Stickney, 334 F. Supp 1341, 1343 (M.D. Ala. 1971).

17. His televised exposé made Willowbrook, and the topic of institutionalization, a national sensation and a topic of public outcry. Even people who knew nothing about disability or institutions had the images of the squalid conditions people with intellectual disabilities had to endure while at Willowbrook projected into their TV screens while unsuspectingly eating dinner. I discuss the exposé as part of a large number of exposés of institutional conditions in chapter 1.

18. Examples of ethnographies of the famous Willowbrook case include Rothman and Rothman, *Willowbrook Wars,* and Goode et al., *A History and Sociology of the Willowbrook State School.*

19. In his most famous decision, in 1973, Judge Judd ordered the U.S. Army to stop the bombing of Cambodia.

20. In *Valvano v. Malcolm* in 1974, for example, Judd held that it was cruel and unusual punishment to confine two people in a one-person cell while awaiting trial. When New York State officials didn't remedy the situation, he ordered them to begin releasing those who had been awaiting trial the longest and had the lowest bail, until the practice of double celling had been stopped. In doing so, Judd rejected officials' complaints that budgetary constraints led to overcrowding and wanted proactive measures to be taken.

21. Taylor, "Institutions and the Law."

22. In *Finney v. Hutto*, 1977, an Arkansas prison was again sued in regard to excessive guard violence and the use of confinement cells. The lower courts declared that "confinement of prisoners in punitive isolation for more than thirty days constituted cruel and unusual punishment and was impermissible."

23. Ruffin v. Commonwealth; U.S. ex rel. Atterbury v. Ragen.

24. The year 1984 is the first year for which data are available. Schlanger, "Beyond the Hero Judge."

25. For further discussion about this case, refer to Malcolm M. Feeley and Edward L. Rubin, *Judicial Policy Making and the Modern State: How the Courts Reformed America's Prisons* (Cambridge: Cambridge University Press, 2000).

26. For example, refer to the chapter by A. Lee, "Prickly Coalitions: Moving Prison Abolitionism Forward," in *Abolition Now! Ten Years of Strategy and Struggle against the Prison Industrial Complex* (Oakland, Calif.: AK Press, 2008), as well as the rest of the contributions in this important anthology marking Critical Resistance's tenth anniversary.

27. Taylor, "Institutions and the Law."

28. David Ferleger and Penelope A. Boyd, "Anti-institutionalization: The Promise of the Pennhurst Case," *Stanford Law Review* 31, no. 4 (1979): 717–52.

29. The decision was based on citing both the equal protection clause of the Fourteenth Amendment and also section 504 of the Rehabilitation Act, which was enacted in 1973 to prohibit discrimination against people with disabilities by entities receiving federal funds. The ruling touched mostly on the right to nondiscriminatory rehabilitation, which the court felt cannot be achieved in a segregated setting—*any* segregated setting.

30. Cited in Taylor, "Institutions and the Law."

31. Pennhurst State School & Hosp. v. Halderman, https://caselaw.findlaw.com/us -supreme-court/465/89.html.

32. I discuss this throughout chapter 2.

33. Schlanger, "Beyond the Hero Judge."

34. Perhaps it was also due to Judge Broderick's tenure as lieutenant governor of Pennsylvania, in which he became familiar with the conditions in mental institutions.

35. Ferleger and Boyd, "Anti-institutionalization," 720.

36. As I discuss in chapter 3.

37. This connection between civil rights and prisoners' rights is well demonstrated in Berger, *Captive Nation*.

38. In 1972, after the public increased interest in prison conditions following the Attica uprising, foundations proposed forming the ACLU's National Prison Project, which became a key player. The Legal Defense Fund of the NAACP has pioneered and focused more on Eighth Amendment violations in prisons and jails, while the ACLU originally focused on due process but later began emphasizing conditions in prisons, especially overcrowding. The organization that brought on litigation based on the federal mandate to desegregate facilities was the Department of Justice's Civil Rights Division. It was not a major player in prison litigation but still played a role in the expansive arena of prison litigation in the 1960s and 1970s. For more of this history, refer to Schlanger, "Beyond the Hero Judge."

39. James B. Jacobs, "The Prisoners' Rights Movement and Its Impacts, 1960–80," *Crime and Justice* 2 (1980): 429–70.

40. The term *jailhouse lawyers* refers to imprisoned people who usually have or had no formal training in law prior to incarceration but as a result of self-teaching become knowledgeable in case law, as well as often informally assisting other incarcerated individuals regarding their cases or conditions of incarceration.

41. Mumia Abu-Jamal, *Jailhouse Lawyers: Prisoners Defending Prisoners: Vol. 5. The USA* (San Francisco: City Lights Books, 2009).

42. Robert T. Chase, "We Are Not Slaves: Rethinking the Rise of Carceral States through the Lens of the Prisoners' Rights Movement," *Journal of American History* 102, no. 1 (2015): 78.

43. Ferleger and Boyd, "Anti-institutionalization."

44. https://www.legacy.com/obituaries/atlanta/obituary.aspx?pid=2907375.

45. The term inspiration porn is attributed to the late Stella Young, especially in her TED talk: https://www.ted.com/talks/stella_young_i_m_not_your_inspiration_thank_you_very_much.

46. Jacobs discusses this dynamic of the worst case scenario in "Prisoners' Rights Movement."

47. Quoted in Jacobs, 453.

48. Rachel Herzing, "'Tweaking Armageddon': The Potential and Limits of Conditions of Confinement Campaigns," *Social Justice* 41, no. 3 (2015): 193.

49. Taylor, "Institutions and the Law," in relation to mental institutions.

50. Spade, *Normal Life.*

51. I am intentionally not settling the debate around the question of transhumanism here and therefore don't claim that this move into legally accounting for selfhood was "good" or "better" than having no such status.

52. Jacobs, "Prisoners' Rights Movement," 432–33, referring to the ruling in Ruffin v. Commonwealth, 62 Va. 790 (1871).

53. Gilmore, "Slavery and Prison"; Davis, "From the Convict Lease System to the Super-Max Prison."

54. Hartman, *Scenes of Subjection*; Patterson, *Slavery and Social Death*; Hortense J. Spillers, *Black, White, and in Color: Essays on American Literature and Culture* (Chicago: University of Chicago Press, 2003); Orlando Patterson, *Slavery and Social Death: A Comparative Study* (Cambridge, Mass.: Harvard University Press, 1982).

55. Chapman et al., "Reconsidering Confinement."

56. People First is a way, advocated for by people with intellectual disabilities, to refer to individuals first and the disability second (such as "people with intellectual disabilities"), to acknowledge the personhood of those with disabilities and their human rights.

57. As Taylor, "Institutions and the Law," points out, the value of many of these cases was to bring attention to the conditions in psychiatric and mental institutions, and as such, they were closer in function to exposés and journalistic accounts.

58. Berger and Losier, *Rethinking the American Prison Movement.*

59. Jacobs, "Prisoners' Rights Movement," 460.

60. Berger and Losier, *Rethinking the American Prison Movement.*

61. As famed sociologist C. Wright Mills claimed in regard to a whole host of social conditions.

62. Liz Samuels, "Improvising on Reality: The Roots of Prison Abolition," in *The Hidden 1970s: Histories of Radicalism,* 21–38 (New Brunswick, N.J.: Rutgers University Press, 2010).

63. Samuels.

64. Emily Thuma, "Lessons in Self-Defense: Gender Violence, Racial Criminalization, and Anticarceral Feminism," *Women's Studies Quarterly* 43, no. 3 (2015): 52–71.

65. Ruthie-Marie Beckwith, "On the Outside Looking In," *IMPACT* 9, no. 1 (1995–96): 8–9; J. O'Brien and People First of Tennessee, *A Chance to Be Made Whole: People First Members Being Friends to Tear Down Institution Walls* (Nashville, Tenn.: People First of Tennessee, 1997).

66. I am indebted here to Steven J. Taylor's nuanced analysis of lawsuits and exposés in the area of deinstitutionalization in *Acts of Conscience: World War II, Mental Institutions, and Religious Objectors* (Syracuse, N.Y.: Syracuse University Press, 2009).

67. Feeley and Rubin, *Judicial Policy Making and the Modern State.*

68. Max Weber, *The Protestant Ethic and the Spirit of Capitalism* (New York: Scribner, 1958).

69. S. P. Sturm, "The Legacy and Future of Corrections Litigation," *University of Pennsylvania Law Review* 142 (1993): 639–738.

70. Foucault, *Discipline and Punish.*

71. The decarceration–industrial complex is discussed in the introduction of the book.

72. Sheryl A. Larson, Amanda Ryan, Patricia Salmi, Drew Smith, and Allise Wuorio, *Residential Services for Persons with Developmental Disabilities: Status and Trends through 2010* (Minneapolis: University of Minnesota, Research and Training Center on Community Living, Institute on Community Integration, 2012).

73. Drinkwater, "Supported Living."

74. Joshua Guetzkow and Eric Schoon, "If You Build It, They Will Fill It: The Consequences of Prison Overcrowding Litigation," *Law and Society Review* 49, no. 2 (2015): 401–32.

75. Samuels, "Improvising on Reality."

76. Eric Cummins, *The Rise and Fall of California's Radical Prison Movement* (Stanford, Calif.: Stanford University Press, 1994).

77. Jonathan Simon, *Mass Incarceration on Trial: A Remarkable Court Decision and the Future of Prisons in America* (New York: The New Press, 2014).

78. Wacquant, "Class, Race and Hyperincarceration."

79. Puar, *Right to Maim.*

80. Ellen M. Barry, "Women Prisoners on the Cutting Edge: Development of the Activist Women's Prisoners' Rights Movement," *Social Justice* 27, no. 3 (2000): 168. Much of the overview of cases presented here comes from her excellent review. Ellen Barry is the founding director of legal services for prisoners with children, co-chair of the National Network for Women in Prison, and legal counsel on many class action lawsuits on behalf of women who are incarcerated.

81. A classic example of the centrality of gender/sexuality (and race) to any critical analysis of imprisonment can be found in Davis, *Are Prisons Obsolete?,* and in the more recent Ritchie, *Invisible No More.*

82. Ritchie, *Invisible No More,* 3.

83. Berger and Losier, *Rethinking the American Prison Movement.*

84. Nicole Hahn Rafter, *Partial Justice: Women, Prisons, and Social Control,* 2nd ed. (New Brunswick, N.J.: Transaction, 1990).

85. The most often discussed cases were litigated regarding facilities in Michigan and Kentucky. In *Glover v. Johnson* (1979) in Michigan, the incarcerated women won major relief based on equal protection rights. The other case, *Canterino v. Wilson* (1982), could be seen as a reform of prison conditions case but also interpreted as a decarceration case. In the original ruling, the court ordered to reduce overcrowding in the prison for women and eliminate the level system in the prisons, which the court found to make the women docile and childlike. But on appeal in 1989, the court rejected the original ruling for lack of evidence, and things in the prison remained status quo.

86. Rafter, *Partial Justice.*

87. Rafter.

88. Ritchie, *Invisible No More.*

89. Elizabeth Whalley and Colleen Hackett, "Carceral Feminisms: The Abolitionist Project and Undoing Dominant Feminisms," *Contemporary Justice Review* 20, no. 4 (2017): 456–73.

90. See E. Bernstein, "Carceral Politics as Gender Justice? The 'Traffic in Women' and Neoliberal Circuits of Crime, Sex, and Rights," *Theory and Society* 41 (2012): 233–59. Victoria Law discusses the term *carceral feminism* in her 2014 article in Jacobin: https://www.jacobinmag.com/2014/10/against-carceral-feminism/.

91. Thuma, *Lessons in Self-Defense.*

92. Angela Davis, *Abolition Democracy: Beyond Prisons, Torture, Empire* (New York: Seven Stories Press 2005).

93. "INCITE!-Critical Resistance Statement," *INCITE!* (blog), July 31, 2018, https://incite-national.org/incite-critical-resistance-statement/; Brady T. Heiner and Sarah K.

Tyson, "Feminism and the Carceral State: Gender-Responsive Justice, Community Accountability, and the Epistemology of Antiviolence," *Feminist Philosophy Quarterly* 3, no. 1 (2017).

94. Ritchie, *Invisible No More.*

95. Beth Richie as well as the work of INCITE! Women of Color against Violence offers a critique of this kind of "carceral feminism" that calls for equality that results in punitive measures.

96. The *Fiandaca* case is of interest not only because it took the parity argument to an extreme (the establishment of a whole new site of incarceration) but also because of its less discussed connection to disability and deinstitutionalization. After the court ruling, New Hampshire debated where to house this new women's prison. It offered to transform a unit in Laconia, its downsized "institution for the retarded," to house the new prison. On appeal, the court reversed the ruling, not because it did not find merit in the equal protection argument, but because New Hampshire Legal Assistance (NHLA), who represented Mary Ann Fiandaca and twenty-two other female New Hampshire prison inmates, also represented the residents at Laconia State School and Training Center, which the court found to be a conflict of interest.

97. Dean Spade's work is pivotal for discussions of the administrative legal control of gender. A pioneering text of the intersection of gender nonconformity and imprisonment, from an abolitionist lens, is Eric A. Stanley and Nat Smith, eds., *Captive Genders: Trans Embodiment and the Prison Industrial Complex* (Oakland, Calif.: AK Press, 2011).

98. Regina G. Kunzel, *Criminal Intimacy: Prison and the Uneven History of Modern American Sexuality* (Chicago: University of Chicago Press, 2008).

99. Sarah Lamble, "Queer Necropolitics and the Expanding Carceral State: Interrogating Sexual Investments in Punishment," *Law and Critique* 24, no. 3 (2013): 229–53.

100. M. Bassichis, A. Lee, and D. Spade, "Building an Abolitionist Trans and Queer Movement with Everything We've Got," in Stanley and Smith, *Captive Genders*, 15–40.

101. https://www.olmsteadrights.org/iamolmstead/history/item.5403-Lois_Curtiss_Story_Continued.

102. The conditions that have to be met for the *Olmstead* decision to take hold are as follows: (1) when professionals determine that such placement is appropriate; (2) the people desire such placement; and (3) the placement can be reasonably accommodated, taking into account the resources available to the state.

103. Samuel R. Bagenstos, "Past and Future of Deinstitutionalization Litigation," *Cardozo Law Review* 34 (2012): 1.

104. Mary C. Cerreto, "Olmstead: The Brown v. Board of Education for Disability Rights—Promises, Limits, and Issues," *Loyola Journal of Public Interest Law* 3 (2001): 47–78.

105. Bagenstos, "Past and Future."

106. *Incitement Newsletter* 23, no. 1 (2010).

107. *Incitement Newsletter.*

108. It is also striking that the man in the photograph is unnamed, and I am not sure if he knows he appears in ADAPT's campaign for freedom.

109. https://www.legacy.com/obituaries/atlanta/obituary.aspx?pid=2907375.

110. Kimberlé Crenshaw, "Mapping the Margins: Intersectionality, Identity Politics, and Violence against Women of Color," *Stanford Law Review* 43 (1990): 1241.

111. A prime current example of the necessity to create solidarity and coalitions between prison justice and disability justice as well as prisoners' rights and disability rights can be found in Talila A. Lewis and Dustin Gibson, "The Prison Strike Challenges Ableism and Defends Disability Rights," *Truthout*, September 5, 2018, https://truthout.org/articles/the-prison-strike-is-a-disability-rights-issue/.

112. Jacobs, "Prisoners' Rights Movement," 430.

113. Ribet's work is important as it focuses on a neglected aspect of the disabling effects of incarceration—the trauma of sexual abuse while incarcerated. Beth Ribet, "Naming Prison Rape as Disablement: A Critical Analysis of the Prison Litigation Reform Act, the Americans with Disabilities Act, and the Imperatives of Survivor-Oriented Advocacy," *Virginia Journal of Social Policy and the Law* 17 (2009): 296.

114. Ribet.

115. Since the passage of the ADA, cases like *Clarkson v. Coughlin*, brought on behalf of deaf inmates in New York in 1995, and *Pennsylvania Department of Corrections v. Yeskey* (1998), in which the department was sued under the ADA for refusing to allow a prisoner to participate in a motivational boot camp because of his history of hypertension, show that prisoners began using the ADA as a way to seek relief or decry prison conditions, and the courts agreed that the ADA covers correctional institutions.

116. Simon, *Mass Incarceration on Trial*.

117. Simon.

118. James Kilgore coined the term *carceral humanism* in his *CounterPunch* article "Repackaging Mass Incarceration," http://www.counterpunch.org/2014/06/06/repackaging-mass-incarceration/.

119. For example, fiscal constraints and realignment leading not to a massive release but to a transfer to county custody and out-of-state facilities. See Liat Ben-Moshe and Erica R. Meiners, "Beyond Prisons, Mental Health Clinics: When Austerity Opens Cages, Where Do the Services Go?," https://www.politicalresearch.org/2014/10/09/beyond-prisons-mental-health-clinics.

120. Olmstead, 527 U.S. 581 at 609–10, Kennedy, J. concurring judgment. Emphasis mine. ("Him" and "His" is in the original, even though both plaintiffs were women.)

121. A similar conundrum occurs regularly in euthanasia cases, where it is often hard to distinguish between chronic and terminal illness and progressive disabilities.

122. Knopp and Prison Research Education Action Project, *Instead of Prisons*.

123. Morris, *Penal Abolition*.

124. Herman Wallace was one of the "Angola 3" and was put in solitary confinement for forty-one years. He was granted compassionate release on October 1, 2013, and died a few days later (outside of prison) of liver cancer.

125. Institutional reform litigation, however, also led to the retrenchment of the carceral state, ushering in the governable iron cage and gender-responsive, gay affirmative and accessible types of incarceration. Political scientist Marie Gottschalk, examines progressive groups or social movements that may have unwittingly aided in the construction of the carceral state as key players that have been overlooked in previous analyses of the growth of the penal state. She focuses on four pockets of activism in particular: the victims' movement, the prison rights movement, the women's movement (especially in relation to the criminalization of domestic violence), and opponents of the death penalty. Gottschalk demonstrates how each movement inadvertently brought forth changes that concluded in more draconian punishments and increased incarceration. For example, opposition to the death penalty brought forth life sentences without parole as well as legitimated the view that public opinion should be central in any penal policy and helped strengthen the deterrence argument in crime control discourse. Similarly, Moms against Gun Violence ushered in gun control measures that increased criminalization of those already most affected, particularly youth of color. The victims' rights movement had no parallel in other industrialized countries at the time, and it made crime victims and those accused and their rights a zero-sum game pushing for policies like "three strikes" laws. Of course, these were aided by structures that are deeply American, such as the shallowness of the welfare state, and deep social and economic inequalities based on gender, race, and sexuality, which led these activists to the arms of "law-and-order" ideologies to deal with such inequities. Gottschalk, *The Prison and the Gallows.*

126. Puar, *Right to Maim.*

127. M. S. Salzer, K. Kaplan, and J. Atay, "State Psychiatric Hospital Census after the 1999 Olmstead Decision: Evidence of Decelerating Deinstitutionalization," *Psychiatric Services* 57, no. 10 (2006): 1501–4.

128. K. C. Lakin, R. Prouty, B. Polister, and K. Coucouvanis, "States' Initial Response to the President's New Freedom Initiative: Slowest Rates of Deinstitutionalization in 30 Years," *Mental Retardation* 43, no. 3 (2004): 241–44.

129. Spade, *Normal Life,* 20.

130. Chandan Reddy, *Freedom with Violence: Race, Sexuality, and the US State* (Chapel Hill, N.C.: Duke University Press, 2011).

131. As Dan Berger, *Captive Nation,* masterfully demonstrates.

Epilogue

1. Knopp and Prison Research Education Action Project, *Instead of Prisons.*

2. Braddock et al., *State of the States.*

3. I thank Richard Ingram for pushing me on this point.

4. Anne M. Lovell and Nancy Scheper-Hughes, "Deinstitutionalization and Psychiatric Expertise: Reflections on Dangerousness, Deviancy, and Madness (Italy and the United States)," *International Journal of Law and Psychiatry* 9, no. 3 (1986): 361–81.

5. Rose, *Governing the Soul.*

6. Fabris, *Tranquil Prisons.*

7. Parsons, *From Asylum to Prison.*

8. This was not the case in institutions for those with I/DD labels, but it was the case for psych hospitals and prisons.

9. Ben-Moshe and Meiners, "Beyond Prisons."

10. Bernard E. Harcourt, "Reducing Mass Incarceration: Lessons from the Deinstitutionalization of Mental Hospitals in the 1960s," *Ohio State Journal of Criminal Law* 9 (2011): 53–88.

11. Marie Gottschalk, "Cell Blocks and Red Ink: Mass Incarceration, the Great Recession, and Penal Reform," *Daedalus* 139, no. 3 (2010): 62–73.

12. Furthermore, Chris Berk, in Harcourt, "Reducing Mass Incarceration," cautions against the use of what he calls "investment talk" or the "language of finance" in emerging discourses on prison reform. The problem with the use of this financial discourse is that it does not contest the interpretation of social cost as inevitable and refers only to financial matters.

13. "Institutions InBrief," https://www.ncd.gov/publications/2012/DIToolkit/Institutions/inBrief/.

14. Kelley Johnson, *Deinstitutionalising Women: An Ethnographic Study of Institutional Closure* (Cambridge: Cambridge University Press, 1998).

15. Gilles Deleuze, "Postscript on the Societies of Control," *October* 59 (1992): 7.

16. Fabris, *Tranquil Prisons.*

17. James Kilgore, "Progress or More of the Same? Electronic Monitoring and Parole in the Age of Mass Incarceration," *Critical Criminology* 21, no. 1 (2013): 123–39.

18. Lamble, *Queer Necropolitics.*

19. Ben-Moshe and Stewart, "Disablement."

20. Gottschalk, *Caught.*

21. American Friends Service Committee, *The Treatment Industrial Complex,* November 17, 2014, https://www.afsc.org/resource/treatment-industrial-complex-how-profit-prison-corporations-are-undermining-efforts-treat-a.

22. Isaacs 2014.

23. Gottschalk, *Caught.*

24. Kilgore, "Repackaging Mass Incarceration."

25. Flyers in possession of the author.

26. Mimi Kim, "Dancing the Carceral Creep: The Anti-Domestic Violence Movement and the Paradoxical Pursuit of Criminalization, 1973–1986," October 14, 2015, https://escholarship.org/uc/item/804227k6; Lamble, "Queer Necropolitics."

27. To borrow from Richie, *Arrested Justice.*

28. Kluth et al., *Access to Academics for All Students.*

29. Reynolds and Elsenman, "Tamms Is Torture."

30. Lovell and Scheper-Hughes, "Deinstitutionalization."

31. Chamberlin, "On Our Own."

32. Peter Stastny and Peter Lehmann, eds., *Alternatives beyond Psychiatry* (Berlin: Peter Lehmann, 2007), 217.

33. "The shifting contours of the carceral state" is a concept many abolitionists are attuned to, but Erica Meiners's work has particularly influenced my thinking on this.

34. I thank Monica Cosby, a fierce Chicago-based abolitionist, for this important point.

35. Dirksen Bauman and Joseph Murray, "Reframing: From Hearing Loss to Deaf Gain," *Deaf Studies Digital Journal* 1, no. 1 (2009): 1–10. More recently: H-Dirksen L. Bauman and Joseph J. Murray, eds., *Deaf Gain: Raising the Stakes for Human Diversity* (Minneapolis: University of Minnesota Press, 2014).

Index

LIAT BEN-MOSHE is assistant professor of criminology, law, and justice at the University of Illinois at Chicago.